Is this a dream I had last night? Some crazy dictionary, half Flaubert's *idées reçues* ..., half Raymond Williams's *Keywords*, half Barbara Cassin's lexicon of untranslatable concepts, with maybe another half of Laplanche and Pontalis dictionary of psychoanalysis? So many halves, but yes, it is true, even if a dream as well. *The Marx through Lacan Vocabulary* is an amazing compendium, assembled by Latin Americans (where all the true Lacano-Marxists flourish)—Christina Soto van der Plas, Edgar Miguel Juárez-Salazar, Carlos Gómez Camarena, and David Pavón-Cuéllar—and startlingly international, with contributors from a dozen countries in Europe, the Middle East, and the Americas. Whether you need to brush up on the distinction between "alienation" and "separation" or parse the difference between the "owner" in Marx and the "master" in Lacan, if you want to suss out how "surplus-*jouissance*" differs from "surplus-value", or *finally* understand those nefarious *mathemes* and four discourses—this is the book for you. Sure to be on the bedside table for every political psychoanalyst and libidinal Marxist—for what better aphrodisiac is there than a dictionary?

**Clint Burnham**, Simon Fraser University, Vancouver, BC, Canada

Aware of how creatively Lacan read Marx, this volume analyzes their reciprocal interaction: Marx critiquing Lacan and Lacan critiquing Marx. The authors send us along an exciting Möbius strip while showing the need for radical critique. This collaborative and plurivocal book is an admirable achievement, an indispensable resource, and a major reference.

**Patricia Gherovici**, Co-founder and Director of the Philadelphia Lacan Group and Associate Faculty, Psychoanalytic Studies Minor, University of Pennsylvania, USA

A direly needed work for both experts and newcomers in the fields of psychoanalysis, Marxism, political and critical theory, and the analysis of ideology and culture. Beyond being a valuable dictionary of terms, this collection offers original theses regarding the pass of Marx through Lacan. The caliber of the contributions is paralleled by the perspicacious selection of concepts.

**A. Kiarina Kordela**, Macalester College, Saint Paul, MN, USA

If invariably a third thing is needed to join the theoretical worlds of Marx and Lacan, a vocabulary is the ultimate *via regia*: language being the messy field of struggle and of truth. Beyond a mere little repertoire of concepts, this fine international collective realizes a clarifying, multifarious, and sometimes unruly intervention paving the ways of how Marxism and psychoanalysis could or should be related in order to confront that other (seemingly more natural and harmonious) couple of capitalism and psychology.

**Jan De Vos**, Professor at Cardiff University, based in Belgium

There are many extremely pressing problems and antagonisms today for which we still need a vocabulary—the right words to name and describe them. Not necessarily new words, but words that resonate powerfully in the contemporary context, concepts that make us see and grasp things differently. *The Marx through Lacan Vocabulary* contributes to this task most admirably.

**Alenka Zupančič**, Professor at The European Graduate School (EGS), and a research advisor and professor at the Institute of Philosophy at the Research Centre of the Slovenian Academy of Sciences and Arts, Slovenia

An indispensable contribution to thinking how Lacan routinely utilized facets of Marx's thought in expanding the critical horizons of psychoanalysis. This invaluable book shows us that we cannot truly appreciate Lacanian psychoanalysis and Lacanian social theory without registering the foundational influence of Marx (as in notions of alienation, automatism, surplus-*jouissance*, political economy, etc.). What emerges from this set of instructive and rigorous essays is not only a Lacanian Marx, but also a properly Marxian Lacanianism. This text will be the standard reference for psychoanalytic social critique for years to come.

**Derek Hook**, Duquesne University, Pittsburgh, USA

*The Marx through Lacan Vocabulary* is not merely the most comprehensive and ambitious survey of the manifold Lacanian encounters and intersections with Marx, which are both inspiring and convoluted. It is a tool most dearly needed in present times, powerfully reminding us of the task and stakes of radical thought in the times of neoliberal slumber and depression.

**Mladen Dolar**, University of Ljubljana, Slovenia

*The Marx through Lacan Vocabulary* is a remarkable and precious tool for all those interested in exploring Lacan's interpretation, appropriation, and transformation of some of Marx's key concepts, as well as an invaluable guide to the many ways in which Lacan's sustained engagement with Marx's text shaped his own thought. As such, it argues convincingly for the need to think together political and libidinal economy, social production and the unconscious, labour relations and language. This collection is also a testimony to the vitality of Lacanian, Marxist, and post-Marxist studies in the so-called Global South, as well as Europe and North America. Scholars, students, and psychoanalysts will use it for years to come.

**Miguel de Beistegui**, ICREA Research Professor, University of Pompeu Fabra, Barcelona, Spain

A dazzling compendium of the non-relationship between Marx and Lacan! As the subtitle of this book suggests, it is a helpful compass that orients the reader in an otherwise overwhelming terrain of what there is in the in-between: between Marx and Lacan, between the libidinal and the political, between theory and praxis.

**Amanda Holmes**, University of Applied Arts, Vienna, Austria

# The Marx through Lacan Vocabulary: A Compass for Libidinal and Political Economies

This text explores a set of key concepts in Marxist theory as developed and read by Lacan, demonstrating links and connections between Marxist thought and Lacanian practice.

The book examines the complexity of these encounters through the structure of a comprehensive vocabulary which covers diverse areas, from capitalism and communism to history, ideology, politics, work, and family. Offering new perspectives on these concepts in psychoanalysis, as well as in the fields of political and critical theory, the book brings together contributions from a range of international experts to demonstrate the dynamic relationship between Marx and Lacan, as well as illuminating "untranslatable points" which may offer productive tension between the two. The entries trace the trajectory of Lacan's appropriation of Marx's concepts and analyses how they were questioned, criticized, and reworked by Lacan, accounting for the wide reach of two thinkers and worlds in constant homology. Each entry also discusses psychoanalytic debates relating to the concept and seeks to refine the clinical scope of Marx's work, demonstrating its impact on the social and individual dimensions of Lacanian clinical practice.

With a practical and structured approach, *The Marx through Lacan Vocabulary* will appeal to psychoanalysts and researchers in a range of fields, including political science, cultural studies, and philosophy.

**Christina Soto van der Plas** is professor of Latin American Literature at Santa Clara University, USA.

**Edgar Miguel Juárez-Salazar** is a professor of Social Psychology at Universidad Autónoma Metropolitana-Xochimilco (UAM-X), Mexico.

**Carlos Gómez Camarena** is a professor at Universidad Iberoamericana, Mexico.

**David Pavón-Cuéllar** is a professor at Universidad Michoacana de San Nicolás de Hidalgo (UMSNH), Mexico.

## The Lines of the Symbolic in Psychoanalysis Series
*Series Editor:* Ian Parker, *Manchester Psychoanalytic Matrix*

Psychoanalytic clinical and theoretical work is always embedded in specific linguistic and cultural contexts and carries their traces, traces which this series attends to in its focus on multiple contradictory and antagonistic 'lines of the Symbolic'. This series takes its cue from Lacan's psychoanalytic work on three registers of human experience, the Symbolic, the Imaginary and the Real, and employs this distinctive understanding of cultural, communication and embodiment to link with other traditions of cultural, clinical and theoretical practice beyond the Lacanian symbolic universe. The Lines of the Symbolic in Psychoanalysis Series provides a reflexive reworking of theoretical and practical issues, translating psychoanalytic writing from different contexts, grounding that work in the specific histories and politics that provide the conditions of possibility for its descriptions and interventions to function. The series makes connections between different cultural and disciplinary sites in which psychoanalysis operates, questioning the idea that there could be one single correct reading and application of Lacan. Its authors trace their own path, their own line through the Symbolic, situating psychoanalysis in relation to debates which intersect with Lacanian work, explicating it, extending it and challenging it.

### Psychoanalysis Under Nazi Occupation
The Origins, Impact and Influence of the Berlin Institute
*Laura Sokolowsky*

### Toward a Feminist Lacanian Left
Psychoanalytic Theory and Intersectional Theory
*Alicia Valdés*

### The Marx through Lacan Vocabulary
A Compass for Libidinal and Political Economies
*Christina Soto van der Plas, Edgar Miguel Juárez-Salazar, Carlos Gómez Camarena and David Pavón-Cuéllar*

# The Marx through Lacan Vocabulary

A Compass for Libidinal and Political Economies

Edited by Christina Soto van der Plas,
Edgar Miguel Juárez-Salazar,
Carlos Gómez Camarena and
David Pavón-Cuéllar

LONDON AND NEW YORK

Cover image: Ana Claudia Flores Ames

First published 2022
by Routledge
4 Park Square, Milton Park, Abingdon, Oxon OX14 4RN

and by Routledge
605 Third Avenue, New York, NY 10158

*Routledge is an imprint of the Taylor & Francis Group, an informa business*

© 2022 selection and editorial matter, Christina Soto van der Plas, Edgar Miguel Juárez-Salazar, Carlos Gómez Camarena and David Pavón-Cuéllar; individual chapters, the contributors

The right of Christina Soto van der Plas, Edgar Miguel Juárez-Salazar, Carlos Gómez Camarena and David Pavón-Cuéllar to be identified as the authors of the editorial material, and of the authors for their individual chapters, has been asserted in accordance with sections 77 and 78 of the Copyright, Designs and Patents Act 1988.

All rights reserved. No part of this book may be reprinted or reproduced or utilised in any form or by any electronic, mechanical, or other means, now known or hereafter invented, including photocopying and recording, or in any information storage or retrieval system, without permission in writing from the publishers.

*Trademark notice*: Product or corporate names may be trademarks or registered trademarks, and are used only for identification and explanation without intent to infringe.

*British Library Cataloguing-in-Publication Data*
A catalogue record for this book is available from the British Library

*Library of Congress Cataloging-in-Publication Data*
A catalog record has been requested for this book

ISBN: 978-1-032-07928-8 (hbk)
ISBN: 978-1-032-07929-5 (pbk)
ISBN: 978-1-003-21209-6 (ebk)

DOI: 10.4324/9781003212096

Typeset in Times
by Deanta Global Publishing Services, Chennai, India

# Contents

*Abbreviations* x
*Contributors* xviii
*Acknowledgements* xxv
*Preface: Marx's homologous, Lacan* xxvi
CHRISTINA SOTO VAN DER PLAS, EDGAR MIGUEL JUÁREZ-SALAZAR,
CARLOS GÓMEZ CAMARENA AND DAVID PAVÓN-CUÉLLAR
*Series preface for The Marx through Lacan Vocabulary:
A Compass for Libidinal and Political Economies* xl

1 **Alienation** 1
BEN GOOK AND DOMINIEK HOENS

2 **Automatism** 16
ELENA BISSO

3 **Bourgeoisie** 23
CARLOS ANDRÉS UMAÑA GONZÁLEZ

4 **Capitalism** 31
ANDREJA ZEVNIK

5 **Communism** 45
IAN PARKER

6 **Consumption** 55
AGUSTINA SAUBIDET

7 **Economy/*Oikonomia*** 63
YAHYA M. MADRA AND CEREN ÖZSELÇUK

| 8 | Freedom/liberty<br>ROQUE FARRÁN | 74 |
|---|---|---|
| 9 | History<br>ADRIAN JOHNSTON | 85 |
| 10 | Ideology<br>NATALIA ROMÉ | 96 |
| 11 | Imperialism<br>LIVIO BONI | 102 |
| 12 | Labour/work<br>SAMO TOMŠIČ | 110 |
| 13 | Market<br>CHRISTIAN INGO LENZ DUNKER | 126 |
| 14 | Master/tyrant<br>FABIANA PARRA | 134 |
| 15 | Materialism<br>DAVID PAVÓN-CUÉLLAR | 142 |
| 16 | Money<br>PIERRE BRUNO | 153 |
| 17 | Politics<br>CARLOS GÓMEZ CAMARENA AND EDGAR MIGUEL JUÁREZ-SALAZAR | 162 |
| 18 | Proletarian/labourer/worker<br>SILVIA LIPPI | 177 |
| 19 | Revolution<br>RICARDO ESPINOZA LOLAS | 188 |
| 20 | Segregation<br>JORGE ALEMÁN AND CARLOS GÓMEZ CAMARENA | 197 |
| 21 | Slavery<br>JUAN PABLO LUCCHELLI AND TODD MCGOWAN | 214 |

| | | |
|---|---|---|
| 22 | **Society**<br>EDGAR MIGUEL JUÁREZ-SALAZAR | 225 |
| 23 | **Superstructure**<br>DANIELA DANELINCK AND MARIANO NICOLÁS CAMPOS | 239 |
| 24 | **Surplus-*jouissance***<br>NADIA BOU-ALI | 246 |
| 25 | **Uneasiness/discontent/unhappiness**<br>NADIR LARA JUNIOR | 256 |
| 26 | **Value**<br>JEAN-PIERRE CLÉRO | 266 |
| | **Annex I. Transliterations** | 276 |
| | **Annex II. What is a *matheme*? Four discourses and mathematics in Lacan**<br>DANIELA DANELINCK AND CARLOS GÓMEZ CAMARENA | 285 |
| | *Index* | 291 |

# Abbreviations

*Seminars, Écrits, Conferences, Interviews, and Letters*
(with abbreviations used in the text)

## Works by Lacan

| | |
|---|---|
| *AE* | (2001). *Autres Écrits*. Paris: Seuil. |
| *AIO* | (1971-1972). An issue of Ones. In: *The Seminar of Jacques Lacan. Book XIX. ...or Worse* (pp. 128–145). Cambridge: Polity Press, 2018 (Also known as "Seminar of The Knowledge of the Psychoanalyst"). |
| *AP* | (1948). Aggressiveness in Psychoanalysis. In: *Écrits* (pp. 82–101), B. Fink (Trans.). New York: W. W. Norton & Company, 2006. |
| *APE* | (1967). Allocution sur les psychoses de l'enfant. In: *Autres Écrits* (pp. 361–372). Paris: Seuil, 2001. |
| *BRP* | (1936). Beyond the Reality Principle. In: *Écrits* (pp. 58–74), B. Fink (Trans.). New York: W. W. Norton & Company, 2006. |
| *CDJ* | (1976). Clôture des Journées de l'École freudienne de Paris. Les mathèmes de la psychanalyse. In: *Lettres de l'École freudienne*, (21). |
| *CF* | (1938). Les complexes familiaux dans la formation de l'individu. Essai d'analyse d'une fonction en psychologie. In: *Autres Écrits* (pp. 23–84). Paris: Seuil, 2001. |
| *CG* | (1975). Conférence à Genève sur le symptôme. *La Cause du Désir*, (95):7–24. |
| *CNA* | (1975). Conférences et entretiens dans des universités nord-américaines. In *Scilicet*, (6/7):5–63. Paris: Éditions du Seuil, 1976. |
| *CPP* | (1967). *Conférence sur la psychanalyse et la formation du psychiatre*. Unpublished. |
| *DDP* | (1972). Du discours psychanalytique. In: *Lacan in Italia (1953-1978)*, L. Boni (Trans.) (pp. 27–40). Milan: La Salamandra, 1978. |

| | |
|---|---|
| *DPP* | (1932). *De la psychose paranoïaque dans ses rapports avec la personnalité*. Paris: Seuil, 1975. |
| *DTC* | (1974). Discourse to Catholics. In: *The Triumph of Religion, preceded by Discourse to Catholics* (pp. 2-53), B. Fink (Trans.). Cambridge: Polity Press, 2013. |
| *DTP* | (1958). The Direction of the Treatment and the Principles of Its Power. In: *Écrits* (pp. 489–541), B. Fink (Trans.). New York: W. W. Norton & Company, 2006. |
| *EC* | (2006). *Écrits*, B. Frink (Trans.). New York: W. W. Norton & Company. |
| *FA* | (1964). Foundation Act. In: J. Copjec (Ed.), *Television* (pp. 97–106), D. Hollier, R. Krauss & A. Michelson (Trans.). New York: W.W. Norton & Company, 1990. |
| *FFI* | (1974). Freud Forever: An Interview with Panorama, P. Dravers (Trans). In: *Hurly-Burly*, (12): 13-21, 2015. |
| *FFS* | (1953). The Function and Field of Speech and Language in Psychoanalysis. In: *Écrits* (pp. 197–268), B. Fink (Trans.). New York: W. W. Norton & Company, 2006. |
| *FPC* | (1950). A Theoretical Introduction to the Functions of Psychoanalysis in Criminology. In: *Écrits* (pp. 102–122), B. Fink (Trans.). New York: W. W. Norton & Company, 2006. |
| *FT* | (1955). The Freudian Thing or the Meaning of the Return to Freud in Psychoanalysis. In: *Écrits* (pp. 334–363), B. Fink (Trans.). New York: W. W. Norton & Company, 2006. |
| *ICM* | (1950). Intervention au 1re Congrès mondial de psychiatrie. In: *Autres Écrits* (pp. 127–130). Paris: Seuil, 2001. |
| *IEM* | (1972). Interventions sur l'exposé de P. Mathis: "Remarques sur la fonction de l'argent dans la technique analytique" au Congrès de l'École freudienne de Paris sur "La technique psychanalytique". In: *Lettres de l'École freudienne*, (9): 195–205. |
| *IL* | (1957). The Instance of the Letter in the Unconscious or Reason Since Freud. In: *Écrits* (pp. 412–441), B. Fink (Trans.). New York: W. W. Norton & Company, 2006. |
| *IM2* | (1970). *Impromptu n°2, Seconde conférence publique de Jacques Lacan à l'Université de Vincennes, 4 June 1970*. Unpublished. |
| *IMX* | (1966). Of Structure as the Inmixing of an Otherness Prerequisite to Any Subject Whatever. In: R. Macksey & E. Donato (Ed.), *The languages of Criticism and the Sciences of Man: The Structuralist Controversy* (pp. 186–200). Baltimore: Johns Hopkins Press, 1970. |
| *KIT* | (1971). Knowledge, ignorance, truth and enjoyment. In: *Talking to Brick Walls: A Series of Presentations in the Chapel at Sainte-Anne Hospital*, A. Price (Trans.). Cambridge: Polity |

|       | Press (Also known as "Seminar of The Knowledge of the Psychoanalyst"). |
|-------|-----|
| KS    | (1963). Kant with Sade. In: *Écrits* (pp. 645–669), B. Fink (Trans.). New York: W. W. Norton & Company, 2006. |
| LD    | (1980). Letter of Dissolution. In: J. Copjec (Ed.), *Television* (pp. 129–131), D. Hollier, R. Krauss & A. Michelson (Trans.). New York: W.W. Norton & Company, 1990. |
| LE    | (1972). L'étourdit. In: *Autres Écrits* (pp. 449–496). Paris: Seuil, 2001. |
| LT    | (1945). Logical Time and the Assertion of Anticipated Certainty. In: *Écrits* (pp. 161–175), B. Fink (Trans.). New York: W. W. Norton & Company, 2006. |
| LTE   | (1971). Lituraterre. In: *Autres Écrits* (pp. 11–20). Paris: Seuil, 2001. |
| MA    | (1980). Monsieur A. In: *Ornicar?* (21–22): 17–20. |
| MDP   | (1933). Motifs du crime paranoïaque. In: *De la psychose paranoïaque dans ses rapports avec la personnalité* (pp. 25–28). Paris: Seuil, 1975. |
| MIN   | (1952). *Le mythe individuel du névrosé, ou poésie et vérité dans la névrose*. Paris: Seuil, 2007. |
| MS    | (1949). The Mirror Stage as Formative of the I Function as Revealed in Psychoanalytic Experience. In: *Écrits* (pp. 75–81), B. Fink (Trans.). New York: W. W. Norton & Company, 2006. |
| MSS   | (1967). La méprise du sujet supposé savoir. In: *Autres Écrits* (pp. 329–339). Paris: Seuil, 2001. |
| N13   | (1945). Le nombre treize et la forme logique de la suspicion. In: *Autres Écrits* (pp. 85–99). Paris: Seuil, 2001. |
| OSC   | (1977). Ouverture de la section clinique. In: *Ornicar?* (9): 7–14. |
| P9O   | (1967). Proposition du 9 octobre 1967 sur le psychanalyste de l'École. In: *Autres Écrits* (pp. 243–260). Paris: Seuil, 2001. |
| PAG   | (1947). La psychiatrie anglaise et la guerre. In: *Autres Écrits* (pp. 101–120). Paris: Seuil, 2001. |
| PAM   | (1971). *Talking to Brick Walls. A Series of Presentations in the Chapel at Sainte-Anne Hospital*, A. Price (Trans.). Cambridge: Polity Press, 2017 (Also known as "Seminar of The Knowledge of the Psychoanalyst"). |
| PEA   | (1976). Préface à l'édition anglaise du Séminaire XI. In: *Autres Écrits* (pp. 571–573). Paris: Seuil, 2001. |
| PEM   | (1967). Psychanalyse et médecine. In: *Lettres de L'École Freudienne* (1): 34–61. |
| PIT   | (1957). Psychoanalysis and Its Teaching. In: *Écrits* (pp. 364–383), B. Fink (Trans.). New York: W. W. Norton & Company, 2006. |

| | |
|---|---|
| PL | (1955). Seminar on "The Purloined Letter". In: *Écrits* (pp. 6–48), B. Fink (Trans.). New York: W. W. Norton & Company, 2006. |
| POE | (1967). The Place, Origin and End of My Teaching. In: *My Teaching* (pp. 1–56), D. Macey (Trans.). London: Verso, 2008. |
| PPC | (1946). Presentation on Psychical Causality. In: *Écrits* (pp. 123–160), B. Fink (Trans.). New York: W. W. Norton & Company, 2006. |
| PRF | (1975). Le plaisir et la règle fondamentale. In: *Lettres de L'École freudienne* (24): 22–24. |
| PT | (1951). Presentation on Transference. In: *Écrits* (pp. 176–185), B. Fink (Trans.). New York: W. W. Norton & Company, 2006. |
| PTH | (1970). Preface of one Thesis. In: Anika Lemaire, *Jacques Lacan* (pp. VII–XV), D. Macey (Trans.). London: Routledge & Kegan Paul Ltd, 1977. |
| PU | (1960). Position of the Unconscious. In: *Écrits* (pp. 703–721), B. Fink (Trans.). New York: W. W. Norton & Company, 2006. |
| QTP | (1956). On a Question Prior to Any Possible Treatment of Psychosis. In: *Écrits* (pp. 445–488), B. Fink (Trans.). New York: W. W. Norton & Company, 2006. |
| RA | (1970). Radiophonie. In: *Autres Écrits* (pp. 407–448). Paris: Seuil, 2001. |
| RDL | (1958). Remarks on Daniel Lagache's Presentation. In: *Écrits* (pp. 543-574), B. Fink (Trans.). New York: W. W. Norton & Company, 2006 |
| RDT | (1969). D'une réforme dans son trou. In: *Figures de la psychanalyse* (17): 181–187, 2009. |
| RSF | (1966). Responses to Students of Philosophy Concerning the Object of Psychoanalysis. In: J. Copjec (Ed.), *Television* (pp. 107–114), D. Hollier, R. Krauss & A. Michelson (Trans.). New York: W.W. Norton & Company, 1990. |
| RXIX | (1972). Report on Seminar XIX. In: *The Seminar of Jacques Lacan. Book XIX. …or Worse* (pp. 215–220), A. R. Price (Trans.). Cambridge: Polity Press, 2018. |
| S0 | (1952-1953). *Le Séminaire. L'homme aux loups.* Unpublished. |
| SI | (1953–1954). *The Seminar of Jacques Lacan. Book I. Freud's Papers on Technique*, J. Forrester (Trans.). New York: W.W. Norton & Company, 1991. |
| SII | (1954–1955). *The Seminar of Jacques Lacan. Book II. The Ego in Freud's Theory and in the Technique of Psychoanalysis*, S. Tomaselli (Trans.). New York: W. W. Norton & Company, 1991. |
| SIII | (1955–1956). *The Seminar of Jacques Lacan. Book III. The Psychoses*, R. Grigg (Trans.). New York: W. W. Norton & Company, 1997. |

| | |
|---|---|
| SIR | (1953). The Symbolic, the Imaginary, and the Real. In: *On the Names-of-the-Father* (pp. 1–52), B. Fink (Trans.). Cambridge: Polity Press, 2011. |
| SIV | (1956–1957). *The Seminar of Jacques Lacan. Book IV. The Object Relation*, A. Price (Trans.). Cambridge: Polity Press, 2021. |
| SIX | (1961–1962). *Le Séminaire. Livre IX. L'identification*. Unpublished. |
| SPT | (1956). The Situation of Psychoanalysis and the Training of Psychoanalysts in 1956. In: *Écrits* (pp. 384–411), B. Fink (Trans.). New York: W. W. Norton & Company, 2006. |
| SQ | (1966). On the Subject Who is Finally in Question. In: *Écrits* (pp. 189–196), B. Fink (Trans.). New York: W. W. Norton & Company, 2006. |
| SSD | (1960). The Subversion of the Subject and the Dialectic of Desire in the Freudian Unconscious. In: *Écrits* (pp. 671–701), B. Fink (Trans.). New York: W. W. Norton & Company, 2006. |
| ST | (1966). Science and Truth. In: *Écrits* (pp. 726–745), B. Fink (Trans.). New York: W. W. Norton & Company, 2006. |
| SV | (1957–1958). *The Seminar of Jacques Lacan. Book V. Formations of the Unconscious*, R. Grigg (Trans.). Cambridge: Polity Press, 2017. |
| SVI | (1958–1959). *The Seminar of Jacques Lacan. Book VI. Desire and its Interpretation*, B. Fink (Trans.). Cambridge: Polity Press, 2019. |
| SVII | (1959–1960). *The Seminar of Jacques Lacan. Book VII. The Ethics of Psychoanalysis*, D. Porter (Trans.). New York: W. W. Norton & Company, 1992. |
| SVIII | (1960–1961). *The Seminar of Jacques Lacan. Book VIII. Transference*, B. Fink (Trans.). Cambridge: Polity Press, 2015. |
| SX | (1962–1963). *The Seminar of Jacques Lacan. Book X. Anxiety*, A. R. Price (Trans.). Cambridge: Polity Press, 2014. |
| SXI | (1964). *The Seminar of Jacques Lacan. Book XI. The Four Fundamental Concepts of Psychoanalysis*, A. Sheridan (Trans.). New York: W. W. Norton & Company, 1998. |
| SXII | (1964–1965). *Le Séminaire. Livre XII. Problèmes Cruciaux pour la Psychanalyse*. Unpublished. |
| SXIII | (1965–1966). *Le Séminaire. Livre XIII. L'objet de la psychanalyse*. Unpublished. |
| SXIV | (1966–1967). *Le Séminaire. Livre XIV. La logique du fantasme*. Unpublished. |
| SXIX | (1971–1972). *The Seminar of Jacques Lacan. Book XIX. ...or Worse*, A. Price (Trans.). Cambridge: Polity Press, 2018. |
| SXV | (1967–1968). *Le Séminaire. Livre XV. L'acte*. Unpublished. |

| | |
|---|---|
| SXVI | (1968–1969). *Le Séminaire. Livre XVI. D'un Autre à l'autre*. Paris: Seuil, 2006. |
| SXVII | (1969–1970). *The Seminar of Jacques Lacan. Book XVII. The Other Side of Psychoanalysis*, R. Grigg (Trans.). New York: W. W. Norton & Company, 2007. |
| SXVIII | (1971). *Le Séminaire. Livre XVIII. D'un discours qui ne serait pas du semblant*. Paris: Seuil, 2006. |
| SXX | (1972–1973). *The Seminar of Jacques Lacan. Book XX. Encore*, B. Fink (Trans.). New York: W.W. Norton & Company, 1999. |
| SXXI | (1973–1974). *Le Séminaire. Livre XXI. Les Non-Dupes Errent*. Unpublished. |
| SXXII | (1974–1975). *Le Séminaire. Livre XXII. RSI*. Unpublished. |
| SXXIII | (1975–1976). *The Seminar of Jacques Lacan. Book XXIII. The Sinthome*, A. Price (Trans.). Cambridge: Polity Press, 2016. |
| SXXIV | (1976–1977). *Le Séminaire. Livre XXIV. L'Insu que Sait de l'Une-bevue s'Aile à Mourre*. Unpublished. |
| SXXV | (1977–1978). *Le Séminaire. Livre XXV. Le moment de conclure*. Unpublished. |
| SXXVII | (1980–1981). *Le Séminaire. Livre XXVII. Dissolution*. Unpublished. |
| TT | (1974). The Third. In: *The Lacanian Review*, E. Ragland (Trans.), (07): 83–112, 2019. |
| TV | (1973). Television. In: J. Copjec (Ed.), *Television* (pp. 3–46), D. Hollier, R. Krauss & A. Michelson (Trans.). New York: W.W. Norton & Company, 1990. |
| VST | (1955). Variations on the Standard Treatment. In: *Écrits* (pp. 269–302), B. Fink (Trans.). New York: W. W. Norton & Company, 2006. |
| YG | (1958). The Youth of Gide, or the Letter and Desire. In: *Écrits* (pp. 623–644), B. Fink (Trans.). New York: W. W. Norton & Company, 2006. |

## Works by Marx (and Engels)

| | |
|---|---|
| BLB | (1852). *The Eighteenth Brumaire of Louis Bonaparte*, C. P. Dutt (Trans.). New York: International Publishers, 1975. |
| CAF | (1882). Carta de Marx a Freud. In: *Revista Subjetividad y Cultura*, (26): 1–15, 2008. |
| CAI | (1867a). *Capital. A Critique of Political Economy*, Vol. I, B. Fowkes (Trans.). London: Penguin, 1990. |
| CAII | (1867b). *Capital. A Critique of Political Economy*, Vol. II, D. Fernbach (Trans.). London: Penguin, 1992. |

| | |
|---|---|
| *CAIII* | (1867c). *Capital. A Critique of Political Economy*, Vol. III, D. Fernbach (Trans.). London: Penguin, 1993. |
| *CGP* | (1875). Critique of the Gotha Programme. In: *Karl Marx & Frederick Engels Collected Works* (Vol. XXIV, pp. 75–99), P. Ross & B. Ross (Trans.). London: Lawrence & Wishart, 2010. |
| *CHP* | (1843). *Critique of Hegel's Philosophy of Right*, J. O'Malley (Trans.). Oxford: Oxford University Press, 1970. |
| *CPE* | (1859). *A Contribution to the Critique of Political Economy*, N.I. Stone (Trans). Chicago: Charles H. Kerr Publishing Company, 1904. |
| *DDE* | (1841). Difference Between the Democritean and Epicurean Philosophy of Nature. In: *Karl Marx & Frederick Engels Collected Works* (Vol. I, pp. 25–107), J. Dirk & S. R. Struik (Trans.). London: Lawrence & Wishart, 2010. |
| *EPM* | (1844). *Economic and Philosophic Manuscripts of 1844*, M. Milligan (Trans.). New York: Prometheus Books, 1998. |
| *EW* | (1975). *Early Writings*, R. Livingstone & G. Benton (Trans.). London: Penguin / New Left Review. |
| *GI* & ENGELS, F. | (1846). The German Ideology. In: *Karl Marx & Frederick Engels Collected Works* (Vol. V, pp. 19–539), W. Lough (Trans.). London: Lawrence & Wishart, 2010. |
| *GR* | (1858). *Grundrisse. Foundations of the Critique of Political Economy*, M. Nicolaus (Trans.). London: Penguin, 1973. |
| *MCP* & ENGELS, F. | (1848). Manifesto of the Communist Party. In: *Karl Marx & Frederick Engels Collected Works* (Vol. VI, pp. 477–519), S. Moore & F. Engels (Trans.). London: Lawrence & Wishart, 2010. |
| *MOS* | (1846). *Marx on Suicide*, E. A. Plaut, K. Anderson, G. Edgcom (Trans.). Evanston: Northwestern University Press, 1999. |
| *OJQ* | (1843). On the Jewish Question. In: *Karl Marx & Frederick Engels Collected Works* (Vol. III, pp. 146–174), C. Dutt (Trans.). London: Lawrence & Wishart, 2010. |
| *PP* | (1847). *The Poverty of Philosophy. Answer to the Philosophy of Poverty by M. Proudhon*, Institute of Marxism Leninism (Trans.). Moscow: Progress, 1955. |

| | |
|---|---|
| *PPO* | (1880). The Programme of the Parti Ouvrier. In: *The First International and After,* (pp. 376–377), D. Fernbach (Trans.). London: Verso, 2010. |
| *PRW* | (1864). A Provisional Rules of the Working Men's International Association. In: *The Bee-Hive Newspaper*, London, November 1864. |
| *TER* | (1862). The Election Results in the United States. In: *Karl Marx & Frederick Engels Collected Works* (Vol. XIX, pp. 263–265), P. Ross & B. Ross (Trans.). London: Lawrence & Wishart, 2010. |
| *TOF* | (1845). Theses on Feuerbach. In: *Karl Marx & Frederick Engels Collected Works* (Vol. V, pp. 3–5), W. Lough (Trans.). London: Lawrence & Wishart, 2010. |
| *VPP* | (1865). *Value, Price, and Profit*, International Publishers (Trans.). Chicago: Charles H. Kerr & Company, 1910. |

# Contributors

**Jorge Alemán** is an Argentinian psychoanalyst and writer living in Madrid. He is a member of the World Association of Psychoanalysis. He is currently the director of the Lacanian journal *Lacan emancipa* (Lacan Emancipates). He has published *Ideología* (NED/Página 12, 2021), *En la frontera. Sujeto y capitalismo* (Gedisa, 2014), and *Horizontes neoliberales en la subjetividad* (Grama, 2016).

**Elena Bisso** teaches psychoanalysis and holds a PhD in psychology at University of Buenos Aires (UBA), Argentina. She practises psychoanalysis. Her PhD thesis proposes a response to the objection that Deleuze made to Lacan on the univocity of the unconscious in 1969, published as *Lacan, Deleuze y Lalangue* (Prometeo, 2017). Her research interests include Freud, Lacan, and their intersection with education and labour studies.

**Livio Boni** is a psychoanalyst, PhD in psychopathology, translator, and researcher living in Paris. Currently he teaches at *Collège international de philosophie*. He has published *L'inconscio post-coloniale. Geopolitica della psicoanalisi* (Mimesis, 2018) and *La vie psychique du racisme* (with Sophie Mendelsohn, La Découverte, 2021). He is also a member of the editorial committee of the journal *Actuel Marx*.

**Nadia Bou-Ali** is Assistant Professor and Director of Civilization Studies Program at the American University in Beirut. She practises psychoanalysis in Beirut. Her research interests include intellectual history, psychoanalysis, and critical theory. She has co-edited the book *Lacan contra Foucault* (Bloomsbury, 2019) and authored the book *Psychoanalysis and the Love of Arabic* (Edinburgh University Press, 2020).

**Pierre Bruno** is a psychoanalyst based in Paris. He is a former professor of psychoanalysis at the University of Paris 8 Vincennes-Saint-Denis, and he is a member of the psychoanalytic association *Le pari de Lacan* (Lacan's Wager) and the editorial board of the journal *Psychanalyse*.

**Mariano Nicolás Campos** is a PhD candidate in philosophy at Universidad de Buenos Aires, Argentina. His research interests are Marx's theory of fetishism and

French and German reception of Marx in the 20th century. Currently he is a professor at Universidad de Buenos Aires. He teaches on the relation between Hegel and Marx and on contemporary authors like Sohn-Rethel, Debord, and Žižek. He has coordinated seminars in hospital institutions on Marxism and Lacanian psychoanalysis. He is the author of the book *El desciframiento del mercado: brillo, automatismo y lógica en Karl Marx* (2021, Prometeo Libros).

**Jean-Pierre Cléro** is Emeritus Professor of Philosophy at the University of Rouen Normandy, France, and Director of the Centre Bentham (Sciences Po, Paris). His areas of research are mathematics, classical English philosophy, and medical ethics. He has translated many books by Bentham, Stuart Mill, Moore, and Harsanyi. He has also published books such as *Lacan in the English Language* (Aguincourt, 2020), *Lacan: Y a-t-il une philosophie de Lacan?* (Ellipses, 2015), *Le vocabulaire de Lacan* (Ellipses, 2012), and *Calcul moral ou comment raisonner en éthique* (A. Colin, 2004).

**Daniela Danelinck** is a PhD candidate in philosophy at Universidad de Buenos Aires, Argentina. She has a doctoral scholarship at the Institute Dr. Emilio Ravignani (CONICET). A self-proclaimed "theoretical psychoanalyst", she has written numerous articles on theoretical or "ultra-lay psychoanalysis". The subject of her current research is the problem of causality involved in Lacan's theory of discourses. She has published *Debería darte vergüenza. Ensayo sobre álgebra lacanaiana* (Heterónimos, 2018). She is also a professor at Universidad Nacional de Tres de Febrero, Argentina, a member of *Entrevenir*, and co-coordinator of the Laboratory of Politics of the Unconscious.

**Christian Ingo Lenz Dunker** is a Brazilian psychoanalyst and full-time professor at Psychology Institute at USP. He is an Analyst Member of School (AME) of the Forum of the Lacanian Field. He is currently coordinating the Laboratory of Social Theory, Philosophy and Psychoanalysis of the USP. He is the author of *Pasión de la ignorancia* (Contracorrente, 2020), *Transformaciones de la intimidad* (Ubu, 2017), and *Structure and Constitution of Psychoanalytic Clinic* (Karnac, 2010). He has won twice the Jabuti Prize in Brazil.

**Ricardo Espinoza Lolas** is a Chilean philosopher, writer, and critical theorist. He is currently a full-time professor at Pontificia Universidad Católica in Chile, where he teaches contemporary philosophy. He has published books such as *Žižek Reloaded: Políticas de lo radical* (Akal, 2018), *NosOtros: Manual para disolver el capitalismo* (Trotta, 2019), and *¡Hegel Hoy!* (Herder, 2020).

**Roque Farrán** practises philosophy in Córdoba, Argentina. He is currently a researcher at Political Theory Studies Program (CIECS-CONICET) where he directs the research group on Materialist Thinking. He has published several books such as *Badiou y Lacan: El anudamiento del sujeto* (Prometeo, 2014), *El uso* *de los saberes* (Borde Perdido, 2018), and *Populismo, Feminismo, Psicoanálisis* (Prometeo, 2020).

**Carlos Gómez Camarena** is a practising psychoanalyst and a member of the Forum of the Lacanian Field in Mexico City. He is a full-time professor and researcher at the Universidad Iberoamericana, Mexico City. His research revolves around mathematics, 20th-century French philosophy, and psychoanalysis. Currently he is co-directing in Mexico the international research project 'Extimacies: Critical Theory from the Global South', financed by the Andrew Mellon Grant Foundation.

**Ben Gook** is Lecturer in Cultural Studies at the University of Melbourne. He was previously an Alexander von Humboldt Postdoctoral Fellow at Humboldt University, Berlin. His research interests include psychoanalysis, affects and emotions, cultural and social theory, screen studies, and cultural studies. In 2015, he published *Divided Subjects, Invisible Borders: Re-Unified Germany after 1989* (Rowman & Littlefield). He is currently working on alienation and disaffection.

**Dominiek Hoens**, PhD (Ghent University), teaches philosophy at the Royal Institute for Theatre, Cinema and Sound (RITCS, Brussels), where he also does research under the heading of "Capital owes you nothing". Recent publications include an edited collection on Marguerite Duras (www.lineofbeauty.org), a chapter on Jacques Lacan in *Routledge Handbook of Psychoanalytic Political Theory* (2020), and several articles on Blaise Pascal.

**Adrian Johnston** is Chair and Distinguished Professor in the Department of Philosophy at the University of New Mexico at Albuquerque and a faculty member at the Emory Psychoanalytic Institute in Atlanta. His most recent book is *Prolegomena to Any Future Materialism, Volume Two: A Weak Nature Alone* (Northwestern University Press, 2019). With Todd McGowan and Slavoj Žižek, he is a co-editor of the book series Diaeresis at Northwestern University Press.

**Edgar Miguel Juárez-Salazar** is Professor of Social Psychology at Universidad Autónoma Metropolitana-Xochimilco (UAM-X), Mexico City. He has published several books and articles on Lacanian psychoanalysis and critical psychology and translated Samo Tomšič's *The Labour of Enjoyment* (Paradiso, forthcoming) into Spanish. His current research revolves around the archival studies on guerrilla political movements in Latin America during the 1960s and 1970s using Lacanian approaches to discourse analysis.

**Nadir Lara Junior** is a psychoanalyst and independent researcher in Brazil. His areas of research interest are Lacanian discourse analysis, critical theory, psychoanalysis, and Marxism. He has co-edited the books *Psicanálise e Marxismo: as violências em tempos de capitalismo* (with David Pavón-Cuéllar, Appris, 2018) and *Análise lacaniana de discurso: Subversão e pesquisa crítica* (with Christian Dunker, Appris, 2019).

**Silvia Lippi** is a psychoanalyst in Paris. She holds a PhD in psychology from Université de Paris 7. Currently she is a psychologist at the health hospital EPS Barthélemy Durand in Étampes, France.

**Juan Pablo Lucchelli** is a psychiatrist and psychoanalyst living in Switzerland. He is a member of the World Association of Psychoanalysis. He is the author of several books on psychoanalysis, including *Introduction à l'objet a de Lacan* (Michèle, 2020) and *Sexualités en travaux* with S. Žižek and J.-C. Milner (Michèle, 2018).

**Yahya M. Madra** is Associate Professor of Economics at Drew University, NJ, USA, and is a psychoanalyst-in-training at the National Psychological Association for Psychoanalysis in New York City. He is a co-editor of the journal *Rethinking Marxism*.

**Todd McGowan** teaches theory and film at the University of Vermont. He is the author of *Universality and Identity Politics* (Columbia University Press, 2020), *Emancipation After Hegel* (Columbia University Press, 2019), *Only a Joke Can Save Us* (Northwestern University Press, 2017), *Capitalism and Desire* (Columbia University Press, 2016), and other works. He is the editor of the Film Theory in Practice series at Bloomsbury and co-editor of the Diaeresis series with Slavoj Žižek and Adrian Johnston at Northwestern University Press.

**Ceren Özselçuk** is Associate Professor in the Department of Sociology at Boğaziçi University, Istanbul. She is an editorial member and managing editor of the journal *Rethinking Marxism*.

**Ian Parker** is Co-director of the Discourse Unit (www.discourseunit.com) and a practising psychoanalyst in Manchester. His books include *Psychoanalysis, Clinic and Context: Subjectivity, History and Autobiography* (Routledge, 2019) and, with David Pavón-Cuéllar, *Psychoanalysis and Revolution: Critical Psychology for Liberation Movements*.

**Fabiana Parra** is a researcher at Instituto de Investigaciones en Humanidades y Ciencias Sociales (IdIHCS) and advisor at Consejo Nacional de Investigaciones en Ciencia y Tecnología (CONICET) in Argentina. She is currently teaching at Universidad Nacional de La Plata (UNLP), Argentina. Her research focuses on ideology, subjectivation, critical politics, Global South feminisms, and intersectionality.

**David Pavón-Cuéllar** is a researcher and full-time professor at Universidad Michoacana de San Nicolás de Hidalgo (UMSNH), Mexico. His latest books include *Más allá de la psicología indígena: concepciones mesoamericanas de la subjetividad* (Porrúa, 2021), *Zapatismo y subjetividad: más allá de la psicología* (with Mihalis Mentinis, Cátedra Libre, 2020), *Psicología crítica: definición, antecedentes, historia y actualidad* (Itaca, 2019), and *Marxism and Psychoanalysis: In or Against Psychology?* (Routledge, 2017).

**Natalia Romé** is Chair Professor in Social Sciences at the Universidad de Buenos Aires, where she is also the Director of the Master in Communication and Culture Studies. She is Senior Researcher in Instituto de Investigaciones Gino Germani, Universidad de Buenos Aires, where she co-coordinates the Program of Critical Studies. She is one of the foundation members of the Red Latinoamericana de Estudios Althusserianos, member of the editing board of *Demarcaciones,* and is part of the Organizing Committee of Althusserian Studies Conferences since 2009. She has also published *La posición materialista. El pensamiento de Louis Althusser entre la práctica teórica y la práctica política* (Edulp: La Plata, 2015) and *For Theory: Althusser and the Politics of Time* (Rowman & Littlefield, 2021).

**Agustina Saubidet** is a psychoanalyst. She teaches and holds a fellowship at the University of Buenos Aires (UBA). The subject of her research for her PhD is the clinical consequences of incest in adults from anthropological, philosophical, and psychoanalytical perspectives. She won the Psychology Faculty Prize 2018 at UBA for her essay "The Anthropological Criticism of the Oedipus Complex: Its Contributions". She works as a consultant and trainer at several health institutions in Argentina.

**Christina Soto van der Plas** is Adjunct Lecturer at Santa Clara University, California. She has a PhD in Romance studies from Cornell University. She has published several articles and essays on Latin American literature in national and international journals. Her non-fiction book, *Curaçao, costa de cemento pueblo de prisión* (FETA, 2019), won the National Prize for Young Chronicle in Mexico. She is also translator of Alenka Zupančič into Spanish for Paradiso Editores. She is currently obtaining her licence to practise counseling psychology and is interested in psychoanalysis. Her book *A Poetics of Transliterature in Latin America* is forthcoming. In her current research project, she is focusing on tracing the corpus, project, and definition of "Latin American Antiphilosophies".

**Samo Tomšič** obtained his PhD in philosophy at the University of Ljubljana, Slovenia. He is currently research associate at the Humboldt University of Berlin, Germany, and visiting professor at the University of Ljubljana. His research areas comprise structuralism, psychoanalysis, political philosophy, and contemporary European philosophy. Recent publications include *The Capitalist Unconscious: Marx and Lacan* (Verso, 2015) and *The Labour of Enjoyment: Towards a Critique of Libidinal Economy* (August Verlag, 2019).

Contributors xxiii

**Carlos Andrés Umaña González** is a practising psychoanalyst. He was a researcher at the Institute of Social Investigations of the University of Costa Rica. Currently he is the Executive Director of *Fundamentes Foundation* and creator of the programme "Prevention Houses for Listening and Developing Art Skills for the Youth in Risk" recognized in 2020 with the National Youth Award "Jorge Debravo" by the Ministry of Culture of Costa Rica. His research focuses on the constitution of subjectivity in the neoliberal period and the relationship between politics and psychoanalysis.

**Andreja Zevnik** is Senior Lecturer in Politics at the University of Manchester. Her research is inspired by psychoanalysis, continental philosophy, and critical race theory and mainly focuses on the production of subjectivities and different political imaginaries in acts of resistance amongst various marginalized groups. Her publications include *Jacques Lacan Between Psychoanalysis and Politics* (with Tomšič, Routledge 2015), *Lacan and Deleuze: A Disjunctive Synthesis* (with Nedoh, Edinburgh University Press 2017), and *Politics of Anxiety* (with Eklund and Guittet, Rowman & Littlefield, 2017).

**Transliteration contributors**

**Abdallah El Ayach** is a researcher at the American University of Beirut working on the problem of language and social mediation in relation to rational cognition and self-consciousness. His research concentrates on Lacanian psychoanalysis, Marxism, and American pragmatism. He also works on the problem of translation of modern philosophy into Arabic, focusing on the translations of German Idealism. He has worked on developing a database, under the name *Naqd*, for critical theory in Arabic including both translations and monographs.

**Hidemoto Makise** is Associate Professor of Life Health Science at Chubu University, Aichi, Japan. He practises psychoanalysis and is one of the directors of Lacanian Society of Japan. He is the author of several articles nf psychoanalysis and the book *Psychoanalysis and Drawings* (Seishin Shobo, 2015).

**Maria Melnikova** is Senior Lecturer in Psychology at the Department of Clinical Psychology, Conflictology and Psychoanalysis, Udmurt State University (Izhevsk, Russia). She is also an editor and translator for the ERGO publishing house, which specializes in the publication of books on the humanities, primarily on psychoanalysis.

**Sergey Sirotkin** is Professor of Psychology, Head of the Department of Clinical Psychology, Conflictology and Psychoanalysis, Udmurt State University (Izhevsk, Russia). He is also the director of the ERGO publishing house, focused on publishing books in the humanities, primarily psychoanalysis.

**Tzuchien Tho** is a philosopher and historian of science. He is currently lecturer at the University of Bristol. Previously, He has been affiliated with the Jan van Eyck Academie in Maastricht (NL), the École Normale Supérieure in Paris (*Rue D'Ulm*), the Max Planck Institute for the History of Science (Berlin), Berlin-Brandenburg Academy of Sciences, the Institute for Research in the Humanities (University of Bucharest), and the University of Milan. He is currently working on a research project on causality in 18th-century physics, focusing on the development of analytical mechanics. He is also currently working on issues related to Badiou's mathematical ontology, the philosophy of algebra, Leibniz's reception in the 20th century, and the critique of contextualism as historical methodology.

# Acknowledgements

Many thanks are due to our editor at Routledge, Ian Parker, for entrusting us with the task of compiling this vocabulary and for his invaluable help during the various stages of its preparation. Concluding this project would have been impossible without the assistance of Ana Claudia Flores Ames and Carla Tirado Morttiz. We are also greatly indebted to Jean-Pierre Cléro for his help on our database of implicit and explicit quotes on Marx in Lacan's seminars and *écrits*. This database was the core and the origin of this vocabulary.

This vocabulary has been part of the international research project 'Extimacies: Critical Theory from the Global South', financed by the Andrew Mellon Grant Foundation (Early Career Program). Many thanks to our colleagues Surti Singh, Ian Morrison, Nadia Bou-Ali, Alejandro Cerda-Rueda, Sami Khatib, and Silvio Carneiro.

Last but not least, we would like to thank all contributors for their devotion, originality, and erudition. Any remaining mistakes, conscious and unconscious, should be attributed solely to the editors of this volume.

Christina Soto wants to thank Cynthia for her patience throughout the process.

Edgar Juárez wants to dedicate this vocabulary to Andrea Huerta for her love and support.

Carlos Gómez Camarena wants to dedicate this vocabulary to his father, a strange businessman who has voted all his life for the Communist Party.

# Preface: Marx's homologous, Lacan

*Christina Soto van der Plas, Edgar Miguel Juárez-Salazar, Carlos Gómez Camarena and David Pavón-Cuéllar*

Jacques Lacan was known for constantly playing with words. He either split them or combined them, used them in an allusive or elliptical way; he often deviated from their narrow definitions and gave them different meanings, depending on the moment in which they appeared. He also exhumed terms that were no longer in use, or coined neologisms for each argument. He used different languages and mixed them, exploited *double entendres*, and never prevented the incessant sliding of meaning. Sometimes, in following his own theory, he took no interest in the signified and only manipulated the literal signifier, favouring the rhythm and musicality at the expense of everything else.

The way in which Lacan used words is apparently incompatible with a vocabulary. How to catalogue a set of such broad, heterogeneous, intricate, volatile, and unpredictable set of words? How to compile concepts if they can be re-read, undone, reinvented, and if the very term "concept" is highly problematic in Lacan's work? The very idea of a vocabulary could be thought to be simply meaningless and seem inadmissible from Lacan's perspective.

We might be under the impression that psychoanalysis, particularly in the Lacanian version, consists of something that cannot be enclosed in its concepts, that exceeds, goes beyond or transcends them. But Lacan himself dismisses this first impression. In his own words, psychoanalysis is something that can be found in "the concepts through which it is formulated and transmitted", something that "endures" through these concepts, and is not "something else", different from them. In such a way, the psychoanalytical "vocabulary" is psychoanalysis itself, and not "a signal of things which would be beyond", not a repertoire of "little labels, designations floating in the unnamed of everyday analytic experience" (*SII*, 24.11.54, p. 14). This experience is constituted internally and configured by the vocabulary, presenting itself and not only representing or reflecting itself in it, since there are no two different planes roughly coinciding with one another. There is only one plane or level and it is made of words.

The peculiar way in which Lacan considers words allows for accessing the also peculiar experience of the analysis. Louis Althusser understood this very well when he remarked that Lacan staged the "language of the unconscious" in the "rhetoric of his words" (p. 32). Lacanian rhetoric is not incompatible with a vocabulary, but rather it already constitutes a vocabulary in its own right, is apparently incompatible with what is often understood by the idea of a "vocabulary", displaying what is at stake in the analytic experience.

Lacan's concepts are fascinating because they ingeniously reveal and unsettle what they are referring to. For Lacan, it is about helping us delve into a reality that can only be grasped when we "designate it by means of our vocabulary" (*SII*, 24.11.54, p. 14). The repertoire of concepts is necessary to pave the way for what they name. This is precisely what Lacan discovers in his reading of Karl Marx, and this is what he uncovers for us through the concepts that guide it, which are the concepts catalogued in this vocabulary.

## Marx *through* Lacan

The concepts included in *The Marx through Lacan Vocabulary* are the ones that we considered to be the fundamental concepts for the Lacanian reading of Marx. Either Marx or different Marxist thinkers used most of these concepts in their work, but Lacan gave them new meanings, inseparable from the Freudian legacy, that ultimately allow us to perceive surprisingly novel perspectives on what they describe. These perspectives can be grasped precisely by virtue of how psychoanalysis is articulated with Marxism in each concept.

The revolution which Lacan addresses in his work, for example, is the same one that Marx and his followers wrote about, but in thinking the revolution also through Freud and his categories, he binds it together with regression and repetition, thus enhancing the conception of the logical drive of the revolution. Similarly, the Freudian theory of the unconscious and its Lacanian correlation with language allow for a more complex understanding of the Marxist concept of alienation. Other concepts included in the Vocabulary function similarly: each one of them gives rise, in fact, to an articulation of Marxism and psychoanalysis, centred on the same object.

It is precisely because they refer to the same object, that Marx's and Lacan's conceptualizations can be articulated in a single concept. Each one of the concepts confirms and reaffirms the homology between the conceptual formulations that converge in it and articulate themselves around its object. Instead of getting confused and muddled as in Freudo-Marxism, these formulations can be comprehended precisely because Lacan knows that they are homologous, they are of the same kind, and they move in the same space of logic. The object to which they refer is constructed logically and for the same reason there is an homology. The homology between Marx and Lacan is what we outlined in the first title for this vocabulary: *Marx : Lacan*. We indicated in such a way that it is Lacan's vocabulary but it is also Marx's. It would be impossible to abstract from Marx concepts that he did not use and that are distinctively Lacanian, such as surplus-*jouissance*, but the concept designates indeed what is at the core of Marx's unravelling of surplus-value.

Each concept corresponds to *what Lacan worked through in what Marx discovered.* Lacan delves deeper into the Marxian discovery and that is his precisely contribution. By delving deeper into Marx's thought, Lacan either confirms, reassesses, specifies, introduces nuances, plays it down, pinpoints, makes more specific or general, clarifies, or contradicts it. Among others, these operations can be appreciated in Lacan's addressing of Marx's concepts, included in the Vocabulary.

The initial name of this project was *"Marx : Lacan Vocabulary"*, which takes up a similar formula proposed by the Argentinian psychoanalysts Jorge Alemán and Sergio Larriera in their book *Lacan : Heidegger,* which "builds relationships with his sayings" and allows us to think of the relationship between Marx and Lacan as a form of thought in "open and discontinuous development". For them, this *non-relationship* between Marx and Lacan has no guarantees, and it is not an easy one. It is a continuous and discontinuous bond at the same time or, to express it in Deleuzian terms, a "disjunctive conjunction". The colon punctuation sign functions as a kind of *matheme,* and emphasizing the non-guaranteed, contingent, conjectural, and certainly not-easy link between these two forms of thought. But we also wanted to avoid the classic Lacanian approaches to psychoanalysis where these connections are punctuated by *"avec",* the traditional "and", or even the *losange* ($\lozenge$) as a paradoxical or fixed form of this relationship. Our collaborators agreed to be part of the project to contribute to the development of this formula.

## From the register to the vocabulary

Lacan commented about the famous *Technical and Critical Vocabulary of Philosophy* by André Lalande (1926)[1] that "[a]ttempts to establish such dictionaries are extremely perilous and yet simultaneously fruitful", because language is "crucial to every problem we examine" (*SVI,* 12.11.58, p. 8). We cannot avoid the problems when dealing with its formulation. Elucidating a concept is as dangerous as it is fruitful because there is a demand to tackle the fundamental theoretical questions where it intervenes and it implies taking a stance facing each and every one of them. The different authors traced in their entries this repertoire of the fundamental concepts through which Lacan reads Marx.

The authors of the entries were chosen primarily for their familiarity with the concepts assigned to them, as well as for their interest and theoretical work that have Lacan's reading of Marx as a compass. The analysis of this reading, carried out by one of us, is at the origin of the Vocabulary. The first step, and the moment when this project was unknowingly born, was a thorough register of Lacan's explicit and allusive references to Marx, including his name, his ideas, and his concepts. The initial version of this register was prepared at the University of Rouen, Haute-Normandie, between 2006 and 2007, and was supervised by Jean-Pierre Cléro, who wrote the "Value" entry for this vocabulary. This version was the basis of the PhD dissertation of its author (Pavón-Cuéllar, 2013) and of many of his publications (cf. Pavón-Cuéllar, 2009; 2014), and it was later enriched by another one of us in the Universidad Michoacana de San Nicolás de Hidalgo, Morelia, between 2013 and

2014, within the framework of a series of research projects with diverse products, including the dissertation of the author that developed them (Juárez-Salazar, 2014).

After those initial and exhaustive uses of the collection and its first supplements, there was still a partial record that remained, a part of the mystic writing board that was firmly opposed to its disappearance or it being condemned to oblivion. That remainder became the basis for all the 28 entries, also tracing a journey through singular, confusing, strange, suggestive, and incisive moments of the relationship between Lacan's teaching and his frequent mentions of the work of Marx and Marxism. Lacan's baroque and unmistakable style produced an enormous number of citations that were, by their very nature, somewhat unclassifiable. The twists and turns of the Lacanian way of transmission, further enhanced by Jacques-Alain Miller's authorization, made this comprehensive collection of quotations an oftentimes unintelligible monster that required weeks of re-reading and ordering. The initial database progressively grew and again each citation was found electronically to be then refined and reclassified, discarding some extremely vague passages that distanced themselves from the relevant connection between Lacan and Marx.

A few years later, when the project of what we called a "dictionary" at the time began to take shape, we found an allusion from Lacan to Marx and Freud that explores what a citation is:

> What does a citation consist in? In the course of a text where you are making more or less good progress, if you happen to be in the right places of the class struggle, all of a sudden you will cite Marx, and you will add, "Marx said". If you are an analyst you will cite Freud and you will add, "Freud said". This is fundamental [*capital*].
>
> (*SXVII*, 17.12.69, p. 37)

Lacan affirms that recurring to Marx and Freud is not an arbitrary matter. However, the real problem with citing is, according to Lacan himself, the enunciation. The enunciation constitutes an "enigma", that impregnable feature of the signifier—anyone can cite and occupy the place of the statement, which is a matter that should at least move us and shake off the plague of knowledge. A "citation" is, effectively, a "half-said", a means of enjoyment, in which we find ourselves already being part of a "*discours*" and a "*structure*". In Lacan's own words, it is in the "enigma" itself that the "interpretation" is at stake, and this is the reason why we decided to define it as a vocabulary, acquiring a contingent nuance (*SXVII*, 17.12.69, p. 37). Along these lines, the re-reading of Marx, Lacan, or even Freud is not only a matter of perspective or operations, but also of enunciations and positions.

In other words, the Vocabulary took shape in a strange way and its interstices, composed by a multitude of citations, were meant to be reworked by various authors. The different ways in which these authors interpreted the citations is what constitutes each one of the entries. Meanwhile, when the corpus of this archive was being formalized, we were also bewildered by the enigma. The clearest example of this is that, at some point, we confused the term "consumerism" with "communism", which sparked, months later, an anxious joke-work and ended up becoming the entry on "communism"—there was certainly some surplus-*jouissance* gained from this joke. When we discovered the mistake we had made, we had to seek two more collaborators, and after discussing their interpretation and takes on the concept. What was originally an entry on "consumerism" was consequently transformed into "consumption" and, in a consecutive accidental dissolution, a new entry appeared: "automatism".

Almost a year before this mythical lapsus, Carlos Gómez Camarena and Christina Soto van der Plas enthusiastically joined the project and, with their help, the database was finally consolidated and the authors of the entries assigned. Christina served not only as an editor but was also responsible for the English edition—which will certainly be followed by editions in Spanish, Portuguese, Italian, French, and probably Russian and Turkish. The initial instructions for the authors were to follow the vocation of an open, contingent, militant writing that reflected their way of opening and reworking the bond between Marx and Lacan. Our Vocabulary goes beyond the accumulative and enjoyable process of gathering knowledge. It is for this reason that our proposal sought, from the very beginning, to appeal to young researchers, Lacanians from the so-called Global South, and also from the well-known European and Anglo-Saxon world, always trying to achieve an equitable percentage of participation. For these same reasons, each entry respects and follows the unique style of each author.

Consequently, in addition to having certain characteristics of indeterminacy in its writing, our Vocabulary is also a way of organizing and systematizing that which sometimes produces enormous gaps in the reading of Marx by Lacan under the attempt of having an impact at the crossroads, impasses, and contingencies of both thinkers. At the same time, the choice of the authors gathered here sought to bring together collaborators whose militancy, academic research, and work from psychoanalysis were also characterized by the significance of recovering the validity of Marx's thought in Lacan's subversive gaze. This approach also focused on the Marxian-Lacanian orientations produced in the countries of the Global South who play a significant role. Most of the authors—18 out of 30—come from this region of the world. It was more difficult to maintain a similar balance in terms of gender—9 out of 30 authors are women. An important pending matter is the participation of Marxian-Lacanian authors from Africa and who are black.

The contributors include authors from four continents: America, Asia, Europe, and Australia; from countries such as Argentina, Mexico, Costa Rica, Chile, Brazil, Turkey, Slovenia, Italy, Lebanon, Belgium, England, France, Australia, and the United States. Ultimately, to enhance the open vocation of a vocabulary—and inspired by the work of Barbara Cassin (2004)—we included in the entries the transliterations and translation of the terms in Turkish, Chinese, Russian, Japanese, and Arabic, assisted by fellow academics, militants, and psychoanalysts from Japan, Russia, Lebanon, and England. The Vocabulary contains an annex with some problems—and opportunities—about the (un)translatability of certain terms into other languages and their possible implications and main bearings for Marxism and psychoanalysis in those languages. Ultimately, due to its nature as a vocabulary, we envision that editions in other languages will contain new entries or forewords by psychoanalysts, Marxists, militants, academic or crucial philosophers in those languages. This was and has been the fate of the important work undertaken by Barbara Cassin (2014b) throughout these years.

The entries that were developed for this volume constitute what we consider fundamental concepts for both theoretical worlds. From alienation to labour, the trajectory takes us through Marx's explanations, interrogations, and analysis that were in their turn also questioned, criticized, and reworked by Lacan, accounting for the wide reach of two thinkers and worlds in constant homology. The core of the project and how it is organized lie in the polyphony and contingency of each one of them and in the clinical-political uses that Lacan highlighted and seized. Each entry also represents some of the interests of the authors and contain their concerns, and for this reason each one has a "Further reading" section with perpendicular works that can help readers explore new routes. In global terms, this collective work allows the reader to explore routes of inquiry into the relationship between the economic-political world and the psychoanalytic world, in addition to detailing Lacan's voyages in search for Marx throughout his entire work.

Regarding the labyrinthine citation process of Lacan's *Écrits*, seminars, interviews, speeches, letters, fragmentary notes, and lectures in English, we have decided to refer to the works in their official English versions (W.W. Norton or Polity Press). To avoid further complexities between the official and unofficial versions, we included at the beginning of our Vocabulary a helpful guide including the abbreviations of Lacan and Marx's works that were used in the entries. As for the unofficial versions, we decided to refer to the original works in French and we followed the well-known and widespread translations by C. Gallagher, A. R. Price, R. Grigg, and their respective collaborators, as well as some other translators whose translations have not been officially published, but are freely accessible online. In this sense, we are very grateful for the editions of internal circulation translated by Cormac Gallagher and other psychoanalysts, whose names are unfortunately unknown to us. In specific cases, several authors directly translated seminars or unpublished writings from French or Spanish, which have not been published in English. In both cases we included in the citations only the abbreviation of the work and the date of the session, if applicable, without a page number. When we use a published version of Lacan's seminars, the citation includes the date of the seminar session cited, and the pagination. Including the date is already a code widely used among those who study Lacan and has been adopted as a response to the fragmentation and little editorial care to which the work of the Parisian psychoanalyst has been subjected. As for Marx's works, we follow the most well-known versions in English (published by Penguin) and the Collected Works.

## On the Vocabulary

The preface of the *Dictionary of Untranslatables* begins by tracing a genealogy to locate the place that this filiation occupies (Apter, 2014, p. VII):

> [It] belongs in a genealogy that includes Diderot and d'Alembert's *Encylopédie* (1751–66), André Lalande's *Vocabulaire technique et critique de philosophie* (1902–23), Émile Benveniste's *Le Vocabulaire des institutions indo-européennes*, Laplanche and Pontalis's *The Language of Psycho-Analysis* (1967, classified as a dictionary), *The Stanford Encyclopedia of Philosophy* (an online resource inaugurated in 1995), and Reinhart Koselleck's *Geschichtliche Grundbegriffe* (a dictionary of political and social concept-history, 2004). Along another axis, it recalls Raymond Williams's short compendium of political and aesthetic terms, *Key-words*, informed by British Marxism of the 1960s and '70s. Unlike these works, however, the *Dictionary* fully mobilizes a multilingual rubric.

Our Vocabulary inscribes itself in the lineage of this same genealogy, including the multilingual rubric—which is what we will call untranslatable, *lalangue*, or misunderstanding. It is also worth noticing that two of these works are directly related with psychoanalysis (Laplanche and Pontalis) and with Marxism (Williams).

Within Marxism and in relation to Marx, there has been a wide variety of glossaries and lexicons, almost all of them made for popular-interest books or for communist parties and, for this very reason, they did not circulate more broadly. The first widely available dictionaries and vocabularies about Marx's work were published in the 1980s—taking a rather critical stance and going against the grain of official Marxism—among which the most prominent are those of Bottomore (1983) *A Dictionary of Marxist Thought*, Bensussan and Labica's (1982) *Dictionnaire critique du marxisme*, and Carver's (1987) *A Marx Dictionary*.

While certainly the *Vocabulaire du marxisme: Français-allemand* (Bekerman, 1981) was a bilingual attempt to address Marxist concepts, it is not based on "the multilingual rubric", that is, it is not based on the equivocal. Other important dictionaries that have been published in the new millennium are the *Dictionnaire Marx contemporain* (Bidet & Kouvelakis, 2001) and *The Marx Dictionary* (Fraser & Wilde, 2011). Another two interesting projects are the historical-conceptual approach to Marxism contained in the *Historical Dictionary of Marxism* Walker & Gray, 2007), and—following the British tradition of keywords—the *Revolutionary Keywords for a New Left* (Parker, 2017), which includes two interesting terms: "psychoanalysis" and "psychologization".

The French collection of vocabularies, in the "Ellipses" publishing house, more recently published three short vocabularies: on Marx (Renault, 2001), on Freud (Assoun, 2002), and on Lacan (Cléro, 2002). The latter was expanded, years later, and published as *Dictionnaire Lacan* (Cléro, 2008).

As for the psychoanalysis dictionaries, the above-mentioned *The Language of Psycho-Analysis* (Laplanche & Pontalis, 1967) and *International Dictionary of Psychoanalysis* (De Mijolla, 2005) are more general psychoanalytic approaches and target an international audience of psychoanalysts. In a line closer to French psychoanalysis the *Dictionnaire de la psychanalyse* by Chemama and Vandermersch (1993), and Élisabeth Roudinesco and Michel Plon's (1997) dictionary with the same title follow a more historical-conceptual understanding. The first dictionary fully devoted to Lacan's work is Saint-Drôme's (1994) *Dictionnaire inespéré de 55 termes visités par Jacques Lacan* [*Unexpected Dictionary of 55 Terms Addressed by Lacan*], and two years later *An Introductory Dictionary of Lacanian Psychoanalysis* (Evans, 1996) was published. This last book is the most famous dictionary on the topic, and is guided by a thesaurus-like structure, almost a database, and was developed during the author's research stay in Buenos Aires.

Finally, there are two unique dictionaries, one due to the specificity of its subject—*Dictionnaire amoureux de la psychanalyse* (Roudinesco, 2017)—and the other due to how close it is to our approach: *Psychanalyser en langues: intraduisibles et langue chinoise* (Cassin & Gorog, 2016). The first one approaches psychoanalysis through the lens of love and the second one relies precisely on the untranslatability of the Chinese language to think about psychoanalytic practice.

This necessary detour allows us to locate our Vocabulary and its stance. Our affiliation is clearly twofold: Marxism and psychoanalysis. But what is unique about this project is that we depart from one author's terms—Marx—to think about how another author makes use of them—Lacan. In addition to this, we also read Lacan through Marx's lens. And we are not dealing only with a closed set of terms—open to the outside—but also of concepts that, given the many misunderstandings, mistakes, transliterations, and untranslatability they have endured, are also open to the inside (of each term).

Although the terms "vocabulary", "dictionary", "glossary", or "thesaurus" are apparently synonyms, they have different meanings and are distinguished by important nuances. While the thesaurus refers to a list of words, to a kind of warehouse or treasury that is sometimes confused with the dictionary, it is instead a kind of search system—classifying the texts in a certain hierarchy, inclusion or order—and it looks more like a database than a dictionary. The word thesaurus, however, comes from "treasure" and it cannot be ignored that it is the same term that Lacan uses when referring to the great Other: "the treasure trove of signifiers" (*SV*, 08.01.58, p. 134).

The lexicon is also a set of words, an inventory of ideas that brings together the expressions of the language from a particular community of speakers. It can even be thought of as a collection of jargon, slang, or argot. In this sense, the lexicon is located on the side of the vernacular, and not of a glossary. The glossary, on the other hand, is a compilation of definitions and explanations of technical terms, generally arranged alphabetically, and dealing with a specialized and sometimes highly technical subject. It aims to introduce technical words for those that are not familiar with a specific domain or world. For this reason, one can find lexicons within travel guides and glossaries at the end of a dissertation, a research project, a book, or an encyclopedia.

A dictionary is neither a lexicon nor a glossary as we have defined. It is a set—constituted in a network—of heterogeneous words and terms to be consulted. The dictionary is a system that offers us the meaning, definition, etymology, spelling, syllabic separation, grammatical form, lexical rules, and correct pronunciation of a word. The dictionary belongs to the realm of the official, to the stability of structures and to agreed-upon linguistic rules and guidelines. It is precisely the opposite of what Lacan called *lalangue* [*the language*] as an integral (or accumulation) of equivocals or misunderstandings that persist in a language (*LE*, p. 490). In other words: while the dictionary is governed by the correct form or standards for pronouncing, writing, defining, *lalangue* is the accumulation of words from other languages, the spelling errors, homophone words, grammatical mistakes, etc. French and Portuguese are two accumulations of misunderstandings and equivocal understandings from Latin. American English or Australian English are two *lalangues* that are equivocals of British English, as much as Mexican Spanish is an integral of misunderstandings different from those of Argentine Spanish, both derived from Iberian Castilian. This is a crucial issue, since the accumulation of grammatical, lexical, phonetic, or etymological mistakes is what makes the bastard become a diamond or a grain of sand turn into a pearl. These are the untranslatables: diamonds that emerge from a single coal. A vocabulary like Cassin's dictionary—like Lalande's—of the 21st century (Courtine, 2005).

A vocabulary *à la* Barbara Cassin has an open vocation. This is an open vocabulary but not in any way. It is not only about the endlessness or the flipside of a closed set, but rather about there being on the inside of each entry, each term, inconsistencies and problematic points or main bearings, which are ultimately the same. For this reason, the vocabulary does not follow the Wikipedia model of a modifiable and open space, because it does not have the main bearing of misunderstandings and untranslatability. A misunderstanding of a phonetic, scriptural, grammatical, or lexical mistake creates a pearl or a diamond: a whole tradition of thought, in the case of Marxism and psychoanalysis. We philosophize or theorize in specific languages. It is not a coincidence that here we are using verbs that point towards "philosophy" and later to "theory". The translators of the *Dictionary of Untranslatables* clarify this point in the introduction (Apter, 2014, p. VIII):

> "Theory" is an imprecise catchall for a welter of postwar movements in the human sciences—existentialism, structural anthropology, sociolinguistics, semiotics, history of *mentalités*, post-Freudian psychoanalysis, deconstruction, post-structuralism, critical theory, identity politics, post-colonialism, biopolitics, nonphilosophy, speculative materialism—that has no equivalent in European languages. What is often referred to as "theory" in an Anglophone context would simply be called "philosophy" in Europe.

In other spaces of the Global South, the question of theory and philosophy are discussed under different disguises and are perhaps more concerned with the validity and criticism of different forms of thought within specific traditions and languages. In this regard, the vocabulary is open to new entries and glosses, but also to the misunderstandings of each term. These misunderstandings, equivocals, and problematic points can be conceived of more as a productive tension rather than as places where the debates become stagnant or paralyzed. The untranslatable of each language is a symptom of each of them, but also a marker, a trait of the instability of meaning, of a performative dimension of language, a temporary condition of translation or even a new way of conceiving of sophistry: not so much as a hoax or a payment in exchange for knowledge but, as in Gorgias's sense, words that performatively create the being. Untranslatable is not "what cannot be translated, but what does (not) cease (not) being translated" (Cassin, 2014a, p. 30). More than words, untranslatables are travelling concepts, misplaced ideas that assign new meanings to old terms and are productive in their ambiguity. Outside of their natural environment, these concepts are located off the power grid of dominant languages and potentially mobilized around the disagreement over their meaning, around their alienation or misrecognition; unfaithful renderings. For this reason, this vocabulary has as a defining trait that in the titles of each entry the reader can also find the transliterations and translations of the terms. In the annexes, the reader will find notes on the transliterations and translations where there are comments on the possible misunderstandings and equivocals in the different languages, the traditions of untranslatability and the grains of sand that become pearls. These notes locate rich veins for Marxism and psychoanalysis in these languages; because we practise, theorize, think, and militate in languages—and not only through languages—but also because "untranslating" is knowing the difference.

Along these lines, the orientation of this vocabulary opposes that of an encyclopedia. The encyclopedia is a compendium of knowledge claiming to be universal and objective, a closed set, a "well-rounded education" (*enkyklo, paideia*) according to its etymology: an "Other of the Other" or Other guarantee, in Lacan's terms. The *Encyclopedia* was also a pedagogical project for political purposes whose main idea was to address citizens to politicize them with the motto demanding: *sapere aude*, dare to know! The project was of course based on opposing science and philosophy to religion and metaphysics. Its core rhetorical trope was the battle of light against darkness. Its co-ordinates were those of a philosophical, literary, and political modernity. Its aim: modernize the citizens. Our Vocabulary has a political ambition, but not in terms of accumulating knowledge or seeking its completion, in light over the shadow. Rather, it is about politicizing through language—and above all through the cross-readings of Marx : Lacan. But in a vocabulary with an open vocation—inwards and outwards—it is not about identities or cultural traditions, but rather about the reserves of misunderstandings, equivocals, and mistakes in a language. And, like the *Encyclopedia*, our Vocabulary also aimed to gather the voice of some of the most important philosophical and cultural figures and authors of Marxism and psychoanalysis.

Finally, a vocabulary is not a handbook seeking to update the knowledge on a specific topic nor is it a compilation of articles. It is also not a keyword, a term coined by the Welsh Marxist Raymond Williams (1976), who launched an entire intellectual tradition based on this type of intervention. The term "keyword" can also be understood as a "pass-word"—as in Spanish or French—that is, as an "abracadabra", a magic word to open closed doors and tear down the walls guarded by the sentry or a "shibboleth", to distinguish one tribe from another. In Spanish it is a *"palabra clave"*, a "clue" that would give us, precisely, a clue for understanding something broader. The linguistic sense of the "Keyword" now lies closer: an index of a word that appears in a text more than once, and that guide or orient the reading of a text—the insistence of the signifier, as Lacan would argue. A "keyword" opens doors in the sense that it reveals the internal structure of an author's reasoning, the conceptual or heuristic weight that a word—or concept—has in the work of an author or his thought. There is a pedagogical desire in such enterprise: to make complex terms accessible to elucidate the simplest ones. But a "keyword" has, let us put it this way, a Gramscian vein in William's work, since it is also *a debate over the cultural and hegemonic sense of a term* and what it means within a community. In all of these senses, our Vocabulary is a "Keyword" or, better yet, a "Key Concept".

In the origin of the term "vocabulary" we find the Latin word *vocabulum*, word, vocable, and that, in particular, has the quality of being *vocative*, that is, to call or summon someone or something, directly addressing them. Ultimately, it is related to the voice; it has to do with the act of directly calling, vouching, summoning, or perhaps even being summoned (as in vocation). In its more current form, we refer to vocabulary when we speak about the acquisition of a lexicon, as a repertoire, to express the twists and turns of a particular language. For our Vocabulary, we wanted precisely to highlight Lacan's calling to Marx and vice versa, and the way in which a concept not only carries a word forward as if it were an empty set to be filled with meaning, but rather is more intimately related to the vocation of the letter as material support that concrete discourse borrows from language. In this instance between the voice and the inscription of thought, keywords, and the untranslatability, our Vocabulary operates as a navigation chart for the libidinal and political economies.

The influence of Marx's thought on Lacan's theoretical and conceptual inquiries generally only focuses on the explicit relationships traced by Lacan in Seminars XVI and XVII, *From an Other to the other* and *The Other Side of Psychoanalysis*. However, throughout Lacan's work, some homologies can be read in the concepts we chose to develop in this vocabulary. But this was not our only wager. It was also about reading Marx through Lacan and sometimes even reading Lacan through Marx. Each author of the entries weighted this relationship differently, and gave a different sense to this "vectorization" of going from one author to the other. In some cases, the concept held more weight on Marx's side than on Lacan's and vice versa. For example, in a single entry, "Slavery", Marx's work was absent, which turned out to be a great discovery since the

Master–Slave axis was asymmetrical in Lacan's work: while the first term was clearly Marxist, the second one came from a Hegelian–Kojèvian tradition. Each entry strains the relationship between Marx and Lacan, but also between reading to the letter and what each author imprints with their characteristic style of reading—not only in their writing, but also because of the Marxist authors that are summoned to highlight an aspect of Marx (Gramsci, Althusser, Lukács, Williams, Luxemburg, among others). Therein lies also the richness of this vocabulary. Some entries were written by two authors, which led to the enhancement of their individual work. The vast majority of the entries are structured as follows: introduction, Marx's thought, Lacan's appropriation of the concept, and conclusions. Since the conception of the project some of the entries had different weight. The editors considered that entries such as "Labour", "Politics", or "Materialism" would be longer entries; "Communism", "Market", or "Money" would be medium in size; while "Bourgeoisie", "Imperialism", "Segregation", or "Value" would be shorter. In the research and editing process, some of these criteria changed when we realized their conceptual weight-bearing was different and there was much more to say about Marx's terms in Lacan. Furthermore, each entry relates to some entries more than to others. This is indicated at the beginning of each collaboration by a directionality that points towards other terms. In this regard, the Vocabulary can be conceived of as a compass with arrows pointing towards different directions, orienting different possible readings of the material.

The academics, researchers, psychoanalysts, and Marxists invited to collaborate belong to different generations and many of them have been researching on this topic for a long time, and their publications have already become classics in this field of study. Other collaborators are younger and have published texts in the last five years that have revitalized the panorama of Lacano-Marxism. For the new generations, it is impossible to conceive of Lacan without the work of Chantal Mouffe, Ernesto Laclau, Slavoj Žižek, Judith Butler, or Alain Badiou. In the case of Jorge Alemán—whose main works have unfortunately not been translated into English—he has had a great influence on most of the Latin American collaborators to this vocabulary. In this sense, the phrase "Lacanian left" has different meanings in the Global North and in the Global South. In the Global North, the work of Yannis Stavrakakis (2007, 2019) is well known, while in the Global South the influence of Jorge Alemán (2009) is unique. In both cases, they provided different readings of the work of Chantal Mouffe and Ernesto Laclau (1985). Finally, it is important to mention that feminism, gender theory, and decolonialism have also had an impact on the authors' readings of this project, so it is not strange to find authors such as Silvia Federici (2004) or Franz Fanon (1952; 1961) cited when debating certain arguments.

There is no doubt that we worked with the best academics and researchers in the complex and rare field of Lacano-Marxism. We summoned a wide variety of contributors from all over the world that have extensively and profoundly devoted themselves to Lacanian psychoanalysis and Marxism. It is not easy to find academics, psychoanalysts, or researchers working in the field of Marxism who read or consider Lacan. Nor is it easy in the Lacanian field for Marx to be read beyond what Lacan said about him. We were demanding and, in the end, this vocabulary also turned out to be an inquiry process and a research device.

Ultimately, this vocabulary aims to offer for academics and readers both of Marxism and of psychoanalysis in general a tool to facilitate the understanding and complexity of the encounters between these two fields, as well as the importance of Marx for Lacanian practice and of Lacanian concepts for the theory and practice of Marxism. In this way our Vocabulary becomes a crucial undertaking for unshackling our debates and to think about the concepts at the intersection of economy, philosophy, epistemology, sociology, and politics from the perspective of Marx in Lacan's reading. Moreover, it aims to sharpen the psychoanalytic perspective and highlight Marx's relevance in understanding the fundamental link between the social and individual dimensions for Lacanian clinical practice.

Santa Cruz, Ciudad de México and Morelia, April 2021

## Note

1 The term *lalangue* precisely comes from a lapsus that Lacan uttered when wanting to mention the name of this vocabulary (Lalande). It gave rise to this ambivalence, coining one of the most famous concepts of Lacan's work (*PAM*, p. 11).

## References

Alemán, J. (2009). *Para una izquierda lacaniana... Intervenciones y textos*. Buenos Aires: Grama.
Alemán, J. & Larriera, S. (1996). *Lacan: Heidegger*. Buenos Aires: Ediciones del Cifrado.
Althusser, L. (1964). Freud et Lacan. In: *Écrits sur la psychanalyse* (pp. 22–53). Paris: STOCK/IMEC, 1993.
Apter, E. et al. (2014). Preface. In: Cassin, B. (Ed.), *Dictionary of Untranslatables. A Philosophical Lexicon*. Princeton, NJ: Princeton University Press.
Assoun, P.-L. (2002). *Le vocabulaire de Freud*. Paris: Ellipses.
Bekerman, G. (1981). *Vocabulaire du marxisme: Français-allemand: vocabulaire de la terminologie des œuvres complètes de Karl Marx et Friedrich Engels*. Paris: Presses universitaires de France.
Bensussan, G. & Labica, G. (1982). *Dictionnaire critique du marxisme*. Paris: Presses universitaires de France.
Bidet, J. & Kouvelakis, E. (Eds.) (2001). *Dictionnaire Marx contemporain*. Paris: Presses universitaires de France.
Bottomore, T. et al. (1983). *A Dictionary of Marxist Thought*. London: Blackwell.
Carver, T. (1987). *A Marx Dictionary*. London: Polity Press.
Cassin, B. (2014a). Traduire les intraduisibles, un état de lieux. In: *Cliniques méditerranéennes*, 2(90): 25–36.
Cassin, B. (Ed.) (2014b). *Philosopher en Langues: Les Intraduisibles en Traduction*. Paris: Rue d'Ulm.

Cassin, B. & Gorog, F. (Dir.) (2016). *Psychanalyser en langues: intraduisibles et langue chinoise*. Paris: Demopolis.
Chemama, R. & Vandermersch, B. (Eds.) (1993). *Dictionnaire de la psychanalyse*. Paris: Larousse.
Cléro, J.-P. (2002). *Le vocabulaire de Lacan*. Paris: Ellipses.
Cléro, J.-P. (2008). *Dictionnaire Lacan*. Paris: Ellipses.
Courtine, J.-F. (2005). Le "Lalande" du XXI$^e$ siècle. In: *L'Agenda de la pensée contemporaine*, (1): 96–100.
De Mijolla, A. (Ed.) (2002). *International Dictionary of Psychoanalysis*. New York: Macmillan.
Evans, D. (1996). *An Introductory Dictionary of Lacanian Psychoanalysis*. London: Routledge.
Fanon, F. (1952). *Peau noire. Masques blancs*. Paris: Seuil.
Fanon, F. (1961). *The Wretched of the Earth*, R. Philcox (Trans.). New York: Grove Press.
Federici, S. (2004). *Caliban and the Witch*. New York: Autonomedia.
Fraser, I. & Wilde, L. (2011). *The Marx Dictionary*. London: Continuum.
Juárez-Salazar, E. M. (2014). *La sociedad en la obra de Jacques Lacan*. Morelia: Universidad Michoacana de San Nicolás de Hidalgo.
Laclau, E. & Mouffe, Ch. (1985). *Hegemony and Socialist Strategy*. London: Verso.
Lalande, A. (1926). *Vocabulaire technique et critique de la philosophie*. París: Presses universitaires de France.
Laplanche, J. & Pontalis, J.-B. (1967). *The Language of Psycho-Analysis*, D. Nicholson-Smith (Trans.). London: Karnac.
Parker, I. (2017). *Revolutionary Keywords for a New Left*. Winchester: Zero Books.
Pavón Cuéllar, D. (2009). *Marxisme lacanien*. Paris: Psychophores.
Pavón-Cuéllar, D. (2013). *Lacan, lecteur de Marx*. Rouen: Université de Rouen.
Pavón-Cuéllar, D. (2014). *Elementos políticos de marxismo lacaniano*. Ciudad de México: Paradiso.
Renault, E. (2001). *Le vocabulaire de Marx*. Paris: Ellipses.
Roudinesco, É. (2017). *Dictionnaire amoureux de la psychanalyse*. Paris: Plon.
Roudinesco, É. & Plon, M. (1997). *Dictionnaire de la psychanalyse*. Paris: Fayard.
Saint-Drôme, O. (1994). *Dictionnaire inespéré de 55 termes visités par Jacques Lacan*. Paris: Seuil.
Stavrakakis, Y. (2007). *The Lacanian Left. Psychoanalysis, Theory, Politics*. Edinburgh: Edinburgh University Press.
Stavrakakis, Y. (Ed.). (2019). *Routledge Handbook of Psychoanalytic Political Theory*. London: Routledge.
Walker, D. & Gray, D. (2007). *Historical Dictionary of Marxism*. Plymouth: The Scarecrow Press.
Williams, R. (1976). *Keywords: A Vocabulary of Culture and Society*. New York: Oxford University Press.

# Series preface for *The Marx through Lacan Vocabulary: A Compass for Libidinal and Political Economies*

## Series preface

This book is an intervention, designed to change the world, and a resource, designed to enable others to take this work forward. It is already an intervention, cutting through the many attempts of psychoanalysts and political theorists to reduce one domain to the other. It is now, in this form as a capacious contradictory text, an invaluable resource for future mapping of the overlapping territories of subjectivity and capitalism.

Marxism was, from the beginning, contemporaneous with psychoanalysis, and its critique of political economy was paralleled by the critique of the subjective economy of life under capitalism that Freud and then Lacan encountered. It is for that reason that Marxism so often appears to be analogous to psychoanalysis, particularly to Lacanian psychoanalysis which is attuned to the operations of language structured through the Symbolic. This Symbolic order structures and warrants the forms of competitive individualism that psychoanalysts encounter in the clinic. Marxism, like so many forms of psychoanalysis, is not only a tool of critique, but is much of the time neutralized and absorbed, recuperated, such that our Imaginary grasp of it does, indeed, turn it into a worldview, making it function as if it were a metalanguage. This book clears a way through the Imaginary lures of ideology, whether that is Lacanian ideology or Marxism turned into ideology. The book reveals contradictions as well as apparent complementary relationships, contradictions that speak of the Real in the realm of subjectivity and political economy. This book enables us to navigate old terrain, and notice what we need to take into account in order to position ourselves as Lacanians who are also necessarily Marxist.

Although this is, formally-speaking, an "edited" book, compiled by Christina Soto van der Plas, Edgar Miguel Juárez-Salazar, Carlos Gómez Camarena, and David Pavón-Cuéllar, it is, in fact, a collective project, and so it is as profoundly Marxist as it is psychoanalytic. It is collective in a number of respects. It relies on the commitment of colleagues who are committed to Marxist and Lacanian practice, a shared commitment to two systems of thought that were each themselves designed to transform what they described. It is grounded in an immense prior work of close reading and collation of points of connection between Marx and

Lacan so the authors of different elements were here able to already be oriented, with compass in hand to map out the terrain.

The book is global in scope, both in its planning and in its execution, with a detailed attention to the way language, fractured into different languages, geographically-historically constructed lines of the Symbolic, enables us to speak of the world but also misleads us about its underlying nature. This book speaks of "libidinal and political economies" that are located at the intersection between different languages, this English edition accompanied by publication in different languages. It is true to the internationalist spirit of both psychoanalysis and Marxism. It is internationalist without succumbing to the temptations of globalization, of the colonization of one realm of thought, or one form of culture, over another.

The wager of the book is that there is a homology between Lacan and Marx, one that has wide-ranging consequences for social theory and clinical practice. It is the relationship between those two systems of thought, of theory and practice interwoven, that is at stake here, a relationship the editors define as a close reading of Marx through Lacan. This is not to reinstate Lacanian psychoanalysis as a worldview or metalanguage through which various precepts of Marx can be reinterpreted, as if we were bad analysts injecting meaning into the words of an analysand, nor, for that matter, to treat Marxism as a metalanguage that could adjust Lacan to the reality of the capitalist society in which psychoanalysis was born and now thrives. Rather, in line with authentic Lacanian psychoanalysis, these explorations of key concepts enable Marx to speak, to speak again, to speak truth about a world that routinely and insidiously separates subjectivity from it.

Psychoanalytic clinical and theoretical work circulates through multiple intersecting antagonistic symbolic universes. This series opens connections between different cultural sites in which Lacanian work has developed in distinctive ways, in forms of work that question the idea that there could be single correct reading and application. The Lines of the Symbolic in Psychoanalysis series provides a reflexive reworking of psychoanalysis that transmits Lacanian writing from around the world, steering a course between the temptations of a metalanguage and imaginary reduction, between the claim to provide a god's eye view of psychoanalysis and the idea that psychoanalysis must everywhere be the same. And the elaboration of psychoanalysis in the symbolic here grounds its theory and practice in the history and politics of the work in a variety of interventions that touch the real.

Ian Parker<br>Manchester Psychoanalytic Matrix

# Chapter 1

# Alienation

Ben Gook and Dominiek Hoens

—Ara.: اغتراب —Chi.: 異化 —Fre.: *Aliénation* —Ger.: *Veräuserung/ Entfremdung/Entäusserung*—Ita.: *Alienazione*—Jap.: 疎外—Port.: *Alienação* —Rus.: *Отчуждение*—Spa.: *Alienación*—Tur.: *Yabancılaşma*

→ *Freedom/Liberty*; *History*; *Labour/work*; *Society*

In Jacques Lacan's writings and seminars, the word "alienation" was frequently used until early 1968, only to disappear almost entirely from them after that year. And although alienation is one of the notions most explicitly discussed in his teaching between 1964 and 1968, in his most direct engagement with Marx's work—the first two lessons of the sixteenth seminar, held in November 1968 (13.11.68; 20.11.68)—alienation does not appear even once. One could speculate this is the case because Lacan wishes to avoid any confusion between his psychoanalysis and a certain Freudo-Marxism *en vogue* at the time, spreading ideas about bourgeois society's alienating suppression of human beings' natural capacities to create and to love. Yet, there is also an *internal* logic to the development of Lacan's theory, which eventually results in the notion's omission.

In Karl Marx's *oeuvre*, we note a strikingly similar trajectory. The term appears throughout his early writings. It is particularly apparent in the so-called *Economic and Philosophic Manuscripts of 1844*, a set of notes unpublished by Marx but posthumously collected and published in the 1930s. Shortly after 1844, Marx turns against the term, notably in *The German Ideology*. Here one can speculate—with some textual basis—about his repulsion towards a prevailing philosophical and political tendency to use the word imprecisely, contributing to ideological mystifications. Still, even as Marx drops the term from his texts, a logic of alienation continues to shape his critique of capitalism and political economy.

## *Alienare* and its Translations

Since the fourteenth century, alienation has been used in English to describe either an estranging *action* or an estranged *state* (Williams, 2015, p. 3). It stems from the Latin *alienare*, meaning to cause to be estranged or to take someone else's

DOI: 10.4324/9781003212096-1

property, then further related to *alienus*, something of, or belonging to, another person or place. One sense of the term (i) refers to being cut off from—or a breakdown of relations with—a group, God, or political authority. A legal sense of the term (ii) comes into the language around the fifteenth century, naming the transfer of ownership (e.g., rights, estates, money) to another. This legal term accrues a negative connotation of a beneficiary's improper transfer or stealthy contrivance. Alienation's negative understanding in this sense of impropriety became dominant, although a technical usage continues to describe legal, voluntary transfer. Alongside alienation as a separation process, a sense emerges to describe the *state* of something alienated (iii). An analogy arises too, as it had in Latin, referring to the insane—or those otherwise understood to have lost mental faculties—as alienated (iv).

The common use of the word up until a century ago typically referred to the legal sense of the alienation from property. Even so, the first sense (i) survived theologically as a state of being separated from the knowledge of God. This sense has overlapped with a general use—via Rousseau—in which people are divided from their nature: we are either estranged from our *original* (historically "primitive") or *essential* (inherent, permanent) nature. If civilisation or modernity is taken as alienation's cause, overcoming alienation thus involves a return to primitivism or some cultivation of feeling and activity that counters civilisation. Estrangement from essential nature is typically seen in either a religious sense of separation from the divine in man or psychological estrangement from some energy (e.g., Reich). So disalienation proceeds in these instances by recovering a connection with the divine or recovering of libido or sexuality. However, such a disalienation is also considered either impossible (i.e., alienation as the price of modernity) or radical (e.g., ending forms of repression, such as capitalism or the bourgeois family). After Marx's early manuscripts began circulating from the 1930s, "alienation" had taken on a psychological character by the 1950s, naming a loss of connection with our deepest feelings and needs, sometimes twinned with social critique (modern work, education, and community). In an era of anti-communism, this criticism lost its Marxian cast, eventually becoming a byword for "menial work" in empirical sociology.

Lacan's French, like English, uses the single word, *aliénation*. However, after the Latinate terminology was imported into Germanic equivalents, philosophical German uses two words to designate alienation. In a philological analysis of Marx's writing, there may be some merit in distinguishing between *Entäusserung* and *Entfremdung*, where the translation from English had settled, after Hegel, into two different senses of alienation. Interestingly, this is then re-translated back into English (and French) following Marx's conceptual labours, adding complications to using a single word to describe what Marx himself intended. Marx occasionally combined senses (i) and (ii), and he was influenced in this by translations in his native German. The German verb *entäussern* corresponds mostly to sense (ii) of alienation (i.e., transfer to another). The verb *entfremden* is closer to (i) notably, the act or state of estrangement between people. *Entäusserung* indicates something projected, objectified, or outside of the self. In this sense, it connotes externalisation or objectification. *Entfremdung* carries the German equivalent of "alien" (*Fremd*), suggesting becoming a stranger to oneself (hence the choice of "estrangement" in English) or submitting to another's power. Marx uses the intensified term *Selbstentfremdung* (self-estrangement) in the fourth thesis on Feuerbach, adding that this means *Selbstzerrissenheit* or inner strife, as well as *Sichselbstwidersprechen* or self-division. Adjudicating the correctness of various translations is beyond our scope here (Ross, 2020). At a minimum, the movement from Latin *alienare* into English to German and back again seems to be a case of foreign contact instilling greater semantic depths—and no shortage of confusion.

## Marx's *Manuscripts* and the Four Estrangements

Marx (*EW*, pp. 322–375) highlights four areas of alienation in his *Economic and Philosophic Manuscripts of 1844*. Capitalism estranges producers from (a) themselves, (b) nature, (c) their products, and (d) others. The conditions of alienation under capitalism are threefold: (i) the division of labour, which deposits people into limited, specialized roles, fragmenting the picture of a social whole; (ii) the market system, in which producers disregard human needs answered by products (use-value) to focus solely on market and profit (exchange-value)—the forking of value here is crucial; (iii) the property system, where producers lose control over work processes and the resulting products, which are given over to the owners of the means of production (i.e., the worker does not belong to himself at work). Alienation's theoretical and critical meaning in Marx can be summed up here as the antagonism between human essence and existence, between human potential and actual human societies. It names the frozen expression of humanity's powers.

Marx, in this period, holds that to be a person is to have a *telos*: namely, a path of self-development. Marx's "self-development" is achieved by labour or work—not, per Hegel, in thought. Work, for Marx, will help deliver social formations to a higher stage. However, labour alienates itself (in objectified labour) and comes to exist in contradiction to workers (in capital, private property). Thus, alienation and work are ambivalent—dialectical—tendencies in capitalist societies, as they cause suffering and private gain, even as they progress society to a higher level.

Much of the explicit theory of alienation in Marx was written before 1850. In this phase, it followed the lead of Hegel and Feuerbach, not least by criticizing their accounts of alienation. Around 1845, Marx was politicized by encountering the German and French proletariats (and later the British, via Engels). This (re-)entry into social struggle coincided with a withdrawal from academic philosophy, moving further into the sphere of journalism. A deeper study of the political economists, alongside the (failed) European revolutions of 1848—so hopefully announced by the *Communist Manifesto* of 1847—saw Marx transition to altered concepts. The moral wrong of alienation shifts to the background as Marx comes to use the descriptive language of political economy; Marx begins to adopt an immanent method that aims to criticise bourgeois capitalism from within its conceptual vocabulary, which typically does not include "alienation". Throughout his corpus, Marx remains attentive to the material conditions designated by "alienation" in the early writings.

Let us consider the iconic form of alienation—work. Marx criticised political economists for collapsing basic human activity (labour) and alienated work (wage-labour, work that generates commodities and capital). In *alienated labour*, the worker objectifies and alienates their essence for a wage. The product of estranged labour is not (simply) a natural object worked on by people to fulfil their needs (use-value) but the objectification of human subjectivity. The worker's subjectivity is separated and incorporated into the material object (use-value), becoming the commodity's body. This intimates the energetics of labour—or an economy of work—apparent in the *Manuscripts*, where Marx also demonstrates the debt to the Hegelian–Feuerbachian critique of religion:

> [T]he more the worker exerts himself in his work, the more powerful the alien, objective world becomes which he brings into being over against himself, the poorer he and his inner world become, and the less they belong to him. It is the same in religion. The more man puts into God, the less he retains within himself. The worker places his life in the object; but now it no longer belongs to him, but to the object. The greater his activity, therefore, the fewer objects the worker possesses. What the product of his labour is, he is not. Therefore, the greater this product, the less is he himself. The externalisation [*Entäusserung*] of the worker in his product means not only that his labour becomes an object, an external existence, but that it exists outside him, independently of him and alien to him, and begins to confront him as an autonomous power; that the life which he has bestowed on the object confronts him as hostile and alien.
>
> (*EW*, p. 324)

The objective conditions of labour are a product of the worker's toil. In other words, wage-labour produces marketplace commodities at the same time as it produces and reproduces itself (i.e., wage-labour) as a commodity (*EW*, p. 324–325). Not only sellable objects are fabricated, then, but the necessary social relationships of capitalism. Marx suggests this in the "estranged labour" section of the 1844 *Manuscripts*, then expanded it in the "simple reproduction" chapter of *Capital*. Likewise, in *Grundrisse*, Marx (*GR*, p. 512) will note "the production of capitalists and wage labourers is thus a chief product of capital's realisation process". He adds that "objectified labour" is posited as "the objectivity of a subjectivity antithetical to the worker, as *property* of a will alien to him".

In the *Manuscripts*, after the long passage cited above, Marx (*EW*, p. 366) adds that alienation:

> appears not only in the fact that the means of my life belong to *another* and that *my* desire is the inaccessible possession of *another*, but also in the fact

that all things are *other* than themselves, that my activity [i.e. labour] is *other* than itself, and that finally – and this goes for the capitalists too – an *inhuman* power rules over everything.

Labour evidently becomes the victim of a power (i.e., dead labour) it itself created. The fundamental contradiction in capitalism is between people (living labour) and capital (dead labour), the inhuman power. This is a literal contradiction: humanity becomes dehumanised, such that humanity is no longer human; alienated labour too is identical to itself and different from itself. It names, then, a sort of uncanny doubling: of people alien to themselves, of work alien from its worker. Under these conditions, human essence is alienated as it is expressed or, better, objectified in wage-labour's products. Existence thereby negates and conflicts with essence, where Marx's "essence" leaves behind prior metaphysics to entail a series of relationships, or an ensemble of social relations. In brief, wage-labour strips the worker of her connections with others:

> When man confronts himself he also confronts *other* men. What is true of man's relationship to his labour, to the product of his labour and to himself, is also true of his relationship to other men, and to the labour and the object of the labour of other men.
>
> (*EW*, pp. 329–330)

In the *Manuscripts*, Marx's most penetrating passages aimed to establish the meaning of human labour's alienation in wage-labour. In this, he was strained between two forms of argument. On the one hand, an objective-structural argument about the historical situation of exploitation—or, put differently, exploitation *as* a historical concept. On the other, the relationship-attitude-experience of the individual. Reflecting these tensions and the working-through of the concerns they entail, the influences and interlocutors in this period include philosophers (Rousseau, Feuerbach, Proudhon, and Hegel) and his first entanglements with political economists (Smith, Say, Ricardo, and Sismondi). The stress fell on phenomenology in the *Manuscripts*, leading to an experiential, materialist or psychological formulation of alienation as a subjective term (felt powerlessness, estrangement, and so on), even as it led on to questions about private property, objectification, exploitation, and a resolution in a humanist communism—the name for human reconciliation with labour, fellow men, and nature. For Marx, alienation is pre-eminently a phenomenon in capitalist social formations, although it was a feature of pre-capitalist societies. Cutting the knot of this contradiction, as for other communists, entails producing a society where private property disappears, and people can labour for themselves, fulfilling their *telos*, and for social utility, fulfilling labour's collective promise.

## Marx's *Capital* and Alienation's Conceptual Displacement

In Marx's writing, alienation can be found in at least five overlapping dimensions with a corresponding (metaphysical) object: theological (God), political (the state), psychological (ruling class ideology), economic (the commodity), and technological (the industrial machine) (Wendling, 2009, pp. 37–38). In each of these domains, with each of these objects, something produced by people comes to dominate them as an alien power over which they have diminishing control. There are various *separations*, one of the basic figures of Marx's thought from beginning to end, marked by its negativity. In combination, these dimensions yield a generalised alienation of the human being from their fellow human beings in capitalist societies.

Put differently, alienation is the historically variable gulf between, on the one hand, multifaceted human capabilities, needs, knowledge, and social relations, all developed progressively by society—that is, objectively—and, on the other, the one-dimensionality, poverty and dependence—experienced subjectively—of the individual producers of that objectified human wealth. The early Marx sought to explain capitalism's moral wrong through the individual's relations to productive activity, the later Marx through the social totality. The Marx of *Capital* focused on the specific character of socio-economic interaction in a capitalist society, namely the commodification of labour-power and transformation (or *subsumption*) of pre-capitalist work into waged labour. This is a scientific theory of material interests, focusing on the capitalist economy's internal contradictions. The conceptual key for this new theoretical departure—whereby explicit reference to "alienation" recedes—will be the commodity. This shift will be necessary for Marx's expanded aims because alienation can descriptively characterize individual experience within a society but cannot characterize total social experience. Marx will begin *Capital* with the commodity as it can fulfil this role in his expanded critique.

Marx's early critical project had been to reveal the material, human roots of the alienated objects by demystifying their metaphysical status and deflating their alienating power. However, in Marx's eyes, critics famously need to do more than interpret this alienated world—they need to change it. More than an imperative against theorizing (i.e., the undialectical dichotomy of theory and praxis), this injunction suggests the need to change philosophy (the great generator of abstractions). Or, rather, an injunction for philosophy to abolish itself through realizing a better social formation. This injunction itself marks a shift in Marx's thinking and his project. Alienation is jettisoned as a category in this shift. Tellingly, Marx (with Engels) will mock the philosophers of alienation in *The German Ideology* and *The Communist Manifesto*. Marx likely rejected the moral terminology, including alienation, for its links to bourgeois ideology, which centred on rational individuals, and that ideology's historical limitation within capitalist society. Alienation had become an ideological concept rather than a lever for theory and praxis.

## Alienation's Marxist Afterlives

For many, and particularly after Althusser's intervention, alienation has been a lynchpin of the shift between an early and a late Marx, or, more proscriptively, a young and a mature Marx. Alienation can be the centre of this periodization as it marks a shift from a human-centred account of suffering in the early years to the impersonal account of forces in the later years. This periodization places the 1844 *Manuscripts* on one side, the *Theses on Feuerbach* and *The German Ideology* as a pivot moment, and the *Grundrisse* and *Capital* on the mature side. Even if the designation of "early" writings is technically unobjectionable, the distinction became a way to suggest these immature texts led to a blind alley.

Following common usage, we continue to use these demarcations, although primarily to distinguish biographical moments. The early/late distinction based on alienation is untenable (Musto, 2010). We could cast the question about the status of alienation in Marx's work as one of the productive ambiguities of Marx's texts—or as Balibar puts it, "a problematic open to all kinds of transformations, reformulations and extrapolations, whose starting point is not the oblivion of Marx's words and sentences but their intrinsic vacillation" (Balibar, 2017, pp. 87–123). Among Marx's worksites open to conceptual labourers, alienation remains one of the busiest.

It is also a worksite beset by decades-long strife and disagreement, and so perhaps better conceived as a *Kampfplatz*. The young Marx's texts stood in a difficult relation to the socialist states' official doctrines, diverging from "dialectical materialist" ("diamat") orthodoxy: the *Manuscripts*' external status is illustrated by their exclusion from the main body of the Marx–Engels *Werke* in the GDR; estrangement and alienation—let alone the trenchant, detailed, and complex critique of Hegel's philosophy—appeared nowhere in the reigning, canonical texts of Engels, Plekhanov, and Lenin; "diamat" distorted Lukacs's (1971) thinking to the point of him disowning in 1967 the problematic of reification, fetishism, and alienation, which he had claimed in 1923 to be "central to the revolutionary critique of capitalism"; meanwhile, abandoned by Marxists, the early works were turned to by existentialists and Catholics in France after WWII. This was also the moment at which Lacan seems to pass beyond an open discussion of alienation.

## Early Lacan: The Stranger in the Mirror

In the early years of Lacan's intellectual journey, including both his doctoral thesis (*DPP*) and brief reports on patients, *aliénation* and *aliéné* (alienated) occur rarely and only concerning psychiatric illness. Here, alienation stems from the prehistory of psychiatry, when during the late eighteenth, early nineteenth centuries, figures like Philippe Pinel applied it to patients who had lost their reason. Due to their illness, they have become *alien* to themselves, and it is the *alienist's* task to treat the patient mentally and get a derailed reason on the right track again (Pouillaude, 2013). In that sense, the psychiatric use of the notion echoes its older juridical meaning—the transfer of property—for the alienated no longer "owns" his most crucial, defining feature (i.e., reason), and it is the physician's goal to unalienate the patient, that is to restore ownership and free use of reason. In twentieth-century psychiatry, the notion falls into disuse because of its unscientific, rather moralizing connotations. Nonetheless, Lacan continues to adopt the notion, although, within his theory, it takes on a meaning unmistakably different from its original psychiatric one.

In a second period, alienation is more prominently present. Inspired by Hegel's *Phenomenology of Spirit*—and particularly Alexandre Kojève's reading of it—Lacan conceives the "mirror stage" to explain how a child acquires a sense of organic unity and "self". Whereas for psychiatry, one is alienated from oneself if one loses reason, for Lacan, alienation is the prerequisite for any reasonable thinking performed by an "I". This is made clear from the outset of his seminal paper, *The Mirror Stage as Formative of the I Function*, as "it should be noted that this sets us at odds with any philosophy directly stemming from the *cogito*" (*MS*, p. 75). The starting point for a reflection on human mental life should not reside in a Cartesian "I think" (*cogito*), but in detailing the necessary conditions for someone to be able to say "I" (Nobus, 1998, p. 111). These conditions, according to Lacan, are incarnated by a mirror presenting an image that the child—supported by a parent—considers an image of himself. However, the "mirror" reflecting one's image *should not* be taken literally, for, besides the mirror, there are peers—the "other" (*autre*) as Lacan puts it—with whom the child can identify. This allows Lacan to refer to Marx in support of his theory of the mirror stage:

> Some of you are, I believe, fairly familiar with *Das Kapital*. I am not talking about the entire text – who's read *Capital*! – but with the first book, which almost everyone has read. A prodigious first book, superabundant, revealing someone – and this is rare – who sustains an articulated philosophical discourse. I urge you to go to the page where, at the level of the formulation of the so-called "theory of the particular form of the value of merchandise", Marx shows himself, in a note, to be a precursor of the mirror stage.
> (*SV*, 27.11.57, pp. 72–73)

And, indeed, the footnote in *Capital* makes a similar argument regarding the acquisition of a human identity:

> In a certain sense, a man is in the same situation as a commodity. As he neither enters into the world in possession of a mirror [*Spiegel*], nor as a Fichtean philosopher who can say "I am I", a man first sees and recognises [*bespiegelt*] himself in another man. Peter only relates to himself as a man through his relation to another man, Paul, in whom he recognises his likeness. With this, however, Paul also becomes from head to toe, in his physical form as Paul, the form of appearance of the species man for Peter.
> (*CAI*, p. 144)

The Hegelian, dialectical aspect of this dynamic is evident: one only finds oneself outside of oneself and because of an other, i.e., a mirror image. The mirror image has a unifying effect on the child's bodily experience—*one* body instead of *many* separate organs—but that does not produce a stable identity. On the one hand, nightmarish fantasies haunt the child about the dissolution of his virtual unity into fragmented body-parts, and on the other hand, unity does not involve unicity. As Lacan puts it in *Family Complexes in the Formation of the Individual*: "Before the ego affirms its identity, it blends with the image that forms and primordially alienates it" (*CF*, p. 43). The ego is not only alien to itself—it is first and foremost an *exterior* image—it continuously runs the risk of vanishing in (the image of) the other. Here one can think of the phenomenon known as transitivism—the one child's crying provokes the other's tears—or, more generally, of emotional contagion, which obscures the moment when precisely the emotion started and who was the first to express, for instance, anxiety. A second alienation is needed to have a more stable experience of *self*—namely, the moment when the other seems to desire and enjoy what the ego does not have. To illustrate this, Lacan repeatedly discusses a scene taken from Augustine's *Confessions*: "I have seen and experienced an infant who was jealous: he could not yet speak, but he grew pale and gave a nasty look to another infant who was sharing his milk" (Augustine, 2019, p. 7). Although the mother's milk fuels the mutual identification of the one child with the other—the desire of the one becomes the desire of the other—it also functions as the third element that minimally yet crucially differentiates the one child from the other. The other does not only *have* the desired object, as a sign of the mother's love, the object also turns him into someone who really *is*. The enjoyment may be merely supposed, from the jealous infant's perspective—marked by lack and desire—the scene involves the other child as someone whose being is complete.

This second alienation—the identification with the other qua desire, involving the (imagined) loss of the object of rivalry—creates a difference between the one and the other child, yet that does not change the fact, according to Lacan, that the ego is constituted by nothing else than "a series of alienating identifications" (*FT*, p. 347). This intuition has clinical implications—the psychoanalyst's aim cannot consist in strengthening the patient's ego—but should also be understood as a critical stance vis-à-vis "the utilitarian conception of man" that reinforces "the promotion of the ego in our existence […] leading to an ever greater realisation of man as an individual, in other words, in an isolation of the soul that is ever more akin to its original dereliction" (*AP*, p. 99).

## Symbolic Alienation as a Structural Solution to the Imaginary Deadlock

If our relating to ourselves and others is imaginary—for relying on (mirror) images—and consists in complexifying, but also immutably perpetuating the alienated relation of human beings with themselves, can one think of a way out of this closed, paranoid universe? Can one fathom, simply put, the possibility of unalienation, different from the total destruction of mirroring others and entering a hellish universe made up of fragmented bodies? During one period of his teaching, Lacan seems to be convinced there is such a solution, and its name is "the symbolic". In what is arguably one of his most essential writings, *The Function and Field of Speech and Language in Psychoanalysis*, Lacan states that "it is always in the relation between the subject's ego [*moi*] and his discourse's *I* [*je*] that you [the psychoanalyst] must understand the meaning of the discourse if you are to unalienate the subject" (*FFS*, p. 250). Although the human individual has a sense of self because of his "erotic relationship in which he fixates on an image that alienates him from himself" (*AP*, p. 92), this "self" is supplemented by what Freud called "the other scene" and Lacan rephrases as the Other. This Other—with a capital O, to distinguish it from the other, the fellow human being—is language. It is language not in its instrumental capacity for communication and expression but rather as an alien domain where the subject is spoken (or spoken about). Besides the *ego*, an *I* is situated within an unconscious linguistic, symbolic universe. So, instead of focusing on the ego and its demands (for help, love, and understanding), the psychoanalyst should reckon with a supposed, hidden "I", subjected to symbolic laws and signifiers that determine its existence. This analytic process can eventually result in so-called "full speech"—to the detriment of the ego's empty speech—which testifies to taking into account one's symbolic determination *beyond* and *before* any mirroring can occur. The symbolic Other "saves" the human being from a life solely situated on an imaginary plane, and provides a place within a family and social structure. To the extent that the latter is unconscious and approached by the individual in the inevitably "wrong", that is, imaginary way, the obvious question is why this is the case. Why can't the human being choose to be the subject of the symbolic structure that precedes it? Why can't it fully coincide with the symbolic elements that make up its identity? Or, put differently, why is the mention of "unalienate", quoted above, an *hapax legomenon*—a one-off—in Lacan's work? There are three reasons why a plain and simple unalienation is impossible:

1. The symbolic does not undo the imaginary; it supplements rather than sublates or annuls the alienating imaginary dialectic discussed above.
2. The symbolic is made of signifiers which are first and foremost *alien* to the child; sense, meaning, and signification are only a retroactive and—as Lacan will emphasise—illusory effect.
3. To the Other, the subject can ultimately only respond in an imaginary way, that is, via constructing a fantasy (*phantasme*).

To highlight the symbolic's *alien* and *alienating* nature, Lacan provides his audience with the canonical definition of the subject as "that which is represented by one signifier for another signifier" (*SIX*, 06.12.61). The subject is represented in the field of the Other, but remains as such absent from it. Signifiers take care of representation, but there is no natural or other "proper" relation between subjectivity and signifiers. More precisely, the subject is an effect of the signifiers' representational activity, as these provoke the simple question: what are they about, what is their *subject*?

## Not Without Separation

From the 1960s onwards, Lacan distances himself from the idea of the Other as the socially shared, Oedipalized universe, which awaits the subject, for it to occupy a symbolic place. Instead, Lacan highlights the traumatic dimension of the encounter with the Other. This Other first and foremost consists of signifiers that make no sense as such—only being intelligible via their combinations and as an effect—and the subject's *appearance* within the Other is concomitant with the subject's *disappearance*. The following quotation illustrates how cautious Lacan is about a possible misunderstanding of his use of alienation:

> One has to admit that there is a lot of this alienation about nowadays. Whatever one does, one is always a bit more alienated, whether in economics, politics, psychopathology, aesthetics, and so on. It may be no bad thing to see what the root of this celebrated alienation really is. Does it mean, as I seem to be saying, that the subject is condemned to seeing himself emerge, in initio, only in the field of the Other? Could it be that? Well, it isn't. Not at all – not at all – not at all.
>
> (*SXI*, 27.05.64, p. 210)

Alienation does not concern the loss of a former "self" or a primordial identity or capacity; it consists in a choice—here, Lacan uses the Latin *vel*, a disjunctive "or"—for either "being" or "meaning". This choice is peculiar, for if one were to choose being, there would be no subjectivity whatsoever—for the subject is a subject of signifiers—and both "meaning" and "being" would be lost. Hence, the only option is the forced choice for "meaning", which involves the loss of "being". To illustrate this, Lacan uses the example of the highwayman offering his victim the choice between his "money" or his "life". If the victim were to give his life, the money is lost too; so, the only option is to hand over his money, saving his life, albeit without money. Similarly, the subject is represented in a meaningful way yet loses any being outside or independent of the (meaningful) Other.

A second operation follows alienation: separation. This may sound surprising, for on a general and fundamental level, doesn't alienation consist of separation? For instance, a Christian is alienated to the extent that he lives a life separate from God, or a factory worker has to separate himself from his range of skills to perform the repetitive, numbing, hence alienating actions that are expected of him (Leopold, 2018). However, as argued above, the subject in Lacan is an *effect* of alienation. It does not *precede* this operation. So the ensuing "separation" intensifies the primordial alienation by imagining what was lost via the alienation. Alienation and separation are neither opposed nor identical but involve, firstly, an "alienating" splitting (*fente*) of the subject—it "exists" in between two signifiers—and, secondly, a "separating" resplitting (*refente*) of the subject, to the extent that the subject imagines and therefore relates to an object, i.e., the entire being that presumably got lost because of the first operation. As Dany Nobus succinctly puts it: "Lacan considers the two operations of alienation and separation to be circular, yet non-reciprocal: they are circular, because one leads to the other, ad infinitum, but at the same time they are non-reciprocal, because one does not compensate for the other" (Nobus, 2013, p. 181; see also *PU*, p. 714).

Like alienation in the imaginary—which involved the identification with an alienating image and the alienating loss of an object of enjoyment (milk)—symbolic alienation involves two moments: (1) the representation of the subject in the field of Other (alienation), and (2) the phantasmatic relation to an object that would restore one's full being yet is lost (separation). Its mere role of sealing alienation may explain why Lacan discusses "separation" only during a brief period of his teaching (1964). Yet, if one takes a closer look at the following years, 1965–1968, one can conclude that, for Lacan, separation is the most crucial aspect, which from then on is simply named alienation.

## The Other's Stupidity

Separation is the constitution of an object that supposedly incarnates one's being "before" alienation. However, this "being" is not only imagined; it is also a reply to the Other. In alienation, one chooses "meaning" and becomes the subject of the Other, which raises the question of what one is for this Other beyond the signifiers it represents the subject with. This confrontation with the *Other's desire* leads the subject to invent an object that would be an adequate response: the object *a*. I do not know what I am for the Other. However, the phantasmatic answer allows one to "forget"—repress—the Other's traumatic dimension and reduce the *O*ther to the *o*ther.

> I am linked to the human Other by something which is my quality of being his *semblable* and the result is that what remains of the anguishing *I don't know what object I am*, is, fundamentally, *misrecognition*. There is a misrecognition of what the *a* is in the economy of my human desire, [which turns the structure of desire into a] fundamental alienation.
> (*SX*, 03.07.63, p. 325)

This object belongs neither to the subject—for it got lost in the alienating operation—nor to the Other—for it is supposedly what the Other qua *desire* desires. In spatial terms, the object *a* is what stands in between subject and Other, relating the one to the other and differentiating them. In that sense, the object *a* refers to both alienation (the being that got lost) and separation (the object that *causes* the desire of the Other).

Before alienation disappears from his work, Lacan qualifies it as the "pivotal point" of his theory. This pivotal point concerns the Other's incompleteness, which Lacan first conceptualizes as the desire of the Other, then as object *a* and finally as *pas-tout*. It would exceed the limitations of this entry to detail this trajectory, but the political importance of this is made clear by Lacan himself. "The fact of alienation does not consist in our being taken up, made up, represented in the Other; on the contrary, it is essentially grounded in the Other's rejection" (*SXIV*, 18.01.67). This does not mean that one can reject the Other, live without or outside this alienating dimension, but one can make evident that the Other's "gift" of meaning is made of meaningless signifiers. As meaning is what makes life into a life one can intersubjectively share and feel at home in, the absence of meaning inherent to the elements that produce meaning—signifiers—is usually avoided. It is the psychoanalyst who, by a specific way of listening and intervening, brings to the fore the stupid (*bête*), meaningless signifiers that govern unconsciously one's life. However, this specific production of signifiers that *undo* meaning can also occur outside of the psychoanalyst's consulting room. There are moments when the signifier appears as a proper name—without a direct meaning and isolated from other signifiers. Take, for instance, "worker". There is a whole difference, Lacan explains, between the word "worker" in the paternalist phrase "they are good workers" and in "workers of the world, unite", the famous line from Marx and Engels's *Communist Manifesto*. In the first phrase, a predicate (good) gets connected to a subject (worker) and, thereby, the latter is identifiable (and disappears under) the combination of the two signifiers, good and worker. In the second phrase, however, no difference is made between good or bad workers; one is merely invited to identify with one signifier without knowing its precise meaning (*SXV*, 07.02.68). "Worker" in this sense, on the one hand, affirms the Other's primacy—there is no unalienated subject, for any subject is a subject of the signifier—yet, on the other, as a "stupid" signifier, it suspends all the usual meaning produced between two or more signifiers. It *rejects* the Other qua meaning as an isolated, empty signifier and makes the subject appear as that undetermined object that causes the Other's incompleteness.

At this stage of his teaching, Lacan points out the homology between his object *a* and Marx's *Mehrwert*, the value the capitalist extracts from the labourer's work (*RA*, p. 434; *SXVI*, 20.11.68; see also Tomšič, 2015). Qualifying the object *a* as a *plus-de-jouir*—a wordplay on *plus*, a lost (*plus*) enjoyment (*jouir*) turned into a surplus (*plus*) of enjoyment—one should draw two conclusions: (a) the alienation involved is fundamental, because constitutive of the subject; (b) it also does not rule out the possibility that a subject chooses the meaningless aspect of the signifier it is subjected to and incarnates the very obstacle to any supposedly all-embracing Other.

**Post-Lacanian Developments**

A recent uptick in interest in alienation has seen leading voices in both Marxist (Balibar, 2017, 2018, 2020; Harvey, 2018; Musto, 2010) and Lacanian (Ruti,

2017, 2018a, b; Tomšič, 2019; Verhaeghe, 2018; Žižek, 2017) debates writing about the term. This accords with a certain rhythm of attention to the idea, somewhat mirroring the phases of focus and disavowal—or at least terminological shapeshifting—we have noted in alienation's trajectory in Marx and Lacan's thought. The previous highpoint of the debates around alienation—the 1960s and 1970s—occurred as Lacan was using the concept. The term reached the peak of popular currency and critical infamy at this moment, particularly in the French debates, as Althusser attempted to banish it from the Marxist lexicon—even as he could never entirely be done with it himself. We can ground these historical periods in materialist concerns. The late 1960s into the 1970s were a period of capitalist crisis. The attention to alienation today looks to follow the global financial crisis of 2007–2008. Among those Lacanian scholars cited as working on the idea today, the Marxist sense of alienation is perhaps even more apparent than in Lacan's writing. As such, a greater materialist impulse in the critique of capitalism has entered the theorization of alienation today.

**Further reading**

Balmès, F. (2011). *Structure, logique, aliénation. Recherches en psychanalyse*. Toulouse: Erès.
Jaeggi, R. (2014). *Alienation*, F. Neuhouser & A. E. Smith, (Trans.). New York: Columbia UP.
Laurent, E. (1995). Alienation and Separation. In: R. Feldstein, B. Fink and M. Jaanus (Eds.), *Reading Seminar XI. Lacan's Four Fundamental Concepts of Psychoanalysis* (pp. 19–38). Albany: State University of New York Press.
Sayers, S. (2011). *Marx & Alienation. Essays on Hegelian Themes*. London: Palgrave Macmillan.

**References**

Augustine (2019). *Confessions*, Th. William (Trans.). Indianapolis: Hackett Publishing Company.
Balibar, É. (2017). *The Philosophy of Marx*, C. Turner (Trans.). London: Verso.
Balibar, É. (2018). Philosophies of the Transindividual: Spinoza, Marx, Freud. In: *Australasian Philosophical Review*, 2(1): 5–25.
Balibar, É. (2020). *Spinoza, the Transindividual*, M. G. E. Kelly (Trans.). Edinburgh: Edinburgh University Press.
Harvey, D. (2018). Universal Alienation. In: *TripleC*, 16(2): 424–439.
Leopold, D. (2018). Alienation. In: E. Zalta (Ed.), *The Stanford Encyclopedia of Philosophy*. https://plato.stanford.edu/archives/fall2018/entries/alienation/.
Lukács, G. (1971). *History and Class Consciousness: Studies in Marxist Dialectics*, R. Livingstone (Trans.). Cambridge: MIT Press.
Musto, M. (2010). Revisiting Marx's Concept of Alienation. In: *Socialism and Democracy*, 24(3): 79–101.
Nobus, D. (1998). Life and Death in the Glass. A New Look at the Mirror Stage. In: D. Nobus (Ed.), *Key Concepts of Lacanian Psychoanalysis* (pp. 101–138). London: Rebus Press.

Nobus, D. (2013). That Obscure Object of Psychoanalysis. In: *Continental Philosophy Review*, 46: 163–187.
Pouillade, E. (2013). Épistémologie de l'Aliénation et Antériorité. In: *L'Evolution Psychiatrique*, 78: 189–205.
Ross, L. (2020). On Disentangling Alienation, Estrangement, and Reification in Marx. In: *Rethinking Marxism*, 32(4), 521–548.
Ruti, M. (2017). *The Ethics of Opting Out: Queer Theory's Defiant Subjects*. New York: Columbia UP.
Ruti, M. (2018a). *Distillations: Theory, Ethics, Affect*. New York: Bloomsbury Academic.
Ruti, M. (2018b). *Penis Envy & Other Bad Feelings: The Emotional Costs of Everyday Life*. New York: Columbia UP.
Tomšič, S. (2015). *The Capitalist Unconscious: Marx and Lacan*. London: Verso.
Tomšič, S. (2019). *The Labour of Enjoyment: Towards a Critique of Libidinal Economy*. Berlin: August Verlag.
Verhaeghe, P. (2018). Beyond Alienation. In: *Psychoanalytische Perspectieven*, 36: 421–433.
Wendling, A. E. (2009). *Karl Marx on Technology and Alienation*. New York: Palgrave Macmillan.
Williams, R. (2015). *Keywords: A Vocabulary of Culture and Society*. Oxford: Oxford UP.
Žižek, S. (2017). *Incontinence of the Void: Economico-Philosophical Spandrels*. Cambridge: The MIT Press.

# Chapter 2

# Automatism

*Elena Bisso*

—Ara.: اوتوماتزم —Chi.: 自動性 —Fre.: *Automatisme* —Ger.: *Automatismus* — Ita.: *Automatismo* —Jap.: 自動性 —Port.: *Automatismo* —Rus.: *Автоматизм* —Spa.: *Automatismo* —Tur.: *Otomatizm*

→ *Capitalism*; *Market*; *Superstructure*; *Surplus*-jouissance

Automatism is the automatic quality of industrial production in capitalism as well as of the functioning of Capitalist discourse. An important characteristic in both cases is that the subject is dispensed with. This concept allows us to understand why the Capitalist discourse formalized by Lacan has the particularity of self-consuming and self-consummating in an incessant and vertiginous wheel, unlike the four discourses whose movement operates through quarter-turns. It is for this reason that authors such as Jorge Alemán (2013) consider that there is no Capitalist discourse but rather a capitalist device. The key to such reading of automatism is found in the argument deployed by Althusser (1965) in *Reading Capital*. It is a matter of conceiving specific social relations as dependent on the functions of the production process. Thus, automatism in the capitalist production process is the typical mode of Capitalist discourse.

Both the market—as a form of social bond—described by Marx and the unconscious in Lacan are structured as a language. It is for this reason that the psychoanalyst correlated surplus-value with surplus-*jouissance* (*SXVI*, 13.11.68). By means of this homology—and insofar as the capitalist system and discourses are forms of production—it is possible to abstract automatism as a common characteristic. This is why it can be affirmed that in Capitalist discourse the automatism of the process of production of capital is at stake. However, it is necessary to specify how automatism is found in Marx's *Capital* as well as the different uses of "automatism" in Lacan's work, especially automatism as something that constitutes the unconscious itself. We find an important antecedent of this Lacanian homology in his graph of desire—which he designed in 1958—where he compared Marx's surplus-value with the surplus-*jouissance* in psychoanalysis, a graph where he also placed the market in the place of Other of the unconscious (*SXVI*, 13.11.68).

## The central automaton in *Capital*

The development of machinery in the capitalist system occurred by displacing human labour, replacing tools manipulated by men with tools integrated into a machine. This profound change in the world of work has had various consequences on human life, for example, in media and transportation. When tools migrated from instruments of the human body to tools of a mechanical device or machine tool, the driving machine acquired autonomy, definitively freeing itself from the barriers of human power (*CAI*, p. 499). One of the effects of the replacement of man by machine was the Capitalist discourse. This change consisted in substituting the place of the employed—as the creator of the product—for the central automaton: "a mechanical monster whose body fills whole factories, and whose demonic power, at first hidden by the slow and measured motions of its gigantic members" (*CAI*, p. 503).

In this way, the workers, grouped or isolated in the manufacture, carry out each of the special processes with their handmade tools; in such a way that the process is designed for the worker's needs. In other words, the worker is included in the process. In mechanical production, the subjective principle of the division of labour disappears, so that the process has become depersonalized and has erased the singular traces of each worker (*CAI*, p. 501). This suppression of the subjective principle of the division of labour is a key variable in the progressive dehumanization that is currently affecting the lives of workers, considering that computing is a contemporary by-product of industrial mechanization.

Automatism implies production through machinery and is the most developed form of production in the capitalist system. Automatism is also the form of the functioning of Capitalist discourse in Lacan's theory. Both the capitalist system and the Capitalist discourse *displace the subject, tending to dispense with it*. Machines replace human labour, producing pathological effects in the workers who manipulate them. Lacan points to the worker's anxiety as one of the effects of his alienation to machines (*FFI*, p. 21).

## Of repetitive creation in the unconscious

The best-known use of the term "automatism" in Lacan's work comes from his critique of Clérambault's notion of "mental automatism" (*SIII*, 27.06.56, p. 362). In his seminar on *The Psychoses* Lacan states that the use of this expression in psychiatry is problematic since not only the psychotic suffers from the involuntary impositions of words in his thought, but language speaks for itself. Many years later, in *Seminar XXIV* (17.05.77), he states that mental automatism comes from the subject itself; it is a structural characteristic and the very nature of the signifier, which has implications for the psychoanalytic conception of the unconscious defined as politics. As Lacan concludes laconically: "the unconscious is politics" (*SXIV*, 10.05.67). The primary identification, inaugural to the Other, is the establishment of the otherness that allows the social bond in the form of discourse.

The logic of the signifier and of the unconscious is founded on repetitive creation by the insistence of the language of the Master, of an Other, who possesses the means and contains *jouissance*, as Lacan argued in *The Other Side of Psychoanalysis* (*SXVII*, 18.05.70, p. 124). In the establishment of the unconscious and the subject, there is repetitive creation, there is automatism of that which does not stop not being written. The subject is spoken by its unconscious and the worker is automated by the process of capitalist production; only by unalienating itself does it recover its human dignity. The signifier is introduced as an apparatus of *jouissance* and is comparable to the functioning of a machine, and this figure confirms that the symbolic register commanded by the unary trait is characterized by its automatism (*SXVII*, 14.01.70, p. 48). The analytical operation consists in making the Real a semblance, in the discourse in which the object *a* is the agent, thus provoking the emergence of the divided subject, that is to say, what its clinical and political effect is in the face of the foreclosure of meaning caused by Capitalist discourse. *No meaning returns from capitalist otherness* in its pure demand for endlessness. There is pure demand without desire.

In this way, it is enlightening to think of Capitalist discourse as the automaton that, by inverting the order of the logic of the signifier—as a variation of the discourse of the Master—in its cunning, makes liberation impossible, repeats and repeats without the production of meaning, without otherness or subject of the unconscious. In Capitalist discourse, repetition or automatism is autonomized. There is no Other that repeats and produces the loss that is the surplus-*jouissance*, but rather this repetition disarticulates the subject from its otherness and reifies it in the same way that in the capitalist system of production it produces a machine that autonomizes itself from the machine-tool carried by the worker. If there is a subject of the unconscious it is because there is One who is alienated. And it is precisely in Capitalist discourse that the register of the symbolic is not organized in a logic of meaning, in a logic that affects the subject that emerges between two signifiers that produce meaning. This operation is not possible in the latter case.

Another consequence for ideology can be deduced. It is what Žižek has theorized as automatism in the unconscious. This is a reference to Pascal that has been used by Althusser for his development of the "Ideological State Apparatuses".[1] For Pascal, reasoning is determined by an external "machine" that commands its interiority, nonsensical, automatism of the signifier, in the symbolic plot in which subjects are trapped. Pascal calls for disenchantment, since we humans are as much automaton as spirit. Proofs and arguments are convincing for the spirit. Habit gives strength to the proofs and the automaton commands the spirit without thinking. According to Žižek (1989), Pascal defines the unconscious in the same way as Lacan: the automaton—comparable to the dead and insensible letter—without knowing, directs the mind towards it (p. 34).

## The automatism of Capitalist discourse

It is essential to analyze the time in which Lacan produced the concept of Capitalist discourse. He began the last class of *Seminar XV* by stating that he only showed up to maintain contact with his audience, that he would not do the seminar in its usual way, as he abided by the strike slogan of the *Union of Higher Education*: "for a question of discipline which does not necessarily mean to be at the height of events" (*SXV*, 15.05.68).[2] May '68 was in full swing. This movement began in November 1967 at the University of Nanterre through a student revolt that demanded the reform of exams. In that same session of his seminar, Lacan notes that he had met at his school with one of the ringleaders of the revolution, who told him that they expected psychoanalysts to help them throw bricks. Lacan replied that the place of the analyst is to occupy the function of the object *a*. This precision of Lacan's anticipates the discourse of the Analyst whose function is to restore the subject of the unconscious that the Capitalist discourse forecloses.

Lacan's story as a reader of *Capital* is already known, where he points out that the most striking thing about this book is the laughter of the capitalist. Indeed, when Marx writes about the "process of labor and the process of capitalization", the capitalist laughs as he foresees the case where the cost of the daily maintenance of labour power costs only half a working day, even if the worker works a whole day, where the value created by its use for a whole day is twice as great as the daily value of it—a great good fortune for the buyer—and never a detriment or disadvantage to the seller (*CAI*, p. 300). It will also be surplus-value that smiles on the capitalist with the captivating charm of something created out of nothing by the worker, who invests labour power, and which generates no value for himself (*CAI*, p. 325).

Lacan, a reader of Marx, shines in *Seminar XVI*, describing the laughter of the capitalist in *Capital* as the somewhat sinister response of a fantasmatic character or figure who laughs at the discovery of surplus-value in the face of the exploited, of the man who has only rudimentary instruments: his joiner, the lathe, and the milling machine thanks to which he is going to perform marvels, including exchanging services (*SXVI*, 04.12.68). The asymmetry of the figures of the capitalist and the worker is such that the laughter of the capitalist is a revealing event—a figure that has become almost mythical in Lacan's reading of Marx. This commotion is a way of signaling a mode of *jouissance*. The capitalist's laughter is almost an interpretation of the figure of the worker, a reading that appears in Lacan at a time of great social upheaval and trade union struggles (*SXVI*, 04.12.68).

It can be noted that this reading is simultaneous with May '68, where Lacan deals with the question of work and capitalism, right in the middle of the student and worker's revolt. His reading is slightly prior to the seminar he will conduct the following year, *The Other Side of Psychoanalysis*, which is traditionally linked to the social question due to the elaboration of the discourses. The most fruitful antecedent of this elaboration appears in the last session of *Seminar XV*, in which he proposes that the revolution should be of interest to the analyst. This interrogation raises the question of what a psychoanalyst would do when facing an event like this. It is Lacan himself who elaborates his four discourses very soon after. This is the moment when Lacan took the logic of the signifier as far as possible to formalize four modes of the social bond. One of them—the discourse of the Master—also expresses the logic of the unconscious itself and is constituted precisely by the automatism of the subject. In this same period Lacan elaborates the homology between the automatism of the industrial production of the capitalist system and the functioning of the Capitalist discourse, which appears in 1968 and is developed in his seminars *From an Other to the other* and *The Other Side of Psychoanalysis*. With this elaboration he read his time: the year 1968 and its consequences. It is here that Lacan points out that a psychoanalyst must read its contemporary subjectivity.

Capitalist discourse is constituted by two variations of the discourse of the Master. The first consists in the disruption of the places of the $S_1$ and the divided subject, the latter remaining in the place of the agent. And the second is the inversion of the vector whose meaning remains as descending, which determines a circularity, unlike the four discourses established in 1969. Alemán and Larriera (1996) have referred to this circularity as a "sinister circle" (p. 178). They describe Capitalist discourse as a perverse form of discourse since in the "small deviation" where the $S_1$ and the divided subject are inverted, a subject-master, an anomaly occurs and has ethical consequences in the field of the social. In their interpretation, there is a radical distortion, in that civilization is subordinated to science and technique because the unconscious and its effects are ignored: desire and subject. In this way, both technical and scientific discourse reject the subject and consume the Capitalist discourse (Alemán & Larriera, 1996, p. 178). In their reading, the capitalist subject—tributary of the acephalous will that performs—does not know impossibility and lives in a world populated by commodities (Alemán, 2013, p. 148). We call this circularity, for the purposes of this vocabulary, "automatism" and then correlate it with the automatism of capitalist production. It is this functioning of automatism in Capitalist discourse that is described by Lacan in his so-called *Milan Discourse*—delivered on 12 May 1972—when he states that this discourse "runs too fast, on wheels, and is consumed so well that it is consumed" (*DDP*, p. 36).

## Capitalist discourse dispenses with the subject

Automatism in discourse and in capitalist production has certain effects on workers. Lacan located the worker's anxiety as one of them in an interview for the *Panorama* newspaper in Rome, Italy, on 21 December 1974. When asked about anxieties in the plural and, specifically, whether they are linked to the social field and its conditions, Lacan answered that there is the anxiety of the scientist in the face of his own discoveries, as well as that of the worker "enslaved to the assembly line like the rowers on a galley" (*FFI*, p. 21). Thus, the worker becomes a cog in the machinery created by humans. The need to earn a living wage prevents him from separating himself from the production process in which he is frankly "enslaved". This last image illustrates the alienation of the subject from the capitalist production machine and is the source of research in the field of work psychopathology by Christophe Dejours, psychiatrist and psychoanalyst, who classifies these psychopathological entities as severe mental disorders (SMDs), musculoskeletal disorders, caused by the mechanization and automation of procedures, not only in line-workers but also in other workers occupying administrative and managerial positions (Dejours, 2010).

After 1970—and especially after the 1973 oil crisis—work processes were redesigned and the Taylorist–Fordist paradigm went into crisis due to its high costs, and employment contracts became more flexible, giving rise to what is known as teleworking, a modality in which the employee is available without time limits. Economic crises in the capitalist system bring about innovations being applied to the production system and one of these was the development of information and communication technologies (ICTs) and its application in the rationality of production. One of the effects of teleworking was "to render workers invisible" workers, for employers, society in general, and legal institutions, producing great savings for companies.

The development of teleworking follows the same mode of automatism as industrial production, since computer devices produce a new commodity: that of knowledge. This form of production determines workers who know no time limits and are captured by global communication channels through the internet. The contemporary form added to the automatism of industrial production is that of the production of knowledge in the field of informatics by means of the devices created by this new form of production.

## Consequences of automatism in the Capitalist discourse

Lacan homologized surplus-value with surplus-*jouissance*. The object *a* is the central concept of this articulation. Based on this, there is a correlation between the automatism of industrial production and Capitalist discourse, where the symbolic register becomes relevant, the same as that which establishes the unconscious and its variant "*Yad'lun*"[3] through the creative automatism of $S_1$. It is possible to specify three consequences of the automatism of Capitalist discourse: ethical, clinical, and functional.

The ethical consequences arise in the face of the alienation of the worker from the machinery, which currently occurs in the computer devices that are part of the production process of knowledge. Lacan pointed out the anxiety of the worker riveted to the assembly line, or man as a cog in the machine, having thus inverted the original logic in which it is man who governs what he has created. The contemporary form of this anxiety is that of the hyperconnected worker in remote work, for being attached to the computer device. As for the clinical consequences, the system tends to dispense with the subject, which has the effect of reifying the subject and annulling the conditions for the emergence of desire, which affects contemporary symptoms such as *karoshi*—sudden death due to overworking—extreme exhaustion, addictions, and anorexia. Recalcati (1997), a Lacanian psychoanalyst, has interpreted the latter as a rebellion against the imperative of consumption, exposing its extreme thinness as an obstacle to the capitalist system. The functional consequences of automatism in Capitalist discourse are its self-consumption, as described by Lacan in a vertiginous circuit of self-consummation.

## Notes

1 In the term "Ideology" in this vocabulary, one will find reference to the "autonomization of the processes of consciousness", which is a feature of automatism.
2 Capitalist discourse is usually introduced in Lacan by saying that this expression appears in *"On Psychoanalytic Discourse"*, but this is not precise. In the first class of *Seminar XVI* (20.11.68), only six months after May '68, Lacan will formulate for the first time the expression "Capitalist discourse".
3 *Yad'lun* is an expression coined by Lacan that stands for a signifier produced through the iteration of a subject (1971–1972, 15.03.72, pp. 109–114). "I was fomenting no thought of the One, but on the basis of the fact of saying *y a dl'Un*," says Lacan (*RXIX*, p. 215), indicating that it is precisely a strange One that does not permit a global unification, but a "unary trait": a trait which allows repetition. *Yad'lun* has been mainly translated as "there is something of One" or "There is such a thing as One", as Fink does in his translation of *Seminar XX* (p. 5, footnote 5). As Adrian Price, translator of *Seminar XIX*, explains: "The written form *Yad'lun* is an attempt to capture the concentrated pronunciation of *Y a de l'Un*, itself an informal contraction of *Il y a de l'Un*. Thus, not only does the content of the expression indicate the prominence of the One, but its very form presents as a unitary element" (*SXIX*, pp. 240–241, endnote 1 of Chapter IX).

## Further reading

Alemán, J. (2012). *Soledad: común. Políticas en Lacan*. Buenos Aires: Capital Intelectual.
Dejours, C. (Ed). (2010). *Psychopathology of Work. Clinical Observations*, C. Williamson (Trans). London: Karnac, 2015.
Laval, C. & Dardot, P. (2009). *The New Way of the World: On the Neoliberal Society*, G. Elliot (Trans). London: Verso, 2013.

## References

Alemán, J. (2013). *Conjeturas sobre una izquierda lacaniana*. Buenos Aires: Grama.
Alemán, J. & Larriera, S. (1996). *Lacan: Heidegger*. Buenos Aires: Ediciones del Cifrado.
Althusser, L. (1965). From Periodization to the Modes of Production. In: L. Althusser & É. Balibar (Eds.), *Reading Capital* (pp. 209–223), B. Brewster (Trans.). London: New Left Review.
Dejours, C. (Ed). (2010). *Psychopathology of Work. Clinical Observations*, C. Williamson (Trans). London: Karnac, 2015.
Recalcati, M. (1997). *L'ultima cena: anoressia e bulimia*. Milan: Bruno Mondadori.
Žižek, S. (1989). *The Sublime Object of Ideology*. London: Verso.

# Chapter 3

# Bourgeoisie

*Carlos Andrés Umaña González*

—Ara.: برجوازية —Chi.: 資産階級 —Fre.: *Bourgeoisie* —Ger.: *Bürgertum* —Ita.: *Borghesia* —Jap.: ブルジョアジー —Port.: *Burgesia* —Rus.: Буржуазия —Spa.: *Burguesía* —Tur.: *Burjuvazi*

→ *Capitalism*; *Money*; *Society*; *Tyrant/master*

The word "bourgeoisie" comes from the Latin *burgus* that comes from the Germanic *burgs*: small city and fortress. Its Spanish derivative *burgo* (1087) refers to: suburb, small and late medieval city from Eastern Europe; appearing as well as a modality of being in *El Cantar del mío Cid* (poem that narrates the life of Rodrígo Díaz de Vivar the Campeador—or *caballero* in Spanish—around 1200) as *burgalés*: demonym used to address the inhabitant of the burg. Finally, established as bourgeois and middle-class (in French *bourgeoisie*): inhabitants of the burgs, the bourgeois.

## A minimum notion

As evoked in this introduction, the definition of a category initially demands the tracing of basic lines of origin in order to understand it. After tracing these, it is possible to problematize, as far as possible, the contradictions and limitations that it presents as a heuristic tool. In addition, we must mention that we are facing a category where two authors meet: Lacan and Marx, whose theoretical paths, objects of analysis, and practices are particular, and, despite the accurate indication of its homology (Tomšič, 2015),[1] a vital difference prevails between their interlocutions. This relationship has been framed by Alemán (2019) through his anti-philosophy and its *insignificant devices* (Alemán & Larriera, 2009); these do not intend to introduce the homologations and distances of Marx and Lacan to a system of thought or philosophical tradition, but to capture a singularity, in this case, the concept of *bourgeoisie*, starting from the "theoretical rigor together with the urgencies and conclusions of the historical reality that determines us" (Alemán, 2019, p. 16).

For Engels and Marx, the bourgeoisie constitutes the social class that prevails as dominant in a mode of production defined as capitalism. This domain is carried out when the bourgeoisie, as a class, possesses the means to produce and transform capital, thus appropriating the world of the living—the time, the life of workers, and the ecological dimension—to transform it into a dead world: capital that gets accumulated on the basis of exponential growth in the absence of limits. It is possible to understand the origin of the bourgeoisie by following the thesis of the dialectic movement of history, in which the main idea is that "The history of all hitherto existing society is the history of class struggles" (*MCP*, p. 482). It is in this way that feudalism, as a previous period, conceives of the bourgeois outside of the lordly and ecclesiastic control that was being dissolved in favour of the opening up of commercial exchanges unknown at that time due to the novelty of their magnitude and dynamics:

> The discovery of America, the rounding of the Cape, opened up fresh ground for the rising bourgeoisie. The East-Indian and Chinese markets, the colonization of America, trade with the colonies, the increase in the means of exchange and in commodities generally, gave to commerce, to navigation, to industry, an impulse never before known, and thereby, the revolutionary element in the tottering feudal society, a rapid development.
>
> (*MCP*, p. 485)

This revolutionary element, along with particular artistic practices and new forms of knowledge, introduced a gradual stabilization of a class that produced, reproduced, and transformed reality at an unprecedented pace. This initially revolutionary class established control once it discovered the practice of accumulating capital.

## The domination of the bourgeoisie

For Marx and Engels, the production, the reproduction, and the material transformation of a specific society implies, in the field of representations, that

> The class which has the means of material production at its disposal, has control at the same time over the means of mental production, so that thereby, generally speaking, the ideas of those who lack the means of mental production are subject to it.
>
> (*GI*, p. 59)

This mental or spiritual power is produced upon the conviction of a particular conception of the world, "hence of the relationships which make the one class the ruling one, therefore, the ideas of its dominance". In such a way, ideology from the Marxist perspective will have a structural economic correlate, which universalizes its conception by infiltrating "art, law, economic activity, in all the manifestations of personal and collective life" (Gramsci, 1971, p. 12).[2]

Based on the previous framework, Marx (*GR*) points out that there are specific ideological illusions in the bourgeois operation. The idea of individual freedom in human rights, as well as the economic fantasy that fetishizes the field of the market, are two of these illusions. Another critique is added on an epistemic level: denouncing the political economy and its alleged neutrality and economic inevitability. The latter becomes magnified if we consider the legal dimension, which tries to disengage, politically speaking, or religion, which has been known for mutating its general values in the case of bourgeois society. The former is also related to the proposal of the French Physiocratic School and its divergence from political sovereignty and economical science. Up to this point, we have reviewed both the notion of bourgeoisie from Engels and Marx and its ruling effect; let us move on towards the intersection of Marxist development and the work of Lacan.

## The bourgeoisie within Lacanian transmission

In Lacan's work, the category of bourgeoisie comes up on multiple occasions. In brief, for the purposes of establishing this category, we will emphasize four key references in the "period" that goes from 1966 to 1972. This delimitation acquires meaning if one considers that Lacanian transmission during this period was challenged by the impact of the youth riots and the cultural changes resulting from the revolutions that took place at that time. Throughout these years, concerns appear regarding discursivity, the social bond, the idea of revolution, *jouissance* in societal dispositions, the invention of the symptom, and, in broader terms, the relationship between psychoanalytic practice and civilizing dynamics and, therefore, the interrelation of psychoanalytic practice and the Marxist field.

From the start, it must be noted that it is not possible to locate in Lacan a definition of "bourgeoisie". While Marx and Engels analyzed the material conditions that allowed the emergence of the bourgeoisie (the production, the transformation, and the innovation of capital) as well as the ideologic operation carried out by this class, Lacan was interested in the operation of the bourgeoisie in an approach that, anchored in the economy under the assumptions of Engels and Marx, focuses its attention on the psychic dimension, meaning "an economic problem of great importance, that of the relationship between desire and jouissance" (*SXIII*, 20.04.66).[3] His analysis does not present an unhistorical nor a formalized condition, instead, it emerges from a specific symbolic articulation of a historic *moteriality* that allows the apprehension of a singular subjection from the significant materialism. *Moteriality* [*moterialité*] stands for a materialism of words, as indicated by the Lacanian neologism derived from materiality [*materialité*] and word [*mot*] in French (*CG*, p. 13).

For Lacan it is modern science, the immanent episteme within the bourgeoisie, that produces a definition of the subject in capitalism. Science reaches this production through the development of a universalizing psychology, resulting from the economic bourgeois order and its diverse variations of the production of knowledge. It is a transition of economy that, backed by science, advances towards the *psi* field, that is, the *psi* as Foucault understood it, notion to which Lacan did not subscribe to at the time (*DPP*, p. 68):

> Academic psychology, being the latest arrival in the exact sciences and having thus appeared at the height of the bourgeois civilization that supports the body of these sciences, could only trust naively in the mechanistic thought that proved its worth so brilliantly in the sciences of physics. [...] Likewise, the historical progress of a psychology such as this, when it takes the experimental critique of the hypostases of religious rationalism as its starting point, culminates, with the most recent psycho-physics, in functional abstractions the reality of which reduces with ever greater rigour to measuring solely the physical yield of human labour.

Therefore, for Lacan, mechanical thought, transmitted by the economic progress of the bourgeoisie, determines the *psi* field as a positive science. What the subjects have at hand to subjectivize (making here reference to the difference that Alemán (2019) points out from Lacan regarding Foucault's proposal (1982–1983)), and, in the first instance, what subjectivizes them when entering the chain of signifiers that precedes them, will be characterized in structural terms as coming from a mechanistic concern, a naive concern that allows us to see that Lacan does not have a mechanism or its physics as the target of his critique, but rather the extrapolation of these to "any psychological hypothesis of the subject's relations with language" (*SXIII*, 20.04.66). This relationship enables the link between bourgeois society, in which the family appears in a dominant position, and Oedipal knotting as symbolic resolution (*P9O*):

> Let's observe the place that Oedipal ideology such that it has in some way dispensed sociology, for a century now, from taking a stand, as it ought to have done before, on the worth of the family, the family such as it exists, the petit-bourgeois family in civilization, –i.e., in the society conveyed by science.

At this point we will have to emphasize the use of the word "ideology": what does Lacan want to say with this? He elevates the Oedipal effects of the familial configuration to ideology and to the sociological institution, effects that seem to support their legitimacy again in scientific knowledge. But we must go further by asking ourselves, how can one articulate the mechanistic extrapolation to the *psi* field with what is at stake in the "Oedipal ideology"? To follow up on the former, a triad is profiled from bourgeois society: science, psychology, and family. Where to read the excesses of this establishment? What escapes the bourgeoisie, the "science-driven society"?

## *Jouissance* and pleasure in bourgeois society

By referring back to a comparative exercise in which the issue of *jouissance* in ancient times is shown, Lacan brings to attention the topic of the *jouissance* of the Master in *Seminar XIII* (20.04.66):

> One looks after private properties; one does not make them work so bloody hard as in regimes of liberty. Which means, that the problem of jouissance in the ancient world was resolved and, in a way, that I think you see clearly, the beings devoted to jouissance, to pure and simple jouissance, were the slaves as, moreover, everything indicates.

The Master enjoys this *jouissance* through the body and life of the slave: "the problem of jouissance was resolved in Antiquity" (*SXIII*, 20.04.66), as stated by Lacan. This is a disposition of the *psychic class economy*; the other is not that much of a subject, it is a pure object of *jouissance*. It is the emergence of capitalism that structurally disrupts and modifies the past: "Undoubtedly the problem of *jouissance* will be posed for us in different terms, and certainly in terms that, given the fact of capitalism, are a little more complicated" (*SXIII*, 20.04.66); here the subject renews its condition (extended *res cogitans*, business paradigm, the enlargement of the I), habilitating the modalities of the *jouissance* by registering it in a particular discourse: the University discourse, the discourse of science. Thus, this freedom collects for the subject, before the powers of production, a *plus-de-jouir*, typical of the civilizing model, a singular surplus in relation to its own scarcity. This connection that gets established between freedom and beyond the pleasure principle, is not registered by the bourgeoisie; in contrast, a kind of deafness is going to be presented by Lacan (*SXVI*, 15.01.69):

> Those listeners were bourgeois listeners [...] in other words, they absolutely didn't have the faintest idea about what the pleasure principle is. The pleasure principle is a reference from the morality of antiquity. In antique morality, pleasure, which consists precisely in making as little as possible of it, *otium cum dignitate*, is an asceticism. It may be said that this pleasure joins up with the pleasure of pigs [...]. What can that have to do with the idea that the bourgeois man forms of pleasure or, moreover, the idea he forms of reality?

In this comparison, the model of the bourgeois subject cannot be found immersed in the pleasure principle ruled by the *otium cum dignitate* (leisure with dignity); on the contrary, and as we saw in the previous quotation, the liberty that is acquired in the frame of reference of capitalism offers the latest range in which the issue of pleasure reappears with the possibilities of having diverse trajectories. Considering this, civilization expects to compress itself in a dyad: reason/pleasure, oriented towards the ascesis of the latter, an unsustainable operation tailored for "bourgeois digestion" (*SXVI*, 15.01.69). It is a civilizing ambition that intends to suffocate and to silence that which will always be present in the bond, what exceeds it, meaning the *jouissance*. The excess escapes the control of economic science, the quantifiable field, the science that intends to produce a subject in the absence of its *jouissance*, a delimited subject with precision, there "where science maintains it sutured, by the sheer strength of arithmetic", there where Descartes "splits being, which, from its two butt ends ['I am thinking', 'therefore I am'], cannot conjoin but in manifesting the torsion it has undergone in its knot. Causation? Turnaround? Negativity?" (*SXIII*, 20.04.66). This quotation can be expanded from a passage from a previous seminar: "is our aim to arrive at a unified field, and to turn men into moons?" (*SII*, 25.05.55, p. 241).

This complex operation of silencing the excess will end, according to Lacan (*DDP*, p. 32), in a discursive articulation, particularly *jouissante*, without a cut. We face a return of the things that the "stubborn ears" did not wish to hear: what breaks the sutures of science as a support of bourgeois civilization. This is the outcome that Lacan traces from the project of the bourgeoisie: the Capitalist discourse in which the subject is finally subsumed by the merchandise when he locates himself precisely in this position, the position of the subject as an interchangeable element (human capital!), entrepreneur of himself, dealing with its anxiety in the addicted consumption (without a break) relative to a circularity of acquirable objects, that is to say, what it can buy and even buy himself.

## The bourgeoisie in Marx : Lacan

For Lacan, psychological science is the product of the "peak of the bourgeois civilization", and his fundamental thinking would entail the particular idea of subjectivity linked to other sciences of the epistemic bourgeois scheme. This Lacanian indication agrees on a broader scale with the critique of the ideologic operation conducted by Marx, where he states that the freedom registered in liberal rights is determined by the political economy in the last instance. It is in this way that, according to both authors, the bourgeoisie produces a specific approach to subjectivity that obliterates the place of the subject as an ideological product, forcing him into the kingdom of the "*I-cracy*" (*SXVII*, 21.01.70, p. 63). In this way, the notion of freedom that is questioned by Marx is the same as of the modern subject that resonates with the critique presented by Lacan of the typical psychology of the bourgeois civilization; they both posit a question for the matter of the scientific illusion of the centralization of the "I", thereby permitting an eccentric movement out of it.

Conversely, we find that, from this idea of psychology, Lacan refers to the bourgeois ambition of circumscribing the psychic dimension exclusively to the field of reason as being "stubborn ears". It is, among all this, that beyond the pleasure principle seems to be escaping from the familiar, social, and (as a last resort) scientific comprehension of this psychological civilizing. The issue of *jouissance* opens the discussion about the particular era of the discursive configuration of capitalism. This is, without a doubt, a possibility that Lacan takes into account, departing from the Freudian conceptualization, but also, thanks to the discovery of the surplus-value in Marx, that particular form of *jouissance* in capitalism, as well as the response obtained from the subjects about it: the *plus-de-jouir* which allows them to find a resolution for an inexorable scarcity derived from the permanent acquisition of their lives by capital.

To conclude, we must consider an irreconcilable difference between both authors. We talked about the historic conditions of the formation of the bourgeoisie. For Marx and Engels (*MCP*), the bourgeoisie is constituted as the last dominant class in history, until the revolution wins freedom for the working class and the construction of a new society without a dominant class. Departing from the idea of a particular subject irreducible to the symbolic configurations of any era, Lacan (*SXIII*, 20.04.66) will not share this hypothesis. On the contrary, there is no possibility, from psychoanalytic Lacanian theory, of considering a completed horizon or a dissolution of the structural gap that determines its subject. The gap that reveals itself is ahistorical, perpetual, and constitutive. This affirmation has a considerable impact for the notion of ideology in which Marx defines it as biased, as a false universal to surpass, and that, from the reading of Lacan in the intermingling with Marxism (e.g., Althusser, Pêcheux, or Žižek) is, however, a perpetual condition, since: "the eternity of *the unconscious* is based, in the last instance, on the eternity of *ideology* in general" (Althusser, 1969, p. 176). Nevertheless, this does not prevent Lacan from considering the overcoming of the bourgeoisie as a ruling class, even if the other economy, the psychic one, does not foretell harmony for the future, not even with the toolkit of Marxism at its disposition:

> One cannot scour clean the plague of excrement which the order of social exploitation, which takes its stand on this opening in the subject, and therefore does not create, whatever may be thought about it, even in Marxism, alienation, in the order therefore of social exploitation.
>
> (*SXIII*, 20.04.66)

## Notes

1 See Lacan (*SXVI*, 13.11.68).
2 Our translation.
3 Translation by A. Price.

## Further reading

Althusser, L. (1969). *On the Reproduction of Capitalism*, G. Goshgarian (Trans.). London: Verso.
Lacan, J. (1965–1966). *Le séminaire. Livre XIII. L'objet de la psychanalyse*. Unpublished [Lesson of 20/04/1966].
Sombart, W. (1916). *El apogeo del capitalismo*. México: Fondo de Cultura Económica, 1984.

## References

Alemán, J. (2019). *Capitalismo: crimen perfecto o emancipación*. Barcelona: NED Ediciones.
Alemán, J. & Larriera, S. (2009). *Desde Lacan: Heidegger. Textos reunidos*. Madrid: Ediciones Miguel Gómez.

Althusser, L. (1969). *On the Reproduction of Capitalism*, G. M. Goshgarian (Trans.). London: Verso, 2014.

Foucault, M. (1982–1983). *The Government of Self and the Others*, G. Burchell (Trans.). New York: Picador Editions, 2011.

Gramsci, A. (1971). *El materialismo histórico y la filosofía de Benedetto Croce*. Buenos Aires: Nueva Visión.

Tomšič, S. (2015). Homology: Marx and Lacan. *S: Journal of the Circle for Lacanian Ideology Critique*, 5: 98–113.

# Chapter 4

# Capitalism

*Andreja Zevnik*

—Ara.: رأس المال —Chi.: 資本主義 —Fre.: *Capitalisme* —Ger.: *Kapitalismus* —Ita.: *Capitalismo* —Jap.: 資本主義 —Port.: *Capitalismo* —Rus.: *Капитализм* —Spa.: *Capitalismo* —Tur.: *Kapitalizm*

→ *Consumption*; *Economy*; *Market*; *Surplus-jouissance*; *Value*

## Introduction

Capitalism is not a core concept in Lacan's psychoanalysis. However, the idea has played a significant role in the development of his theory from the mid-1960s when Marx and his critique of political economy became significant reference points for Lacan in particular in the re-conceptualization of the subject and the social bond (as it is conceptualised in the theory of the four discourses). Lacan in his post-1969 texts reorients his theory of language from an exclusive attachment to structural linguistics to the critique of political economy. The move, Lacan claims, is down to Marx's theory of production, which departs from discursive asymmetry and social non-relations to which structural linguistics is attached (Tomšič, 2012, p. 101). This new attachment to the theory of production intertwines Lacan's earlier work on the unconscious subject and Marxist thinking about the capitalist labourer bringing the transformation of the subject that psychoanalysis strives to achieve in line with the political question of social change. In *Television* (*TV*, p. 16) Lacan states that the goal of psychoanalysis is a way out of the Capitalist discourse. Psychoanalysis—in Lacan post 1960s outlook—has the same universal goals as Marxism. Politically, Lacan's turn towards Marx and the notion of capitalism can be aligned with the changes in the political sphere. The collapse of the Bretton Woods system the 1960s and 1970s saw a gradual decline of this monetary system and the end of the gold standard. Lacan saw this move as a triumph of religion—(capitalist) abstractions become the driving forces of economy, inaugurating the neoliberal era and the self-regulating market economy. For as long as things can be exchanged "the hypothesis of money breeding money will persist" (Tomšič, 2015a, p. 48). Lacan's turn towards Marx and the notion of capitalism and capitalist production also brings together the Freudian libidinal economy with Marx's political economy. The intersection of Marx and

Freud is also where Lacan's thought most significantly overlaps the libidinal and the political, the *objet petit a* and the surplus-value, where his rethinking of *jouissance* and social relation inevitably lies.

## Defining capitalism: an (im)possible task?

Perhaps one of Lacan's first definitions/expositions of capitalism can be traced back to his text *Kant avec Sade* (*KS*, p. 656):

> Especially regarding a certain equivocal notion that has been gaining ground about the relation of reversion that supposedly unites sadism with a certain idea of masochism – it is difficult for those outside such circles to imagine the muddle this notion creates. We would do better to learn from it the lesson contained in a fine little tale told about the exploitation of one man by another, which is the definition of capitalism, as we know. And socialism, then? It is the opposite.

This definition of capitalism is significant for two reasons: the first is the evocation of the relationship between sadism and masochism (to which we will return); the second is the alignment of psychoanalysis with a Marxist understanding of market economy and capitalist exploitation. For Marx (*CAI*) capitalism is production based on the private ownership of the means of production, where the worker produces commodities that are exchanged on the market for a greater value. The value of the worker's labour is greater than what the capitalist bought it or. This—as both Lacan and Marx acknowledge—is the source of surplus-value. Capitalist society, for Marx, is best described by the circuit of commodity production. The famous formula M–C–M' of commodity production is focused on M–M' (producing surplus) whereby the input into the production of commodities (including the price of labour) is outweighed by the commodity's market price. Specific to the capitalist mode of production is that inputs and outputs of production are supplied by the market—and as such are commodified. The technology and the worker (organization of labour) in the capitalist mode of production have been commercialized. Lacan (*SXVI*, 20.11.68) agrees with Marx that the market is the source of surplus-value. This is the excess that supports and drives capitalism.

Lacan's use of Marx's critique of political economy and capitalism concerns the libidinal economy of the subject and its social bond. For example, Lacan accords Marx the discovery of the "surplus", that being surplus-value in capitalism or surplus-enjoyment/*objet petit a* in the libidinal economy (*SXVI*, 20.11.68). Inasmuch as the impossible attainment of *objet petit a* drives the subject, surplus drives capitalism. Bringing Marx and Freud together (most explicitly in *Seminar XVI*) Lacan shows how unconscious production of *jouissance* and the social production of value follow the same logic and display similar structural contradictions: for example, not repression of productive potentials of sexuality, drives, or desires but the insatiable demand for production—production for the sake of production (*SXVI*, 20.11.68). Capitalism for Lacan and Marx rejects the paradigm of negativity. It attempts to avoid castration or the intervention of language that splits and decentralizes the subject (*SSD*, 1960). "Surplus-*jouissance* responds, not to *jouissance*, but to the loss of *jouissance*" (*SXVI*, 15.01.68). The logic of capitalist production appears to guard against entropy, or better, it seeks to compensate for the intervention of the signifier into the libidinal. In *Seminar XVII* Lacan states that: "when the signifier is introduced as an apparatus of *jouissance*, we should thus not be surprised to see something related to entropy appear, since entropy is defined precisely once one has started to lay this apparatus of signifiers over the physical world" (*SXVII*, 14.01.70, p. 49).

Capitalism also introduces a different form of power—liberal power that changed the character of power from what Lacan calls positive power (with direct consequences) to liberal power which can also be seen as camouflaged or anarchic power (*SXVI*, 19.03.69). The Russian revolution attempted to return to positive power but failed. The transformation into liberal power was sustained by capitalism's attachments to the modern function of science.

Lacan's reflections on capitalism touch on a number of interrelated points. They highlight the capitalist attachment to libidinal (desire for excessive enjoyment), whereby capitalism presupposes that all of us have a relation with enjoyment (*SXVI*, 21.05.69). Similarly, they point to the structural impossibilities/contradictions presented by the capitalist system. In particular, Lacan questions the possibility of liberation that comes either with or as a reaction (resistance) to capitalism. In that way, Lacan considers capitalism useful as a structural logic. In *Seminar XVI*, for example, he states that "capitalism is of use, but the things it produces aren't" (*SXVI*, 19.03.1969), pointing precisely to the effects capitalist logics (or what Lacan later also called "Capitalist discourse") has on the formation of the subject and the social bond. A year later, in *Seminar XVII*, he clearly links the effects of capitalist logic to the formation of the social bond.

## Capitalism in Lacan's work

While a more systematic engagement with capitalism and capitalist logics only appears in Lacan's *Seminars XVI* and *XVII* between 1967 and 1970, Lacan's earlier work suggests he was intrigued by the phenomena. For example, in *The Function and Field of Speech and Language*, Lacan credits capitalism with a creation of reality, which results in a combination between exact and subjective science. Specifically,

> the ever freer play of mathematical law [… and] the brazen face of capitalist exploitation, [...] although they seem to come from radically different realms, their effects come to constitute our subsistence, precisely by intersecting there in a double reversal: the most subjective science having forged a new reality.
>
> (*FFS*, p. 236)

In this way capitalism is credited with the emergence of the new science and constitutes a break with the Ancient (Greek) world: a shift that was predicated on the change in what can be counted, the relationship with "private property", and the place of *jouissance* in the system of production. In *Seminar XIII*, Lacan explicitly states that: "Socrates did not engage in social criticism nor did Freud. It is no doubt because both one and the other had the idea from where there was situated an extraordinarily important economic problem, that of the relationships of desire and of *jouissance*" (*SXIII*, 20.04.66). In 1966 Lacan had already begun to connect capitalism with *jouissance* (a move which launched the development of the theory of discourses and the formations of the social bond). The problem of *jouissance* in the Ancient world was resolved by the figure of the slave—in an almost Hegelian Master/Slave dialectic—also the figure of *jouissance*. With modern science and modern industry, the problem of *jouissance* needed a different resolution. The figure of the slave could no longer exist as private property. The slave, for Lacan, could not be mistreated, as "he was capital" (*SXIII*, 20.04.66). Thus, for modern industry to work "it was necessary that slaves should not be private property. One looks after private properties, one does not make them work so bloody hard as in regimes of liberty" (*SXIII*, 20.04.66).

Further in *Seminars XIV* and *XV* Lacan's observations continue to focus on the effects of the changed reality brought about by capitalism. While references are scarce, Lacan focuses on the calculability or the production of value in capitalist reality. First, the foundation of the object of merchandise is reliant on a misidentification between the exchange-value and use-value. The exchange-value is falsely identified as use-value (*SXIV*, 12.04.67). Second, Lacan challenges the significance Marx attaches to class consciousness, seeing it as nothing but "the number". He very pointedly asks:

> Why should class consciousness be so sure of its orientation [...] when it even knows nothing or knows very little about the theory, when class consciousness functions, [...] if it is reduced properly to those who belong to the level defined [...] by the term of 'the class' excluded from capitalist profits?
> (*SXIV*, 19.04.67)

Lacan was sceptical of the invocation of Marxist thought in militancy or protests. He saw "revolution"—as a form of political project in the 1960s—as a reaffirmation of capitalist logic, not its challenge. In that sense, class consciousness, for Lacan, was a naive concept of militancy rather than a significant analytical tool.

Scepticism for the militant aspects of Marx's thought somewhat disappears in *Seminar XVI* where Lacan shows how Marx derives surplus-value, a key analytical component on which psychoanalysis and Marxism overlap. As Lacan states:

> Marx starts from the function of the market. His novelty is the place that he situates labour in it. It is not the fact that labour is new that allows his discovery, is it the fact that it is bought; that there is a labour market. This is

what allows him to demonstrate what is inaugurating in his discourse – what is called surplus value.

(*SXVI*, 13.11.68)

He further goes on suggesting that: "we know about, or rather that we know very badly, because it is not sure that taking power resolved what I will call the subversion of the capitalist subject expected from this act" (*SXVI*, 13.11.68). Here, Lacan cautions about the transformative potential of militancy, even if grounded in the Marxist thought of that time. A "hysteric" refusal of the master does not end in revolution but in the re-institution of a new master. This statement needs to be taken alongside the provocation/graffiti—"Structures do not walk on the streets"—that appeared in Paris during student protests and that—allegedly—challenged the insistence on structuralism/structures when considering political action. If anything, then, Lacan's *Seminar XVII* shows how structures do precisely that—walk on the streets—and how structural shifts can account for social outbursts. Lacan clearly demonstrates the significance of social structures for political change/action. He highlights his reading of structure and militancy by showing how Marx himself was a structuralist, and that this is something that perhaps his followers, caught up in militant actions, all too often forget. He states: "The important thing is what Marx is designating and what his approach means. Whether his commentators are structuralist or not they still seemed to have demonstrated that he for his part is structuralist" (*SXVI*, 13.11.68).

Finally, the remarks on militancy and structures suggest a shift in Lacan's thinking about the Other. As a result of capitalist logic Lacan moves away from thinking about the Other in a Saussurean linguistic way to the Other of *jouissance*, which is embedded in Marxist thinking about production. The logic of capital as embodied in the faith of postmodern markets further led Lacan to state that "the Other doesn't exist". Capitalism or the logic of capital introduce religious components through the notion of fetishism and allow Lacan to show how religion triumphs over science and emancipatory politics. The inexistence of the Other—or the inexistence of the market in Marxist terms—is supported by abstractions. The Other and the market are upheld by fantasies whereby faith in the Other maintains the existence of the Other; or whereby "the money breeding money" (Tomšič, 2015a) maintains the illusion of the market. The logic of capitalism shows how the Other and the market—as two cornerstones of psychoanalysis and political economy respectively—are supported by faith—a blind belief in their existence and necessity.

So what can be extrapolated from Lacan's development of the concept? Lacan, for once, assumed a critical stand towards contemporary social order; he repeatedly challenged the dominant logics and ideologies of which capitalism is central. Lacan is thus no doubt critical of capitalism, even though he sees its use, but he is equally critical of Marxism (or a particular incarnation of it). In fact in *Talking to Brick Walls* he states that (*PAM*, 6.01.72, p. 90):

> History has shown that the discourse [of the Master] was alive and kicking […] until a particular infection […] it turned into the discourse of the capitalist, of which we wouldn't have had the faintest idea had Marx not set himself to completing it, to giving it its subject, the proletariat. Thanks to this, the discourse of capitalism has flourished in every nation-state that has taken a Marxist form.

Whether that is more of a critique of how Marxism has been used in the social field and less of Marx's thought as such remains unclear. Psychoanalysis is then the intervention into the capitalist reality, an intervention into the capitalist rejection of castration. The antidote for capitalism—castration—thus comes in the form of the Analytic discourse (*PAM*, 6.01.72, p. 91), and psychoanalysis is tasked with finding an exit from capitalism (*TV*, p. 16). In tasking psychoanalysis with this "revolutionary" goal Lacan turns psychoanalysis from a subjective science (a practice concerned with the analysis of individual symptoms) to a social theory concerned with addressing social symptoms understood as structural articulations of subjects' protests against capitalist modes of enjoyment.

## Capitalism as a theoretical tool

Lacan's focus on Marx's critique of political economy and Freud's discovery of the unconscious to which he devotes a good part of *Seminar XVI* is significant for two reasons: it signifies Lacan's second (re)turn to Freud which is indebted to Marx; and its signifies a refocusing/abandonment of structural linguistics. Marx thus allows Lacan to move away from structural linguistics as a mode of representation to a theory of language as "discursive production". Following Marx, Lacan can remove the bar between the language and the signified, as we can observe in his study of Joyce, where language loses its grammatical consistency and the production of meaning is secondary to the production of enjoyment. The focus of discursive production which became central to Lacan's teaching post 1968 has a number of immediate implications for Lacan's theory; most significantly it shapes the way Lacan can now think of the subject and the structural product of the social bond.

Bringing together Freud's unconscious and Marx's critique of political economy (and more specifically capitalism) allows Lacan to develop a new theory of the subject. Much has been written about the centrality of sexuality in Freud's thinking; what remains important in this context are the characteristics of "sexuality": it is decentralized, relational in-existence, fictitiousness, castrating, in rejection of negativity. And these characteristics align themselves with those of capitalism. Sexuality—like capitalism—is driven by the imperative to enjoy which in turn leads to its commodification. The famous Freudian sexual repression appears as repression through commodification. In capitalism, commodification becomes the capitalist form of repression that has its consequences for sexuality and subjectivity. But as Lacan shows, such repression through commodification does not achieve its goal. Enjoyment received from the commodities cannot substitute for the superegoical imperative to "Enjoy!". He writes:

> What differentiates the discourse of capitalism is *Verwerfung*, the fact of rejecting, outside all the fields of the symbolic. [...] What does it reject? Well, castration. Any order, any discourse that aligns itself with capitalism, sweeps to one side what we might simply call [...] matters of love.
> (*PAM*, 6.01.72, p. 91)

What the Capitalist discourse reveals is that commodification rejects castration and strives to enjoy completely, through commodities. Inasmuch as fantasies support this striving to "Enjoy!", the subject inevitably encounters negativity, either through the experience of dissatisfaction due to the lack of enjoyment received by the commodities or through the intervention of the surplus-*jouissance* in the body. What counts for capitalism is sex as pure enjoyment without negativity or limitation; and a production of enjoyment through enjoyment itself (like money breeding money). "If [...] he hadn't computed this surplus jouissance, if he hadn't converted it into surplus value, in other words if he hadn't founded capitalism, Marx would have realised that surplus value is surplus jouissance" (*SXVII*, 11.03.70, p. 141).[1] This capitalist logic of enjoyment is unsustainable without commodities as substitutes to the real of *jouissance*.

Marx shows how capitalism turns everyone into a desubjectivized labour power through the production of value and the production of enjoyment. In *Seminar XVI* Lacan sees it as a move towards proletarianization or the proletariat as the only universal subject position achieved through the absolutization of the market and the introduction of surplus enjoyment (*SXVI*, 20.11.68). For capitalism everyone is translatable into labour-power or as Lacan says: "The proletariat [...] it means that labour is radicalised to the pure and simple level of merchandise" (*SXVI*, 12.02.69). By translating surplus enjoyment into surplus-value Lacan's theory of the subject (and psychoanalysis) meets Marx's critique of political economy. Arguably, this coupling leads towards emancipatory politics (Tomšič, 2015b, p. 152).

The theory of four discourses developed in *Seminar XVII* is most directly and noticeably influenced by Marx's thought. It would be impossible to summarize the details of the theory here, thus the focus remains on the explicit intervention capitalism makes into the matrix of the four discourses. Capitalism in the theory of four discourses needs to be understood as performing a double function. First, the capitalist production overlaps with discursive production, leading Lacan to develop a dynamic structuralism by formalizing discourses into a matrix allowing for a quarter turn between the elements producing language (Tomšič, 2015b, p. 157). The second is the change in the Master discourse itself and arguably a development of a distinct structure of Capitalist discourse. In doing so, Lacan (*SXVII*, 17.12.69, p. 31) explicitly says that Marxism did not succeed in challenging the persistence of the Master's discourse; while the structure of the *mastery* has changed (from that of the Master discourse to the discourse of the University) its prevalence has been maintained.

The strife of the "old" Master discourse should be understood in the following way: the four elements that can be isolated and that construct language are: signifiers $S_1$, $S_2$, a subject $S$, and the object $a$ produced in the discourse. The four positions that these objects occupy are: master signifier, knowledge, *jouissance*, and the subject (read clockwise); the relationships between the elements can also be read as: desire, Other, loss, and truth (*SXVII*, 18.02.70, pp. 92–93). The old Master discourse can be read in a Hegelian way as a relationship between the Master/Feudal lord ($S_1$) and the Slave ($S_2$); whereas for Lacan, the slave as the subject is the bearer of knowledge (Schema 1 and Schema 2)

For Lacan, the intervention of capitalism into this structure introduces a modification at the level of knowledge. The Master discourse under capitalism can be read as the Capitalist ($S_1$) and the proletariat ($S_2$) in the place of knowledge. The $S_2$ here is specified "as being, not knowledge of everything [...] but all knowing. [...] Understand this as what is affirmed as being none other than knowledge, which in ordinary language is called bureaucracy" (*SXVII*, 17.12.69, p. 31). However, the positioning of the proletariat poses a certain problem. Lacan says that the proletariat has been dispossessed, and that this dispossession is the foundation

## Discourse of the Master

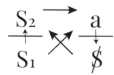

*Schema 1* The Master discourse. Source: Schema adapted from Lacan (*DDP*, p. 40).

## Discourse of the University

$$\frac{S_2}{S_1} \overset{\longrightarrow}{\times} \frac{a}{\$}$$

*Schema 2* The University discourse. Source: Schema adapted from Lacan (*DDP*, p. 40).

for attempted revolution (*SXVII*, 17.12.69, p. 32). The schema represents this as a gap in the circle: the production of the subject and the object cannot be brought into relation unless the relation is sought via the capital (the relation via commodities). This break in the structure allows Lacan to develop four discourses and he consequently began reading capitalism within a different discursive structure. The move to knowledge signifies Lacan's move to the University discourse, where $S_2$ operates as a Master signifier.

Reading capitalism through the University discourse allows Lacan to state that capitalist exploitation frustrates the master signifier (knowledge), because it renders its knowledge useless. In a move of subversion, what is returned to him is Master's knowledge, "what remain in effect is the essence of the master, namely that he does not know what he wants. [… T]his is why all he has done is change masters" (*SXVII*, 17.12.69, p. 32). The consequences of this shift are worth quoting at length (*SXVII*, 17.12.69, p. 32):

> There you have what continues the true structure of the Master's discourse. The slave knows many things, but what he knows even better still is what the master wants, even if the master doesn't know it himself, which is the usual case, for otherwise he would not be a master. The slave knows what it is, and that is what his function as slave is. This is also why it works. […] The fact that all-knowing has moved into the place of the master is something that does not throw light on it, but rather makes a little bit more obscure what is at issue, namely, truth. How does it come about that there is a master's signifier in this place? For this is well and truly $S_2$ of the master, revealing as it does the bare bones of how things stand under the tyranny of knowledge. […] Now the sign of truth is somewhere else. It is to be produced by what has come to be substituted for the ancient slave, that is, by those who are themselves products, as we say, consumables every bit as much as the others. "Consumer society", we say. "Human material", as it was called at one stage.

So what does this tell us about "the subject" or what Lacan meant when invoking "consumer society"? The Capitalist in the University discourse strives to produce subjects of value. In 1968, students—amongst others—demanded a reform in the education system based on "credit points". Lacan made numerous references in his lectures to the consequences that this has on the production of knowledge. It quantifies knowledge, subsuming it to the logics of value and capitalist production: "for reasons that have nothing to do with the virtue of this discourse credits pass progressively from a use value to an exchange value" (*IM2*). Addressing the production of capitalist subjectivities further he states that the students will play the function of surplus-value and sustain the style of exchange and market that capitalist society constitutes.

Discourse of the Capitalist

$$\frac{\$}{S_1} \times \frac{S_2}{a}$$

*Schema 3* The Capitalist discourse. Source: Schema adapted from Lacan (*DDP*, p. 40).

The logic of capitalism thus alters the structure of mastery and turns it into one aligned with the University discourse. Later—though this is contested—Lacan develops a third iteration of the Capitalist discourse, departing from the initial structure which allows for only four turns. In his intervention in Milan (*DDP*) he introduced a new "fifth" structure. This new iteration swaps the places of the $S_1$ (Master) and the subject ($\$$). Arguably (Tomšič, 2015a, p. 204) this established a relation between the subject of representation and the object of production. "The subject of capitalism is now no longer located in labour-power but in capital itself. In this way Lacan formalizes the central thesis of political-economic fetishism: money labors (in both meanings of the word)" (Tomšič, 2015b, p. 59) (Schema 3).

This new structure allows for two sets of relations: one of representation ($\$$, $S_1$, and $S_2$) and another of production ($S_1$, $S_2$, and $a$) between which there is no gap. As Tomšič (2015b) shows, this intervention anticipates financialization, which suggests a substitution of the contradiction between capital and labour with the productive split of capital. The relations between the elements also suggest that we are dealing with a transformation in a Master discourse; one which resembles the core fantasy of capitalism—the rejection of negativity. However, as Tomšič shows:

> This fantasy of completeness undoubtedly echoes Marx's point regarding fetishism and for this reason cannot represent an actual discursive formation but formalizes the appearance of capital as self-engendering entity, the appearance that traverses all stages of fetishism and that echoes the rejection of castration, which nevertheless persists behind this fantasmatic veil.
>
> (p. 160)

## Contestations of/in the Capitalist discourse

Tomšič's discussion of capitalism as a "fifth discourse" indicated that questions whether Lacan meant this formulation to be understood as an independent/fifth discourse or only a perversion of the discourse of the Master remain unresolved.

If Tomšič argues for the latter, others either embrace the possibilities of this new structure (Mura, 2015; Pavón-Cuéllar, 2009) or remain less interested in whether this is indeed a separate structure, but instead interrogate its consequences, for example, in relation to surplus or interpellation. The surplus as a distinct capitalist conception intervenes in psychoanalysis at a number of different levels; its significance is how it opens up theorization of subjectivity with constraints and possibilities of emancipation.

In *Seminar XVI* Lacan traces the homology between *jouissance* and surplus-value. Capitalism activates the same *jouissance* for "the purpose of its incessant drive for accumulation" (Bianchi, 2010, p. 36). The aimlessness and drive for production for the sake of accumulation characterize both libidinal economies. By putting *jouissance* in relation to the surplus-value, *jouissance* becomes quantifiable/valorized. The structure of the University discourse—a representation of capitalist logic—reveals a removal of the obstruction central to surplus-*jouissance*, which allows for a repetition of enjoyment as "possible". This stands in direct position to *jouissance* in the Master discourse where repetition appears as impossible (in turn, enjoyment derives precisely from the impossibility of its attainment). The enjoyment that emerges in the University discourse is a semblance: "Lacan goes as far as to call it now 'an imitation of surplus jouissance'" (Zupančič, 2006, p. 171). The logic of capitalism empties the impossibility at the core of *jouissance*, making everything (appear as if they) run smoothly. We appear to be enjoying only that this is not quite the case. The inoperability of enjoyment (the imperative of: "Enjoy!") is suffocating. The semblance of enjoyment that capitalism introduces is nothing but a semblance. It appears as if "Impossible is possible" (p. 171) and yet it is not. The semblance of surplus-*jouissance* is attached to material objects of desire, which are not some "primordial incestuous lost object on which desire remains forever transfixed [...] but a purely formal object that causes us to desire objects that we encounter in reality" (Žižek, 2016a, p. 127). Capitalism sustains itself by endlessly producing those little objects of desire upon which the attainment of *jouissance* relies and which create the impression that the impossible is possible. However, such objects deprived of their surplus (coffee without caffeine etc., as Žižek famously writes) are impotent. In contrast, a life of pure surplus-*jouissance* is impossible to live. *Jouissance* requires "mediation", it can have "the semblance of an external superego, but also the plasticity of something that can be re-shaped, and morphed into something else" (Bianchi, 2010, p. 137). By introducing the duality of *jouissance* in capitalism Bianchi sees a potential for a re-inscription of the social bond. By working through the symptom he ponders on the possibility of creating a different mode of production, desire that exists outside of the logic of capitalism.

By positioning the surplus in sex and capitalism Zupančič similarly explores the position of the subject in capitalism. In *What is Sex?* she brings into the forefront the notion of "non-relation" in capitalism and sex. She states that: "social relations of power –domination, exploitation, discrimination– are first and foremost forms of exploitation of the non-relation" (Zupančič, 2017, p. 30).

Capitalism starts with two revolutionary ideas: "the economic relations do not exist" and "the non-relation could be profitable". The second idea is particularly revolutionary as it depends on a logic in which wealth can increase itself. The profitability of the non-relations derives from the mode of production, as Marx had already developed. It lies precisely at the point where labour enters the markets only as another commodity which is for sale. Thus, "what makes the products (labour power) also appears with them on the market as one of the products, objects for sale" (p. 33). This is the moment of structural negativity that capital exploits. It is not that capitalists are stealing from the workers as they are "employing them to make the negativity/entropy of the system work for them, the capitalist" (p. 33). Labour power as a commodity is the point that marks constitutive negativity of the system. The subjects entering this non-relation (those selling their labour) need to be free agents selling their "property, [their] commodity" (p. 33). This brings us back to the proletariat as being the truth of capitalism, or what Tomšič (2015a) called a symptom of capitalism. The proletariat is not a social class but a constitutive negativity in capitalism. What can the proletariat do as a point of negativity (rather than social class)? It can name what Zupančič called "the symptomatic point of this system, its disavowed and exploited subjectivity" (p. 34).

In the third iteration of the subject position within Capitalist discourse of surplus and *jouissance* Lacan introduces the idea of a "student as a helot". "And the first to collaborate with this [...] are you, for you, fulfil the role of helots of this regime. [...] The regime is putting you on display. It says: 'Look at them enjoying!'" (*SXVII*, 3.12.69, p. 208). The student—through acts of resistance—performs the function of the regime against which it rebels. The student is in a position of the regime's *jouissance*, in a position of perversion, as Tomšič (2015a, p. 227) notes. He further explores the role of perversion in the position occupied by the students. In acts in which students exhibit *jouissance* they offer themselves to the regime's gaze. As the subjects of capitalism, their performance creates a continuity between *jouissance* and labour, putting them in a position of the surplus-object. As Tomšič (2015a, p. 228) shows, "the students demand for jouissance without castration is the productive ground for the jouissance of the system. Life without boredom and enjoyment without restriction inaugurates a new, more radical and invisible form of exploitation". He further continues to show how masochism (which Lacan invokes in his first mention of capitalism in *KS*) is key to the capitalist foreclosure of castration and how masochism is not only a perversion but also a perversion that is defined by the absence of shame. The subject who can enjoy its position as an object is the true master.

> Sadism reveals the truth of jouissance [...] whereas masochism avoids the moment of this discontent by taking the pleasure as an immediate source of pleasure, thereby establishing the alliance between sexuality and the rejection of castration through the commodity form.
>
> (Tomšič, 2015a, p. 229)

Starting with the students' display of *jouissance* to the regime's gaze, Tomšič (p. 229) concludes that the perfect subject of capitalism is a masochist. As they can enjoy being a commodity among other commodities, "while assuming the role of surplus labour, the position of the object that willingly satisfies the system's demand". The capitalist imperative to "Enjoy!" is thus not an imperative to enjoy in fulfilling your pleasures but an imperative to suffer and to enjoy it.

## A hysteric capitalist?

Not entirely independently from the University discourse, another interpretation of capitalism emerges in the context of the Discourse of the Hysteric. The interpretation either appears as a figure of (unsuccessful self-revolutionizing) resistance to the capitalist system, or as a hystericized mastery. The student helot who performs resistance—its individualised *jouissance*—for the gaze of the Master might be a perfect capitalist figure of "hysterical" op/positions. Its resistance is subsumed into reinstating the regime it is opposing. Žižek explains this position well when he states that: "the explosion of the hysterical capitalist subjectivity that reproduces itself through permanent self-revolutionizing, through the integration of the excess into the 'normal' functioning of the social link (the true 'permanent revolution' is already capitalism itself)" (Žižek, 2016b, p. 495). The hysteric opposition is subsumed by the ability of capitalism to change, adapt, and re-create itself.

However, it is impossible to see capitalism in the Hysteric's discourse, without acknowledging the products of capitalism in the University's discourse. Is the hysteric a proletariat who provokes its Master/the capitalist or is the reverse the case? Is the capitalist a hysteric who is "caught in the internal self-propelling cycle of extended reproduction provoking its own true Master, the Capital itself" (Žižek, 2016b, p. 490)? Žižek sees the dependency and the tension between the University and the Hysteric running across both poles of the class antagonism, splitting each into two. Equally, he sees that the capitalist is split into two and only functions if it oscillates between the University and the Hysteric. For Žižek (2016b, p. 490) this is a "parallax"—the opposition between a hysteric desire and a perverse drive of capitalism. The overlapping element of the desire/drive is the subject who is a product of the University discourse and an agent of the Hysteric discourse, and simultaneously knowledge ($S_2$), which is a product of the Hysteric discourse and an agent in the University discourse.

Hysteric logic is a logic of subject-expansion, whereas the logic of the University is the logic of knowledge domination. Žižek proposes that the University and Hysteric are two incarnations of Capitalist discourse only due to the failure in the Master discourse: the Master as hystericized and devoid of its authority. It can no longer appear as dominating, exploitative, and yet it requires means which the subjects continue to produce for its benefit. The authority appears as desubjectivized, hidden in allegedly neutral expert-driven bureaucracy.

The University–Hysteric nexus does not produce an emancipated subject. What it does well is to explain the interplay between the subject—*jouissance*—and mastery (be it in the form of knowledge or hystericized authority). This is also what Zupančič and Tomšič outlined when speaking about the non-relation and a disallowed exploited subjectivity.

Is there a way out of capitalism and Capitalist discourse? While Žižek provides us with a political reading of the Discourse of the Analyst, Lacan arguably never suggested that. Is working through the symptom a "way out" of capitalist modes of production? The introduction of capitalism ultimately radicalized psychoanalysis; it aligns it with a critique of social reality that expands it into (either/both) radical politics and a distinct theory of crisis.

## Note

1 Slightly modified translation.

## Further reading

Pavón-Cuéllar, D. (2009). *Marxisme lacanien*. Paris: Psychophores.
Tomšič, S. (2015). *The Capitalist Unconscious: Marx and Lacan*. London: Verso.
Žižek, S. (1989) *The Sublime Object of Ideology*. London: Verso.

## References

Bianchi, P. (2010). The Discourse and the Capitalist. Lacan, Marx and the Questions of the Surplus. In: *Folozofski vestnik*, XXXI(2): 123–137.
Mura, A. (2015). Lacan and Debt: The Discourse of the Capitalist in Times of Austerity. In: *Philos. Today*, 59: 154–177.
Pavón-Cuéllar, D. (2009). *Marxisme lacanien*. Paris: Psychophores.
Tomšič, S. (2012). Homology: Marx and Lacan. In: *S: Journal of the Jan van Eyck Circle for Lacanian Ideology Critique*, 5: 98–113.
Tomšič, S. (2015a). *The Capitalist Unconscious: Marx and Lacan*. London: Verso.
Tomšič, S. (2015b). Psychoanalysis, Capitalism and the Critique of Political Economy: Towards a Marxist Lacan. In: S. Tomšič & A. Zevnik (Eds.), *Jacques Lacan between Politics and Psychoanalysis* (pp. 146–163). London: Routledge.
Žižek, S. (2016a). Object *a* in Social Links. In: J. Clemens & R. Grigg (Eds.), *Jacques Lacan and the Other Side of Psychoanalysis* (pp. 101–128). Durham: Duke University Press.
Žižek, S. (2016b). Can One Exit from The Capitalist Discourse Without Becoming a Saint? In: *Crisis and Critique*, 3(3): 481–99.
Zupančič, A. (2006). Surplus Enjoyment as Surplus Jouissance. In: J. Clemens & R. Grigg (Eds.), *Jacques Lacan and the Other Side of Psychoanalysis* (pp. 155–178). Durham: Duke University Press.
Zupančič, A. (2017) *What Is Sex?* Cambridge: MIT Press.

# Chapter 5

# Communism

Ian Parker

—Ara.: شيوعية —Chi.: 共產主義 —Fre.: *Communisme* —Ger.: *Kommunismus* —Ita.: *Comunismo* —Jap.: コミュニズム —Port.: *Comunismo* —Rus.: *Коммунизм* —Spa.: *Comunismo* —Tur.: *Komünizm*

→ *Freedom/liberty*; *Labour*; *Proletarian*; *Revolution*

The term "communism" in both Marx's and Lacan's work has at least three meanings. It refers to a future society beyond capitalism and to the political movement organized around the mobilization of the working class that opposes capitalist society now. This double usage is complicated by a third meaning, attached, by advocates and detractors, to the identity of those who wish for a future communist society and/or those who build the communist movement: these are the "communists".

In both authors, "nature" and "culture" are intertwined in such a way that cannot be resolved through facile dialectical sublation. Conceptualization of the possible and impossible relationship between the two terms is made more opaque by the different valences in German, French, and English. This difficulty has been noted by numerous authors attempting to translate Marxist and Lacanian analysis from one "culture" to another and to thereby determine what "nature" means in different specific circumstances.

In both Marx and Lacan, of course, there are additional contextual and temporal factors. The meanings of "communism" and "communist" are structured by contemporary nineteenth and twentieth century debates concerning politics and the direction of the treatment, and the meanings mutate during the course of each author's work.

## Marx on communism

There is a trajectory in Marx's work, from a phenomenologically oriented and humanist-inflected notion of communism in which the abolition of private property is intimately linked to the end of alienation and to the self-conscious appropriation of nature, to a structural-historical critique of political economy which

DOI: 10.4324/9781003212096-5

is more cautious about specifying blueprints for a future post-capitalist society (Balibar, 1994). Emphasis thereby shifts from what is possible to what is made almost impossible, what must be overcome. There is, in his early work, an overriding concern with the real movement forward of history from "primitive communism" in pre-class society to a form of communism that assimilates the experience and wealth of previous development. There is then, in the later work, detailed analysis of the forms of production and a corresponding reification of nature that blocks that movement forward, blocks the realization of communism, an analytic account that also puts the notion of universal "needs" in question (Mandel, 1967).

The publication history of Marx's texts, including the "discovery" after his death of some earlier more humanist works, have exacerbated the always-already retroactive character of Marxism. What "communism" was and what it could be, as well as who is qualified to argue for it, are profoundly governed by this history, a scholarly and activist history in readings of Marx as "ecosocialist", for instance, which call for revision of the caricature, and usually anti-communist, accounts of the movement as being necessarily "Promethean". In those accounts, "communism", in the form of a future society or in the actual practices of societies governed by "communist parties", is accused of valuing industrial development and scientific progress over attempts to live in and with and against alienated nature (Kovel, 2002).

There is thus an oscillation, among opponents and supporters of "communism", between holistic ideals, of what communism promises when it heals the rift between culture and nature that is opened up by class society and intensified by capitalist exploitation, and technical solutions that could only hope to engineer a pragmatic compromise and maintain the gains already achieved. The notion that there will be a historic return, on a higher level of social development, to once-existing "primitive" communism thus repeats an eschatological motif in many radical political reform movements. This universalized ideal of communism is actually questioned by Marx, and increasingly so in his notes on natural science; here the analysis of different economic forms of the "metabolic" relation between culture and nature opens to a "communist" conception of how that may be managed in a non-exploitative way (Saito, 2017).

Whether or not this shift of emphasis in Marx's work represents an "epistemological break"—even, perhaps, effectively a turn from phenomenology to structuralism—there are consequences for the notion of communism as a type of society and communism as the movement towards that society. These consequences are materialized in the figure of the "communist" and the political movement that figure adheres to, supports, speaks for, and drives forward. Marx, throughout his work, from first to last, stressed that "interpretation" of the world was only of significance if it thereby entailed changing that world (*TOF*). Marxist analysis, as such, was designed to transform what it was applied to, only functioning as analysis insofar as it brought about and reflected upon change.

The historically mediated consequences of Marx's own shift of emphasis are thus embedded in and reflect changes in the conduct of the communist movement itself. These changes are not only subjective, concerning how the "communist" articulates their relationship to communism, but also institutional—how a "communist" activist operates as part of the political apparatuses that advocate communism. In the early days of the movement, in which Marx was an active protagonist, the "communists" should, as an ethical imperative, not operate as a party with "interests separate and apart from the proletariat as a whole" (*MCP*, p. 497). This formulation is the dominant ethos of the activist and strategic *Communist Manifesto* in 1848. That is, communism as a future society is already germinal and must be self-consciously realized to some extent, insofar as that is possible, in the movement as such (Rowbotham et al., 2013).

Correlative with the formation of the First International in 1864 and the internal managerial disputes which Marx presided over, adherence to the cause became more structured, manifested in the programme of the organization, and it called upon professions of identity among those involved, as "communist". Communism as real movement of history tended to be disconnected from communism as future society, with a symptom, we might say, of that shift deposited in the identity of the separate individuals still loyal to the organization. Organizations and individuals came to embody "communism", arguing amongst themselves at least as much as with outsiders about what the political process and timescale would be that would allow this communism to be instituted, for the now reified programme to be implemented (*CGP*).

There were two materially effective forms of separation between competing institutionally structured domains of activity after Marx's death, forms of separation through which Marx was read and interpreted which also bear on the meanings of "communism" and "communist". This means that the "Marx" and the notions of "communism" that Lacan encounters and responds to in the twentieth century are very different from the three meanings of communism in the nineteenth. The retroactive effects of discoveries and re-interpretations of key texts are mediated by these two forms of separation.

The first of these forms of separation takes place through the emergence of academic institutions, universities that specialize in the reification and transmission of knowledge that is often set against practical understanding and immediate social change. Specification of what "communism" is or could be is thus reduced to speculative or positivist programmes of research, depending on whether the academic orientation is "philosophical" or "social-scientific". On the one hand, the "communist" is treated as an anomaly, an enthusiast if not a fanatic who is out of place in the academic institution, while on the other hand, the universities do provide a place for communists to carry on some version of their work when they have taken refuge there from the outside, sometimes hostile world.

Academic conceptions of "communism" as a future society, and sometimes of the "communist" accused of abnormal attachment to a clearly formulated idea of what the future might look like, thus repeat and exacerbate the actual political debates that were occurring in the Second International—this after Marx's death. Here a politically instrumental gap opens up between a minimal set of reforms that can be hoped for under capitalism and a more grandiose vision of what will eventually be realized in the far-distant future. The reforms will be implemented by the social-democratic parties, the leaders and members of which sometimes call themselves "Marxist", and they will console themselves with a more elaborate strategic long-game which perpetually defers the foundation of a communist society. In the process, communism as the real movement virtually disappears from the scene, is made redundant (Lenin, 1901).

The second of the forms of separation that come to determine how Marx and the notion of communism will be understood is instituted in the tradition of the Third International under Stalin. Now communism as the real movement of history is systematically subordinated to, effectively replaced with, the "party" as bureaucratic apparatus that then demands obedience from the "communist" who is charged with speaking for the party and for the supposedly post-capitalist society that is actually being constructed in the Soviet Union (Trotsky, 1936).

Marx's own 1875 distinction between a first stage in the transformation of society after the overthrow of capitalism, "socialism", and a longer-term goal in which there could finally be forms of free association that could be called "communist", is then taken as justification for the limited horizons of a regime attempting to build this socialism in one country (Stalin, 1924). This "socialism" in the midst of a hostile capitalist world is thus set against a future communist society which would be "international", the international society that unites the human race.

The two forms of separation intermesh with and reinforce each other, with the effect that communism as movement, communism as future society, and the communist as activist—part of the movement and avatar of the future—are split apart. A series of dividing practices in the academic institutions of the capitalist world, in which the communist as militant is excluded, come to mirror dividing practices in the "communist" world in which there are either apparatchiks or provocateurs, those who are loyal to or those who contest the systematically distorted conceptions of communism being circulated there. Those who contest it and attempt to retrieve a notion of communist practice as "transitional" include revolutionary communist militants of the Fourth International (Trotsky, 1938).

## Lacan on communism

This is the contradictory context in which Lacan speaks of communism, and thereby diagnoses what it has become as a vision of a future state of being, as an institution designed to bring it about, and as a form of identity among adherents of the cause.

The urtext of the Marxist tradition is, of course, written by Marx, sometimes supplemented by an often-contested reading of Engels, while the urtext of the Lacanian tradition is, to a large extent, written or spoken by Lacan, sometimes now supplemented by an often-contested reading of Jacques-Alain Miller, but at a deeper more fundamental level written by the founder of psychoanalysis, to whom Lacan "returns"—Freud. It is Freud, not Lacan, who is closer to being contemporary with Marx and, then, the social-democratic Second and Stalinist Third International. It is between avid readers of those two writers that a long-standing dialogue began that then travelled through the different emerging traditions of so-called "Freudo-Marxism", traditions that Lacan is then responding to when he speaks of "communism" (Pavón Cuéllar, 2017).

When Freud (1930), in *Civilization and its Discontents*, refers to communism, it is to declare that he is agnostic about the economic advantages of it, but to argue that "the psychological premises on which the system is based are an untenable illusion" (p. 113), and an "idealistic misconception of human nature" (p. 143). Freud's lengthiest discussion of it three years later is of communism functioning as a "worldview", during which he, of course, makes it clear that psychoanalysis itself should not be considered as being such. The subordination of scientific or political programmes of research to a worldview would give to it a religious character in which there would be a combination of illusion and conformist group psychology (Freud, 1920). Freud (1933) wants to steer psychoanalysis clear of this temptation of a worldview, and suspects that "communism" is already prey to that (p. 180).

There is, again, in his debate over the causes of war with Einstein, the same year, reference to the impossibility of overcoming underlying "human aggressive impulses", and that they can merely be channelled (Einstein & Freud, 1933, p. 212). Freud's sardonic comments about the probability of communism being characterized by persecution comparable with that of the Jews under Nazism rather than perpetual peace should also be read in the context of the increasing distaste for psychoanalysis as a bourgeois decadent fake science in the late 1920s and Stalinist 1930s Soviet Union (Miller, 1998).

By the time Lacan trained as a psychiatrist and then a psychoanalyst in the 1930s there was an open breach between supporters of the Soviet Union, of this actually existing "socialism in one country", including apologists for the Stalinist show-trials, and those who were accused of being "Trotskyite-fascists" by Moscow and the French Communist Party, the PCF, including participants in the surrealist movement with which Lacan was at one time associated and for which he wrote. The PCF becomes the dominant intellectual force on the left after the Second World War, challenged after the Sino-Soviet split by Maoist-influenced theorists. These currents insist upon "communism" as an ideal and, even more so, as performative fidelity to a cause represented by state institutions in either the Soviet Union or China and relevant loyal party institutions.

If there could be communism, it would neither, as far as Lacan is concerned, entail the end of conflict—that possibility is decisively opposed at Lacan's access point to Hegelian phenomenology—nor the kind of mutual recognition that would dissolve human aggression into transparent intersubjective dialogue (Kojève, 1969). The displacement of the human being from being the centre of the universe, apex of nature or master of consciousness, also means that the most humanist hopes of Marx that the enlightened communist human being "will move around himself as his own true sun" are quite impossible. Those humanist hopes are those in which, for example, his vision of communism is the obverse of religion, but tied to the coordinates of the very worldview it pits itself against: "Religion is only the illusory sun which revolves around man as long as he does not revolve around himself" (*CHP*).

Not only do Copernicus, Darwin, and Freud progressively break open narcissistic illusions of control but also completeness and what Lacan decries as the idea that there is a perfect circular motion at play in which we might discover ourselves. This "geocentrism", Lacan argues, is at play in the popular illusions about a communist future, but it is, he says, "reactionary". Galileo, arguing for a Copernican shift in astronomy, may have been progressive, and lauded by erstwhile communists like Arthur Koestler for that, but Lacan notes that Galileo did not go far enough "when faced with a prejudice as solid as the perfection of circular motion" (*SVIII*, 21.12.60, p. 92).

Such circularity is of a piece with the idea that there is a progressive journey towards enlightenment, an illusion that brings together enthusiasts for science as a worldview and enthusiasts for communism, a happy combination illustrated, Lacan says, by Flaubert. Lacan here acknowledges that scientists and communists have something in common with psychoanalysts who take the materiality of signification seriously, which is precisely why we need to be wary of scientism or "belief in progress", which Lacan characterizes elsewhere as "*progressisme*" (*SXVI*, 12.02.69). For Lacan, "The signifier is matter transcending itself in language. I leave you the choice of attributing that sentence to a Communist Bouvard or a Pecuchet exhilarated by the marvels of D.N.A." (*RSF*, p. 112).

The illusion of circularity is complemented by the illusion of intersubjectivity, transparent dialogue which not only characterizes what some hope for under communism, but also invites colleagues to imagine they might have fruitful dialogues with communists but are then disappointed. This complaint is the burden of Lacan's disagreement with Merleau-Ponty who wishes to have a "dialogue with communism" and is then surprised that "we don't understand one other" (*SII*, 19.01.55, p. 77). This observation comes at a point in Lacan's work when he is beginning to distance himself from the ideal of "intersubjectivity" in analysis. The phenomenological Merleau-Ponty thinks we must understand communism, Lacan says, and is attached to this idea because he believes that "*the foundation of language is that it is universal*". It will depend very much, though, Lacan continues, on what this universality rests, whether on communication or ruptures in recognition and "the death instinct" (*SII*, 19.01.77, p. 83).

Marx had, in *Capital*, summed up the ideological infrastructure of capitalist society and the forms of political economy he set himself against as "Freedom, Equality, Property and Bentham" (*CAI*, p. 280). Marx's reference here is to the utilitarian Jeremy Bentham, a philosopher emblematic of what Lacan refers to a number of times in *Seminar VII* as "the service of goods" (*SVII*, 06.07.60, p. 318). This moral framework, in which costs and benefits of courses of action and the correlative fair distribution of commodities is supposed to lead to human happiness, is counterposed to a properly psychoanalytic ethical stance.

For Lacan in that Seminar, however, "the service of goods'" is also, perhaps even more so, to be found in the domain of an apparently "post-revolutionary perspective", a "communist future" which, far from transcending the kind of society Marx was describing, actually only succeeds in "perpetuating the eternal tradition of power." Worse, while that "communist future" is only present in a "part of the world" that "has resolutely turned in the direction of the service of goods," it differs from Creon—the city ruler Antigone defies—only in aiming to "embrace the whole universe" (*SVII*, 06.07.60, p. 318). Here again we would be caught in the trap of a worldview, a political-economic programme and form of society masquerading as a worldview.

Lacan's comments on the nature of communism as an institution, of the party form and obedience to it, take up Freud's arguments about group psychology, illusion, and worldview (Freud, 1920). The failure of "Communist society" to displace "fundamental relationships", particularly that "the necessity of marriage was not even touched by the effects of the revolution", testifies, according to Lacan, to the power of the kind of deeper human proclivities that Freud had already adverted to (*SIX*, 14.03.62). However, this argument is now being made by Lacan in a context where the Soviet Union is a dominant ideological force and the PCF is functioning as if it were a kind of church. There are thus explicit references to the Christian ethos of communist organizations.

With respect to the state, Lacan argues that the only interest of the "communist revolution" in Russia "is to have restored the function of power", though it is "not easy to hold onto" in conditions where "capitalism reigns" (*SXVI*, 19.03.69). Turning to the party apparatus of the PCF, a more immediate competing institution set against that of his own psychoanalytic school, Lacan refers to the "communist church" and its "ecclesiastical authors" who are "excellent workers" who are devoted to "service as such", a form of service which then "necessarily leads to lies" (*SXVI*, 12.02.69). Apparatchiks of this church then include "the communist priest" from whom we receive "moral propositions" (*SXVI*, 20.11.68). This institution, "communism", pretends to be an alternative to the Gaullism it pits itself against after the Second World War, but this is merely a "game" between the two forces, avatars of "civilization", and here Lacan refers to crusades against Byzantium and other contemporary "crusades" that perpetuate such games (*SXVI*, 26.03.68).

There is then a significant shift away from these critical comments about the Christian moral frame governing the activity of the communists after Lacan comes into conflict with the International Psychoanalytical Association, with allusions in his seminar to currents in Judaism as a problem. In *Seminar X*, a year before what Lacan will frame, in a deliberate reference to Spinoza's exclusion from his own Jewish community, "excommunication" from the IPA (*SXI*), the moral "pharisaism" of communists is condemned. This self-righteousness of "communist pharisaism" is emblematic not just of a particular kind of political stance— that "sum of habits, good or bad, wherein a certain established order finds its comfort and security" (*SX*, 28.11.62, p. 31).

Lacan draws a very clear connection here between the worst of a moralizing "psychiatric milieu" and "communist pharisaism". Lacan will rail against the IPA, but in Seminar X he also describes the difficulty in making his speech heard to "the utterly particular reservations of the communists"; this "non-reception", he claims, is why he has been devoting himself to making himself heard within "the analytic milieu" (*SX*, 28.11.62, p. 31). In 1970, in *Radiophonie*, Lacan complains not only that he has had to face "non-reception" by communists, but accounts for that by claiming that they set themselves against the "bourgeois order" as "against-society", so "counterfeiting" everything that this order makes "honourable": "work, family and country" (*RA*).[1]

When Lacan turns to the figure of the communist, the jaundiced picture he paints of communism as such, as an illusory utopian ideal of direct unmediated communication, and of the state and party institutions that betray that ideal as they demand "service" from their adherents, is layered with another series of pathologizing motifs. The Communist Party functions ostensibly as mere example, but a symbolically potent example nonetheless, of an institution that someone might join "just to piss off her father". The conceptual question that is being addressed here, the relation between the ideal ego and the ego ideal, recurs later in the same *Seminar VIII*, when a youngster might contemplate annoying father by "brandishing her Communist Party card" (*SVIII*, 31.05.61, pp. 340–341).

## Conclusions

The connection and disjunction between Marx and Lacan at the point of the signifier "communism" turns around their shared and opposing conceptions of the relationship between culture and nature. This complex contradictory relationship is configured in Marx first, in line with dominant "communist" and anti-communist representations of his work, by the promised future utopian healing of the rift between the two that is now characteristic of class society and then, in a deeper reading of his articulation of nineteenth century debates in the social and natural sciences, by way of his utilization of the notion of "metabolism". The relationship between culture and nature is reconfigured in Lacan through a classically Freudian specification of the drive as operating on the border of the physiological and the psychical, a reading refracted through his three-register reading of what "civilization" and its "discontents" amounts to. The relationship reappears in quasi-anthropological conceptions, from Hegelian phenomenology via Kojève and then structuralism—borrowed from Lévi-Strauss—of the way that nature is transformed into culture (Lévi-Strauss, 1958).

The question is whether the continuing and necessary "metabolic" relationship between human beings and nature opens up the horizon for a vision of communism that does not pretend to resolve all contradiction between the two while ending every antagonistic relationship between human beings. At stake here is the way "nature" operates in relation to culture, to different forms of culture (Elias, 1994). The semiotic slippage between the three connotations of "communism" and "communist" is partly what is at stake in dialogue between Marxists and Lacanians. For Marxists this slippage usually enables a necessary dialectical movement between the present and the future, encouraging activity, change. Lacanians, in contrast, often facilitate characterization of what is presented as a rival "worldview", encouraging pathologization, fixity, which is set against possibilities of change and a form of universality that transcends nineteenth-century conceptions, conceptions that both Freud and Marx were confined within and tried to escape.[2]

## Notes

1 Translated by Jack W. Stone.
2 Jacques-Alain Miller claims, in his Marginalia on *Seminar VI*, that the dictum that "There cannot be satisfaction of one person without the satisfaction of all" is "Lacan's version of communism, as inspired by Kojève" in *Seminar VI* (p. 511).

## Further reading

Mandel, E. (1971). *The Formation of the Economic Thought of Karl Marx*. London: New Left Books.
Saito, K. (2017). *Karl Marx's Ecosocialism: Capital, Nature, and the Unfinished Critique of Political Economy*. New York: Monthly Review Press.
Tazi, N. (Ed.). (2005). *Keywords: Nature: For a Different Kind of Globalization*. New York: Other Press.

## References

Balibar, É. (1994). *The Philosophy of Marx*. London: Verso, 2017.
Elias, N. (1939). *The Civilizing Process*. Oxford: Blackwell, 1994.
Einstein, A. & Freud, S. (1933). Why War? In: *The Standard Edition of the Complete Psychological Works of Sigmund Freud* (Vol. XXII, pp. 195–217), J. E. Strachey (Trans.). London: Vintage, 2001.
Freud, S. (1920). Group Psychology and the Analysis of the Ego. In: *The Standard Edition of the Complete Psychological Works of Sigmund Freud* (Vol. XVIII, pp. 65–143), J. E. Strachey (Trans.). London: Vintage, 2001.
Freud, S. (1930). Civilization and Its Discontents. In: *The Standard Edition of the Complete Psychological Works of Sigmund Freud* (Vol. XXI, pp. 57–145), J. E. Strachey (Trans.). London: Vintage, 2001.
Freud, S. (1933). New Introductory Lectures on Psycho-Analysis. In: *The Standard Edition of the Complete Psychological Works of Sigmund Freud* (Vol. XXII, pp. 1–181), J. E. Strachey (Trans.). London: Vintage, 2001.
Kojève, A. (1947). *Introduction to the Reading of Hegel: Lectures on the Phenomenology of Spirit*, J. Nicholson (Trans.). New York: Basic Books, 1969.
Kovel, J. (2002). *The Enemy of Nature: The End of Capitalism or the End of the World?* London: Zed Books, 2007.
Lenin, V. (1901). *What Is to Be Done?* New York: International Publishers, 1969.

Lévi-Strauss, C. (1958). *Structural Anthropology*. M. Layton (Trans.). Harmondsworth: Penguin.

Mandel, E. (1967). *The Formation of the Economic Thought of Karl Marx*. London: New Left Books, 1971.

Miller, M. (1998). *Freud and the bolsheviks: psychoanalysis in imperial Russia and the Soviet Union*. New Haven: Yale University Press.

Pavón Cuéllar, D. (2017). *Marxism and Psychoanalysis: In or Against Psychology?* London: Routledge.

Rowbotham, S., Segal, L. and Wainwright, H. (1979). *Beyond the Fragments: Feminism and the Making of Socialism*. Pontypool, Wales: Merlin, 2013.

Saito, K. (2017). *Karl Marx's Ecosocialism: Capital, Nature, and the Unfinished Critique of Political Economy*. New York: Monthly Review Press.

Stalin, J. (1924). *Foundations of Leninism*. Beijing: Foreign Languages Press, 1965.

Trotsky, L. (1936). *The Revolution Betrayed: What Is the Soviet Union and Where Is It Going?* M. Eastman (Trans.). New York: Doubleday, Doran, and Company, 1937.

Trotsky, L. (1938). *The Death Agony of Capitalism and the Tasks of the Fourth International*. Sidney: Resistance Books, 1999.

# Chapter 6

# Consumption

*Agustina Saubidet*

—Ara.: استهلاك —Chi.: 消費—Fre.: *Consommation*—Ger.: *Verbrauch/Konsum* —Ita.: *Consumo* —Jap.: 消費 —Port.: *Consumo* —Rus.: *Потребление* —Spa.: *Consumo* —Tur.: *Tüketim*

→ *Automatism*; *Labour/work*; *Market*; *Slavery*

## Marx in Lacan

The preconception that Marxism and psychoanalysis do not get along—already current in Freud's day—apparently grew stronger in the 1990s. This tension, present in Lacan's times too—particularly since May '68—crystallized due to Deleuze, along with Derrida and Foucault, and fostered a gap between the fields of psychoanalysis and social studies. Nevertheless, when reading Lacan's work, it is easy to find the opposite.[1]

There are two early examples. In a clear reference to the section "The Fetishism of Commodities and the Secret Thereof" in *Capital*, Lacan examines the commodities' fetishist value, attained less from its *use-value* (linked to a human need) and more from its *exchange-value* (an object considered as a commodity). The fetish value remains hidden in capitalism behind the money value: this is what Lacan will define as "fetish-object" or "screen-object" (*SIV*, 21.11.56, p. 24). The following year, Lacan regards *Das Kapital* as "a prodigious first book, superabundant" (*SV*, 27.11.57, p. 72), and he "urges" us to revise the first section on the particular subjects of the commodities value, the quantitative value relationships, and *the universal equivalent*. Marx's name is in every single one of Lacan's Seminars, except for *Seminars VIII, XII*, and *XIII*, and he goes so far as to say that Marx is a structuralist (*SXVI*, 13.11.68). Rather than being a scholarly or an isolated reference—or a minor writer—Marx happens to be for Lacan not only a philosopher and a poet (*SXXV*, 20.12.77), but also a cornerstone thinker for psychoanalysis, almost to the extent of Saussure, Lévi-Strauss, Aristotle, Hegel, and Spinoza. The most well-known moment of this connection happened between 1968 and 1971, when he brought forward the concept of "surplus-*jouissance*" based on a comparison between psychoanalysis and Marxism. His four discourses are a conclusion of this. Marx is still a reference for him even after the *Letter of Dissolution* (*MA*,

18.01.80). In his final versions, Lacan regards Marx as the creator of the symptom (*SXXII*, 18.02.75; *CNA*; *LD*, 18.01.80). Lacan's insistence on Marx is at times tinged by Levi-Strauss's ink, and sometimes refracted by Althusser's magnifying glass.

There are two issues that should be highlighted. First, when revisiting Marx's works, it is important to note that Lacan deals mostly with his first, most philosophical writings: *On the Jewish Question* (*OJQ*); *Economic and Philosophic Manuscripts* (*EPM*); *The Poverty of Philosophy* (*PP*); *A Contribution to the Critique of Political Economy* (*CPE*). The second issue is not only that Lacan links psychoanalysis to Marx, but also, at least in two seminars (*SVI*, 17.12.58, p. 123; *SXIV*, 12.04.67), he does so by using *The Elementary Structures of Kinship* (Lévi-Strauss, 1949), a book that will be paramount throughout his work. The liaison provided by Lévi-Strauss's *The Elementary Structures* enabled Lacan to connect value theory and the concept of Marxist *surplus* to the field of psychoanalysis (Saubidet, 2018).

## From the exchange of goods to women as objects of consumption

From Lacan's perspective, the common ground of psychoanalysis, economics, and anthropology are women's bodies considered as commodities, objects of exchange and usufruct between men; bodies with exchange value, enjoyment value (*SXIV*, 12.04.67). Men could also be considered exchange commodities between different groups of women, yet that would not change the form of exchange (Lévi-Strauss, 1956). "Man" and "Woman" are effects of discourse. Therefore, it is not a question of biology, it is a question of how bodies have been semanticized and signified according to different periods, culture, social status, and division of labour.

This matter had already been addressed by Lacan in *Seminar IV* when discussing Dora's case regarding the exchange of goods and gifts. Similarly, in 1971 there is another key phrase: "You shall not covet the wife of your neighbor nor his ox, nor his ass, and anyway there is an enumeration which is precisely that of the means of production" (*SXVIII*, 19.05.71).

This triple liaison between Lacan, Marx, and Lévi-Strauss has gone unnoticed, and has been subsequently overshadowed, which has led to the clinical misunderstanding between *jouissance* and surplus-*jouissance* [*plus-de-jouir*], as well as to the omission of a father's version linked to "female daughters": the father as a donor (*donateur*) (*SIV*, 23.01.57), as a proxy of the mother's father or likewise of the group that has granted a gift (Lévi-Strauss, 1949), prior to the symbolic father in *Seminar V*. This father fulfils a pre-Oedipal role, essential to the structure; that is to say, the father occupies the place of the fourth element that is in a position to donate, to grant, and to circulate his goods—including his daughters. This leaves on the subject not only a symbolic trace standing for the origin of mutual circuits of exchange—a clearly anti-capitalist function of the father—but also provides particular ways of regulating pleasure, as Lacan puts it: "'Usufruct' means that you can enjoy (*jouir de*) your means, but not waste them" (*SXX*, 21.11.72, p. 3).

So far, we have considered how, in the forms of exchange, women circulate among men as commodities, as Mauss (1950),[2] Lévi Strauss (1949, 1950), and Lacan (*SVI*) himself point out. Therefore, we wonder: are women in the capitalist mode of production viewed as objects of consumption, accumulation, and usufruct? This is the central issue of the term "consumption" concerning this entry.

## What is consumption for Marx?

Unlike classical economists—who consider production, distribution, exchange, and consumption as separate and independent terms—for Marx these four instances are different stages of the same unit, that is to say, they are a whole. Consumption is then the last step, in which "the product drops out of the social movement, becoming the direct object of the individual want, which it serves and satisfies in use" (*CPE*, p. 275). Consequently, production turns immediately into consumption and vice versa. The way the object is consumed is a direct consequence of how it was produced, distributed, and exchanged. "A mutual interaction takes place between the various elements. Such is the case with any organic body" (*CPE*, p. 292). If there is no consumption, there is no production; if there is no production there is no consumption because it an object would be lacking. Only in its consumption does the product really transform into a product. According to this account, consumption is the source of the need for a new production, subsequently becoming the internal cause of production, its prerequisite: "No wants, no production. But consumption reproduces the want", Marx states (*CPE*, p. 279).

Hence, production creates consumption by providing its substance, its object; but this is not an object of chance, it is a specific object that should be consumed in a specific way. Hence, as production creates the object, it also creates the consumer and the ways to consume it. Likewise, this very production creates the need for this object. Thus, production not only produces an object for a subject, but also a subject for an object. Accordingly, production and consumption, in their creation, create each other.

In line with Marx's logic, every capitalist society has forms of consumption according to their forms of production in order to attain a particular form of profit, the *surplus*, based on the exploitation of the body of the other, the surplus of production accumulating in the hands of those that do not produce it, but who nevertheless have rights over it for the sole cause of being the owners of the means of production. *Surplus* therefore is free labour and its accumulation turns into *capital*, something impossible without the idea of private property. The problem is not so much profit as such but the excessive lucre on the other's body. In other words, exchange is not accumulative, but colonization is.

Although money is the principal mode of production of *surplus*, Lacan (*IEM*) warns us that it is not the only way to produce it. Hence, a subject—as an effect of discourse—submerged in a capitalist society, carries that form of relation based on exploitation obtaining *extra profit* by the usufruct of the other's body. This usufruct can also be based on their time, space, knowledge, and know-how, and not necessarily on money. Moreover, a subject can exert the very same exploitation on their own body.

In this regard, the issue of women as objects of usufruct is addressed by Silvia Federici (2004, 2018) in her latest research. She not only explores the role of proletarian and bourgeois women supporting the capitalist system by their labour and reproductive capacities but also redeems from oblivion what happened to certain women, deemed to be "witches" (doctors, midwives, sorcerers). In the transition from the Middle Ages to capitalism, these women, prior to their extermination, had their knowledge stolen (Federici, 2004); this colonization and accumulation of wealth allowed the bourgeoisie to create the discourse of modern patriarchal, colonialist, and capitalist science, with the ability to overthrow God, thereby attaining political power. The latter must not be ignored, since Lacan himself enunciates that psychoanalysis operates on the subject of modern science (*ST*, p. 729), i.e., when capitalism has crystallized and spread as a mode of production generating a type of subject inherent to it.

## Consumption by alternative non-capitalist forms

Likewise, in the realm of capitalist societies, other modes of production that are universal coexist and relate to each other. Namely, the *potlatch*, a concept that Lacan borrows from Marcel Mauss in several passages of his work (*SIV*, 23.01.57; *SVII*, 18.05.60; *SXIX*, 09.02.72, 19.04.72). "These forms of exchange have a practice conceived to have a salutary function in the maintenance of intersubjective relations" provided that "miraculously" (*SVII*, 18.05.60, pp. 234–235) some things escape the typical logic of disposal, use, and distribution of commodities in the capitalist modes—based on accumulation and deprivation.

Unlike these capitalist modes, the *potlatch*'s ethic resides in granting gifts to make friends (Amigo, 2015); that is to say, exchange and contractual forms by means of mutual gifts (Mauss, 1950) which do not use accumulation to generate capital. Instead, they circulate mutual benefits and compensations from *giving* to *receiving* and *giving back*, since those who collect a gift are bound to return it. This has a clinical and political direct consequence: it is important to take into account how these verbs function in every subject inhabiting the capitalist mode.

Far from "primitive", the forms of exchange such as *potlatch* are universal, complex, and essential to the survival of a group, and capitalism is entrenched in these forms and others. Their specific feature is that they involve the entire culture's symbolic life; consequently, they are considered a *total social fact* (Mauss, 1950, Lévi-Strauss, 1950, Alberti & Méndez, 1993).

The *potlatch* has many faces. It can be close to the idea of *gift* and is simultaneously connected with the idea of destruction and wealth consumption through a ceremony, a public ritual in which goods are destroyed, consumed, and squandered

(*SVII*, 18.05.60, p. 235). By the logic of the *potlatch*, the more you lose, destroy, and consume, the more you have. You can only have as much as you can lose. That is how value becomes evident: in the giving without limit. The gift is an act of love but, likewise, the more you grant, destroy, and consume the more power you get, express, use, and exert: the power of giving and receiving. Consequently, rank in society, a place in the hierarchy, is earned. In conclusion, the apparently irrational acts of losing, donating, destroying, squandering, and consuming in excess actually provide a social hierarchy for the subject (Bataille, 1949).

To put it succinctly: destruction in the *potlatch* determines a position of power and hierarchy, a greater social value and prestige; and the act of yielding or granting women is one of the most important ones (Mauss, 1950; Lévi-Strauss, 1949, 1950). In these systems, single men are regarded as greedy outsiders, since anyone accumulating goods for himself and being unwilling to grant or exchange them with the community is severing his ties with it. Conversely, capitalism considers gifts and wealth consumption as loss.

## Between Marx and Lévi-Strauss: political economy in the Dora case

Going back to Lacan on Marx and Lévi-Strauss, we begin with the following situation: Dora is trapped as an object of exchange between two men, Mr. K. and Dora's father. "Dora is thus offered up defenseless to Herr K's attentions, to which her father turns a blind eye, thus making her the object of an odious exchange" (*PT*, p. 178), being placed as the fourth element making possible the relation between the other three terms. This quadripartite (quaternary) structure[3] can only function if Dora is completely objectified.

The second situation appears in *Seminar IV*, when Lacan states (*SIV*, 23.01.57):

> Dora rebels absolutely and starts to say, *my father is selling me to someone else*. In effect, this is a clear and excellent assessment of the situation, to the extent that it has been kept in this half-darkness. As a matter of fact, from the father's standpoint, allowing Frau K.'s husband to carry on his courting of Dora over these long years in a sort of veiled tolerance has been a way of repaying his indulgence. […] Dora finds herself having slid into the role of a mere object.

The father sells Dora to Mr. K. in exchange for Mrs. K. who, according to Mr. K., is worthless. The problem of this scene lies not only in the complexity of Dora's place—due to the absence of the mother as an object of desire for the father's gaze—but something underlying, an interpretation of political economy that has not been highlighted enough. In the fiction of the normative monogamist Oedipus, one thing is Dora's father being a widower or a divorced man and quite another is that the father may "rent" his daughter in exchange for another woman—being already married to one. This reveals the amorous, ideal, and normative Oedipal structure of modern monogamy and shows the most palpable economic materialist aspect of the bourgeois capitalist mode of production in which this quadripartite system is settled, connected to *the elementary structures of kinship*: the side benefit from the objects over which "men" feel like "owners", endorsed by the civil code of the time (*MOS*). Of course, it must be considered that the interpretation of Dora's case is intrinsic to a different time, a time related to the bourgeoisie, the patriarchal and colonialist mode—from the nineteenth century to the beginning of the twentieth century—centred in private property of men over daughters, women and wives. Under these regimes, polygamy "is not allowed".

Let us examine Dora's father. The father keeps the power for himself, as it accumulates and usufructs for himself three goods: Mrs. K. (his married lover), Dora's mother (whom he keeps socially as his wife), and his daughter Dora (whom he rents). From each one he gains something. *But Dora is not one more constituent of the series of her father's women*, she is his daughter and that is why she occupies another genealogic place. Similarly, even if Dora may want to, she could not bond to Mr. K. because he already has a wife: *it is neither an exchange nor a gift*.

Considering the *potlatch* system, this capitalist logic portrays a false donation, a false liaison, because in order to have an alliance there must be the loss of an object, a gift, something to give away. And this is the main point: Dora's father never loses his property and usufruct rights over his daughter and wife, thus there is no exchange; instead, he profits from his daughter's body for himself. Without the idea of *private property*, a form of capitalist appropriation linked to the civil code of the time, this would not have been possible: again it is evident how the Law is part of the *superstructure* of this political economy. Then this an enjoyment of private entities arranged between two men, trying, in the case of Dora's father, to achieve some complicity with Freud in order to make Dora stop standing in the way of his relationship with Mrs. K.

Another element to take into consideration is that Dora, in terms of value, is worthless, and it is Mr. K. who lets her know it. The exchange of an object for another is possible, to begin with, because there is a value ratio between them. The phallus as a *universal equivalent* allows some equivalence between Dora and Mrs. K. If one of the objects is worthless—in this case Mrs. K. is nothing for Mr. K.— the other is too, because nobody exchanges what is not worthy. Consequently, Dora verifies that she is worthless to her father, she is not phallically signified, and that is why she cannot be donated. In her place, she is withheld to provide some *surplus* for her father and Mr. K.

This version of the patriarchal, accumulative, and greedy father does not seem very close to an ideal Oedipus complex, but rather to its most incestuous version, closer to capitalist grammars much more dramatically expressed in the bourgeois classes, where love proves unable to veil the *plus-de-jouir* that the discourse establishes. The father, in his position of bourgeois male—even when he is a proletariat—intends to enjoy without giving anything. The very bourgeois women, in this case Mrs. K. and Dora's mother, are the main accomplices of these masters, because they are also interested in profiting from the benefits granted by these positions (de Beauvoir, 1949).

As Lacan states, the exchange value only functions on the outside, when a commodity is exchanged for another (*SXVI*, 30.04.69). When it is kept inside, in a warehouse, preserved, not being consumed, its use value is prohibited, that is, it cannot be used to satisfy a need from the inside (*SXVI*, 30.04.69). Clearly, the latter does not occur in Dora's case, where the weak are exploited by the strong, "where individual interest is mocked, and where the lies of the rich are changed into truth", where "rank will be reduced to a commodity of exploitation, a shameless source of profits" (Bataille, 1949, pp. 74–75). Women in the realm of these types of societies have become a commodity, from the legal idea of *possession*, by which they lose their value as subjects, transformed into objects for pleasure with exchange value (*SXIV*, 12.04.67). Certainly, Dora's case analysis by Lacan is the best example available to understand this logic.

Undoubtedly, with regard to consumption, Lacan follows Marx. He was able to see how societies of consumption reproduce—just as in its forms of liaison, alliance, and exchange, as well as in its *superstructure*—their production modes based on the exploitation of one body by another for attaining surplus and its consequences in the enjoyment policies of each subject. Likewise, Marx with his clinical regard could see the jealous man as a private owner and the woman as part of the inventory (*MOS*).

Translated from Spanish by Laura Hermanoff

## Notes

1 Of course, it was highly criticized. On this matter I suggest reading Gayle Rubin (1975).
2 "Commodity" is considered as a circulating good, whereas "property" was a term chosen in the translations of Mauss; both stress the idea of property and therefore the Graeco-Latin idea of *"bien"* is lost.
3 This idea of "a four-class system" is present throughout Lacan's work, and was borrowed from the kinship atom in *The Elementary Structures of Kinship* by Lévi-Strauss.

## Further reading

Rubin, G. (1975). The Traffic in Women: Notes on the Political Econony of Sex. In: Rayna Reiter (Ed.), *Towards an Anthropology of Women* (pp. 157–210). New York: Monthly Review Press.
Marx, K. & Engels, F. (1846). The German Ideology. In: Karl Marx & Frederick Engels *Collected Works* (Vol. V, pp. 19–93), W. Lough (Trans.). London: Lawrence & Wishart, 2010.
Saubidet, A. (2019). Cuando la mujer se vuelve parte del inventario. In: *Narraciones*, 1: 63–74.

## References

Amigo, S. (2015). *Los fracasos del fantasma*. Buenos Aires: Letra Viva.
Alberti, B. & Méndez, M. L. (1993). *La familia en la crisis de la Modernidad*. Argentina: Libros de la Cuádriga.
Bataille, G. (1949). *The Accursed Share: An Essay on General Economy*, R. Hurley (Trans.). New York: Zone Books, 1991.
De Beauvoir, S. (1949). *The Second Sex*, C. Borde & S. Malovany-Chevalier (Trans.). New York: Vintage Books, 2011.
Federici, S. (2004). *Caliban and the Witch: Women, the Body, and Primitive Accumulation*. Nueva York: Autonomedia.
Federici, S. (2018). *El patriarcado del salario*, M. Catalán (Trans.). Buenos Aires: Tinta Limón.
Lévi-Strauss, C. (1949). *The Elementary Structures Of Kinship*. J. H. Bell et al. (Trans.). Boston: Beacon Press, 1969.
Lévi-Strauss, C. (1950). *Introduction to the Work of Marcel Mauss*. F. Baker (Trans.). London: Routledge, 1987.
Lévi-Strauss, C. (1956) The Family. In: H. Shapiro (Ed.). *Man, Culture and Society* (pp. 261–285). New York: Oxford University Press.
Mauss, M. (1950). *The Gift: Forms and Functions of Exchange in Archaic Societies*, I. Cuninson (Trans.). London: Cohen & West, 1966.
Saubidet, A. (2018). El Marx que usó Lacan: aportes del marxismo al psicoanálisis lacaniano. In: Universidad de Buenos Aires (Ed.). *Memorias XX. Congreso internacional de investigación y práctica profesional en psicología* (pp. 699–704). Buenos Aires: UBA-Facultad de Psicología.

# Chapter 7

# Economy/Oikonomia

Yahya M. Madra and Ceren Özselçuk

—Ara.: اقتصاد —Chi.: 經濟 —Fre.: *Économie* —Ger.: *Wirstschaft/Oeconomie* —Ita.: *Economia* —Jap.: 経済 —Port.: *Economia* —Rus.: *Экономика* —Spa.: *Economía* —Tur.: *Ekonomi*

→ *Bourgeoisie*; *Capitalism*; *Money*; *Value*

Economy is a polyvalent concept that is central to Lacan's discourse both as the locus of his return to Freud and as his persistent engagement with Marx throughout his *Séminaires* if not in his *Écrits*. The term *économie* in French refers simultaneously to the discipline that studies the economy and that which is the object of such a field. To these two, one must add, following Frédéric Langer's (2014) entry for the *Dictionary of Untranslatables*, three additional connotations in French which also exist in some modified form in English: a virtue of prudence leading to "economizing" behaviour; the outcome of the exercise of that virtue; and, more typically, an organization of parts of a whole, an arrangement of resources, or an internal ordering (*nomos*). In fact, the most frequent usage of the term "economy" in Lacan's *Écrits* and *Séminaires* will fall under this final connotation—such as the "psychic economy", "libidinal economy", "subjective economy" (determined by the unconscious), "constitutive economy of the different neurosis", and so on.

Lacan's enduring interest in *économie* is an ongoing investigation and crossreading of two threads that he finds in his return to Freud. Together they define a sequence of theoretical problematics on the division of both the subject and the structure where, in each iteration, Lacan reworks his analytical discourse in relation to and as a critique of the philosophical discourses that provide foundation to the discussions of economy and the economic. The first thread begins with Freud's "quantum of affect" (the origins of which can be traced back to as early as the *Project* (1895) and which goes through successive "paradigms of jouissance" as the privileged conceptual site on which Lacan revised his own discourse on "libidinal economy" (Miller, 2019)). The second thread begins with Freud's dream work (as formulated in the *Interpretation of Dreams* in 1900) as a general model for analysis of all formations of the unconscious (symptoms, parapraxes, and jokes) through the dual logics of condensation and displacement all the way through to the homology between surplus-value and surplus-*jouissance*. These two threads are always intertwined and attain their most succinct formalization in *Seminar XX*: "the signifier is the cause of jouissance" (19.12.72, p. 24). In this formula, Lacan conjoins the two distinct notions of *économie* that circulate throughout Freud's texts, the affective flows of the "economic approach" and the signifying network of "substitutive representations" (Freud, 1924, p. 150; cf. Kornbluh, 2014, p. 146). Already in Freud's work on dream interpretation, the notions of condensation and displacement, the grammar of unconscious substitutions, were understood to carry "economic overtones" and interpretation was conceptualized to aim at activating the flow of affective quanta across "associative chains" (Laplanche & Pontalis, 1973, p. 128).

In this entry, Lacan's engagement with *économie* will be read as a sustained "critique of political economy" where not only the sovereign subject of theoretical humanism (with the construct of *homo economicus* being its paradigmatic specimen) is dismembered into partial drives, and reduced to the stupid *jouissance* of the body, but also the realist model of value, where price (*qua* signifier) is supposed to represent, under conditions of equilibrium, the underlying fundamentals[1] (*qua* signified), is turned inside out in a rather accurate reading of Marx on the retroactive (*après coup*) constitution of value in *Capital*. The former, the critique of theoretical humanism, was clearly intended by Lacan, but more explicitly highlighted by Jacques-Alain Miller who, in the "Classified Index of the Major Concepts" of *Écrits*, included the entries for "*the ideology of freedom*" and "*the ideology of free enterprise*" (*EC*, p. 857). According to Miller, for Lacan, the "modern ego" could only be "the paranoiac subject of scientific civilization, whose imaginary is theorized by a warped psychology in the service of free enterprise" (p. 852). The latter, the critique of theoretical structuralism, is what enables Lacan to formalize Freudian partial objects, via Marx's notion of surplus-value, into object *petit a* and to push structuralism to its real limits in various paradigms of *jouissance*.

When searching for the traces of *économie* in Lacan's Seminars and *Écrits*, it is necessary to look beyond the word itself, to the metonymic networks of associations structured around a series of encounters and formalizations where he articulates a "critique of political economy" whether he directly refers to the economy or not: his critique of ego psychology and the L-schema; his emplacement of the ethics of psychoanalysis ("*Ne pas céder sur son désir*") against the utilitarian "*service des biens*"; the deconstruction of drives into partial objects (gaze, voice); the critique of the Hegelian notion of alienation through the vel of alienation as a constitutive moment in a subject's access to language (logic of the signifier); the homology between value and signifier and surplus-value and surplus-*jouissance*; the four discourses as the logics of social link and the Capitalist discourse as the fifth, false discourse; formulae of sexuation as the formalization of the sovereign logic of exception (as the modern logic of corporate appropriation) and the one-by-one logic of non-all as an immanent critique of the regime of value (real abstraction); and finally the clinic of the *sinthome* under late capitalism.

## Critique of theoretical humanism

### Critique of ego psychology

In Lacan's early seminars, *économie* appears both as a domain of study of structural anthropology and as a relational structure. Louis Althusser, in his first encounter with Lacan, brought attention to Lacan's critique of ego psychology, where the humanist psychological self, "centered in an 'ego'" (Althusser, 1964, p. 31) is displaced by rallying the notion of elementary structure borrowed from Levi-Strauss's structural anthropology, the quintessential discourse on symbolic exchange, and, in particular, the economy of women as objects of exchange.[2] Already in *Seminar II*, in 1955, Lacan declared that psychoanalysis is not a humanism and noted his surprise that "laboratory scientists should still entertain the mirage that it is the individual, the human subject [...] who is truly autonomous" (12.01.55, p. 68). This sentiment of the Freudian field found its echo in the Marxian field, when in *Freud and Lacan*, Althusser (1964) welcomed the notion of the human subject which is "decentered, constituted by a structure that, too, has a 'center' solely in the imaginary misprision of the 'ego'" (p. 31). For Lacan, ego psychology's reliance on the ego's supposed capacity for observation constrains the analytical experience into the imaginary register where the analysand's ego, normatively, must align with (or better yet mirror) the analyst's ego (*SII*, 25.05.55, p. 241). At this point in Lacan's work, Freud's economic approach figures in through the concept of libido which allows one "to speak of desire in terms which involve a relative objectification [...] a unit of quantitative measurement" which is essentially immeasurable but allows one "to unify the variation in qualitative effects" (*SII*, 18.05.55, p. 221). Desire is sexual and it is, in its intensity, that which manifests itself "at the joint of speech, where it makes its appearance, its sudden emergence, its surge forwards" (p. 234). In other words, desire functions as the libidinal force that propels the chain of signifiers along the metonymic axis. To the extent that desire is that which is left over from the subject's demand for recognition by its others, it is caught between the imaginary and the symbolic, where these two registers are in a relation of juxtaposition. On one side, there is the Imaginary, "the plane of mirror, the symmetrical world of the *egos*". On the other side, there is "the wall of language" that brings an order (*nomos*) and names the imaginary objects (ego and its others) within an organized system, the Symbolic (*SII*, 25.05.55, pp. 244–246). For Lacan, the aim of analysis, at this stage of his discourse, is to enable the subject "to name, to articulate, to bring this desire into existence" (*SII*, 18.05.55, p. 228) by "progressively discovering which Other he is truly addressing, without knowing it" (*SII*, 25.05.55, p. 246). Here, Lacan submits Freud's economic approach into the grid of a sobering and perhaps even liberating understanding of the economy borrowed from structuralist anthropology and linguistics. The economy in the sense of a relational structure functions as a critical grid through which the economic model of pleasure is rehauled.

## Critique of utilitarianism and theory of fictions

Six years later, in *The Ethics of Psychoanalysis*, Lacan will turn the critical edge of the now overhauled, beyond-the-pleasure-principle version of the economic model, articulated through the category of *jouissance* [defined in this Seminar as "not purely and simply as the satisfaction of a need but as the satisfaction of a drive" (*SVII*, 04.05.60, p. 209)], back to a utilitarian notion of economy *qua* service of goods (*service de bien*), where "the greatest utility for the greatest number" (*SVII*, 11.05.60, p. 229) is the good that is strived for. Jeremy Bentham stands at the crossroads of Lacan and Marx, so close to the immoderate dimension of satisfaction and yet so far from it. On the one hand, Bentham, in his *Theory of Fictions*, approaching "the question at the level of the signifier", opens the concept of use (utility, use-value) to social division and distribution, severing its ties from the sphere of "predetermined needs" (*SVII*, 11.05.60, p. 228). Yet, on the other hand, there is something excessive in Bentham's and in the utilitarian calculus of pain and pleasure that incessantly, obsessively, strives to squeeze life out of this division of use into signifier and signified by way of controlling it, by filling it up, by bringing it back under a panoptic episteme that reconciles the (knowing) subject with the (known) object under the sovereignty of reason and discipline of the senses (Miller, 1987). For Marx [and Engels] of *The German Ideology*, Bentham's theory of utility "reflected the desire to reduce all relations to the relations of exploitation" and its articulation marked the assertion of the conditions of existence of bourgeoisie as those of the whole society (*GI*, pp. 412–415). In *Capital*, Marx summarized this insight with the formula of the fetishism of commodities: "Freedom, Equality, Property and Bentham" (*CAI*, p. 280). In *Seminar VI*, a year before his *Ethics* seminar, Lacan was already working with the idea of a homology between the theory of utility as a fetishism of the commodities and the signifying logic.[3] He noted,

> the very first step of Marx's analysis of the fetishistic nature of commodities consists precisely in broaching the problem from the level of the signifier [...] The relations between values are defined as signifying relations, and all subjectivity, and possibly even that of fetishization, comes to be inscribed within this signifying dialectic.
>
> (*SVI*, 15.04.59, p. 313)

However, Lacan's discourse criticizes this fetishistic service of commodities not because it is a drive for the generalization of utilitarian calculus but rather because it is bound to fail on account of *"jouissance* use". "To exercise control over one's goods", as it means "to have the right to deprive others of them", "entails a certain disorder". It is important to "recognize that the depriving agent is an imaginary function" and that disorder stems not from the depriving other but rather from depriving oneself from enjoying on the path of desire under the command of the good (*SVII*, 11.05.60, pp. 229–230). It is this kind of deprivation "that leads us to demand the same dissatisfaction of others" (Copjec, 2002, p. 174), namely, to envy. This dialectic of rivalry and envy, the evil jouissance of *Civilization and Its Discontents* (*SVII*, 20.03.60, pp. 184–185) is bound to derail any attempt at a utilitarian distributional justice. "There's absolutely no reason why we should make ourselves the guarantors of the bourgeois dream" (*SVII*, 29.06.60, p. 303).

## Montage of drives and vel of alienation

The critique of theoretical humanism, as embodied in the autonomous ego of the ego psychology, continued in *Seminar XI*, achieving a particular clarity around a division of the subject between the Real of the partial drives, now conceived through the metaphor of surrealist *"montage"* (*SXI*, 06.05.64, p. 169) and the Symbolic network of signifiers where a signifier "is that which represents a subject for another signifier" (p. 207). The critique of political economy operates at both sides of the division, where once again two distinct notions of economy, the affective and the linguistic, conjoin, disjunctively, in the category of the drive. On the side of the Real, the unified and structured subject of theoretical humanism (whether it be *homo psychologicus* or *homo economicus*) is reconceived as a distributed vector field of partial drives circling (deriving satisfaction) around now proliferating objects (breast, faeces, gaze, voice) and failing to represent the totality of the sexual tendency of the subject, let alone being organized around an aim of biological reproduction. In recent years, some have correlated this notion with the solipsistic economic man of neoclassical marginalism, who optimizes his consumption function by consuming each commodity up to an amount where the (marginal) benefit (satisfaction) derived from the last unit in each commodity is equal to the others.[4] While the marginal calculus governing the actions of *homo economicus* in early twentieth-century neoclassical theory subordinated the bodily "satisfaction" to a rational mind and hence remained in the humanist epistemology of *homo psychologicus*, a much more radical fragmentation and decentring of the subject, arguably echoing Lacan's deconstruction of subjects into partial drives incessantly seeking satisfaction, can indeed be found in the Bourbakist formalism of post-war general equilibrium theory (Ruccio & Amariglio, 2003). On the side of the Symbolic register, we have a far-reaching commentary on the category of alienation. At first glance, this is indeed a criticism of some of the humanist conceptions of alienation found in the Marxian field (including in Marx's own formulations). Alienation, for Lacan, describes the *forced* choice faced by the subject whose access to *meaning* (and hence to Symbolic order *qua* big Other) necessarily entails the loss of its *being*. Unlike the classical Marxian notion of alienation which can be overcome in a post-capitalist society, Lacanian alienation is a "constitutive" condition that results from subject's acquisition of language *qua* structure (Tomšič, 2015, p. 53; Žižek, 2017, pp. 226–227). Yet, the example Lacan invokes in the seminar points towards a particular instance of forced choice (*freedom or death!*) that also interested the Marx of *Capital* immensely. Lacan notes, "[f]reedom, after all, as you know, is like the *freedom to work*, for which the French Revolution, it seems, was fought" (*SXI*, 27.05.64, p. 213).[5] The Bourgeois Revolution marks the emancipation of the serfs from their feudal ties. But, as Marx would remind us, the newly liberated proletariat

> must be free in the double sense that as a free individual he can dispose of his labour-power as his own commodity, and that, on the other hand, he has no other commodity for sale, i.e., he is rid of them, he is free of all the objects needed for the realization [*Verwirklichung*] of his labour-power.
>
> (*CAI*, pp. 272–273)

And it is precisely this insight that Lacan highlights: "It can also be the *freedom to die of hunger*" (*SXI*, 27.05.64, p. 213).[6] This implicit reference to Marx gives an unexpected ontic quality to the constitutive homology between signifier and (economic) value that runs through Lacan's Seminars and *Écrits*.[7]

## Critique of structuralism

### Homology between surplus-value and surplus-*jouissance*

So far, what we have highlighted in Lacan's discourse has been his critique of theoretical humanism (*qua* critique of political economy), a critique that he shared with Althusser, mobilizing a number of key structuralist models and strategies to displace the subject from its sovereign position. *Seminar XVI* is a turning point where Lacan candidly acknowledges what he is taking from the structuralist movement that was ridiculed in May 1968 ("Structures don't march on the streets!") and from Althusser in particular, namely, his idea of absent cause that exists only in its effects (also referred to as "structural causality" or "metonymic causality").[8] With this Seminar, Lacan moves from the disjuncture between the affective economy (*jouissance*) and signifying economy (signifier) to versions of their articulation and locates the place of object *a* in the structure of the signifying chain, as a "being of thought" (*SXVI*, 13.11.68). Elsewhere, Miller (2007) describes the impossible ontological status of this "being of thought" as being a "third term" between a "corporeal specimen" and "logical consistency" (p. 29). Lacan's precise debt to Marx (or more precisely to Althusser) is the homology he constructs between the "place" and "essential function" of surplus-*jouissance* (*plus-de-jouir*) and surplus-value, in their respective fields. At the level of conceptual operation, the terms function as the "scissors' mark of discourse" (*SXVI*, 27.11.68), as the master signifiers that inaugurate, respectively the analytical discourse (Lacan) and the critique of political economy (Marx). In Marx's critique of political economy, surplus-value, as the unpaid portion of living labour, desubstantialized through value-form, functions as an absent cause, only visible in its effects and ontologically immeasurable (Roberts, 1996). Yet it is also that which (*qua* object *a*) propels the competitive compulsion to *siphon* it *off* from less efficient firms and distribute it to more efficient ones. The impossibility of value-form to fully reconcile with itself, its constitutive failure to allocate resources in the "right way" (the crisis ridden nature of the capitalist value-form circulating through the circuits of capital, with its disjunctive and imbricated moments of production, distribution, consumption) is where the homology comes to its own (Henderson, 2013; Malabou, 2002). If Lacan is integrating the affective economy (*jouissance*) within the functioning of the signifying economy (value-form), this is an integration that holds the signifying chain to a permanent subversion, unravelling and transformation "from within" as there is always a surplus that either exceeds its localization (i.e., the *impossibility* of the appropriation of surplus-value in a capitalist firm) or falls short of its truth (i.e., the competitive battles around and on the distributions of surplus-value rendering is always *inadequate*).[9] As partial objects (breast, faeces, voice, gaze) that fragment the body of the subject are further formalized into an impossible object (surplus-*jouissance*) that displaces the structure from within (*extimate*-ly), Lacan, in his final decade, proceeded to produce an affectionate yet truly incisive immanent critique of structuralism.

## Four discourses and the Capitalist discourse

In *Seminar XVII*, Lacan introduces four discourses that further formalize the relation between the signifying and the affective economies around (non-)relations of *impossibility* and *impotence*. On the side of the signifying economy, starting with the discourse of the Master, Lacan marks the disruptive function of *truth* ($) as the cause of the constitutive *impossibility* of social link ("a signifier represents a subject for another signifier") that always fails to communicate the meaning. This formalization evokes the logic of suture where the barred subject, through *repression* (*Verdrängung*), enters the symbolic order (constitutive alienation) at the expense of being. On the side of affective economy, where knowledge ($S_2$) functions as a means of *jouissance* for the Master, the *product* of this communication, the object *a* (qua surplus-*jouissance*) is barred from the *truth*, is never adequate to it ("one takes *jouissance* by morsels" (*SXVII*, 11.03.70, p. 108)). The *impotence*, or the inability of the product to meet the need articulated in demand, Lacan argues, is constitutive ["one can try to conjoin this production with needs, which the needs one fashions—there is nothing doing" (*SXVII*, 10.06.70, p. 174)]. This disjunctive articulation of signifying and affective economies restages Marx's critique of value-form where surplus-value is only visible in its effects and disruptive of the reconciliation of value with itself (through the crises generated by the central imbalance of capitalist value-form described above) but goes beyond by traversing the fantasy of a socialist economy where needs (represented by $S_1$) are matched to abilities (*savoir* represented by $S_2$) in a harmonious manner.[10] This is not an anti-socialist position, rather a provocation to post-capitalist politics—in the spirit of a critique of political economy—to take this constitutive impossibility of economic value as its starting point. In response to the deficit of symbolic investiture provoked by the constitutive crisis of value-form (or more formally, the *impossibility* in signifying economy as disjunctively mediated through the *impotence* in affective economy), capitalist society managed "to allow itself a relaxation of the university discourse" (*SXVII*, 10.06.70, p. 168). This counter-clockwise shift, from the discourse of the Master to that of University, hides the master signifier ($S_1$) under knowledge ($S_2$)—the hidden truth of the contemporary technocratic regimes of biopolitical governmentality being the corporate sovereignty enacted through the ruthless capitalist appropriation by the Board of Directors, Trustees, and other modern masters. This truth is further occluded in the fifth discourse that Lacan (*DDP*) articulated in his Milan Discourse where a closed circuit loops forever, without impossibility or impotence, to offer an endless series of morsels of enjoyment (lathouses, commodities, interfaces, fixes, cures, rewards, and so on) for the satisfaction of the subject.[11] Arguably, when Lacan argued a year before in *Seminar XVII* that "surplus value is a memorial to surplus *jouissance*", as its "homogenous equivalent" (11.02.70, p. 81), he was referring to this semblant status of morsels of enjoyment, the topic of *Seminar XVIII*.

## *From the logic of exception to logic of not-all*

In *Seminar XX*, we find the succinct formula, "the signifier is the cause of jouissance" (12.19.72, p. 24). At this point in his discourse, Lacan thinks of the relation between the signifying and affective economy as one of performativity and develops the concept of *lalangue*, as his departure from structuralism, to point at the beyond of language, where enjoyment achieved through homonymy (the function of *signifiance,* translated by Fink as "signifierness") opens up to the unconscious knowledge, producing effects on the subject through affects (*SXX*, 26.06.73, p. 139).[12] As much as it is a critique of structuralism, it is also a criticism of Marx in whose work, according to Lacan, "use value serves only as an ideal point in relation to exchange value, to which everything is reduced" (*SXX*, 10.04.73, p. 97). To the extent that, for Lacan, "jouissance is what serves no purpose" (*SXX*, 12.12.72, p. 3) Marx's discourse on value does appear to remain within the structuralist frame. Yet, it is possible to find the excess of affect in Marx not only in the impossibility of value-form discussed above, but also in the logic of disavowal that operates in commodity fetishism (Žižek, 1989), in the logic of drive that governs the compulsion to accumulate (McGowan, 2013), in the place of subversive proletarian truth against adaptation to capitalism (Pavón-Cuéllar, 2011), or in the logic of value as sublimation *qua* objectification that elevates an unassimilable surplus of (labour) activity to the status of *Das Ding* (Henderson, 2013, p. 139). It is also possible to bring in the formulae of sexuation that Lacan develops in *Seminar XX* (having already introduced them in *Seminar XIX* and *L'Étourdit*) in conversation with Marx's analysis of appropriation, more precisely, the articulation of appropriation and distribution, as the exception to the "exchange of equivalents" which sets up the capitalist universe of an internally dislocated relation between production (social labour, abilities) and consumption (social reproduction, needs). With the logic of exception, Lacan memorializes Freud's myth of the primordial father in the formal language of structure and topology. The logic of exception constitutes an "all" that satisfies the condition of "compactness", a "limited, closed, supposedly instituted space [...] an intersection extending to infinity" (*SXX*, 12.12.72, p. 9). The concept of economy in high modernist general equilibrium theory is a homogeneous space of commodities which is also a closed set that allows for no entropy; a closed nomos.[13] But what makes an economy capitalist is not the fact that it is posited as a closed set of homogenous commodities, but rather the moment of decision (or, each moment of knotting), the act of appropriation of surplus-value by one of the many names-of-the-father (the Board of Directors, the CEO, the Entrepreneur, the President, the Despot). On the other hand, Lacan argues that closed sets are covered with open sets that exclude their own limits. This leads him from the infinity within bounds of limit to that of a finite series counted one by one (*une par une*)—or to that of the logic of not-all. In the *Critique of the Gotha Program*, Marx (*CGP*) deconstructs the bourgeois ideology of equal exchange that characterizes the programme under the axiom "from each according to his abilities to each according to his needs". "From each [...] to each" is often approached as an ideal principle which announces that the organization of social labour would be solved and the surplus of value would disappear under socialist (associative) production (p. 87). However, precisely because Marx goes to great pains to strike at the hollowness of the assertion that workers have the exceptional rights to the whole proceeds of their labour, it can be read as a half-said (*mi-dire*) that puts a communist know-how into use by registering not only the singular formation of needs and abilities but also their radical separation, and from there, forges a relation where there is none, each by each. This logic of non-all will eventually lend itself to a clinic of the *sinthome*, where the stability of the subject is predicated upon how their symptom knots the Real, the Symbolic, and the Imaginary together, in a singular manner (*SXXIII*, 16.12.75, p. 44). This is a clinical modality that supplants the discontinuous diagnostic structures (neurosis, perversion, psychosis) and proposes to attend to each symptom (including the Oedipus complex), each knot one by one (*SXXIII*, 18.11.75, p. 13). Whether this is Lacan's accommodation to the realities of late capitalism or his manner of pointing at the possibility of forging post-capitalist ways of being is a question that can only be taken up one by one.

## Notes

1 The fundamentals that anchor price will change from "labor embodied" in nineteenth-century classical political economy to "individual preferences represented through utility functions" in early twentieth-century canonical Neoclassical Economics (Ruccio & Amariglio, 2003).
2 See, in particular, Lacan's allusion in 1951 to "the most elementary social exchanges" that "Dora names as the grounds of her revolt" (*PT*, p. 181).
3 The first time Marx appears in Lacan's *Seminars* is in 1957, in *Seminar V* in the context of his reading of Freud's *Jokes and Their Relation to Unconscious* (see *SV*, 27.11.57, p. 73 and 04.12.57, p. 87). And in *Seminar XIV*, Lacan (12.04.67) would declare that structure, the proposition that "the subject is a fact of language (*fait de langage*), is

something to do with language (*fait du langage*)", is the contribution of both Marxism and psychoanalysis to science.
4 See, e.g., Birkin (1999); for a cogent critique of this position, see Kornbluh (2014).
5 Emphasis added.
6 Emphasis added.
7 While it is possible to read this homological articulation as Lacan's ontologization of capitalism, this would be misleading as capitalist commodity relations are one form of organizing the economy. Yet, it is also true that capitalist commodity relations, as a mode of subjection, has a tendency to present itself as a totalizing ontological project that has a claim on the social ontology as such. See Özselçuk & Madra (2021).
8 See Althusser et al. (1965, pp. 334, 344).
9 See Ruccio and Amariglio (2003).
10 See in the same Seminar 18.02.70, p. 92 and 11.03.70, p. 108.
11 Translation by J. W. Stone.
12 For the centrality of performativity in Lacan's late discourse, see Cassin (2020).
13 See, e.g., Koopmans (1957) and Debreu (1959).

**Further reading**

Bruno, P. (2019). *Lacan and Marx. The Invention of the Symptom*. J. Holland (Trans.). London: Routledge.
Chakrabarti, A., Dhar, A. & Cullenberg, S. (2012). *World of the Third and Global Capitalism*. Delhi: Worldview Publications.
Rouse, H. & Arribas, S. (2011). *Egocracy. Marx, Freud and Lacan*. Zürich: Diaphanes.

**References**

Althusser, L. (1964). Freud and Lacan. In: O. Corpet & F. Matheron (Eds.), *Writings on Psychoanalysis. Freud and Lacan* (pp. 7–32), J. Mehlman (Trans.). New York: Columbia University Press, 1996.
Althusser, L., Balibar, É., Establet, R., Macherey, P. & Rancière, J. (1965). *Reading Capital* (The Complete Edition). London and New York: Verso, 2015.
Birken, L. (1999). Freud's "Economic Hypothesis": From Homo Oeconomicus to Homo Sexualis. *American Imago*, 56(4): 311–330.
Cassin, B. (2020). *Jacques the Sophist: Lacan, Logos, and Psychoanalysis*, M. Syrotinski (Trans.). New York: Fordham University Press.
Copjec, J. (2002). *Imagine There's No Woman. Ethics and Sublimation* (pp. 158–176). Cambridge: The MIT Press.
Debreu, G. (1959). *Theory of Value. An Axiomatic Analysis of Economic Equilibrium*. New Haven and London: Yale University Press.
Freud, S. (1895). Project for a Scientific Psychology. In: *Standard Edition of the Complete Psychological Works of Sigmund Freud, 1886–1899* (Vol. I, pp. 282–346), J. Strachey (Trans.). London: Hogarth Press, 1981.
Freud, S. (1900). The Interpretation of Dreams. In: *Standard Edition of the Complete Psychological Works of Sigmund Freud*, (Vol. V, pp. 339–627), J. Strachey (Trans.). London: Hogarth Press, 1981.
Freud, S. (1924). Neurosis and Psychosis. In: *Standard Edition of the Complete Psychological Works of Sigmund Freud, 1923–1925*, (Vol. XIX, pp. 148–153), J. Strachey (Trans.). London: Hogarth Press.

Henderson, G. (2013). *Value in Marx: The Persistence of Value in a More-than-Capitalist World*. Minneapolis: University of Minnesota Press.
Koopmans, T. J. (1957). *Three Essays on the State of Economic Science*. New York: McGraw-Hill Book Company.
Kornbluh, A. (2014). *Realizing Capital. Financial and Psychic Economies in Victorian Forms*. New York: Fordham University Press.
Langer, F. (2014). Economy. In: B. Cassin (Ed.), *Dictionary of Untranslatables. A Philosophical Lexicon* (pp. 243–245), S. Rendall, et al. (Trans.). Princeton: Princeton University Press.
Laplanche, J. & Pontalis, J. B. (1973). *The Language of Psychoanalysis*, D. Nicholson-Smith (Trans.). London: Hogarth Press.
Malabou, C. (2002). Economy of Violence, Violence of Economy (Derrida and Marx). In: L. Lawlor and Z. Direk (Eds.), *Jacques Derrida: Critical Assessments of Leading Philosophers* (pp. 180–198), J. Lampert & O. Serafinowicz (Trans.). London and New York: Routledge.
McGowan, T. (2013). *Enjoying What We Don't Have. The Political Project of Psychoanalysis* (pp. 52–78). Lincoln and London: University of Nebraska Press.
Miller, J.-A. (1987). Jeremy Bentham's Panoptic Device. In: R. Miller (Trans.). *October*, 41(102): 3–29.
Miller, J.-A. (2007). Reading of the Seminar From an Other to the Other. In: B. Fulks (Trans.), *Lacanian Ink*, 29: 8–61.
Miller, J.-A. (2019). Six Paradigms of Jouissance. In: *Paradigms of Jouissance. Three Interventions by Jacques Alain-Miller* (pp. 11–77), J. Haney (Trans.). London: London Society NLS.
Özselçuk, C. & Madra, Y. M. (2021). In the Void of Formalization: The Homology Between Surplus Value and Surplus *Jouissance*. In: P. Kingsbury & A. J. Secor (Eds.), *A Place More Void* (pp. 267–284). Lincoln: University of Nebraska.
Pavón-Cuéllar, D. (2011). Marx in Lacan: Proletarian Truth in Opposition to Capitalist Psychology. In: *Annual Review of Critical Psychology* 9: 70–77.
Roberts, B. (1996). The Visible and the Measurable: Althusser and the Marxian Theory of Value. In: A. Callari & D. F. Ruccio (Eds.), *Postmodern Materialism and the Future of Marxist Theory: Essays in the Althusserian Tradition* (pp. 193–211). Hanover: Wesleyan University Press/University Press of New England.
Ruccio, D. & Amariglio, J. (2003). *Postmodern Moments in Modern Economics*. Princeton: Princeton University Press.
Tomšič, S. (2015). *The Capitalist Unconscious. Marx and Lacan*. London: Verso.
Žižek, S. (2017). *Incontinence of the Real. Economico-Philosophical Spandrels*. Cambridge: The MIT Press.
Žižek, S. (1989). *The Sublime Object of Ideology*. London: Verso.

# Chapter 8

# Freedom/liberty

Roque Farrán

—Ara.: حرية —Chi.: 自由 —Fre.: *Liberté* —Ger.: *Freiheit/willkür* —Ita.: *Libertà* —Jap.: 自由,自由 —Port.: *Liberdade* —Rus.: *Свобода/вольность (воля)* —Spa.: *Libertad* —Tur.: *Özgürlük/özgürleşme*

→ *Alienation*; *Politics*; *Revolution*; *Slavery*

As a good materialist thinker, Lacan conceives, in the first place, the determination of the subject for causes that it ignores and that can only be cleared in a second moment with a certain amount of freedom. Freedom in Lacan is linked from the beginning to psychic causality and madness, without identifying itself with the latter entirely, for it rather constitutes its limit. To understand this complex position, we can trace how freedom emerges and unfolds in different moments of Lacan's thinking: in relation to the dialectical progress of the analysis, to the determinations of the logic of the signifier, to *jouissance*, to the axiomatic relation of the subject and to the Borromean knot. It is, without a doubt, a topic that is halted precisely when the expression "freedom of thought" is analyzed. Lacan's relation to Marx's and Hegel's thought is evident as well as prominent, although it has a singular modulation when it comes to the problem of madness.

## Freedom, between the imaginary and the symbolic

Lacan writes in the classical *On Psychic Causality* the following: "Not only can man's being not be understood without madness, but it would not be man's being if it did not bear madness within itself as the limit of his freedom" (*PPC*, p. 144). The role of the limit is mentioned here as a way to give an account of freedom's ambiguity because the mad person is the one that believes he/she is free while ignoring the causes that determine him/herself to be the way they are. But, at the same time, madness is not a voluntary affair nor is free will, which is why he further clarifies: "It is certainly true – to interrupt this serious talk with something humorous from my youth, which I wrote in a pithy form on the wall in the hospital staff room – that 'Not just anyone can go mad'" (*PPC*, p. 144). Even Lacan himself considers the possibility of being mad (there is no better way of verifying the

DOI: 10.4324/9781003212096-8

opposite than by asking yourself this question) in his heated discussion of Henri Ey's work:

> Having arrived at this point in my talk on the causality of madness, mustn't I be careful so that heaven may keep me from going awry? Mustn't I realize that, after having argued that Henry Ey misrecognizes the causality of madness, and that he is not Napoleon, I am falling into the trap of proposing as ultimate proof thereof that I am the one who understands this causality, in other words, that I am Napoleon?
>
> (*PPC*, p. 145)

Thus, he shows that a mad person is not the one that believes he is a king or is Napoleon even while being so—according to the common example—but rather the one that identifies him/herself with his/her own existential position to such an extent that he/she ignores the dialectical relationality that constitutes him/her (given the case, this can also be either a psychiatrists or a psychoanalyst). Such inquiry will go very far, to the point that it will be taken up in *Seminar XXI* (11.12.71):

> There is somewhere, in an article called *La causalité psychique*, a place, a place around which a certain number of people have sparred like that, where I knot – because this is what is at stake, liberty and madness – where I say that the one cannot be conceived of without the other, which, of course disturbs people, because all the same, they think immediately, anyway that I am saying freedom is madness.

Of course, as we mentioned before, it is not a matter of simply identifying one with the other—freedom = madness—but rather of avoiding the making of this equivalence. In order to do this, it is important to know what we are talking about when we use the word freedom, and to avoid reducing it to common sense, which is pierced by both will and free will, so that it can regain its philosophical dimension. If we go back to Barbara Cassin's *Dictionary of Untranslatables*, we can see that the oldest notion of freedom, which can be found in modern thinkers such as Spinoza, Hegel, or Marx, resonates with Lacan's thinking. According to Cassin (1994, p. 252):

> "Liberty" looks back to the Latin *liber* and *libertas*, as well as to the Greek eleutheros (ἐλεύθερος), eleutheria (ἐλευθερία): Latin and Greek can effectively be superimposed on the linguistic plane and have (via the old Venetian *(e)leudheros), the same root *leudh–, 'to grow, to develop,' from which come seemingly heterogeneous terms like *Liber* (Lat.), the ancient god of the vine, *liberi* (Lat.), "the children" who are well born, legitimate, and *Leute* (Ger.), "people." Hence the insistence on the ethnic stock and on growth.

The idea that freedom in antiquity had a positive connotation, which was linked to a sense of belonging to a community and its immanent growth or development, was very important. This is so because, in the first place, it distances itself from the idea of reducing the individual to an isolated subject and to its own will of decision-making. In the second place, the notion of freedom is linked to the idea of development, which can be seen in a dialectical way, be it in terms of *imagos*, signifiers, axioms, or knots, as Lacan will show. Madness is a limit to freedom when the subject thinks that it is without any social bonds or independent from them, which is where the subject is constituted as such; also when the subject cannot develop or enrich the imaginary identifications through a symbolic unfolding that reformulates them historically. In this way, Lacan follows modern thinkers such as Spinoza, Hegel, and Marx.[1] When Lacan concludes his early text on psychic causality, he warns us of a danger that we are confronted with nowadays: induced madness through computational calculations and algorithms that manipulate the *imagos*:

> In concluding, I hope that this brief discourse on the imago will strike you, not as an ironic challenge, but as a genuine threat to man. For, while our ability to realize that the imago's unquantifiable distance and freedom's minute blade are decisive in madness does not yet allow us to cure it, the time is perhaps not far off when such knowledge will allow us to induce it. While nothing can guarantee that we will not get lost in a free movement towards truth, a little nudge will suffice to ensure that we change truth into madness. Then we will have moved from the domain of metaphysical causality, which one can deride, to that of scientific technique, which is no laughing matter. Here and there we have seen the beginnings of such an enterprise. The art of the image will soon be able to play off the values of the imago, and some day we will see serial orders of "ideals" that withstand criticism: that is when the label "true guarantee" will take on its full meaning. Neither the intention nor the enterprise will be new, but their systematic form will be (*PPC*, p. 156).

## Freedom in the order of the signifier

The primary form of alienation of "the subject's being" that Lacan identified in terms of *imagos*, which he suggested treating analytically following the symbolical-dialectical progression of the truth, will find similar formulations when it reaches the linguistic paradigm. In *The Function and Field of Speech and Language in Psychoanalysis* he writes:

> Let's be categorical: in psychoanalytic anamnesis, what is at stake is not reality, but truth, because the effect of full speech is to reorder past contingencies by conferring on them the sense of necessities to come, such as they are constituted by the scant freedom through which the subject makes them present.
> (*FFS*, p. 213)

This methodological warning would inscribe itself in the symbolical determination that both linguistics and structural anthropology would help elucidate:

> And this suggests that it is perhaps only our unawareness of their permanence that allows us to believe in freedom of choice in the so-called complex structures of marriage ties under whose law we live. If statistics has already allowed us to glimpse that this freedom is not exercised randomly, it is because a subjective logic seems to orient its effects.
>
> (*FFS*, p. 229)

Thus, madness was yet again defined as "negative freedom", which would be like saying it is some sort of "denied freedom" by not letting it unfold or develop dialectically:

> In madness, of whatever nature, we must recognize on the one hand the negative freedom of a kind of speech that has given up trying to gain recognition, which is what we call an obstacle to transference; and, on the other, the singular formation of a delusion which – whether fabular, fantastical, or cosmological, or rather interpretative, demanding, or idealist – objectifies the subject in a language devoid of dialectic.
>
> (*FFS*, p. 231)

Later on, freedom can be found linked to that particular oscillation between the idea of *being free* in a delusional tone and the narrow margin in which freedom is verified and exercised according to the analytical rule. These are two examples taken from *On a Question Prior to Any Possible Treatment of Psychosis* that oscillate between the socio-cultural plane and the analytical work:

> I will not deny that I have seen enough on this score in our time to wonder about the criteria by which this man – with a discourse on freedom that must certainly be called delusional (I devoted one of my seminars to it), with a concept of the real in which determinism is no more than an alibi that quickly becomes anxiety provoking when one tries to extend its field to chance (I had my audience experience this in a preliminary experiment), and with a belief that unites men, half the universe at least, under the symbol of Father Christmas (which no one can overlook) – would stop me from situating him, by legitimate analogy, in the category of social psychosis which, if I am not mistaken, Pascal established before me.
>
> (*QTP*, p. 480)

Social psychosis, which can be associated with a scientific subjectivity that forecloses the emptiness and the symbolic game of overdetermination while at the same time dissociating the belief in freedom and the alibi of a determinism of the real that does not transform the subject, can be verified also in the clinical and in the analytical work:

> Everything that can be said about the association of ideas is mere dressing up in psychologistic clothing. Induced plays on words are far removed from it; because of their protocol, moreover, nothing could be less free. The subject invited to speak in analysis does not really display a great deal of freedom in what he says. Not that he is bound by the rigor of his associations: they no doubt oppress him, but it is rather that they lead to a free speech, a full speech that would be painful to him.
>
> (*DTP*, pp. 514–515)

This is so since truth requires the subject to be implied in its *parole* and a specific way of assuming the determination of the symbolic which opens up the possibility of a rigorous type of freedom.

Then in *Kant with Sade*, the intersection of the subjective and the social is present again and it is related, nonetheless, to the idea of revolution, where freedom is conceived of precisely as desire: "it is the freedom to desire that is a new factor, not because it has inspired a revolution—people have always fought and died for a desire—but because this revolution wants its struggle to be for the freedom of desire" (*KS*, p. 663). In *Position of the Unconscious*, the logical dilemma shows its political and dramatic dimension:

> This disjunction is incarnated in a highly illustratable, if not dramatic, way as soon as the signifier is incarnated at a more personalized level in demand or supply: in "your money or your life" or "liberty or death." It is merely a question of knowing whether or not (*sic aut non*) you want to keep life or refuse death, because, regarding the other term in the alternative, money or liberty, your choice will in any case be disappointing. You should be aware that what remains is, in any case, diminished: it will be life without money and, having refused death, a life somewhat inconvenienced by the cost of freedom.
>
> (*PU*, pp. 713–714)

## Freedom of thought

Thus, we get to the widely spread delusional freedom (social psychosis), to the narrow freedom of the *parole* (verified in the analysis) and the revolutionary freedom of desire. We get to the problematized "freedom of thought". Once again it is important to think about freedom in all its complexity, in this case between the objective and the subjective, the norm, transgression and utopia. Lacan's commentary on Hegel (which also refers to Plato and Thomas More) is invaluable in order to capture the complexity that incites freedom in the modern era. In *Seminar XVI*, Lacan writes:

What does freedom of thought mean? How the devil can people even consider that there is a value inscribed in these three words? As a first approach, let us spell out that if thought has some reference, if we consider it in what we could quickly call its objective relationship, naturally there is not the slightest freedom. The idea of freedom in this quarter of objective references has all the same core point around which it arises. It is the function, or more exactly the notion of the norm. From the moment that this notion comes into play, there is introduced correlatively that of exception, indeed even that of transgression. It is here that the function of thinking can take on some sense by introducing the notion of freedom. In a word, it is by thinking about Utopia that, as its name states, is a place that is nowhere, *no place*, it is in Utopia that thinking would be free to envisage a possible reform of the norm. This indeed is how in the history of thinking from Plato to Thomas More things have been presented. With regard to the norm, the real locus in which it is established, it is only in the field of Utopia that freedom of thought can be exercised. This indeed is what results in the works of the last of those that I have just named, namely, the very creator of the term *Utopia*, Thomas More. And moreover, by going back to the one who put forward, who consecrated under the function of the Idea the term of norm, Plato. Plato at the same time constructs for us a Utopian society, the Republic, where there is expressed freedom of thought with regard to the political norm of its time.

(23.04.69)

While from an objective point of view freedom refers to that which has no place, utopia is *par excellence*, on the subjective side, and in its problematic location, that freedom which finds its opportunity (not in thinking but in knowing):

Pulling back from this, not going to involve myself in developments that would send us astray with respect to what we have to question, I will ask how there is expressed in this register what is involved in freedom of thought. Here Hegel is a reference point that is not simply convenient but essential. In this axis that interests us, he prolongs the inaugural *cogito*. Thinking surrenders itself if one questions the centre of gravity of what is qualified there as *Selbstbewusstsein*. I know that I think. The *Selbstbewusstsein* is nothing else. Only what he adds to Descartes, is that something varies in this *I know that I think*, and this is the point where I am. This, I was going to say by definition, in Hegel, I do not know. The illusion is that *I am where I think*. Freedom of thought here, is nothing other than what Hegel forbids me to think about, which is that *I am where I want to be*. In this respect, what Hegel reveals, is that there is not the slightest freedom of thought. The time of History is necessary so that at the end, I think at the right place, at the place where I will have become Knowledge. But, at that stage, there is absolutely no longer any need for thinking. [...] It is clear from Hegel's demonstration that I cannot think that I am where I want. But it is no less clear in looking closely at it that it is this and nothing else that is called thinking. So that this *I am there where I want* which is the essence of freedom of thought as a stating is properly what cannot be stated by anyone.

(*SXVI*, 23.04.69)

This is perhaps where one could read the Marxist utopia of achieving communism not so much as a suggestion of *another place* but in the destruction or revocation of all existing places and social classes so that the enunciation of the libertarian essence can be possible (we should return to Badiou's dialectic between the *horlieu* and the *esplace* in Hegel, Marx, and Lacan in his *Theory of the Subject* (1982)).[2]

The complexity of the role of thinking and freedom in its enunciation is constantly problematized by Lacan, who goes back to it through the street interpellations that made him think all the time. In *Seminar XIX*, Lacan states:

> The other day, as I was leaving the latest session up at the Panthéon, someone questioned me – he might be here again – on the subject of whether I believed in freedom. I told him he was being funny. And then, as I am always fairly weary, I broke off. But this doesn't mean I wouldn't be prepared to confide in him personally on this matter. The fact is, I seldom speak about freedom, and so this question was his initiative. Knowing why he asked me this would not be unwelcomed to me.
>
> (04.05.72, p. 131)

Even if he finds it funny, this is something that interpellates him and to which he goes back repeatedly in order to say something about it.[3] After sharing this anecdote, he asserts his axiomatic conceptualisation:

> There is one facet of knowledge about truth that derives its strength from entirely neglecting its content. This hammers home how the signifying articulation is its time and its place, and it does so to such an extent that something is shown which is nothing but this articulation. The *monstration* of this articulation, in the passive sense, finds itself assuming an active sense and imposing itself as a *demonstration* to the speaking being who, in this instance, can only acknowledge, for the signifier, not merely inhabiting it but being no more than its mark. The freedom to choose one's axioms, that is to say, the point of departure chosen for this demonstration, consist solely in undergoing its consequences as a subject, consequences that, for their part, are not free.
>
> (*SXIX*, 10.05.72, p. 154)

The freedom to choose one's own axioms, even though one undoubtedly will suffer from its consequences, is very important when it comes to the subject's real freedom. After having said this, he asserts one of his usual provocations by going back to the street address and by implicating the Vatican (always mindful of the places of enunciation) as well, for it exemplifies what he is talking about:

> There are people who like me a bit in practically every corner, even in the wings of the Vatican. Why not, after all? There are some great people there. For the person who questioned me about freedom, I shall say that only freethinkers I know are in the Vatican. For my part, I'm not a freethinker. I'm forced to stick to what I've been saying, but over there in the Vatican, what ease they have! You can understand how the French Revolution was helped along by the abbots. If you knew what liberty they have, my dear friends, it would send a shiver down your spine. I try to bring them back to the hard line, but there is no way. They outflank me. For them, psychoanalysis is old hat. You can see what use freethinking has. They're clear-sighted.
> <div align="right">(<i>SXIX</i>, 01.06.72, p. 174)</div>

## The knot of freedom

Freedom is topologically explained in relation to the Borromean knot and the orders or dimensions of experience of the speaking being (the real–the imaginary–the symbolic). In his last seminars, freedom is shown in its entirety: the cut that lets the different orders *loose* is madness itself or is related to it; a female analyst can cope better with the unconscious because of its *free movements*, which works in a suitable way among the knotted orders. In *Seminar XXI*, Lacan says, "And this is why, this is why the best case consists, the case that I have called 'freedom', namely, that if there is something normal, it is because, when one of the dimensions fails you for some reason or other, you should go, you should really go mad" (11.12.73).

In *Seminar XXII* he follows up on it:

> It is certain that what I am saying does not quite go in the direction, despite everything, of what women can, nor take their chance, if one can call that a chance in a kind of integration into the categories of the man. I mean, neither power, nor knowledge, in fact they know about them, they know so much more about them, in short, is that not so, from the very fact of being *a* woman that it is to this indeed that I take off my hat. And the only thing that astonishes me, is not so much as I said like that on occasion, that they know better how to treat the unconscious, I am not too sure. Their category with respect to the unconscious is very obviously of a greater force, they are less bogged down in it. They treat it with a savagery, indeed a liberty of approach which is quite gripping for example in the case of Melanie Klein. It is something that, like that, I leave to the meditation of each one and women analysts are

certainly more at ease with respect to the unconscious. They busy themselves with it, they do not busy themselves with it, it must be said, without it being, without it being at the expense – it is perhaps here that the idea of merit is upset – that they lose something of their chance in it which, simply by being one among women is in a way without measure. If I had – which obviously would never come into my head –, if I should have to localise somewhere the idea of liberty, it would obviously be in *a* woman that I would incarnate it. *A* woman, not obligatorily anyone whatsoever, because they are *not-all* and the *anyone whatsoever* slides towards the *all*.

(11.02.75)

Lastly, in *Seminar XXIII* (16.12.75, p. 38) he clarifies and specifies the tension between limit and freedom that creates madness in the causality of the speaking subject due to the fact that it is knotted to three irreducible dimensions:

> The fact that the first two are loose from one other – this is the very definition of the Borromean knot – enables me to sustain the ex-sistence of the third, that of the real, in relation to the free-roaming imaginary and symbolic. In *sisting* outside the imaginary and the symbolic, the real butts into, plays into, something that is of the order of limitation. Once it has been tied to the other two in Borromean fashion, from that moment forth the two others resist it. This is a way of saying that the real only enjoys ex-sistence to the extent that it encounters, with the symbolic and the imaginary, a point of arrest.

In conclusion, even if the problem of freedom is present in all of Lacan's teachings, there is no substantial conceptual treatment of it, which is no different from the Enlightenment tradition into which Lacan inscribes himself. Freedom is rather present in relation to his analysis of other theoretical and methodological topics, such as the signifying determination, *jouissance*, desire, the logic of the not-all or the Borromean knot. All in all, the word "freedom" is closer to the Hegelian dialectic than to the Marxist one although, as we mentioned before in a footnote, it is also conceptually related to the latter in terms of the treatment of the symptom and madness as hypostasis of the subject. Even if Marx invented the symptom, how to address the symptom seems not diverge: once more, the knowing what to do there among the knotting of the unconscious that Lacan ends up transferring to the female position anticipates our current times in terms of the feminist power, as the previous quote from *Seminar XXII* affirms: "if I had to localise somewhere the idea of liberty, it would obviously be in *a* woman that I would incarnate it" (10.12.74). At this point it is clear that Lacan articulates, as the modern and materialist thinker that he was, both the individual as well as collectivity through the problem of freedom, and that is why his work on the clinic implied also a reading of the social, the political, and the philosophical plane. It is not a matter of erudition but of the material constitution of the subject.[4]

Translated from Spanish by Carla Tirado-Morttiz

## Notes

1 Lambruschini (2017) considers the following: "Both authors [Marx and Hegel] manifest a rejection of the contractualists' atomism that considered society and the State as emergent from a voluntary agreement among individuals that are isolated from one another, as well as of the political economists' liberalism that explained the common good as a natural result of the interaction of individual selfishnesses in the economic sphere. In relation to these considerations, Hegel and Marx seem to return to the ideas of Aristotle and Rousseau: from the former, his conception of Man as a *zoon politikon* and the *polis* as an organic totality that comes before its members, from the latter, his conception of 'general will' as a reality that is substantially different from the mere addition of individual wills or of the will of most. Both Hegel and Marx consider the individual as an essentially social being that develops while living with others and that can only be self-fulfilled within an intersubjective structure. Life with others is a reality in itself and a premise for individual development. For them the common interest is superior to and irreducible to the current particular interests of a civil society and freedom in the community is a precondition of individual freedom" (p. 161). Unfortunately, like in most of his work, the reference to Spinoza is missing, although he is a crucial predecessor of all materialist conceptions that question the liberal dichotomy that opposes the individual to a collectivity.

2 Žižek's Lacanian reading of "How did Marx invent the symptom?" in *The Sublime Object of Ideology* (1989) is also present at this point, when he shows that for Marx the constitution of the subject through specular recognition with the other was very clear (p. 18). This way commodity fetishism implies the substantialization of the subject ("an effect of the network of relations") that was believed to be independent from the social relations that constituted him (Marx gives the example of the King (p. 20)). This is in order to show that the bond of serfdom in capitalism underwent a complex web of relations that did not simply substitute the relations among people by relations among things, as it is generally affirmed, but rather that it repressed some and thus transformed the others (as in hysterical conversion), maintaining the idealisation and the belief of freedom in the ignorance of the symptom (the point of subversion of all bourgeois liberties: the need of the worker to sell *freely* his work for a livelihood). Žižek's quote summarizes this: "With the establishment of bourgeois society, the relations of domination and servitude are repressed: formally, we are apparently concerned with free subjects whose interpersonal relations are discharged of all fetishism; the repressed truth – that of the persistence of domination and servitude – emerges in a symptom which subverts the ideological appearance of equality, freedom, and so on. This symptom, the point of emergence of the truth about social relations, is precisely the 'social relations between things'" (p. 22).

3 Althusser mocks the naive freedom that comes with liberal ideology and defines the subject as constituted by ideology, almost mockingly repeating the term "freely": "the individual *is interpellated as a (free) subject in order that he shall submit freely to the commandments of the Subject, i.e. in order that he shall (freely) accept his subjection*, i.e. in order that he shall make the gestures and actions of his subjection 'all by himself'. *There are no subjects except by and for their subjection*. That is why they 'work all by themselves'" (Althusser, 1970, p. 269).

4 In my own reading of Lacan I try to show the mutual dependence of psychoanalysis, philosophy, and politics. The following text can be reviewed for further information: Farrán (2014, 2018, 2021).

## Further reading

Foucault, M. (1978). *The Courage of the Truth. The Government of the Self and Others II*, G. Burchell (Trans.). New York: Palgrave Macmillan, 2011.

Spinoza, B. (1677). *Ethics Proved in Geometrical Order*, M. Silverthorne (Trans.). Cambridge: Cambridge University Press, 2018.

## References

Althusser, L. (1970). Ideology and Ideological State Apparatuses. In: *On the Reproduction of Capitalism* (pp. 232–271), G. M. Goshgarian (Trans.). London: Verso, 2014.

Badiou, A. (1982). *Theory of the Subject*, B. Bosteels (Trans.). London: Continuum.

Cassin, B. (1994). Eleutheria. In: B. Cassin, et al. (Eds.). *Dictionary of Untranslatables: A Philosophical Lexicon* (pp. 250–256), E. Apter, J. Lezra & M. Wood (Trans.). Cambridge: Princeton University Press, 2014.

Farrán, R. (2014). *Badiou y Lacan: el anudamiento del sujeto*. Buenos Aires: Prometeo.

Farrán, R. (2018). *Nodaléctica: un ejercicio de pensamiento materialista*. Buenos Aires: La Cebra.

Farrán, R. (2021). *La razón de los afectos: populismo, feminismo, psicoanálisis*. Buenos Aires: Prometeo.

Lambruschini, P. (2017). Sobre la libertad. Un contrapunto entre Hegel y Marx. In: *Izquierdas*, 34: 159–182.

Žižek, S. (1989). *The Sublime Object of Ideology*. London: Verso.

# Chapter 9

# History

*Adrian Johnston*

—Ara.: تاريخ —Chi.: 歷史 —Fre.: *Histoire* —Ger.: *Geschichte* —Ita.: *Storia* —Jap.: 歴史 —Port.: *História* —Rus.: *История* —Spa.: *Historia* —Tur.: *Tarih*

→ *Imperialism*; *Master/tyrant*; *Materialism*; *Proletarian*

Jacques Lacan never tired of reminding his variegated audiences that he was a psychoanalyst whose teachings are addressed first and foremost to other analysts and analysts-in-training. In line with this, the Freudian field is the Alpha and Omega of Lacan's reflections regarding an incredibly wide range of topics related to nearly every discipline and concern within the expanses of human knowledge and culture. The topic of history is no exception. As with so many other topics, what Lacan has to say about history, as both a discipline and this discipline's explanatory jurisdictions, begins and ends with psychoanalysis. He muses both about the implications of Sigmund Freud's discoveries for the interpretation of historical phenomena and about what lessons history holds for the theory and practice of analysis.

In the 1955 *écrit*, *Variations on the Standard Treatment*, Lacan goes so far as to grant that, "The modern notion of history will be [...] necessary to the analyst if he is to understand the function of history in the subject's individual life" (*VST*, p. 299). Indeed, for Lacanian psychoanalysis, the subject of analysis, the analysand with his/her speaking unconscious subjectivity, "is as such historicized from one end to the other" (*SII*, 01.06.55, p. 255). This subject's very "soul" (*l'âme*) is "constituted by the history of a word" (or the words of a "discourse" [*discours*]) (*YG*, p. 626). When it comes to the analysand as subject, "it is only the perspective of history and of recognition that allows a definition of what counts for the subject" (*SI*, 27.01.54, p. 35). His/her symptoms crystalize an entire history (*SV*, 18.06.58, p. 440). Or, as Lacan puts it in his key 1953 manifesto *The Function and Field of Speech and Language in Psychoanalysis*, "What we teach the subject to recognize as his unconscious is his history" (*FFS*, p. 217). Furthermore, he points out that a broad base of socio-cultural historical knowledge was crucial to Freud as an analytic thinker and clinician (*FT*, p. 362).

Conversely, the field of history cannot but be reciprocally altered by being put into dialogue with psychoanalysis. On the one hand, Lacan readily concedes, speaking as an analyst, that, "we always have a lot to learn from the history of signifiers" (*SV*, 20.11.57, p. 46) – with etymology being one of the historical disciplines Lacan has in mind as crucial to Freudian analysis (although, for Lacan (*SII*, 15.06.55, p. 285), language is just as much saturated with history as history is saturated with language). Yet, on the other hand, the Lacanian theory of the signifier promises in turn to instruct a history bound up with mediums of signification a thing or two—"*man's relationship to the letter* [...] calls history itself into question" (*YG*, p. 623).

A now-standard periodization of Lacan's teaching, one pioneered by Jacques-Alain Miller and Alain Badiou, distinguishes between an early (1930s–1940s), middle (1950s), and late (1960s–1970s) Lacan. Like nearly all such chronological schemas, this neat-and-clean partitioning of the Lacanian intellectual odyssey into distinct phases risks concealing at least as much as it reveals. Nonetheless, this particular periodization is not without its illuminating virtues. My reconstructions below of the various things Lacan says about history reinforce the impression of a palpable difference specifically between the middle- and late-period Lacan. The Lacan of the 1950s, with his "return to Freud" via Saussurian structuralism, characteristically relies on his register of the Symbolic in articulating a theory of history valid both within and beyond psychoanalysis. In this context, the knowledge-domain of history and its objects of inquiry are seen to be mediated by linguistic structures and dynamics as per a distinctively Freudian account of language.

However, beginning in the 1960s, Lacan's examination of history shifts from its being situated at the intersection of Freudianism and structuralism (as in the 1950s) to becoming dominated by issues arising at the crossroads between psychoanalysis and Marxism. This is likely a result of the confluence of two factors: one, the late Lacan's promotion of the register of the Real, a register he sometimes associates with materiality in several senses, to a position of equal or greater importance *vis-à-vis* the Symbolic (with the latter register previously having enjoyed a certain hegemony because of the middle-Lacan's structuralist leanings); and, two, Lacan coming to feel an obligation to respond to Marxist ideas and preoccupations thanks to the influences of contemporaneous events and interlocutors. Such intertwined influences as Freudo-Marxism, May '68, and Louis Althusser and his Maoist students at the *École Normale Supérieure* (ENS) inspire the late Lacan to assess the possible interfacings of analysis and historical materialism.

The 1950s-Lacan, in line with his more classically structuralist Freud-*avec*-Saussure programme, insists upon the Symbolic nature of history. That which is historical is transmitted in and by signifiers. As narrative, history unfurls as nothing other than chains of signifiers. History is what gets recorded within the Symbolic register, what receives recognition and memorialization by big Others as symbolic orders (originally as patriarchal sociolinguistic systems) (*SI*, 19.05.54,

p. 197). As Lacan sweepingly asserts in *Seminar III*, "all history is by definition symbolic" (16.11.55, p. 13). This insistence upon history as Symbolic persists in Lacan's teaching beyond the 1950s (*SVIII*, 21.12.60, p. 78; *SIX*, 20.06.62; *DTC*, pp. 21–22).

The correlative flip side of the structuralist Lacan's reduction of history to signifiers is his pronounced distaste for, or even dismissal of, references to anything prehistorical *qua* preceding recorded history. In *Seminar III*, Lacan curtly remarks, "I'm not interested in prehistory" (*SIII*, 27.06.56, p. 306). History as such is, for Lacan, born with the signifier (*SXIII*, 08.12.65). Hence, whatever preceded this birth, what came before linguistic recording, can be only one of two things for speaking subjects always-already entangled in and mediated by symbolic orders: either the void of an unknowable "x" or a projection backwards from the present onto this forever-lost-and-inaccessible past of confabulations, fictions, just-so stories, myths, etc.[1]

The (seemingly) prehistorical, under the shadow of the retroactivity of the Symbolic colouring everything related to it by the *parlêtre*, must appear as anticipating properly sociolinguistic elements, as already being made in the image of signifying and recorded history (*SPT*, p. 392). In a Kantian-style critical gesture, Lacan forbids as epistemologically out of bounds both phylogenetic inquiries into the origins of language as well as ontogenetic hypotheses about the preverbal psyches and experiences of persons, including analysands (*SIR*, p. 17). This brings him into conflict not only with certain psychoanalytic figures such as Sándor Ferenczi (a wild phylogenetic speculator) and Melanie Klein (an equally bold ontogenetic speculator). It also puts Lacan at odds with Freud himself, who, from time to time, indulged in speculations about both phylogenetic as well as ontogenetic prehistories prior to the advent or acquisition of language.

In *Seminar IV*, the middle-period Lacan makes explicit something implicit in his treatment of the subject of history throughout the first three years of *Le Séminaire*: his reliance on Freud's concept of "screen memories" [*Deckerinnerungen*]. Freud, in the concluding paragraph of his 1899 essay devoted to this concept, ventures that, "It may indeed be questioned whether we have any memories at all *from* our childhood: memories *relating to* our childhood may be all that we possess" (Freud, 1899, p. 322). For Lacan, and in an implicit reversal of Ernst Haeckel's "ontogeny recapitulates phylogeny", what holds for the individual's life history also holds for collective social history. Historical memory always deals with the past-as-presently-recollected, rather than with a pure past-in-itself as it really was. As Lacan puts it in *Seminar I*, "History is not the past. History is the past in so far as it is historicised in the present – historicised in the present because it was lived in the past" (*SI*, 13.01.54, p. 12).

For the sake of exactitude, it should be noted in passing that the Lacan of the mid-1950s actually distinguishes between "memory" [*mémoire*] and "remembering" [*remémoration*] (Johnston, 2005, pp. 44–45). In *Seminar II*, he contrasts, on the one hand, memory as an organism's manner of retaining changes to its functioning induced by previous experiences, with, on the other hand, remembering as the Symbolic's chains of signifying elements on their own encoding and preserving an enduring order and its laws of operation (*SII*, 11.05.55, pp. 218–219). Remembering is the retention of the past in and by signifiers as a matter separate from any living mind's capacity, with its sentience or sapience, for holding onto and recalling prior experiences. Both the unconscious-structured-like-a-language and history proper *qua* Symbolic fundamentally are about remembering rather than memory for the Lacan of the Saussurian return to Freud. When I use the English word "memory" below, especially in connection with Symbolic history, it usually is meant to designate Lacanian *remémoration* (and not *mémoire*).

That noted, when the Lacan of the first seminar quoted a moment ago says "historicised in the present because it was lived in the past", he alludes to a thesis occasionally surfacing in his work. According to this thesis, the past that can be accessed as history in the present is accessible thus because this past itself, during its own present, already is historicized as it transpires in its own moment of initially occurring. This thesis is the conclusion of two premises: first, to be set down in signifiers is to be historicized through being Symbolically recorded in forms subsequently retrievable, at least in principle, in the future; second, Symbolically mediated speaking subjects live their lives always in the process of rendering themselves and their experiences in the guise of signifiers.

Therefore, Lacan concludes, such subjects are continually historicizing themselves from moment to moment during the very flow of their ongoing existences (*FFS*, p. 217). In *The Function and Field of Speech and Language in Psychoanalysis*, Lacan states, "Events are engendered in a primal historicization – in other words, history is already being made on the stage where it will be played out once it has been written down, both in one's heart of hearts and outside" (FFS, p. 216). Later in the same *écrit*, he likewise speaks of "the constitutive subjectivity of the primal historicization in which events are humanized" (*FFS*, p. 238). The 1957 *écrit, Psychoanalysis and Its Teaching* similarly describes analysis as concerned with the "history of a life lived as history" (*PIT*, p. 366). And, *Seminar XVI* relatedly proposes that human history is the history of humans dealing with history (27.11.68).

Picking back up the thread of the role of the Freudian account of memory in Lacan's conceptions of history, Freud's screen memories and the generalizations he makes about all memory on their basis involve another notion already in place at this early point in his career, namely, "deferred action" (*Nachträglichkeit*, which becomes Lacan's *après-coup*). In line with this notion, historical recollection, whether on the order of ontogeny or phylogeny, always brings with it the effects of the present retroactively altering the past. In a certain sense, all histories are histories of the present. Starting in his early seminars, Lacan (*SI*, 13.01.54, p. 14; 27.01.54, p. 42) recurrently emphasizes just this. What historical thinking often takes for discovered memories of the past are really misrecognized aspects of this thinking, aspects retrojected by it into a supposed preceding time (*SXIX*, 17.05.72, p. 158). With the history of any given content of the past being a matter of a series of retroactions on this content by subsequent times which themselves form a historical sequence, any "history of x" needs to be redoubled by a "history of the history of x" taking into account the historical unfolding of "x"'s successive historicizations (*SXV*, 21.02.68).

The early Lacan elevates the historical dynamic of the retroaction of the present on the past to an absolutely central position in the subjectivity of the *parlêtre*—"The subject's centre of gravity is this present synthesis of the past which we call history" (*SI*, 27.01.54, p. 36). This Lacan, in line with his Saussurian recasting of psychoanalysis, grounds Freud's *Nachträglichkeit* in the structuralist theory of the signifier (as itself a rendition of the Freudian "ideational representation" (*Vorstellung*)). What the founder of psychoanalysis reveals through an examination of the workings of memory, this temporal dynamic of a backward-flowing action of the after upon the before, Lacan ascribes to the logic of signifying chains. To take the most elementary example, in any "S is P" sentence, its post-copula predicate-term ($P$), with the arrival of the punctuation point of the sentence's period at its end, retroactively determines the status of its pre-copula subject-term ($S$). Indeed, for Lacan, this *après-coup* dimension of signifiers' logic is what makes history, precisely as Symbolic, always retroactive.

In the 1907 paper *Creative Writers and Day-Dreaming*, Freud brings the temporal category of the future into his considerations of the reciprocal interactions between past and present already delineated in his earlier reflections regarding memory. With respect to fantasies (including daydreams), Freud (1907) observes:

> they fit themselves in to the subject's shifting impressions of life, change with every change in his situation, and receive from every fresh active impression what might be called a "date-mark." The relation of a phantasy to time is in general very important. We may say that it hovers, as it were, between three times – the three moments of time which our ideation involves. Mental work is linked to some current impression, some provoking occasion in the present which has been able to arouse one of the subject's major wishes. From there it harks back to a memory of an earlier experience (usually an infantile one) in which this wish was fulfilled; and it now creates a situation relating to the future which represents a fulfilment of the wish. What it thus creates is a day-dream or phantasy, which carries about it traces of its origin from the occasion which provoked it and from the memory. Thus past, present and future are strung together, as it were, on the thread of the wish that runs through them.
>
> (pp. 147–148)

He soon adds that, "the wish makes use of an occasion in the present to construct, on the pattern of the past, a picture of the future" (Freud, 1907, p. 148). Insofar as the present is (also) the continual influx and arrival of the future, the notion of the retroaction of the present on the past (i.e., the *Nachträglichkeit* operative for the pre-1907 Freud in the two-trauma model of hysteria, mnemic re-transcriptions, screen memories, and the dream-work)[2] already tacitly entails what Freud here makes manifest in 1907. The past remains permanently open to being rewritten by countless future times.

In line with the Freud of *Creative Writers and Day-Dreaming*, Lacan too stresses the crucial role of the future in historical phenomena both analytic and extra-analytic. With reference to Freud's German, he emphasizes that history has to do not with "*Entwicklung*"—this would be "development" as a linear chronological movement, a one-way progression from past to present, through a successive series of phases/stages—but, rather, with "*Geschichte*" [history] (*SI*, 07.04.54, p. 157). "*Geschichte*" hints at the importance of the future through its linguistic links with such other German words as "*schicken*" (to send) and "*Schicksal*" (vicissitude as "destiny" *qua* a not-limitless range of determinate possibilities to come) (*SII*, 08.12.54, p. 43). The post/pseudo-Freudian tendency to turn psychoanalysis into a developmental psychology concerned with a hierarchy of the phases/stages of an *Entwicklung* ignores and eclipses Freud's replacement of a simplistic image of time as unidirectional linear chronology with a much more subtle and sophisticated model of temporality involving multi-directional interactions between past, present, and future.

For Lacan, the subject of Freudian *Geschichte* is caught within a complex dance between the past and the future. Psychoanalysts commonly are assumed to be obsessed with the past (patients' bad childhoods, etc.). Against this assumption, Lacan maintains that, if anything, the future is privileged by analysts in their labours (*SI*, 07.04.54, p. 157). More precisely, he foregrounds the tense of the future anterior:

> What is realized in my history is neither the past definite as what was, since it is no more, nor even the perfect as what has been in what I am, but the future anterior as what I will have been, given what I am in the process of becoming.
> (*FFS*, p. 247)

Throughout his career, Lacan (*SIII*, 15.02.56, p. 156; 18.04.56, p. 203; *SIX*, 24.01.62; *SX*, 12.12.62, p. 62) repeatedly reflects on the place of history in the analytic cure. In his view, all forms of psychopathology dealt with by analysis, from neurotic to psychotic pathologies, could be said to involve missing or non-integrated signifiers in subjects' histories (whether these signifiers are lacking due to repression, disavowal, foreclosure, or other defence mechanisms). The middle-period Lacan's notion of "full speech" brings with it the idea that analysis heals by enabling analysands verbally to fill in the gaps of their life-historical narratives made by the blows of repressions and/or other defences (*SV*, 08.01.58, p. 136). Indeed, for this Lacan, "The unconscious is the chapter of my history that is marked by a blank or occupied by a lie: it is the censored chapter" (*FFS*, p. 215). In overcoming analysands' defensive forgetfulness and assisting them in (re-)finding the missing signifiers in the chains of their histories, analysis, as "the talking cure", transforms their histories by working in and through the languages in which these histories are narrated and re-narrated (*IL*, p. 438).

Even during the 1950s supremacy of the signifier, and despite this middle period's wholesale subsumption of history under the register of the Symbolic, aspects of history evoking the register of the Real already come to light. In *Seminar I*, Lacan acknowledges that, "Integration into history evidently brings with it the forgetting of an entire world of shadows which are not transposed into symbolic existence" (*SI*, 19.05.54, p. 192). At both the ontogenetic and the phylogenetic levels, this acknowledgement suggests that the genesis of linguistically recorded history brings with it a sort of primal repression (*Urverdrängung*), rendering whatever came before this genesis (i.e., prehistory) an inaccessible Real (as "an entire world of shadows") (*SVIII*, 31.05.61, p. 336).

Likewise, and again already during the era of Lacan's more classically structuralist orientation, traumas are seen to show up as holes in the fabric of the speaking subject's life-historical tapestries (*SI*, 19.05.54, p. 197; *SIII*, 25.01.56, p. 104). As such, traumas, these brutally lawless contingencies, are another Real relative to Symbolic history. The gaps, shadows, and holes marking both primal and secondary repressions as well as traumas (not to mention death too) (*FFS*, pp. 262–263) cause historical narratives' chains of signifiers to be punctuated by recurring returns of these negative factors. These instances of the Real are responsible for certain repetitions traversing the sequences of subjects' Symbolic histories (*SXVI*, 04.06.69).

In line with the impression of a shift in Lacan's thinking at the end of the 1950s and beginning of the 1960s, *Seminar VII* contains some pivotal statements by Lacan about history indicating changes of mind on his part. One moment therein is emblematic of this. In the 11 May 1960 session of the seventh seminar, Lacan approvingly refers to a book he was then in the middle of reading: Jean-Paul Sartre's (1960) *Critique of Dialectical Reason*. Of course, this book is the centrepiece of the later Sartre's partial, qualified conversion to Marxism. Lacan's comments on this occasion praise the Sartrean concept of scarcity, with its materialist implication that human history is organized around zero-sum struggles for control of limited resources and goods (*SVII*, 11.05.60, pp. 226–227).

Lacan makes similar references to the *Critique of Dialectical Reason* in *Seminar X* (14.11.62, pp. 7-8; 28.11.62, pp. 33–34). And, already in the *écrit*, The Situation of Psychoanalysis and the Training of Psychoanalysts in 1956, he claims that Freud's materialism, unlike "naturalist materialism", contains within itself distinctively human (i.e., non-natural) Symbolic history (*SPT*, p. 390). This claim, whether intentionally or not, echoes Marx's contrast, in the first of his eleven *Theses on Feuerbach* (*TOF*), between his own materialism and a "contemplative" materialism running from the ancient Greek atomists to Ludwig Feuerbach.

The combination of Lacan's mid-1960s stay at the ENS coupled with the impact of May '68 leads Lacan, starting in *Seminar XVI*, to deepen his engagement with Karl Marx and Marxism. During this same time, he also draws upon his Kojévian background so as to make Marxist-pleasing references to how the labouring slaves of G.W.F. Hegel's "Lordship and Bondage" chapter of the *Phenomenology of Spirit* are the real subjects who truly make history (*SXVI*, 23.04.69; *SXVII*, 11.02.70, pp.

79–80; 10.06.70, pp. 170–172; *PIT*, p. 372). In *Seminar XVI*, Lacan leans heavily on the Althusserian version of Marx (especially as per 1965's *Reading Capital*), with its structuralization of historical materialism mobilized against "historicist" depictions of Marxism. Doing so enables Lacan's earlier account of history as Symbolic to seem to be squared with historical materialism—"History such as it is included in historical materialism appears to me to conform strictly to structural exigencies" (*SXVI*, 20.11.68). As part of the later Lacan's crediting of Marx with having invented the specifically psychoanalytic concept of the symptom *avant la lettre* (*SXVIII*, 16.06.71), the Lacan of *Seminar XVII* proposes that Marx's historical materialism interprets historical events in a manner akin to how analytic interpretation addresses analysands' symptoms (03.12.69, p. 204).

During the 1970s, Lacan adds some additional twists and caveats to his reading of Marx and the Marxist tradition. In *Seminar XX*, he recasts Marxism as a "gospel" of a new history (09.01.73, p. 30).[3] Historical materialism is here portrayed as prophetic rather than explanatory or predictive. To be more precise, Lacan argues that if Marxism is "true", this will be a matter of it ushering in a new history *à venir*. The "truth" of Marxism resides not in its ability accurately to decode and describe the past up through the present, but, instead, in its power to change the future of social history. Put differently, Marxist historical materialism will have been true—this would be a truth in the temporal key of the future anterior—if it succeeds at remaking subsequent history in its own image and according to its own visions (*SXXV*, 20.12.77; *ST*, p. 738).

In the 1957 *écrit The Instance of the Letter in the Unconscious, or Reason Since Freud*, Lacan declares himself to be agnostic in adjudicating between, on the one hand, his "In the beginning was the Word" of the signifiers inaugurating history *qua* Symbolic and, on the other hand, Marxism's "In the beginning was the Deed" of labour as per historical materialism (*IL*, p. 414). Even during his later turning of more serious and sympathetic attention to Marxism, he still evinces some ambivalence and hesitations *vis-à-vis* the Marxist tradition. As I will argue in a moment, Lacan's reservations apropos historical materialism would qualify, but not rule out, a Lacanian embrace of Marxism.

In *Seminar XII*, Lacan expresses scepticism apropos more economistic permutations of Marxism. In particular, he is suspicious of a story about human history writ large according to which economic laws rule this history in the same way that physical laws rule the material universe. Lacan worries that, as with Laplace's demon in physics, such economic history in Marxism renders everything under the historical sun predictably played out in advance (*SXII*, 19.05.65). Similarly, in *Le savoir du psychanalyste*, he indicates, after reminding his listeners about Marx's anticipation of the analytic concept of the symptom, that analysis envisions a different dialectical dynamic to history than that put forward by historical materialism (*PAM*, 02.12.71). But, alas, Lacan does not specify the precise contours of this other historical dialectic tied to Freud's findings.

As the immediately preceding already hints, Lacan would object to any Marxism presupposing or positing a teleological organization of history. Indeed, he overtly rejects any picturing of history as a "linear evolution" (*SXIII*, 19.01.66). He casts doubt on anyone purporting to possess knowledge of the ostensible laws of history (*FFS*, p. 216). And, Lacan vehemently repudiates associating history's unfolding with providential development (*ST*, p. 743).

At one point in *Seminar VIII* Lacan combines his opposition to history-as-teleology with an equally fierce opposition to history-as-hermeneutics. The acts marking and making history are not governed by an undertow of purpose (as per teleology) and/or meaning (as per hermeneutics) (*SVIII*, 31.05.61, p. 336). *Seminar XI* points to the Holocaust as one horribly massive refutation of a hermeneutic imputation of meaning to the arc of human history (no history, as well as no poetry, after Auschwitz) (29.04.64, p. 153; 24.06.64, p. 275). *Seminar XV, contra* the commonplace view of history as meaningful, portrays it instead as a mere hectic "crush" (*bousculade*) of aleatory encounters without underlying rhyme or reason (*SXV*, 24.01.68). Then, in the twentieth seminar, Lacan bluntly states, regarding historical investigation as a search for meaning, "I can't stand [...] History". The hermeneutical History-with-capital-H is, for this Lacan, a barely disguised form of religious faith in a benevolent God, no more, no less (*SXX*, 16.01.73, pp. 45–46).

Admittedly, certain instances of vulgar Marxism are guilty of turning historical materialism into a teleology and/or hermeneutics (as with both the Second International and Stalinism). Yet, starting with Marx himself, the more sophisticated and thoughtful elements of the Marxist tradition carefully avoid such vulgarities in handling history. For example, two variants of Marxism with which Lacan is familiar, those of the later Sartre and Althusser, share in common, despite their major differences, the opening up of historical materialism to contingencies disrupting the reign of any meaningful purpose in social history. That is to say, there are permutations of historical materialism eschewing both long-term teleologies and an underlying "meaning of it all" to history. These would be the permutations offering the greatest degree of compatibility with Lacanianism, given Lacan's views about history.

At several points, the later Lacan associates history with hysteria— "history is hysteria" (*SXXV*, 20.12.77). He even enshrines this association in the neologisms "*hystoire*" (*PEA*), "*hystorique*" (*SXXIV*, 14.12.76), "*hystorisation*", and "*hystoriser*" (*PEA*). But, what does Lacan's equation of history with hysteria (as "hystory") actually mean? What is he getting at here?

My best guess is that Lacan has in mind how hysteria, on Freud's account of it, involves a "*proton pseudos*" as a falsification of the remembered past (Freud, 1895, pp. 352–359). This same early Freud, in his *Studies on Hysteria* co-authored with Josef Breuer, famously proposes that "*Hysterics suffer mainly from reminiscences*" (Freud, 1893, p. 7). One ought to note that the hysterical subject suffers not from the past as such, but, rather, from "reminiscences" as subsequent recollections of this past. These recollections introduce symptom-generating distortions, fictions, lies, and mistakes into the hysteric's life-historical record.

With an awareness of memory's proneness to falsifications as emphasized in Freud's model of memory and related processes, Lacan, throughout his work, warns of historical narratives' unacknowledged reliances on fantasy, fiction, folklore, myth, and the like (*SIV*, 26.06.57, p. 391). I suspect that Lacan believes this psychoanalytic recasting of history as hystory contains two crucial lessons. First, histories, instead of being seen as furnishing direct insights into how things objectively were, in and of themselves, must always be construed as consisting at least as much of fantasies and fictions projected back onto the past as of the realities and facts of the past *an sich*. Second, just as Freud (1897, pp. 259–260) quickly comes to appreciate that fantasmatic, fictional pseudo-memories can have just as much of an impact on the psyche as real, factual memories, the confabulations and fabrications of Lacanian hystory shape the contours of actual history as itself—for Lacan, a history of how humans narrate and cope with history (in part through falsities, lies, and myths).

Finally, Lacan, across the arc of his intellectual itinerary, walks a fine line between transcendental and historical sensibilities. More precisely, he seeks to incorporate historical dimensions into psychoanalytic metapsychology without, for all that, simply historicizing this metapsychology without remainder. Lacan's fidelity to Freud includes resistance to reducing everything analysis puts forward as holding for the human psyche in all times and places to historically localized and transient constructs. Arguably this puts him in the good company of, among others, Hegel and Marx.

The more transcendentalist side of Lacan proposes that such entities as fantasy and desire (or, more broadly, the fundaments of the libidinal economy) function as trans-historical motors of the movement of history itself (*SVI*, 10.06.59, p. 434; *SVII*, 04.05.60, p. 209). Yet, the more historicist side of Lacan is willing, for instance, to go so far as to emphasize the historically emergent character of the very foundations of classical bivalent logic, starting with its law of identity (A = A) (*SIX*, 06.12.61; *FT*, p. 358). Lacan's oscillations between transcendentalism and historicism leave a lot still to be done both in terms of interpreting and reconstructing his own theoretical framework as well as in terms of re-examining Lacanianism and Marxism with respect to each other.

## Notes

1 See Johnston (2013, pp. 59–77).
2 See Johnston (2005, pp. 5–22).
3 See Adrian Johnston, *Infinite Greed: Money, Marxism, Psychoanalysis*, New York: Columbia University Press (under review).

## Further reading

Althusser, A. (1966). Three Notes on the Theory of Discourses. In: F. Matheron (Ed.), *The Humanist Controversy and Other Writings* (pp. 33–84), G. M. Goshgarian (Trans.). London: Verso, 2003.
Copjec, J. (1994). *Read My Desire: Lacan Against the Historicists*. Cambridge: MIT Press.

Johnston, A. (2012). On Deep History and Lacan. In: *Journal of European Psychoanalysis*, 32: 91–121.
Žižek, S. (1997). The Abyss of Freedom. In: S. Žižek & F. W. J. Schelling (Eds.), *The Abyss of Freedom/Ages of the World* (pp. 1–104), Ann Arbor: University of Michigan Press.

## References

Freud, S. (1893). Studies on Hysteria. In: *The Standard Edition of the Complete Psychological Works of Sigmund Freud* (Vol. II, pp.1-310), J. E. Strachey (Trans.). London: The Hogarth Press, 2001.
Freud, S. (1895). Project for a Scientific Psychology. In: *The Standard Edition of the Complete Psychological Works of Sigmund Freud* (Vol. I, pp. 281–393), J. E. Strachey (Trans.). London: The Hogarth Press, 2001.
Freud, S. (1897). Letter 69 Extracts from the Fliess Papers. In: *The Standard Edition of the Complete Psychological Works of Sigmund Freud* (Vol. I, pp. 173–280), J. E. Strachey (Trans.). London: The Hogarth Press, 2001.
Freud, S. (1899). Screen Memories. In: *The Standard Edition of the Complete Psychological Works of Sigmund Freud* (Vol. III, pp. 299–322), J. E. Strachey (Trans.). London: The Hogarth Press, 2001.
Freud, S. (1907). Creative Writers and Day-Dreaming. In: *The Standard Edition of the Complete Psychological Works of Sigmund Freud* (Vol. IX, pp. 141–154), J. E. Strachey (Trans.). London: The Hogarth Press, 2001.
Johnston, A. (2005). *Time Driven: Metapsychology and the Splitting of the Drive*. Evanston: Northwestern University Press.
Johnston, A. (2013). *Prolegomena to Any Future Materialism, Volume One: The Outcome of Contemporary French Philosophy*. Evanston: Northwestern University Press.
Sartre, J.-P. (1960). *Critique of Dialectical Reason*, A. Sheridan (Trans.). London: Verso, 2004.

Chapter 10

# Ideology

*Natalia Romé*

—Ara.: ايديولوجيا —Chi.: 意識形態 —Fre.: *Idéologie* —Ger.: *Ideologie* —Ita.: *Ideologia* —Jap.: イデオロギー —Port.: *Ideologia* —Rus.: *Идеология* —Spa.: *Ideología* —Tur.: *İdeoloji*

→ *Automatism*; *Politics*; *Society*; *Superstructure*; *Uneasiness*

## Introduction

It cannot be said that the term *ideology* occupies a decisive place in Lacan's teaching. Instead, he appeals to it as part of the theoretical heritage of contemporary Western thought and of the French intellectual atmosphere of the 20th century (cf. Roudinesco, 1993; Descombes, 1979; Milner, 2002). In some cases in his work, the term acquires the characteristics of a concept (*SXIV*, 12.04.67); in others, it moves in the domain of a certain academic or politically informed common sense (*FPC*, 1950). But, in general, it is not the main object of a reflection but is rather mobilized in the name of an argument associated with other problems. This does not mean that its invocation is arbitrary or entirely irregular. On the contrary, it is possible to recognize in the Lacanian appeal of the category of *ideology* regularities that provide significant elements for understanding not only the dialogical threads that give shape to his thinking process and make it possible to recognize the inter-discourse that operates in the transmission of his teaching but also, and especially, to understand some central epistemological and conceptual threads. Beyond the diverse theoretical associations that this term raises, from historical materialism to linguistics and ethnology, it is possible to notice that its reference implies a certain "taking a stance" that we could call materialist, which means criticizing humanist, positivist, empiricist tendencies and mystified forms of thought. These forms are also associated with the interrogation for a non-metaphysical criterion of what is true and with distrust against any imaginary denial of the opacity of language.

This is by no means accidental. As Balibar argues, the term has a controversial philosophical genealogy that goes back to Bacon and Locke, and to two classic contrasting sources: the Platonic "forms" (*eide*) and the "simulacra" (*eidôla*) of Epicurean philosophy (Balibar, 1993). The positive development of the concept of ideology is associated, in the French tradition, with a practical exercise of criticism of the given order of beliefs or knowledge that make up what is usually called the conjuncture. Since its appearance in 1801 in the book *Élements d'Idéologie*, by Destutt de Tracy, the concept of *ideology* and its development formed a unit with practical operations of critique in a realistic or materialistic, anti-theological or anti-metaphysical sense, presented as a denunciation or an effort to understand the invisible threads that connect knowledge and power, philosophy and subordination. Thus, in the first developments concerning a *science of the genesis of ideas*, by Cabanis, in dialogue with Volney and Tracy, as well as in the writings of Auguste Comte in his *Cours de Philosophie Positive* of 1830, or as Émile Durkheim, in *Les Règles de la méthode sociologique*, of 1895, this category comes to name an intellectual effort aimed at establishing the *non-ideal causes* of ideas, individual or collective (Chauí, 2001, pp. 27–37; Quantin, 1987).

## The Marxist concept of ideology

The materialist position associated with the concept of *ideology* brings together, in Karl Marx, the critique of the 18th century mechanicist materialisms and that of the German idealist tradition, with a complex theory of history, guided by the epistemic principle of the primacy of practice over theory and the theoretical principle of the primacy of social relations of production. If we can find in this thought a basis for a positive theory of ideology, it is nevertheless necessary to underline that it is only produced as an effect of its controversial approach to particular ideological formations (Althusser, 1967, pp. 219–248).

In this sense, *The German Ideology* (*GI*), written with Friedreich Engels, is a milestone, where the double functioning of this category can be appreciated: on the one hand, as a concept of the constitutive mechanisms and contradictions in which a certain state of consciousness takes shape and functions socially, based on the conjunction between a certain social division of labour and what can be identified as intellectual difference, linked to the archaic or anthropological division between manual and intellectual labour (Balibar, 1993, pp. 35–56); on the other hand, *The German Ideology* puts forward that in order to have access to the history of social being, understood as the development of production and traversed by the social division of labour, it is necessary to settle accounts with the various forms of dominant ideology—the Hegelian in Germany, for instance. Critique (of the case) is thus a condition of knowledge and forms a unity with it: ideological formations imply an inversion of the real (as it operates in the Hegelian juridical-state universality) and an autonomization of intellectual products (as can be seen in the claim to universality of idealist philosophy), where the trace of the material and historical origin of ideas is lost, and their historical condition denied.

*The German Ideology* is a kind of critical theory of "social consciousness" (*Bewusstsein*), based on the historical conditions that determine its form with a causality that is eccentric to it. It is a theory intended to simultaneously understand the dependence of the forms of consciousness with respect to the social being (*Sein*) and the historical processes of its alienation; that is, of its becoming autonomous with respect to that being, causing an illusory world to emerge. History as the genesis of social consciousness that produces the abstraction of consciousness, offers a theory of misrecognition or illusion, which would be the reverse of the theory of knowledge, allowing a double approach to the ideological, as a social process and as a process of thought (Balibar, 1993). It is thus possible to locate in Marx a non-psychological and anti-humanist critical theory of consciousness, ungraspable in the terms of an interiority closed on itself and perfectly cut off from the transindividual dimension of history.

An epistemological critique and a theory of domination (where the concept of ideology is co-extensive with that of dominant ideology), which identifies dominance and universalisation, coexist in *The German Ideology*. This reveals an internal tension between two tendencies within the text itself that reinscribe its long controversial genealogy *eide/eidôla*. The critique of abstract units and their marking by the concrete contradictions that divide them is obstructed by a certain restitution of the abstract immediacy of the labour relationship with nature, which preceded the unequal division of labour and which may be restored once the latter has been abolished. Thus, we read a kind of inverted Platonism, where "the production of ideas, of conceptions, of consciousness, is at first directly interwoven with the material activity and the material intercourse of men—the language of real life [...] as the direct efflux of their material behaviour" (*GI*, p. 36). Therein lies the idealistic temptation of the Hegelian critique of *alienation* (pr. lat. *alienus*), inseparable from the *Philosophy of History*, understood as a reflective process of the Spirit behaving as a consciousness (cf. Hyppolite et al., 1970).

Perhaps this tension, in a somewhat irresolvable sense, lies at the basis of Marx's abandonment of the term *ideology* and its replacement by other categories, especially that of *fetishism*; although Engels will return to ideology in Ludwig Feuerbach and the End of Classical German Philosophy (1888).

## Fetishism

Marx returns to old questions to formulate them differently, on this occasion, within the framework of their inscription in the fabric of relations organized under the logic of the capitalist relationship of depriving the direct producers of their means of production. The critique of *alienation* takes on a new shift from an association of the problem of *ideology* with the political problem of domination, to the association of *fetishism* with the economic problem of value and exploitation. By reading fetishism in the phenomena of the social and subjective life of his European contemporaries, Marx, like Freud, marks a twist in the history of the term—which appears for the first time in Charles de Brosses's 1756 essay *Histoire des navigations aux terres australes*, referring to the ritual objects of civilizations considered primitive (Iacono, 1992). It questions the progressive temporality that orders cultural differences and the hierarchy of cults, organized according to the growing abstraction of their objects. The result of this critique of European positivist universality is a theory of material production and the transindividual consistency of the Universals or Ideas, which restores the inherent power of the "*phantasmagoria*" of the commodity, in the society that presumes to have freed itself from the enchantment of the world.

Previously mentioned in the *Rheinische Zeitung* and the *Grundrisse*, among others, it is in the first chapter of *Capital* where fetishism finds an original conceptual development associated with the commodity. It is defined there as the way in which a social relationship takes on the *phantasmagorical* form of a relationship between things. Inscribed in the framework of the theory of value, the concept of commodity fetishism assumes the open tensions around that of *ideology*, but advances beyond its limits, with a material, transindividual, and relational conception of social objectivity, where Marx assumes the specific social and subjective efficacy of the appearance order. Far from constituting a distorted perception of reality, fetishism is the way in which reality necessarily appears in the framework of capitalist social objectivity. It thus offers the possibility of thinking about the complexity of a double process, in which the becoming object of social relations—and of their subjective aspects—through a process of *reification* or objectification, paradoxically coincides with the generation of modes of subjection; that is, the production of "economic subjects" (owners, consumers, etc.) with respect to which empirical individuals are abstract. If this development maintains its dialogue with the critique of *alienation* (cf. Lukács, 1923; Marcuse, 1964), the crucial step Marx takes in *Capital* consists in his deduction of the fetishist investment from the logic of relational thirdness that supports his theory of value, on which structuralist interpretations will be based (Balibar, 1993; Milner, 2002). In this way, any restitution of the assumption of transparency of social relations, of labour, or of praxis is hindered (cf. Althusser, 2014).

## Uses in Lacan

Early on, Lacan mobilized the semantic universe of the theory of Marxist ideology, not always with rigorous references and sometimes in an ironic or critical way, where winks, assumptions, clarifications, and demarcations, even slips and failures, abound. Thus, the various mentions of the problem seem to take up again a dialogue with Marxism or with certain Marxists that has occurred, on occasion, offstage.

The term is invoked with a variety of meanings, but in general, is associated with a critique of different forms of idealism and humanism (*FPC*; *RA*; *SXVI*, 19.03.69). In this sense, Lacan is part of that long genealogy that we could call materialist—an adjective he soon received due to the Spinozist influences of his doctoral thesis, by René Crevel and Paul Nizan (Roudinesco, 1993, p. 52)— although he prefers to call his position "realistic" (*SXVI*, 30.04.69). This continuity seems, however, to be marked by a slide from an ambiguous and imprecise attitude towards Marxist thought to clearer references supported by the reading of Marx's writings. This path makes his approach to ideology grow in complexity and precision, from a vague and notional use to its consideration as a concept, consecrated in the conference *An Issue of Ones*, where Lacan risks a definition of what he understands by ideology and establishes a link with his theory of discourses (*AIO*, 04.05.72); possibly due to its rather cultural and social approach to the atmosphere of a certain French heterodox left in which PCF dissidents, surrealist artists, and other personalities have been gathering since the 1930s.

Since the 1950s, references to the term pivot between the Hegelian theory of *alienation* and the idea of universal abstraction and intellectual difference that run through *The German Ideology*. Thus, his critique of humanism can be read in *A Theoretical Introduction to the Functions of Psychoanalysis in Criminology*, with ironic references to "some Marxists" who fail to grasp the profound critique of idealism that lies in the concept of identification that, before aiming at the revelation of a content, strives to reconquer its form (*FPC*). Likewise, in *The Instance of the Letter in the Unconscious, or Reason Since Freud*, Lacan ironically counters the illusion of linguistic transparency that gravitates to a certain social and historical approach to language, where the evocation of certain passages of *The German Ideology* is quite palpable, as is his ludic reference to Stalin's famous refusal to think of language as a superstructure (*IL*; more about the Stalinist theory of language cf. Groys, 2005). In both cases, the reference to the field of the Marxist notion of ideology seems not so much an operation of reading as a critical intervention that aims to leave the supposedly historicist perspectives in the field of the imaginary, in accordance with both Lévi-Straussian commentaries on history and political thought, and with the debates framed in the *Annales School*.

In the 1960s this position changed. There is a more careful approach to the problem of ideology and fetishism, less concentrated on pointing out possible deviations and more interested in a theoretical reading of Marx's writings (*SXIV*, 10.05.67; *SXV*, 07.02.68). But the crucial point of the encounter is to be found in Lacan's reading of the first part of *Capital*, leading to the concept of surplus-*jouissance*. This theoretical encounter is registered in the first lecture of *Seminar XVI*, where Lacan not only seems to find in Marx a more complex treatment of the problem of discourse (*SXVI*, 13.11.68) but also a topology that anticipates his notion of *extimacy*: "What is this inside that seems to make completely enigmatic what is en-closed in it? Is it not, in his way, with respect to the essence of currency, a completely external inside?" (*SXVI*, 23.04.69). But sketches of this articulation were anticipated in *Seminar XIV*, where Lacan evoked the theory of value and flirted with that of reification, to finally adopt a structuralist reading of fetishism (*SXIV*, 12.04.67). In his lecture of 12 April 1967, Lacan leaves the invisible threads of his reading operation exposed by a parapraxis, when he attributes to Marx's *Philosophical Manuscripts* a sentence that corresponds to the introduction of *Das Wesen des Christentums* by Feuerbach, compiled in French by Althusser, whose introduction is included in the volume *Pour Marx* under the title *Philosophical Manuscripts* that Lacan reads and comments on with its author in his correspondence dated 12 October 1965 (cf. Althusser, 1993). During the same seminar, Lacan will offer a definition of the concept of ideology that evokes the Althusserian reading of *Capital* (1967), by affirming the symptomatic condition of truth and defining the symptom as the significance of the *discrepancies between the real and the ideology* and by stating that perception is the model of ideology and its screening in relation to reality.

The trajectory in which the category of ideology grows conceptually, in Lacan's reading of Marx, reaches its highest moment in 1972 when it is invoked to consolidate his concept of discourse: "this sort of structure that I have been designating with the term *discourse*. Through discourse, which is the pure and simple effect of language, a social bond is precipitated. […] is even what is conventionally known as *ideology*" (*AIO*, 04.05.72). In this case, Lacan suggests a possible association between his concept of University discourse and what Marxism criticizes as idealist philosophy, rediscovering the critical power that the Marxist category of ideology implies since *The German Ideology*.

## Further reading

Althusser, L. (2011). *On the Reproduction of Capitalism*, G. Goshgarian (Trans.). London: Verso, 2013.
Pêcheux, M. (1975). *Language, Semantics and Ideology. Stating the Obvious*, H. Nagpal (Trans.). London: Macmillan, 1982.
Žižek, S. (1989). *The Sublime Object of Ideology*. London: Verso, 1989.

## References

Althusser, L. (1967). Marxism and Humanism. In: *For Marx* (pp. 219–248), B. Brewster (Trans.). London: Verso, 2005.
Althusser, L. (1993). *Écrits sur la psychanalyse: freud et Lacan*. Paris: Stock/IMEC.
Althusser, L. (2014). *Philosophy for Non-Philosophers*, G. Goshgarian (Trans.). London: Bloomsbury, 2017.
Althusser, L., Balibar, É., Establet, R., Macherey, P. & Rancière, J. (1967). *Lire le capital*. Paris: PUF, 2008.
Balibar, É. (1993). *The Philosophy of Marx*, C. Turner (Trans.). London: Verso, 1995.
Chauí, M. (2001). *O que é ideologia*. São Paulo: Editora Brasiliense.
Descombes, V. (1979). *Modern French Philosophy*, L. Scott-Fox & J. Harding (Trans.). Cambridge: Cambridge University Press.
Engels, F. (1888). *Ludwig Feuerbach and the End of Classical German Philosophy*. Beijing: Foreign Languages Press, 1976.
Groys, B. (2005). *The Communist Postscript*. London: Verso, 2010.
Hyppolite, J. et al. (1970). *Hegel et la pensée moderne*. Paris: PUF.
Iacono, A. (1992). *Le fétichisme. Histoire d'un concept*. Paris: PUF.
Lukacs, G. (1923). *History and Class Consciousness: Studies in Marxist Dialectics*, R. Livingstone (Trans.). Cambridge: MIT Press, 1971.
Marcuse, H. (1964). *One-Dimensional Man: Studies in the Ideology of Advanced Industrial Society*. New York: Beacon Press.
Milner, J.-C. (2002). *Le périple structural figures et paradigme*. Paris: Verdier.
Quantin, P. (1987). *Les origines de l'idéologie*. Paris: Economica.
Roudinesco, E. (1993). *Lacan. Jacques Lacan: An Outline of a Life and History of a System of Thought*, B. Bray (Trans.). Oxford: Blackwell Publishers, 1999.

# Chapter 11

# Imperialism

*Livio Boni*

—Ara.: إمبريالية —Chi.: 帝國主義 —Fre.: *Impérialisme* —Ger.: *Imperialismus* —Ita.: *Imperialismo* —Jap.: 帝国主義 —Port.: *Imperialismo* —Rus.: *Империализм* —Spa.: *Imperialismo* —Tur.: *Emperyalizm*

→ *Bourgeoisie*; *Capitalism*; *Master/tyrant*; *Money*

The term "empire" occasionally appears in Lacan's Seminars from the 1950s, either in a metaphorical sense—to designate a hold and its extent (*SI*, 19.05.54, p. 196)—or referring to its meaning in Roman or Byzantine antiquity (*SV*, 11.12.57, p. 107). It is nevertheless not surprising that it is in *Seminar XVI* and *Seminar XVII*—where Lacan confronts, in his own way, Marx's concepts—that one finds the most significant mentions of the term, including, for instance, its explicit pairing with the category of imperialism.

Thus, in the session of 7 May 1969 (*SXVI*, 7.05.69), Lacan outlines a genealogy of the imperium as an emporium, as "an order of the Other thanks to which the real takes on the status of world, cosmos". Ancient science, he explains, relies on the possible "harmony" between "knowledge and power", hence the fact that the Empire in antiquity is presented as an ordering principle of the world, of extensibility of a rational "calculation"—of which the emporium is an essential organ, under the symbolic aegis of the One. These remarks echo the Heideggerian analysis of the Latin triumph of the ratio as "calculation", and Lacan insists that, consequently, one must be interested in the moments and places where "there is no counting", that is to say, the times where there is a fundamental disagreement between power (imperium) and the accounting order (emporium). In the same session, therefore, he changes the perspective quite unexpectedly and presents it almost accidentally when he is talking about the shift from the Roman Empire to post-colonial India:

> I have not yet gone to see it but there is, it appears, a film by Louis Malle on Calcutta. In it you see a great number of people dying of hunger. That is what the real is. Where people are dying of hunger, they die of hunger. There is nothing lacking. Why do people start talking about lack? Because they

formed part of an empire. Otherwise, it appears, there would not even be a Calcutta. Because it appears – I am not enough of a historian to know but I accept it because we are told that – without the requirements of this Empire there would have been no conurbation in this place. Modern empires allow their dimension of lack to manifest itself precisely in the fact that knowledge achieved a certain growth in them, no doubt a disproportionate one, with respect to the effects of power. The modern empire has also this property that everywhere it stretches its wings, this disconnection also appears. And it is uniquely in the name of this that one can make of the famine in India a motive to incite us to a subversion or a universal revision of something, the Real!

(*SXVI*, 13.11.68)

There are three propositions that emerge from these first assertions: the form of the Empire is a form of political rationality inherited from ancient metaphysics and their interest in the One as what brings harmony into the world (cosmos); modern Empires worsen the discrepancy between knowledge (counting/*compter*) and power (mastering/*maîtriser*); as this "disjunction" aggravates, it authorizes the revolutionary discourse, and for this discourse the imbalance is the real itself of the system.

It is possible to recognize here several correspondences with the Marxist conception of imperialism, traced by Lacan: the discontinuity between the empire-form linked to the slave mode of production, specific to the Empires of antiquity, and modern imperialism based on the accumulation by dispossession, inseparable from colonial conquest and the establishment of unequal development. One can also find in *Seminar XVII* the explicitly formulated idea according to which Marxian theory denominates a "real" point, in particular through the theory of surplus-value (*Mehrwert*), as an intrinsic point of imbalance of the capitalist order, where a certain knowledge (counting/*compter*) overdetermines power in the sense of the *arché* (beginning, origin). Lacan designates as an "essential turn" the passage of the function of symbolic distribution of pre-modern Empires: "the one who knows how to count can divide up, he distributes, and by definition the one who distributes is just. All empires are just"—"an open tear" that is introduced by the capitalist mode of production:

> it is a matter of defining how this disjunction operates, and to name it as such. So that people do not think it can be warded off in some episodic fashion or other by changing whoever is in power. To say that everything is all right because it is those who up to now were oppressed who are now going to exercise it, for example.
>
> (*SXVI*, 7.05.69)

Lacan consolidated this approach a year later in one of the last sessions of *Seminar XVII*, where, in the process of developing his theory of the four discourses, he returns to the anthropological transformation consisting in the progressive replacement of the discourse of the Master by the Capitalist discourse. He describes the transformation in terms that are translatable to Marxian language:

> Something changed in the Master's discourse at a certain moment in history. We are not going to bore ourselves finding out if it was because of Luther, or Calvin, or some traffic or other of ships around Genoa, or in the Mediterranean Sea, or somewhere else, because the important point is that from a particular day on, surplus pleasure can be calculated, can be counted, totalised. Here what is called "the accumulation of capital" begins.
> (*SXVII*, 10.06.70, p. 177)

Therefore, from the moment when the politico-symbolic economy of *jouissance* is no longer organized in "*rerum concordia discors*" (See *SVII*, 4.05.60, p. 210) of the pre-capitalist imperial order, but in processes of accumulation that are both deeply asymmetrical and indebted to a strict counting, the discourse of the Master is gradually transposed, in the same de-counting (*décomptage*), into the production of surplus-value henceforth designating a surplus-enjoyment. Lacan declares that establishing the precise historical origin is not worth the trouble, hence favouring a *structural* analysis. It was a way to discard Fernand Braudel and Max Weber's hypotheses on the origin of capitalism and its "spirit". For the German sociologist, the anthropological-religious origin is inseparable from the Protestant Reformation and for the historian of the *École des Annales* the origin is linked to the competition between city-states and nation-states in the Mediterranean of the 15th century. However, the genealogy of capitalism is not of interest for Lacan, but rather its almost formal logic, centred on this point of the real, surplus-value, the fundamental "symptom" of capitalism for which Marx was the best clinician, as Lacan recognizes, while contesting the idea that the "truth" of such discovery implies the effective power of Marxist theory, that is to say, its political force. It is almost the opposite because the Capitalist discourse is dissociated from the discourse of the Master and places the real of surplus-value in an analytically incontestable position, which becomes difficult to conceive of dialectically. "Imperialism" becomes, therefore, the name which designates the "negative effects of such a mechanism", without being able to designate it in a more exhaustive and effective way:

> Do you not feel, in relation to what I stated earlier about the impotence to connect surplus value with the master's truth, that we are gaining ground here? I am not saying that the latter is decisive but the impotence of this junction is all of a sudden emptied out. Surplus value combines with capital – no problem, they are homogeneous, we are in the field of values. [...] What is striking and what no one seems to see is that from that moment on, by virtue of the fact that the clouds of impotence have been aired, the master signifier only appears even more unassailable precisely in its impossibility. Where is it? How can it be named? How can it be located, except, of course through

its murderous effects? Denounce imperialism? But how can this little mechanism be stopped?

(*SXVII*, 10.06.70, p. 178)

Therefore, if there was a definition of imperialism to be deduced from Lacan, it would designate not the reality of capitalism—which resides in the production of surplus-value—or even its symbolic status, because capitalism does not fit well within the old imperial figure of an incarnated master representing the point of ultimate harmony between counting (*comptage*) and authority, but rather only its pathological side, its harmful, possibly macroscopic, derived effects, as in the cases of the above-mentioned famines in India, but by no means does he get to the heart of the matter.

Everything seems to point to the fact that Lacan is recognizing and accentuating the internal division of the Marxian and Marxist paradigm, dividing it in an analytical level, able to rigorously name the object of a capitalist desire—surplus-value—and the level of practical ethics, or politics, where one targets pathological figures of this same "mechanism", almost forgetting that every nation-state has a certain degree of imperialism, whether it is properly colonial or internal:

> Beginning from the core, national units form out of the overall structure of the world-economy, as a function of the role they play in that structure in a given period. More exactly, they form against one another as competing instruments in the service of the core's domination of the periphery. This first qualification is a crucial one, because it substitutes for the "ideal" capitalism of Marx and, particularly, of the Marxist economists, a "historical capitalism" in which a decisive role is played by the early forms of imperialism and the articulation of wars with colonization. In a sense, every modern nation is a product of colonization: it has always been to some degree colonized or colonizing, and sometimes both at the same time.
> 
> (Balibar & Wallerstein, 1988, p. 89)

In other words, even though the Lacanian *insight* into the Marxist theory of imperialism is oblique—it proceeds from a topic of discourse—it agrees with the evolution of the category of imperialism in Marxist theorization. Marx designated at the beginning, the "highest stage of capitalism" (Lenin, 1917), whose actual expression were the wars between imperialist powers. In the second part of the 20th century, after the end of the colonial empires and World Wars, Marxism recognizes an intrinsic component of the logic of the State, including the socialist state, and therefore the slogan "Down with imperialism!" functions more like a performative denunciation than a true political identification.

That said, Lacan provides us with another clue in *The Other Side of Psychoanalysis*, where he envisages another meaning of imperialism, encompassing its ideological dimension and its relationship to colonialism:

> Very shortly after the last war [...] I took into analysis three people from the high country of Togo, who had spent their childhood there. Now, I was not able, in their analysis, to find any trace of tribal practices and beliefs. They had not forgotten them but they only knew them from the point of view of ethnography. It has to be said that everything was designed to separate it from them, given what they were, courageous little doctors who were trying to make their way into the medical hierarchy of France, and do not forget we were still at the colonial stage. What they knew about it then from the point of view of the ethnographer was more or less what you find in the newspapers, but their unconscious functioned according to the good old rules of the Oedipus complex. This was the unconscious that they had been sold along with the laws of colonisation, an exotic, regressive form of the discourse of the Master, in the face of the capitalism described as imperialism. Their unconscious was not that of their childhood memories – you could feel that – but their childhood was retroactively experienced in our *fam-il-ial* categories [...] I defy any analyst to contradict me, even if he were to go out into the field.
>
> (*SXVII*, 18.02.70, pp. 91–92)

Here it is possible to confirm the fact that imperialism, far from appearing as the *extreme version* of capitalism, constitutes for Lacan only an "exotic" and "regressive" form, that is, the form of colonialism. One could almost argue, paraphrasing and reversing Lenin's formula, that imperialism is here reduced to an "infantile disease" of capitalism. However, one should remember, especially in the prior quote, the weight that Lacan gives to *subjective* colonization. Imperialism, therefore, also has *anthropological* relevance. The identification with the colonial master functions as the Oedipus complex of the colonized subject, concealing his memory and his affects which could be incompatible with an Oedipal self-representation. And what is even worse, he decodes them after the fact in an Oedipal logic. It is not a problem of cultural uprooting or of the simple Westernization of the elites of the colonized countries, but of an unconscious identification of the colonized with the family novel of the master, ensuring that his own history is not readable except if it is related to that of the master. This means that even national emancipation runs the risk of being just another way of staying within the path traced by the colonial master, that is to say, of defining oneself always in relation to categories—such as "Nation"—that are inseparable from the colonial enterprise, captivating everything that precedes them. It is possible to find this logic of the Oedipal and familial over-coding, which is part of all imperialism, as an ample discussion in the *Anti-Oedipus* (Deleuze & Guattari, 1972).

In the same vein, if we leave the Seminars aside, we find in the text of a conference by Lacan on 22 October 1967 before an audience of psychiatrists, a new distinction between Empire (in the old sense of the term) and imperialism, which consolidates at the same time what had been established and provides a new perspective through the notion of "segregation":

> The factor at stake here is the most burning issue of our times in so far as this era is the first to have to undergo the calling into question of every social structure as a result of the progress of science. This is something which we are going to be contending with, not only in our domain as psychiatrists but in the furthest reaches of our universe, and in an ever more pressing fashion: with segregation. Mankind is entering a period that has been called "global", in which it will find out about this something that is emerging from the destruction of an old social order that I shall symbolise by the Empire whose shadow was long cast over a great civilisation, such that something very different is replacing it, something that carries a very different meaning, the imperialisms, whose question runs as follows: what can we do so that human masses which are destined to occupy the same space, not only geographically, but sometimes in a familial sense, remain separate?
>
> <div align="right">(<i>APE</i>)</div>

One can find here the first allusions to the important motive of segregation which Lacan will put forward in his teaching at the beginning of the 1970s, particularly concerning racism, a phenomenon that for him was not destined to fade away with the end of the colonial era, but rather seemed to become more relevant. The notion of segregation and its polysemy and subtleties will not be analyzed here, but it is important to note nevertheless that Lacan uses it as a counterpoint to the humanist ambition of anti-psychiatry, seeking to put an end to psychiatric segregation. In the midst of the climate of general liberation preceding May '68, for Lacan, the discourse of science emerges paradoxically as triumphant behind the appearance of this device, promising unprecedented forms of segregation already prefigured by the Nazi camps and the Stalinist gulag (*CPP*). What must be noted here is, once again, the difference that Lacan traces between Empire as an "ancient order", tending towards the One, while assuming its internal discrepancies, and "something that carries a very different meaning, the imperialisms", which appear on the horizon of history as hardly related to the past, but related instead to the "planetary" future, as a reaction to the unification/homogenization of the world, within a "the same space, not only geographically, but sometimes in a familial sense". This last mention seems to suggest that imperialisms will not disappear when the European "Age of Empires" of the 19th century is achieved, but rather that it will reappear, on a larger scale, from the very fact that now there is a shared space governed by the same ideals of universality, that is to say, void of all other forms of belonging and self-representation, which will revive a complementary need for differentiation. Some commentators put forward the hypothesis that Lacan may have been aware of Kojève's unpublished texts on "The Latin

Empire" ("*L'empire latin*"), written during the summer of 1954, where the philosopher and future diplomat considered the opportunity to create an imperial bloc between the countries of Southern Europe—Spain, France, and Italy, "Imperial Union of related nations" ["*union impériale de Nations apparentées*"]—in order to compensate for the economic influence of Germany in the future of Europe, and to escape the alternative of having to choose between the "Anglo-Saxon Empire" and the "Slavo-Soviet Empire" (see Kojève, 1945).

A final allusion, *Seminar XVIII*, concludes the series of Lacanian remarks on Empire and imperialism in the years 1967–1970. It deals with the evocation of an almost legendary episode in Chinese history, the burning of books, and the living burial of hundreds of scholars by the last ruler of the Qui dynasty in the third century BC:

> He was someone. He had the books burned. This Tsin had understood things, he was an emperor, it did not last twenty years. Right away writing started up again, and all the more painstakingly, anyway I will spare you the different forms of Chinese writing because the essential relationship of the writing with what was used to inscribe it, the quill, is absolutely superb.
>
> (*SXVIII*, 10.03.71)

What is alluded to here is the fact that Qui Shin Huang, the first Chinese emperor, had seen fit to attack the authority of Confucian scholars for establishing and centralizing his power on a large scale but, paradoxically, he only paved the way for the reign of the Han dynasty, inaugurating the history of the Middle Empire as an empire of the letter, lasting for more than two millennials. This critique of the imperial function of writing overlaps with Lacan's critique of bureaucracy, of the "discourse of the University", and more generally of the seizing of power by a system that does not leave behind any remains of the inscription of knowledge. But how could one not also see, at the same time, a disenchanted appreciation of the legacy of the other great revolt against the alienation of power operating through knowledge, Maoism, and particularly the Cultural Revolution, which had just come to end in an impasse, and whose titanic anti-imperialist mobilization already seemed to announce a revival of the Empire?

Translated from French by Christina Soto van der Plas

## Further reading

Badiou, A. (2009). The Cultural Revolution. The Last Revolution. In: *The Communist Hypothesis* (pp. 101–168), D. Macey & S. Corcoran (Trans). London: Verso, 2010.

Fanon, F. (1961). *The Wretched of the Earth*, R. Philcox (Trans.). New York: Grove Press, 1963.

Heidegger, M. (1957). *The Principle of Reason*, R. Lilly (Trans.). Indianapolis: Indiana University Press, 1991.

# References

Balibar, E. & Wallerstein, I. (1988). *Race, Nation, Class*, É. Balibar & C. Turner (Trans.). London: Verso, 1991.

Deleuze, G. & Guattari, F. (1972). *Anti-Oedipus. Capitalism and Schizophrenia*, R. Hurley & H. R. Lane (Trans). Minneapolis: University of Minnesota Press, 1983.

Kojève, A. (1945). Outline of a Doctrine of French Policy (August 27, 1945), E. de Vries (Trans.). In: *Policy Review*, 126: 3–40, 2004.

Lenin, V. I. (1917). *Imperialism. The Highest Stage of Capitalism*. Sydney: Resistance Books, 1999.

Chapter 12

# Labour/work

Samo Tomšič

—Ara.: عمل —Chi.: 勞動 —Fre.: *Travail* —Ger.: *Arbeit* —Ita.: *Lavoro* —Jap.: 労働 —Port.: *Trabalho* —Rus.: *Труд (Работа)* —Spa.: *Trabajo* —Tur.: *İş*

→ *Capitalism*; *Economy*; *Materialism*; *Slavery*; *Value*

## The labour of the unconscious

Although the notion of *Arbeit* (work, labour) played a significant role in Freud's theory and practice ever since the *Interpretation of Dreams* (1900), psychoanalysis was never included among theories of social labour.[1] After this initial step, Freud examined other types of mental work, most notably joke-work, work of mourning (Freud 1917), and work of repression (Freud 1915b), thus expanding his initial thesis, according to which mental processes can and should be viewed as productive labour. Freud's theory of mental apparatus more or less explicitly equated thought and labour, proposed something like a "labour theory of the unconscious", and in doing so stumbled upon the problematic of abstract labour.[2] Before moving on to the way Lacan's teaching addressed these issues, it is worth recalling some of the basic features of Freud's framework.

*Arbeit* (work, labour) is a relational concept, which in psychoanalytic framing cannot be discussed independently from its product, *Lust*. This second term is commonly translated as "pleasure", although a more appropriate choice may be "lust". Such terminological choice would not only echo the religious problematic of "deadly sin", but it would also directly address the critical Freudian turn in the history and theory of pleasure. Rather than distinguishing it from its opposite, pain or unpleasure, Freud was preoccupied with a problematic continuum or intertwining between pleasure and unpleasure. In Freud's critical theory of pleasure, *Lust* no longer stands for a univocally pleasurable feeling accompanying the satisfaction of needs, demands, or desires as a more or less accidental side-product. Rather, pleasure appears as an essential product generated by the ongoing mental activities.[3]

In the *Interpretation of Dreams,* the unconscious labour thus creates the conditions of possibility for satisfying unconscious desire. It does this, not by reworking dream content, but rather by manipulating its expression, hence its form. Dream-work explicitly unfolds in a conflicted field and must mediate between the unconscious desire and the mechanisms of censorship and repression, which complicate its path towards satisfaction. In a famous passage, Freud writes that dream-work

> does not think, calculate or judge in any way at all; it restricts itself to giving things a new form. It is exhaustively described by an enumeration of the conditions which it has to satisfy in producing its result. That product, the dream, has above all to evade the censorship.
>
> (Freud, 1900, p. 506)[4]

This absence of thinking, calculating, and judging makes the unconscious mechanisms qualitatively distinct from conscious thought. It is due to these "absences" that the unconscious can be described as abstract labour, or in Lacan's occasional wording, as an "ideal worker", who "knows what it has to do" (*TV*, p. 19; *SXIX*, p. 219).[5] Still, this formulation must not distract us from the Freudian insight that the unconscious labour is explicitly embedded in a psychic conflict and must be approached from two opposing aspects. On the one hand it certainly generates the conditions for pleasurable satisfaction by striving to produce a compromise between the repressed unconscious tendency and the mental instances exercising censorship. On the other hand, and because it unfolds in a conflicted field, the unconscious labour equally marks the experience of an ongoing compulsive activity that the affected subject cannot master and that inevitably pushes him or her into a state of exhaustion.

Freud provided two names for the unconscious tendency demanding pleasurable satisfaction: desire and drive.[6] The pleasure produced in the ongoing unconscious activity in turn shows that satisfaction contains a fundamental dislocation. For Freud explicitly remarks that, while every satisfaction is experienced as pleasurable, the pleasure accompanying the satisfaction of unconscious force, such as, precisely, the drive, cannot always or continuously be experienced as pleasurable. The experience of satisfaction thus involves the phenomenon of "pleasure that cannot be felt as such" (*Lust die nicht als solche empfunden werden kann*) (Freud, 1920, p. 220),[7] hence a pleasure that is subjectively experienced as its negative, unpleasure. The complication in pleasurable satisfaction, its experience as disturbing, splitting, or alienating the conscious mind, suggests that there is something involuntary, compulsive, and eventually threatening in the pleasurable satisfaction that the mental apparatus works on. There is an intimate link between unconscious labour and compulsion, which brings the psychoanalytic conceptualization of intellectual labour in direct proximity with Marx's critique of political economy, where labour is equally understood as the central compulsive social activity, in which the link between exploitation and production of value is exemplified.[8] In capitalism, labour stands for the ongoing presence of compulsion in an individual's life, and one could argue that Freud's exposure of the compulsive character of unconscious labour in its own way traces the mental consequences of this universal capitalist compulsion.

Freud (1925, p. 127) leaves hardly any doubt that production of pleasure is an ongoing process, comprised in every apparently "useful" or "meaningful" mental activity:

> Our mental activities pursue either a useful aim or an immediate yield of pleasure (*Lustgewinn*). In the former case what we are dealing with are intellectual judgments, preparations for action or the conveyance of information to other people. In the latter case we describe these activities as play or fantasy. What is useful is itself (as is well known) only a circuitous path to pleasurable satisfaction.

The recognition of the double character of mental activities—pursuing usefulness (meaningful actions) and striving for pleasure-gain—is indeed crucial. Both activities are inseparably intertwined, or rather, they are two sides of one and the same process, whereby Freud's main point is that usefulness is eventually only a detour for production of pleasure. Philosophies of consciousness and philosophies of the mind downplayed, rejected, or entirely overlooked this problematic production, which explains why the Freudian framing had to encounter such strong resistance and rejection in philosophical and scientific circles. For the latter, the main aim of cognitive processes is not simply production of meaningful utterances, but even more crucially, production of knowledge. Contrary to these centralized and normative conceptions of the mind, Freud decentralized the mental apparatus by recognizing the double character of thinking, the "useful" (meaningful) and the "useless" (pleasurable). Moreover, rather than simply pointing back to the mechanist framework, Freud's deployment of "apparatus" places the accent on the compulsive and involuntary aspect of intellectual labour and conceives the mental as a *dysfunctioning* rather than functioning "machine".

To repeat, Freud determined two forces, whose satisfaction requires ongoing production of pleasure and therefore continuous unconscious labour. *The Interpretation of Dreams* still called this tendency desire (or rather, "wish", *Wunsch*), whereas subsequent works shifted the focus onto the drive (*Trieb*).[9] In his early work, Freud highlighted more the ciphering achievement of the unconscious labour, focusing on operations such as condensation and displacement of mental content that Lacan eventually translated into two fundamental linguistic operations, metaphor and metonymy. If dreams and other unconscious phenomena could be compared to a text, this immediately suggested that the main achievement of unconscious labour consisted in producing ciphers and manipulating form. One could compare this achievement with the function of style. But while in the *Interpretation of Dreams* the conflictual character of unconscious satisfaction remains restricted to the discussion of censorship, the displacement from desire to drive overtly pushes the compulsive aspect of production of pleasure to the foreground. Now the conflict does not come from without the repressed force in question, but is instead built in this very force itself. Understood as "constant force" (*konstante Kraft*), the drive brings together perpetual satisfaction and the impossibility of satisfaction, a satisfaction that never comes to an end.[10]

Due to this virtual endlessness of the drive's satisfaction, Jean-Claude Milner argued that Freud's theory of mental apparatus circulates around a problematic parasitism of the infinite on the finite. This parasitism is coded in the very German term: the negative prefix *un-* in *Unbewusst* (unconscious) behaves in the same manner as in *Unendlich* (infinite).[11] Infinite is a feature that disturbs finitude from within, thus preventing it from ever being truly finite, making it always-already to go beyond itself. The infinite could be described as a way of finitude to overcome itself, become destabilized or thrown out of joint. The same goes for the relation between consciousness as a figure of finitude, and the unconscious as what disturbs and decentralizes consciousness from within. In Freud's setting, the constant force of the drive behaves in the same manner in relation to the body, perpetually unsettling it from within. The unconscious labour is an expression of this disturbance, even its manifestation.

In a crucial passage, Freud (1915a, p. 122) remarked that the drive must be understood as the "measure of the demand made upon the mind for work in consequence of its connection with the body".[12] The ongoing work in the mental apparatus is therefore driven by a specific complication in the connection of the mind with the body. Furthermore, *Arbeit* is merely one Freudian name for this problematic connection, the other one being precisely *Lust*. In both cases we are dealing with the fusion of the corporeal and the mental, or as Lacan would say, symbolic, a process in which this distinction is no longer operative and which moreover shows why Freud insisted on the double character of *all* intellectual activities. This is also the reason why Freud spoke of the drive as a border phenomenon between body and mind, since it is ultimately a material force anchored in a symbolic element (*Vorstellungsrepräsentanz* in Freud, signifier of enjoyment in Lacan).

It is crucial that the drive comes in the guise of a demand for work. This specification already hints at a feature that became central in Freud's mature doctrine of drives, compulsive repetition. Freud's mention of "play" and "phantasy" in the earlier quote should therefore not mislead us in believing that mental work unfolds spontaneously and without tensions. Rather, the unconscious labour is one aspect of the ongoing tension in the psychosomatic nexus. The suggestion that all mental activities comprise production of pleasure indicates that this activity is open for complications, which introduces in the subject's mental and physical life a most problematic constraint. For this reason, translating *Lust* with "pleasure" is all the more misleading, since pleasure indeed points towards free play of imagination or fantasy. In contrast, the notion of "lust" does not simply link back to the problematic of "sin", which would impose the duty of confession (this was Foucault's critique of psychoanalysis in the first volume of *The History of Sexuality*); instead, the psychoanalytic demystification of the "deadly sin" isolates the rational kernel of this religious problematic, which consists in the link between "lust" and labour, pinpointed in the very idea of compulsive repetition. What religion still mystified in terms of sinful action, psychoanalysis revealed as an essentially compulsive, involuntary mode of enjoyment, in which mental processes are embedded in an ongoing productive activity, which takes no regard for the subject's self-preservation (Freud 1927). For this reason, psychoanalysis, which is, in difference to confession, equally understood as a demand for work, aims at transforming enjoyment rather than its moral condemnation. The analytic work actively intervenes in the problematic nexus of the mental and the corporeal that Freud pinpoints in the phenomenon of the drive. The activity that Freud described as working-through is thus transformative work consisting of the analysand's activity of speaking and the analyst's activity of interpreting—a "collaboration" in the strong meaning of the term, a social bond guided by the combination of the analysand's "demand for the cure" and the analyst's "demand for work". If Lacan declared psychoanalysis to be a social bond, this inevitably comes with an unambiguous "work-contract".[13]

## A second return to Freud through Marx

*Arbeit* and *Lust* entertain another significant connection. Not only does Freud relate them to one another to the extent that *Lust* is defined as the most essential product of unconscious labour, they are also notions that call for a reference to natural sciences. Freud's epistemological wager was that psychoanalytic theory or "metapsychology" would obtain solid foundations in energetics, the notion of *Arbeit* being already adopted from this scientific framework. However, the crucial significance of *Arbeit* lies less in the fact that it orients psychoanalysis towards the laws of thermodynamics.[14] Rather, the link between *Arbeit* and *Lust* introduces the economic dimension, which stands in direct continuity with social economy. Freud already conceived *Lust* as an essential surplus-product of mental work, and it was only a question of time that Lacan's re-reading of Freud would stumble upon this connection.

This took place after Lacan already proposed a clarification of the Freudian concept of *Lust*, as well as its new translation. In order to avoid the misunderstanding promoted by the established French and English terminology—pleasure, *Plaisir*—Lacan's first step consisted in translating *Lust* with *jouissance*, which displaced the accent from the opposition pleasure–unpleasure to their problematic intertwining, as well as to the involuntary aspect of pleasure that the word *jouissance* addresses more directly (similarly to the English "lust"). In the late 1960s another correction was added, when the neologism *plus-de-jouir*, surplus-enjoyment, was coined in homology with the economic notion of surplus-value (translated into French as *plus-value*). This neologism explicitly translates Freud's term *Lustgewinn*, where enjoyment is already unambiguously understood as profit (*Gewinn*), hence as surplus-product resulting from the nexus between the mental and the corporeal. With his move, however, Lacan supplemented Freud's epistemological wager with a political one, in which critique of political economy began playing a strikingly similar role as energetics in Freud, thus adding to Freud's epistemology an even more explicit critical turn.

With his second clarification of the function of *Lust*, Lacan had to stumble upon the double character of work in the social context. This double character concerns the point that Marx (*CAI*, p. 138) already made with regard to the double character of commodities, use-value and exchange-value:

> On the one hand, *all* labour is an expenditure of human labour-power, in the physiological sense, and it is in this character of being equal, or abstract, human labour that it creates and forms the value of commodities. On the other hand, *all* labour is an expenditure of human labour-power in a particular form and with a definite aim, and it is in this character of being concrete useful labour that it produces use-values.

The silent background of the distinction between abstract and concrete labour (or between labour and work) is again energetics, from which the notion of *Arbeitskraft* migrated into social sciences and eventually into psychoanalysis. Marx refers to this scientific framing by speaking of the expenditure of labour-power in the physiological sense. That this expenditure is a matter of economic calculus and of abstraction is accounted for through the reference to value: production of abstraction. On the other hand, we have the expenditure of labour-power as concrete bodily or mental experience. The main effort of Marx's mature critical project consisted in examining the negative consequences of this expenditure, the consumption, exhaustion, and, ultimately, destruction of working bodies. In the social-economic context, the double character of commodities and therefore of labour equally exposes a problematic nexus, between sensuous materiality and economic abstraction (exchange-value or what Marx occasionally calls "sensuous suprasensuous"). The deadlock, in which the labouring subject finds itself in this process, is indicated in the double use of the term "all": work is split between abstraction and concretion, assuming double status the whole time and entirely.

This split of labour comprises the novelty in Marx's theory of labour, which is of central relevance for psychoanalysis:

> Marx starts from the function of the market. His novelty is the place in which he situates labour. It's not that labour is new, it's that it is bought, that there is a market of labour. This is what allows Marx to demonstrate what is inaugural in his discourse, and which is called surplus-value.
> (*SXVI*, 13.11.68)

Marx does not simply depart from an economic abstraction, the market, but from the gap between abstraction and the body, which stands at the root of the modern metamorphosis of work into a material-abstract process. To repeat, the labouring body is split between concretion and abstraction, and in this division, it is subjected to the compulsive regime of valorisation, from which another essential economic abstraction results, surplus-value:

> Was surplus-value there before abstract labour, I mean labour from which this abstraction emerges as a social average, was the result of something we will call the absolutisation of the market? [...] It is more than likely that the appearance of surplus-value in the discourse was conditioned by the absolutisation of the market. This can hardly be separated from the development of certain language effects, which is why we have introduced surplus-enjoyment.
> (*SXVI*, 20.11.68)

The introduction of surplus-enjoyment thus recognizes that the same absolutization of an abstract symbolic regime is at stake as in the process analysed by Marx in the economic sphere, a process that ended up producing two central modern abstractions, abstract labour or labour-power and surplus-value. The shift from value to enjoyment suggests that the modern regime of valorisation stands also at the root of a metamorphosis of enjoyment, where the accent is placed on enjoyment in objectified form, enjoyment as the privileged object, around which "libidinal economy" (desire and drive) is organized. Freud (1905, p. 149) drew attention to this development in his own manner, when he somewhat enigmatically remarked:

> The most striking distinction between the erotic life of antiquity and our own no doubt lies in the fact that the ancients laid the stress upon the drive itself, whereas we emphasize its object. The ancients glorified the drive and were prepared on its account to honour even an inferior object; while we despise the drive activity in itself, and find excuses for it only in the merits of the object.[15]

One point is worth retaining from this Freudian description of the metamorphosis of pleasure between antiquity and modernity, namely that the emphasis on the object amounts to a libidinal fixation (fixation of the drive). This has significant consequences for the problem that the unconscious labour and the social labour continuously confront. When this object is defined as surplus, the impossibility of satisfaction becomes explicit: satisfaction becomes indistinguishable from dissatisfaction and the drive becomes fixated on the "more" of value and of enjoyment, hence on its increase or growth. The German term *Mehrwert* (surplus-value) epitomizes this fusion of satisfaction and dissatisfaction. It equally acknowledges growth as an inherent feature of the object. The emphasis on pleasure-gain or surplus-enjoyment in Freud and on surplus-value in Marx reflects this shift from the "premodern" to the "modern" mode of production of value and its corresponding mode of enjoyment.

The body put to work therefore confronts the same deadlock in the economic and the libidinal sphere. Work becomes itself a virtually endless process—surplus-labour, as Marx explicitly puts it, using the term *Mehrarbeit*, which suggests that under capitalist conditions work becomes the process, in which the subject's life is progressively consumed rather than sustained. Surplus-labour is the amount of labour that a worker performs beyond the work necessary for their subsistence. In this respect surplus-labour is convertible into surplus-value. This convertibility overtly pinpoints at the core of modern organization of production a fundamental compulsive dimension, which ultimately comes down to the insatiable demand that the generation of value, its perpetual growth, unfolds without interruption. Following this line of thought, Marx argued that the capitalist mode of production comprises a structural tendency to extend the length of the workday, in other words, to keep bodies embedded and engaged in the production process. It is quite telling that the mature Marx describes this tendency as drive (*Trieb*) and henceforth understands capital as drive of self-valorisation or drive of accumulation.

As already mentioned, the capitalist invention and imposition of abstract labour points towards what Lacan described with the expression "ideal worker". The framework, in which this term is introduced, is indicative:

> Does the unconscious imply that it be listened to? To my mind, yes. But this surely does not imply that, without the discourse through which it exsists, one judges it as knowledge that does not think, or calculate, or judge – which doesn't prevent it from being at work (as in dreams, for example). Let's say that it is the ideal worker, the one Marx made the flower of capitalist economy.
>
> (*TV*, p. 14)

The crucial detail here is the link between the unconscious and listening. In contrast to the sphere of production, in analysis the "ideal worker" begins to speak. This ability to speak corrupts its ideal status, since the worker's speech comes in the guise of protest, complaint, or strike. Better put, the worker's speech demonstrates that the "ideal worker" does not exist. What exists is the worker as a "social symptom", in which the contradictions of the capitalist system obtain their material expression.[16] Hence, the proletarian stands for more than actualization of abstract labour in the living body. Speech and listening unfold on the level of "use-value", where the body affected by abstractions articulates its suffering and addresses the analyst with a demand for cure: "The cure is a demand that originates in the voice of the sufferer", of someone who suffers from the subjection of their body and mind to a compulsive discursive regime (*TV*, p. 7). In analysis, but also in emancipatory politics, a different regime of work enters the picture, for which Freud proposed the expression "working-through" (*Durcharbeiten*). To repeat, this work is essentially collaboration, a work-bond between the analysand's speaking and the analyst's listening and interpreting. The aim of this transformative work is to loosen the imposed absolutization of "certain language effects" (as Lacan somewhat vaguely called them), namely the organization of the symbolic order or of social bond around the demand for surplus-product and the imposition of surplus-labour. In doing so the analytic "co-work" or "working-through" strives to introduce movement in the resistant structure and in the fixation of the drive. It attempts to work on and against the structure's resistance to change, and in doing so to overcome the constraints in which the analysand's mental activities unfold in the present moment.

Lacan's engagement with the problematic of labour can be equally divided into two steps. The first one is epistemological and comprises dispersed comments concerning energetics and its role in Freud's work. Here Lacan remained sceptical towards Freud's epistemological wager that natural sciences would eventually verify his theory of libido. The second step is overtly political and significantly more systematic. It can be localized in *Seminars XVI* and *XVII*, where the references to energetics are reinterpreted through the lenses of critique of political economy, and more specifically by means of the structural reading of Marx's *Capital*.[17] In doing so, Lacan depicts Marx as a paradigmatic worker. One could argue that his entire project of critique of political economy—understood both as theory of capitalism and as practice of organization of political subjectivity—exemplifies the process of working-through. At the core of this process, we find Marx's attempt to expose the totality of social casualties resulting from the capitalist organization of production around the insatiable demand for surplus-value. For this reason, Marx's description of capital as drive must be taken at face value, since it explains the compulsive character of labour in modernity, notably when the drive is understood through the lenses of psychoanalysis as insatiable "demand for work".

Furthermore, Marx provides the first structural glimpse into the problematic nexus of abstract (value) and concrete (body), where the process of work is embedded in endless production that Marx not by chance calls "production for the sake of production". The compulsive structural order, in which the labouring subject must perform its task, exemplifies not only the cruelty of the modern absolutization of the market, but also the subordination of labour to useless production, since the produced surplus-object (surplus-value, surplus-enjoyment) serves no other purpose than to keep the capitalist machinery running. The absolutization of the market indeed comes with the imperative that the labouring subject must sacrifice his or her life for the well-being of economy (the proverbial economic growth).

## Entropy and social bond

This is also the point where the reference to energetics, and more particularly to the notion of entropy, becomes of central significance for Lacan. In an illustrative example, Lacan draws attention to an important deadlock that the modern absolutization of the market imposes onto the labouring subject, placing the latter in an impossible position:

> I defy you to prove in any way that descending 500 meters with a weight of 80 kilos on your back and, once you have descended, going back up the 500 meters with it is zero, no work. Try it, have a go yourself, and you will find that you have proof of the contrary. But if you overlay signifiers, that is,

if you enter the path of energetics, it is absolutely certain that there has been no work. When the signifier is introduced as an apparatus *of jouissance,* we should thus not be surprised to see something related to entropy appear, since entropy is defined precisely once one has started to lay this apparatus of signifiers over the physical world.

(*SXVII*, 14.01.70, pp. 48–49)[18]

The Freudian nexus between the mental and the corporeal is here exemplified in the discrepancy between the epistemic-economic calculus, in which the figure of "ideal worker" operates, and the experience of consumption-exhaustion that affects the "material worker", the body inhabited by abstractions. Because the proletariat unites these two aspects of labour, it assumes the status of a *social* symptom. The accent on the social is crucial, not only because it connotes social bond, but also because it stresses that this bond is traversed by a fundamental tension, non-relation, and contradiction. Freud understood early on that the symptom is a compromise formation, in which the enforcing of two opposing tendencies can be observed. Such understanding of the symptom distinguishes the notion from its medical framework and endows it with critical signification (which, again, can already be detected in the way Marx situates the proletariat in the overall framework of the capitalist production). On the one hand, the symptom is entirely integrated in the existing organization of enjoyment or libidinal economy, thus responding to the demand of the drive. On the other hand, the symptom is also articulated suffering and therefore the means through which the analysand can express their demand for the cure. In this respect, the symptom remains attached to the individual's self-preservation.

Both aspects taken together suggest that the symptom is formed at the point where the absolutization of the market unfolds its full consequences. If Marx and Freud transformed the medical notion of the symptom into a critical notion this means that the symptom no longer bears merely the epistemological signification of a sign of illness, but stands for the sign of an ongoing conflict in the symbolic order and therefore in the social sphere. In this respect each particular symptom preserves its social character. It was this critical connotation of the symptom— sign of a psychic conflict, as the early Freud would put it—that was adopted in the elaboration of the psychoanalytic clinic. Furthermore, in both contexts, the Freudian and the Marxian, the function of the symptom expresses the tension between abstraction and bodily experience that marks the activity of work, be it productive social work or unconscious work. The subject emerges from the discrepancy between the discursive calculus, the quantification of the subject's activity, and the psychosomatic exhaustion.

Lacan frames the absolutization of the market in terms of "overlaying the world with the network of signifiers". This process stands for a joint effort of science and economy, epistemic quantification and economic valorisation. The modern scientific ideal that Descartes framed in terms of domination of nature migrated into the sphere of production and the sphere of enjoyment. In this respect neither surplus-value nor surplus-enjoyment exist outside capitalism; they are conditioned by the transformation of labour into a virtually endless process. In this respect, again, Marx's notion of surplus-labour is the crucial third "surplus-object", which explains the other two. Furthermore, the domination of nature does not mean its domination through labour—labour falls on the side of dominated, hence on the side of "nature". Rather, domination has the meaning of what Lacan calls "reduction of material" (*réduction du materiel*),[19] hence quantification, which is again as much an epistemic as it is an economic process.

It is therefore not by chance that Lacan (*SXVI*, 20.11.68) associates knowledge with value rather than with labour: "Knowledge [...] is not work. It is sometimes worth the work, but it can also be given to you without it. Knowledge, in the extreme, is what we call price". One might think that this statement contradicts Lacan's later remarks on the unconscious as knowledge, which is put to work (unconscious knowledge, which does not think, judge, or calculate, "ideal worker"). However, knowledge that does not know itself is precisely not the same as the quantified knowledge, which determines the "price" and moreover which decides whether productive labour has been accomplished or not (as in Lacan's example quoted above). The unconscious understood as a form of decentralized and non-reflexive knowledge has no place in the modern epistemo-economic regime. Moreover, the unconscious is an unintended effect or side product of quantification and therefore a site of minimal protest of the labouring subject. Seen from this perspective, the unconscious also marks the non-quantifiable part of the subject.

The intervention of energetics in the living bodies, their appropriation for the epistemic and economic calculation, only widens the contradiction and tension between the compulsive symbolic activity and the limits of psychosomatic performance. It would nevertheless be wrong to compare the modern proletarian in Lacan's "thought experiment" with Sisyphus. Not only does the Sisyphus-scenario contain no production of surplus-value; it also misses the impossibility at stake in the capitalist organization of labour. We are dealing with two distinct scenarios: while Sisyphus exemplifies the absurdity of labour, the proletariat, understood as one possible name for the subject of epistemo-economic quantification, exposes the uselessness of labour, but not its absurdity since labour here evidently performs a productive task. Sisyphus repeatedly fails in accomplishing his task and therefore performs work that never amounts to a product. The proletariat, in turn, uninterruptedly brings about a product deprived of usefulness, a useless object *par excellence* that is surplus-value.[20]

Lacan exemplifies the consequences of the absolutization of the market and the gap that separates abstract and concrete work by returning to the notion of entropy. Here the link between surplus and lack is crucial, since it is their interdependence that makes labour in capitalist conditions a virtually endless process, in which the subject is gradually consumed-exhausted. Unlike Sisyphus, the proletariat does not confront the repetition of the same "failure", but rather of the same "success". The impossibility of mapping physiological consumption of labour-power to the economic calculus is most overtly exemplified in the senseless activity of transporting a certain weight in two opposite directions. The result is pure loss, which falls on the side of the subject. This example resonates with Marx's argument that capitalism organizes social production around production of a useless surplus-product, hence making social production a self-sufficient process, for the sake of production; only in such introversion of production surplus-value becomes possible—an "object" that serves no other purpose than to keep the machine of useless production running. But together with the surplus, its flipside, which is loss, is equally produced without interruption. Hence, the impossibility to ever satisfy the drive of capital by means of labour, and the imperative to continuously satisfy it.

With the capitalist absolutization of the market a thorough transformation of the human being takes place, in which entropy becomes the defining feature of modern subject:

> there is a loss of *jouissance*. And it is in the place of this loss introduced by repetition that we see the function of the lost object emerge, of what I am calling the *a*. What does this impose on us? If not this formula that at the most elementary level, that of the imposition of the unary trait, knowledge at work produces, let's say, an entropy. That's spelled *e,n,t*. You could write it *a,n,t,h,* this would be a nice play on words.
> 
> (*SXVII*, 14.01.70, p. 48)

The entropic mode of existence that marks the human being under the capitalist absolutization of the market again crystallizes in the process of work. The paradigm of "entropic human" or "enthropos" is a composition of "ideal worker" and exhausted body. In the guise of work, capitalism imposes a "work morality" organized around the renunciation of enjoyment. More precisely put, capitalism is grounded on the link between renunciation of enjoyment and production of surplus-enjoyment. Just as surplus-value joins capital once it has been extracted from the labouring bodies, the extraction of surplus-enjoyment from the ongoing symbolic activity (speech) migrates into discourse, hence Lacan's talk of enjoyment of the Other rather than of the subject's enjoyment. Surplus-enjoyment hence does not name subjective enjoyment, but specifically modern discursive enjoyment, enjoyment conforming to the capitalist organization of production. For this reason, Lacan could argue that both surpluses stand in homology—but the critical point of this framing is that the entire homology is underpinned by the same deadlock and the same impossibility, in which the subjects put to work find themselves. Embedded in the system of compulsive labour, the subject can only access enjoyment in the form of loss and experience dissatisfaction. It is through the pursuit of surplus-enjoyment that the subject most effectively works for the system, thereby becoming a subject, whose sole experience of enjoyment comes in the guise of entropic loss.

Given the centrality of the problematic link between labour and enjoyment it is no coincidence that another issue related to labour becomes of central importance for psychoanalysis—the strike. In a well-pointed remark, Lacan argues that the strike is not only the most social thing imaginable, but also an expression of respect for social bond. This is the case because in the strike a demand for non-exploitative social bond is articulated; it is in this essential aspect that a strike pays respect to the social. Moreover, the strike is a social action *par excellence*, because it disrupts the essentially anti-social consumption of labour in the capitalist organization of production and its matching libidinal economy. Elsewhere Lacan reminds his audience: "In the strike, the collective truth of work manifests itself" (*SXVI*, 20.11.68). This truth certainly concerns the interdependency of labour, exploitation, and production of surplus-value under capitalism. It demonstrates that under capitalism work ultimately serves anti-social purposes. Furthermore, the strike demonstrates that emancipatory politics, too, comprises its own demand for work, first and foremost work on overcoming systemic resistance and systemic enjoyment, which continuously emerge at the core of the subject, notably in the guise of pursuit of surplus-enjoyment.

Insofar as psychoanalysis in its focus on the link between labour and enjoyment, lack and surplus, contributes to unveiling the collective truth of work, it is itself a practice resulting from a strike. Psychoanalysis links with the disruption of the ongoing unconscious labour, a disruption of the libidinal economy grounded on the vicious circle of reproduction of lack-of-enjoyment and production of surplus-enjoyment. It does so by converting the unconscious labour into a transformative labour, again the Freudian "working-through". What is worked through in analysis is the very deadlock that the speaking being finds itself in when it is absolutely integrated in the discourse, the ultimate aim of analysis being to transform this exploitative integration.

The exit from the capitalist social bond can only be called a progress if it happens to all, Lacan remarked in *Television*. This statement could be interpreted as a specific call to psychoanalysts to forge an alliance—precisely a social and therefore political bond—with Marxists and emancipatory movements, instead of particularizing the suffering continuously articulated by various social groups. Only by means of such alliances psychoanalysis remains faithful to the potential of transformation resulting from the unconscious on strike. But this equally means that psychoanalysis itself must remain open to its own transformation.

## Notes

1 It may be recalled that the longest chapter in *Interpretation of Dreams* contains a detailed account of mental operations that Freud unites under the notion of dream-work (*Traumarbeit*). For a well-pointed discussion, see Mai Wegener (2016).
2 The English distinction between work and labour can be evoked here, since it distinguishes what the German *Arbeit* still thinks together, the double character of labour in capitalism, concrete and abstract. See Engels's footnote to Karl Marx (*CAI*, p. 138). For further context, see Samo Tomšič (2015, p. 99ff). From an epistemological point of view, Freud's theory of unconscious labour and Marx's theory of abstract labour can be linked through energetics.

3 Although it must be added that the link between pleasure and thinking can already be found in Aristotle, for whom the "divine" thinking of thinking—an activity that philosophers must aspire to—is precisely a pleasurable activity. However, this intellectual pleasure remains sharply separated from unpleasure. As we know, in Freud the link between thinking and pleasure is marked by compulsion, hence the emergence of unpleasure in the midst of a pleasurable activity.
4 Lacan repeatedly returned to this famous passage.
5 Somewhat surprisingly, Lacan continues, "What does think, calculate, and judge is jouissance". However, as we shall see in the following, thinking, calculating, and judging are here not to be understood in qualitative terms, but as procedures of quantification, such as, precisely, in economic calculus.
6 In the *Interpretation of Dreams*, Freud compares the function of unconscious desire with the role of the capitalist in the organization of social production. This comparison has a surprizing parallel in Marx's work, where the economic category of capital is repeatedly described with the term "drive" (*Trieb*).
7 The formulation describes neurotic unpleasure, hence production of pleasure under the conditions of repression, the most common vicissitude of the drive. It is worth recalling that repression is for Freud the main achievement of unconscious labour, without which the distinction between consciousness and the unconscious is hardly thinkable. See Freud (1915a, pp. 146–158).
8 In this respect, Freud also proposes a "labour theory of enjoyment". Insofar as libidinal production appears as a cause of subjective suffering, its analytical account can be aligned with Marx's critical examination of the link between production of value and exploitation of labour. The shift from labour to its exploitation is a crucial and wide-reaching difference between the labour theory of value introduced by classical political economy and its reformulation in the Marxian framework.
9 This shift is accomplished in 1905 with the parallel publication of *Jokes and Their Relation to the Unconscious* (Freud, 1905a) and *Three Essays on the Theory of Sexuality* (Freud, 1905). The former again places the notion of labour—now in the guise of *Witzarbeit* (joke-work)—at the centre, whereas the latter proposes a theory of sexual development and a polymorph notion of sexuality, which initiated Freud's life-long preoccupation with the drive's destinies (*Triebschicksale*). The question of transformation of a drive-economy (*Triebökonomie*) becomes increasingly important and psychoanalysis itself progressively appears as transformative labour.
10 Freud categorizes the drive as "constant force" in his metapsychological writing on drive and its destinies. Considering Freud's recurrent attempts in linking his concept of the drive and of libido with energetics, one can recall Lacan's remark that "energy is not a substance, which, for example, improves or goes sour with age; it's a numerical constant that a physicist has to find in his calculation, so as to be able to work" (*TV*, p. 18). The drive and energy share the same constancy resulting from a fundamental discursive activity: calculation in the case of the physicist and de/ciphering in the case of psychoanalyst. However, in both cases the discourse manipulates materiality: the physical world and the speaking body, which are here the "object" of calculation and of ciphering.
11 See Jean-Claude Milner (1995, p. 43). To the couple of *unbewusst* and *unendlich*, Milner also adds *unheimlich* (uncanny).
12 The German expression is *Arbeitsanforderung* (demand for work).
13 When founding his psychoanalytic school, Lacan indicated that the same demand for work applies to anybody who wants to associate themselves to the analytic cause: "I don't need a numerous list, but determined workers, such as I already know" (*FA*, p. 100) Lacan's denouncement of the International Psychoanalytic Association (IPA) as a "church"—a denouncement repeated in 1980 in relation to his own *École freudienne de Paris*—is no less crucial. The evocation of "church" suggests a betrayal of the psycho-

analytic demand for work, which turns analysis into a system-conform practice, precisely "confession", striving to implement a normative figure of subjectivity. Lacan's denouncement of IPA as "professional insurance plan against analytic discourse" (*TV*, p. 15) contains the same criticism.
14 For an account of this aspect of Freud's epistemology, see Paul-Laurent Assoun (1981), notably Part II, Chapter III, pp. 145–187.
15 Transl. modified.
16 Lacan famously argued that it was none other than Marx who invented the notion of the (social) symptom. I will return to this issue further below. Critical readers from radical feminism and anti-colonialism underlined that it is necessary to move beyond Marx's focus on the figure of the industrial worker. In other words, the Marxian "symptomatology" must be reworked in a manner that it could be extended to other figures of exploited subjectivity brought about by the capitalist absolutization of the market, the racialized subjects, but also women and children. Exemplary for such extension is Silvia Federici (2004).
17 In this endeavour, Althusser's circle paved the way for Lacan: "Whether these commentators of Marx are structuralist or not, they seem to have demonstrated that Marx is a structuralist. For it is properly from what he is, as a being of thought, to the point where the predominance of the labour market determines it, that the function [...] of surplus-value, emerges as the cause of his thought" (*SXVI*, 13.11.68).
18 For the discussion of entropy, see also Alenka Zupančič (2016).
19 See Lacan (*SXVI*, 20.11.68). Consequently, abstract labour is what is obtained as objectified subjectivity on the background of this reductive operation.
20 This link between uselessness and surplus-value may create the impression that capitalism itself is useless. Here Lacan makes a surprising correction: "I am not saying that capitalism serves for nothing. No. Capitalism serves precisely for something, and we should not forget it. It is the things that it does that serve for nothing" (*SXVI*, 19.03.69). Capitalism serves for augmenting value, but in order to achieve this, the shift from usefulness to uselessness must be accomplished on the level of the product.

## Further reading

Khatib, S. (2021). The Drive of Capital. In: *Coils of the Serpent*, 8: 101–113.
Tomšič, S. (2019). *The Labour of Enjoyment. Towards a Critique of Libidinal Economy*. Berlin: August Verlag.
Žižek, S. (1989). *The Sublime Object of Ideology*. London: Verso.

## References

Assoun, P.-L. (1981). *Introduction à l'épistémologie freudienne*. Paris: Payot.
Federici, S. (2004). *Caliban and the Witch*. New York: Autonomedia.
Freud, S. (1900). The Interpretation of Dreams. In: *The Standard Edition of the Complete Psychological Works of Sigmund Freud* (Vols. IV & V, pp. 1–628), J. E. Strachey (Trans.). London: Vintage, 2001.
Freud, S. (1905). Three Essays on Sexuality. In: *The Standard Edition of the Complete Psychological Works of Sigmund Freud* (Vol. VII, pp. 123–243), J. E. Strachey (Trans.). London: Vintage, 2001.
Freud, S. (1905a). Jokes and their Relation to the Unconscious. In: *The Standard Edition of the Complete Psychological Works of Sigmund Freud* (Vol. VIII, pp. 1–136), J. E. Strachey (Trans.). London: Vintage, 2001.

Freud, S. (1915a). Instincts and Their Vicissitudes. In: *The Standard Edition of the Complete Psychological Works of Sigmund Freud* (Vol. XIV, pp. 109–140), J. E. Strachey (Trans.). London: Vintage, 2001.

Freud, S. (1915b). Repression. In: *The Standard Edition of the Complete Psychological Works of Sigmund Freud* (Vol. XIV, pp. 141–158), J. E. Strachey (Trans.). London: Vintage, 2001.

Freud, S. (1917). Mourning and Melancholia. In: *The Standard Edition of the Complete Psychological Works of Sigmund Freud* (Vol. XIV, pp. 237–258). London: Vintage, 2001.

Freud, S. (1920). Beyond the Pleasure Principle. In: *The Standard Edition of the Complete Psychological Works of Sigmund Freud* (Vol. XVIII, pp. 1–64), J. E. Strachey (Trans.). London: Vintage, 2001.

Freud, S. (1925). Some Additional Notes on Dream-Interpretation as a Whole. In: *The Standard Edition of the Complete Psychological Works of Sigmund Freud* (Vol. XIX, pp. 123–140), J. E. Strachey (Trans.). London: Vintage, 2001.

Freud, S. (1927). The Future of an Illusion. In: *The Standard Edition of the Complete Psychological Works of Sigmund Freud* (Vol. XXI, pp. 1–56), J. E. Strachey (Trans.). London: Vintage, 2001.

Milner, J.-C. (1995). *A Search for Clarity: Science and Philosophy in Lacan's Oeuvre*. E. Pluth (Trans.). Evanston: Northwestern University Press, 2020.

Tomšič, S. (2015). *The Capitalist Unconscious: Marx and Lacan*. London: Verso.

Wegener, M. (2016). Why Should Dreaming Be a Form of Work. In: Samo Tomšič & Andreja Zevnik (Eds.), *Jacques Lacan Between Psychoanalysis and Politics* (pp. 164–179). London: Routledge.

Zupančič, A. (2016). When Surplus Enjoyment Meets Surplus Value. In: Justin Clemens and Russell Grigg (Eds.), *Jacques Lacan and the Other Side of Psychoanalysis* (pp. 155–178). Durham: Duke University Press.

# Chapter 13

# Market

*Christian Ingo Lenz Dunker*

—Ara.: سوق، بضائع —Chi.: 市場/商品 —Fre.: *Marché* —Ger.: *Markt* —Ita.: *Mercato* —Jap.: 市場，商品 —Port.: *Mercado* —Rus.: *Рынок/товар* —Spa.: *Mercado* —Tur.: *Pazar/mal*

→ *Consumption*; *Economy*; *Money*; *Segregation*

The market is the field in which products are exchanged in the form of goods, by buyers and sellers, locally or globally. The market is defined by the movement of goods and capital itself as opposed to the sphere of production, but as the goods originate in labour the market involves the social relations of production (buying and selling labour) and the social division of labour.

Lacan's references to the notion of the market broadly follow a certain deepening of and convergence with Marx's concept, starting with the idea that the market involves a system of exchanges in the field of producing truth, value, and enjoyment. Most of his references to the market are developed in *Seminar XIV*, known for the thesis that the unconscious is politics, and in *Seminars XVI* and *XVII*, where Lacan elaborates his theory of the four discourses by reinterpreting the theses of *Civilization and its Discontents* in the light of Marx and the psychoanalytic notion of *jouissance*. We can then distinguish three critical incidences of the notion of the market in Lacan: the system of formation and transmission of psychoanalysis, the theory of the fantasy, and the conception of the four discourses. Lacan criticizes the corporation of psychoanalysts who dedicate themselves to negotiating their knowledge according to the structure of the market, bringing "scabrous" consequences for practitioners (*PL*). Such consequences concern the status of truth in the field of the market.

This reappears on the assumption that the fantasy, a position of maximum alienation and ignorance of the subject, is composed of operations of negation, inversion, and false universalization. The fantasy is a subjective structure that allows the relations between desire and *jouissance*, between law and pleasure, and between demand and lack, to stabilize, producing a certain identity and proportionality between the subject and the Other, even at the cost of an alienation to object *a*. Lacan describes this alienation using the same terms as in Marx's equation:

the proportion which results from two goods [is] the inverse of price/quantity of goods. [...] The proportion cannot be either of the values of use which fund the price or of the exchange values; [reproducing] the same crap when it comes to the value of the work. [as that which] constitutes the capital.

(*SXIV*, 12.04.67)

Lacan seems sensitive to the criticism that the anthropological foundation of the theory of exchange, derived from Lévi-Strauss, has received from feminist thought, regarding the identification of women with the object exchanged when one considers the primary exchange as an exchange of words.

For Lacan, there is a redoubling of value at the level of the unconscious, which founds any object as a commodity and not exclusively or preferably women. This occurs because:

> There is something that takes the place of the exchange-value, in so far as, from its false identification to use-value, there results the foundation of the object as a commodity; and one can even say more, that capitalism is missing so that it is, which precedes it in many ways, revealed.
>
> (*SXIV*, 12.04.67)

In other words, capitalism makes a false identification in the production of value, which is preceded and conditioned by what Lacan calls the value of *jouissance*, whose psychoanalytical correlate is not the market, as a set of exchanges of goods, nor the corresponding satisfaction of needs:

> we can—I repeat in a metaphor—call the *truth-market*, if, like the last time, you can glimpse that the main-spring of the market is *jouissance-value*. Something is in effect exchanged, which is not the truth in itself. In other words, the link between the one *who speaks* to the truth is not the same depending on the point at which he sustains his *jouissance*. This indeed is the whole difficulty of the position of the psychoanalyst. What does he do? What does he enjoy [*de quoi jouit-il*] at the place he occupies?
>
> (*SXIV*, 19.04.67)

To introduce this metaphor Lacan seems to take seriously the Freudian expression "sex trade", that is, that sexuality is also apprehended by the paradigm of exchanges, since it is of the "demands that desire arises, this indeed is the reason why desire, in the unconscious, is structured like a language" (*SXIV*, 21.06.67).

With the formulation of the principles which would come to govern his own school of psychoanalysis in October 1967, Lacan seems to locate more clearly the social implications of the presence of psychoanalysis in the world. This will lead to three crucial problems for the political horizon of psychoanalysts: the problem of mass identifications in the imaginary, the question of paternal authority in the symbolic framework of the myth of Oedipus, and the real problem of segregation:

"Our coming from common markets will be balanced by the increasingly harsh extension of segregation processes" (*P9O*). Let us remember that the European Common Market came into being in 1957, with the inclusion of Great Britain in 1973, and the embryo of the future European Union with its Euro zone, created in 1999. Lacan's declaration therefore points to the eminently segregated effect of the creation of the common markets, in accordance with the Marxist critique of monopolies associated with the bourgeois cosmopolitanism of production and consumption, the annihilation of national industries, the orientation towards an exportable surplus, the cheapening of supernumerary labour in the fields of raw material production, the effects of the worldwide division of labour. Here Lacan has in mind certain effects of the common market on the economy of enjoyment: racism, oppression of ethnic minorities, natives, migrants, and immigrants, gender inequality and sexual orientation, isolation by psychic suffering. These are particular cases of the false identification between use-value and exchange-value, which make equivalent the position of class with the position of speech.

Lacan criticizes the idealism of those who advocate one: "nostalgia for an unconscious in its first flower, for a practice in its audacious all the time, would be the pure idealism. Simply our realism does not imply progress in the movement which is dubbed with simple succession" (*MSS*). Historical ideologies of a regressive nature would have in common the attempt to return to the natural point of the use-value, as if the exchange-value were only the effect of the market. Their argument is that before the market comes the discourse which becomes the universal means of this inversion. Here it seems to separate itself from the policies of betting on the pacification that would be brought about by the unification of the markets, with the eventual ideological help of the human sciences. It is a false policy because it bets on "wanting to make the *Unheimlich* reassuring was one such falsification, the unconscious being hardly much of a reassurance, by its very nature" (*MSS*). *Unheimlich* is the Freudian expression (Freud, 1919) to designate a kind of anxiety resulting from the corruption of our intuitive oppositions between the familiar and the foreign, between the living and the dead, between the near and the distant. That is, the conflict generated by the social division of labour, the fetishization of merchandise, the ideology of the consistency of the Other as a market, and the extraction of surplus-value will not be resolved by its false universalization, which will make us all family members governed by the same rules and the general equivalence of the calculation of enjoyment. These four functions of the market, with its four psychoanalytic correlates—division of the subject, alienation in the formations of the unconscious, Other without lack, and object to more of *jouissance*—justify the thesis that Marx is the true inventor of the symptom.

> Marx starts from the function of the market. [...] It is not because the work is new that makes its discovery possible, it is because it is bought, it is because there is a work market. This is what enables him to demonstrate what he has said in his inaugural speech and what he will call his added value.
>
> (*SXVI*, 13.11.68)

However, it is not by the simple seizure of power by Marxists that a transformation of the capitalist subject would take place; "it is not sure that taking power resolved what I will call the subversion of the capitalist subject expected from this act" (*SXVI*, 13.11.68). The Lacanian theory of the four discourses starts from the identity between the discourse and the presence of surplus-value in the labour market.

> The identity of the discourse with its conditions [of the labour market]—that's what I hope—will be clarified by what I will say about the analytical march (*demarche*). Not because labour has been something new in the production of goods, not because of the renunciation of enjoyment, whose relationship to labour I will not define here.
> (*SXVI*, 13.11.68)

What is new is not work, nor the renunciation of enjoyment which it presupposes, nor even the constitution of a power by the possibility of choosing which one wants to obey. The principle of an epistemological and historical cut-off

> [i]s that there is a discourse that articulates this renunciation and that makes appear here—for there is the essence of the analytical discourse—what I would call the function of the plus of enjoyment. This function appears because of the fact of the discourse, because of what it proves to be, in the renunciation of the *jouissance*, an effect of the mystical discourse. To mark the things it is necessary to suppose that in the field of the Other there is this market.
> (*SXVI*, 13.11.68)

If the renunciation of *jouissance* and the plus of *jouissance* are effects of discourse, this can only happen because the market has occupied the field of the Other. This means that systems of merit and value, of organization and preference, the ordinal and cardinal structure and discourse retain the means of *jouissance* proper to discourse.

> [I]t is in the discourse on the function of the renunciation of *jouissance* that the term of the object *a* is introduced. The more one enjoys as the function of this renunciation, the more one enjoys the effectiveness of the discourse; he also gives his place to the object *a* in the market, namely in what defines some object of human work as merchandise, so that each object brings in itself something of added value, so that the more one enjoys is what allows the aislamiento of the function of the object *a*.
> (*SXVI*, 13.11.68)

Added value and more enjoyment are not equivalent but superimposed on the discursive process of the market. Everything works as if renunciation, which is structural but not necessarily discursive, created an object which corresponds to it (object *a*). This object is reduced when taken by discourses in a function of reproduction and multiplication: it is the function of the most enjoyable. In the case of the Master's discourse this object is defined as a function of human labour as merchandise. "Was surplus value there before abstract labour", as well as *plus-de-jouissance*? In the case of the Master's discourse, the commodity occupies the place of semblant or dominance, that is to say, as a master and similar signifier ($S_1$): "The commodity is linked to the master signifier, exposing it in this way solves nothing. The commodity is not less linked to that signifier after the socialist revolution" (*SXVII*, 18.02.70, p. 92). In other words, even if the means of production and political governance change, the market tends to persist as a reproduction function of discourse. This reminds us that the market persists, even if we try to regulate the logic of its exchanges in another way. Let us remember that an "absolutization of the market [that] can be considered as a condition for the added value to appear in the discourse" (*SXVI*, 20.11.68).

The absolutization of the market, understood as its mercantile, colonial, and global expansion, has made it possible to give labour its true price. The absolutization of the market seems to be a historical event which has certain language conditions, since

> the letters of the Phoenician alphabet are found, long before the time of Phoenicia, in small Egyptian ceramics in which they served as trademarks. I would like to point out that the letter appeared first in the market, which is typically a speech effect, before it was discovered that it did not use letters [...] something that it had nothing to see with the knowledge of the signifier.
> (*SXX*, 09.01.73, p. 36)[1]

Let us remember that the letter is for the real as well as the signifier is for the symbolic and therefore, by presenting the precedence of the letter in Phoenician commerce, supposedly before capitalism, he is showing how the essential condition of capitalism is not the existence of the market but its absolutization.

> This is how the function of the exchange value is defined in the market; there is the unpaid value in what appears as the fruit of the work, in a value of use; in what the true price of that fruit, is the work, is not paid, until it is paid fairly, in relation to the consistency of the market. This, in the functioning of its capitalist project, is the work not paid, it is the added value. This is the fruit of the means of articulation which constitute the Capitalist discourse of capitalist logic. However, articulated in this way, it is a concerted claim to the "frustration of the worker".
> (*SXVI*, 20.11.68)

The unpaid value, the fruit of labour, is made equivalent to the use-value. This defines the function of the exchange-value, together in relation to the market. Here the homology between the market and the Other is obvious. What is subtracted from the side of the subject reappears completing the Other, giving it consistency. This is the operation already subject to the logic of the fantasy and which now reappears to describe the frustration of the worker. But even this frustration is part and effect of this discourse which puts the subject in the place of his truth. "Notice that I did not say subject although I spoke about the capitalist subject" (*SXVI*, 20.11.68): an important consideration to realize that the capitalist subject is not the only subject, in fact he is only a hidden subject and under the bar of the Master's discourse, here made expression as and support of the Capitalist discourse. It is for this reason that Lacan will see himself obliged to unfold the function of the market when it comes to University discourse: "Knowledge has nothing to do with labour. But in order that something should be clarified in this affair it is necessary that there should be a market, a market of knowledge that knowledge becomes merchandise" (*SXVI* 20.11.68).

Instead of working with the notions of intellectual work and manual work, Lacan opts to unfold the function of the market. Just as the labour market unifies around the commodity as a fetish, the market of knowledge

> unifies science, so much so that it takes its place in a consecutive discourse, reduces all knowledge to a single market, and this is the nodal reference, as we ask ourselves. The price of knowledge follows: the norms which are constituted from the market of science, is nevertheless obtained for nothing. This is what I called surplus enjoying. Starting from knowledge, what is not new but is only revealed starting from the homogenisation of knowledge on the market, one finally sees that enjoyment is organised and can be established as *recherchée* and *pervers*.
>
> (*SXVI*, 20.11.68)

Now it is the master signifier ($S_1$) that occupies the place of truth, just as knowledge ($S_2$) occupies the place of the agent or semblant of this discourse. The appearance of the system of credits (unity of value), as a consequence of the 1968 revolts in France, is an example of how the market of knowledge was being modernized in that country, at the same time as Lacan was thinking about this process. The worker's position of frustration is taken up again, to conceive of the third discourse, which is the discourse of Hysteria. This discourse is known for its potential for questioning and for placing subjective division as semblant and object *a* as truth:

> the revolutionary consequence of this truth, this truth from which Marxist theory has its origin, is precisely capitalism; the revolutionary consequence of theory, part in fact of this truth, namely, that the proletariat, is the truth of capitalism. The proletariat, what do you want to know? It is the work that is

radicalized to the level of pure and simple commerce; what it wants to do, surely, is to reduce it to the mishmash of the work of the same.

(*SXVI*, 12.02.69)

To say that the proletariat is the truth of capitalism is to think of the symptom as truth. In this case, the market is the place of its fundamental alienation, both as a dissociation of means and ends, and as a lack of knowledge of its own position and conscience. The theory of the four discourses thus reveals the theory of the three markets, leaving open what kind of market equivalent would exist in the case of the psychoanalyst's discourse.

A possible way forward can be found in the discussion of the use-value and exchange, with connection to the notions of inside and outside. We know that the simple opposition between the inside and the outside has been the subject of the logic of the fantasy by means of topological figures such as the projective plane, the Cross Cap, and the Klein Bottle, where exteriority and interiority communicate with each other, even if they maintain their local value intuitively:

> [L]et us plant the question of knowing what is inside and what is going on when, for example, it is a market. If we have been aware of the naturalness of the market, we can distinguish between its value in use and its value in exchange. The value of exchange rate is infuriating. But for this market, we put it in a deposit. It's where you keep it, where you keep it. The tones of acceptance, when they are bulging, are exchanged, and when they are consumed: value for use. It is very curious that when you are inside you are reduced to its exchange value. In a deposit, by definition, it is not for hours or for consumption. If you keep them. The value of use, inside, is where you expect it, is precisely prohibited, and there is no more than its exchange value. Where it is more enigmatic, it is when it is no more a question of the market, but of the fetish for excellence: of the currency.
>
> (*SXVI*, 30.04.69)

The opposition between being kept or put into circulation, takes up, in an approximate way, the difference between what is of private use and what is of public use, that is, it refers both to the sense of ownership and to the introduction, or strategic retreat in relation to the direct introduction, into the market. The case of money as a fetish, that is, not yet capital, and not yet necessarily integrated into the financial or exchange system, seems to be paradigmatic of this idea that if all capitalism develops in discourses, not everything is understood by discourses. If discourses are forms of social bond and rules of exchange, there is still the whole set of things that resists the exchange-universe of comparison and substitution, which is the universe of "non-relations", such as "social non-relationship" or the object *a*, as that which strictly cannot be exchanged. Also, in the scope of the subject, it is only when it is a question of the experience of recognizing one among others, without qualities or predicates, that one can attest to a discursive mutation in the economy of truth, of exchanges, and of *jouissance*:

> When the species of plus-de-jouir that has to be "this is someone" is recognized, we will be on the path of a dialectical matter that is perhaps more active than the flesh of the Party, emptied as the baby-sitter of history. The psychoanalyst will be able to clarify this path with his own opinion.
>
> (*RA*)

## Note

1 Transl. Modified.

## Further reading

Bruno, P. (2020). *Lacan and Marx: The Invention of the Symptom*. J. Holland (Trans.). London: Routledge.
Parker, I. (2017). *Revolutionary Keywords for New Left*. London: Zero Books.
Pavón-Cuéllar, D. & Lara Jr., N. (2018). *Psicanálise e marxismo*. Curitiba: Apris.

## References

Freud, S. (1919). The Uncanny. In: *The Standard Edition of the Complete Psychological Works of Sigmund Freud* (Vol. XIX, pp. 217–252), J. E. Strachey (Trans.). London: Vintage, 2001.

# Chapter 14

# Master/tyrant

*Fabiana Parra*

—Ara.: سيد / طاغية —Chi.: 霸主/暴君 —Fre.: *Maître/tyran* —Ger.: *Herr/Tyrannei* —Ita.: *Padrone/tiranno* —Jap.: 主人 / 僭主 —Port.: *Mestre/tirano* —Rus.: *Господин/тиран* —Spa.: *Amo/tirano* —Tur.: *Efendi/tiran*

→ *History*; *Imperialism*; *Proletarian*; *Slavery*

## Introduction: avatars of the term

To understand the status that this complex term has in Lacan's thought, it is necessary to refer to the reading that his teacher, Alexandre Kojève, makes of the dialectic of the master and the slave, which constitutes the encounter of Lacan with Marx and Hegel. It also implies accounting for the potential of the historical and theoretical-political encounter of French thought with German thought in the 20th century (Badiou, 2012). Thus, it is necessary to first examine the vicissitudes and winding paths that this notion has followed in German thought in order to measure the magnitude that this encounter implies.

First of all, it should be noted that it is a multifaceted term composed of two terms with different etymological roots. While *tyrant* comes from the Greek *týrannos* meaning "*lord*" and "*master*", rooted in the Proto-Germanic word *Tiwaz* meaning "god" or "lord", *master* has a double origin: it comes from the Latin *dominus*, meaning master, owner, owner, and lord; and from *herus*: master of the house and lord. In the Middle Ages, *dominus* became a feudal title: *lord*, equivalent to *seigneur* in French and to *herr* in German. *Herr*[1] is synonymous with *gebieter* and means "master", "lord", "patron", "owner" (both of oneself: "*Herr seiner Sinne sein*", and of a situation: "*er war Herr der Lage*"). It thus refers to the autonomous status of a free subject ("*sein eigener Herr sein*"). In Old German, *herr* is an adjective meaning "gray-haired", "worthy", and has been used to designate the dignity of the one who, being old, is morally venerable and wise. This referred to the authority exercised by the father of the family considered head of the clan over his own and their servants, as well as to the power over (*Herrschaft über*) his lands and his servants. With this we find that *herr* is at the root of the word *Herrschaft*, equivalent in English to the terms "dominion", "power", "command", "authority", "lordship", referring to

DOI: 10.4324/9781003212096-14

the master as the one who has sovereign power over himself, since they are recognized as wise and as owners. The opposition between the terms *Herr* and *Knecht* is already present as a difference in status between the owner of land and the one who works the land.

In *Phenomenology of Spirit* (1807), more precisely in the section "Independence and dependence of self-consciousness: lordship and servitude" (*Selbstständigkeit und Unselbstständigkeit des Selbstbewusstseins: Herrschaft und Knechtschaft*), Hegel introduces the term *Herr* (master) in dialectical opposition to *Knecht* (slave) to examine a stage of self-consciousness, confronting one consciousness to another in the process of the formation of self-consciousness. From this confrontation, two figures emerge and find themselves in a dichotomous and codependent relationship: the master (*Herr*), who is the one capable of risking his life in order to obtain recognition, and the slave (*Knecht*), who submits to the other for fear of death. The former wins over the latter, who is nonetheless capable of transforming itself and overcoming the very relations of domination. Alexandre Kojève (1942) states that it is necessary to differentiate power (*Herrschaft*) from authority (*Macht*), although he warns that a power devoid of authority "is not necessarily legitimate" (p. 39). Additionally, he distinguishes four pure types of authority through a phenomenological analysis—that of the father, the master, the boss, and the judge—which he links to four irreducible authority theories: by scholasticism, by Hegel, by Aristotle, and by Plato, respectively (Di Pego, 2020, p. 32).

The most widespread sense of *master* is that of "owner", "master", "boss", or "proprietor"—which is equivalent to the French terms *maître* and *propriétaire* and, in German, to *besitzer* and *arbeitgeber*. In other words, it refers to the condition of domination given mainly by the property relationship. On the other hand, the most widespread sense of *tyrant* is that of "monarch", "despot", and "*sápatra*". In French, this distinction is illustrated early on by Étienne de La Boétie's (1576) characterization in *La servitude volontaire*, where the *tyrant* master is one who makes abusive use of power and who "has the power to be bad when he wants to" (p. 45). But, in addition, in this iconic work on the theory of power, the *tyrant* is an absolute king ("one only be master; one only be king") (p. 45):

> Prince, despot or *tyrant*, the one who exercises power desires only the unanimous obedience of his subjects. They respond to his desire, they make his desire for power possible, not because of the terror it might inspire in them, but because, by obeying, they realize their own desire for submission.
> 
> (p. 111)[2]

Arguing against a certain interpretation of the tyrannical master as the "culprit" of the subject's submission, La Boétie (1576) asks rhetorically: "How can we understand that the master-slave relationship, before being that of two really separate terms, is inherent to the subject himself?" And he answers: "The master is not, then, death and the trigger of servitude, he is not the primordial fear [...] this strange desire for servitude is such that it leads to ignoring the ultimate test" (p. 114).

## The dehumanized and dependent master in Hegel

According to Hegelian dialectic, the history of humanity emerges from the confrontation between two self-consciousnesses that seek to be recognized by the other as superior; a confrontation in which neither of the two must be suppressed, but must be preserved and integrated so that the dialectical movement of history may continue. In this framework of dialectical struggle, the figure of the master corresponds to the self-consciousness that risked his life to achieve recognition; his self-consciousness can be reflected in that of the slave who confirms his superiority and, as such, his nature as a free subject. In contrast, the self-consciousness of the slave who submits to the master to preserve his life cannot relate to himself because the master perceives him only as a thing or instrument to satisfy his preferences and needs. Thus, the master relates to himself through the objects created by the slave and through the slave himself, whom he does not recognize as human and to whose life he does not give value. Consequently, he suppresses in the slave's self-consciousness his "subordination to natural existence" (La Boétie, 1576, p. 114). However, the master is not absolutely free and autonomous. Rather, he depends on the slave to exist as such. Along these lines, Tran duc Thao (1965) argues: "the master possesses only an apparent freedom, for his victory has been nothing but an immediate and, ultimately, still animal negation of the natural *being-there*; therefore, he continues to live in desire and pleasure" (p. 36). For this reason, the master is dehumanized, since he obtains recognition from a thing, from something that, due to experiencing fear (*Furcht*) of death, belongs to the status of *non-human*.[3]

According to the famous interpretation of Chapter IV of Hegel's *Phenomenology of Spirit* by Alexandre Kojève (1982), human reality is constituted as such upon the struggle that culminates in the relationship between Master and Slave, between "Tyranny and Slavery", which constitutes "the historical dialectic" (pp. 4–13). Returning to the reading of his master, Lacan (*SXVI*, 11.06.69) affirms that the dominion of the master/*tyrant* is related to that foundational confrontation of the figures of Master and Slave, where the former is capable of risking his life in order to obtain recognition as a worthy human being. The dominion of the *tyrant* master lies precisely in the risk of life and its guarantee "is nothing other than what is in the other, in the slave, as a signifier, to which only the master contributes as a subject, his support being nothing other than the slave's body".

## The owner-master in Marx

For Marx and Engels (*MCP*, p. 482) the motor force of history is class struggle, which confronts oppressors, and oppressed in a dichotomous and hierarchical way. In this context of class struggle, the confrontation is no longer between two consciousnesses, but between "Freeman and slave, patrician and plebeian, lord and serf, guild-master". Marx distinguishes the feudal master lord (*herr*) from the *modern master*, the bourgeois capitalist—while the former's domination is based on personal force (*Macht*), the latter dominates in an anonymous and impersonalized way through capital, which is "a social force". Marx assigns a revolutionary role to this modern master, who replaced the old conditions of oppression based on "idyllic relations" to "resolved personal worth into exchange value" (*MCP*, pp. 486–487).

In this framework of class-divided capitalist societies, the domination of the master—i.e., the owner of the means of production—becomes increasingly depersonalized, unlike non-capitalist, archaic societies, where "the domination (*Herrschaft*) of the proprietor over the propertyless may be based on personal relations" (*GI*, p. 63). However, despite the depersonalization of the relation of domination, for Marx (*CAI*, p. 794) there is a concrete, singular, and particular experience that allows the interpretation of the underlying aspects of the specific relation between master and slave, which is manifested in the "absolute dependence of the working class upon the capitalist class". Marx uses the term "owners" to refer to the owners of the means of production who subjugate the direct producers "to keep the plough in the hand of the owners" (*CAI*, p. 880).

## The *tyrant* master in Lacan

Similarly, for Lacan the dialectic of history continues insofar as "the master is represented by the slave", and insofar as the master as subject is supported by the body of the slave. With these ideas, Lacan goes back to the modern critique of the established order and radicalizes the existential dilemma in which the master finds himself: so fundamentally dependent on the slave to subsist that "if the slave dies, there is nothing left". The master, for Lacan, is not a free subject, but is "as perfectly enslaved as possible" and can do nothing but oppress the slave, who is his ideal (*SXVI*, 18.08.69). Nevertheless, the master obtains a recognition that does not satisfy him since it comes from another who he does not recognize as a worthy human being. For Lacan, what is at stake in this "recognition of man by man" is "a radical negation of natural values", whether expressed "in the sterile tyranny of the master or in the fruitful tyranny of labor" (*AP*, pp. 98–99).

In the framework of the Lacanian reading of the struggle for recognition, the master is the one who has been able to renounce *jouissance* and risk his life for pure prestige. And, therefore, he is the one who will have the privilege of *jouissance* when the struggle to death is over, unlike the slave, for whom the path of work is traced. However, through such a path, "the slave transforms his own nature"[4] and educates himself, transforming the natural world into the historical world.

Nonetheless, for Lacan, "the master is not simply the strongest", since "the struggle of pure prestige at the risk of death still belongs to the realm of the imaginary" (*SXVII*, 20.05.70, p. 152). In this framework, there is a discourse—the analytic discourse—that articulates the master's renunciation of *jouissance* and makes the function of the surplus-enjoyment appear. According to Lacan, this function can be thought of as analogous to surplus-value, that is, as the usurpation of *jouissance*. Let us recall that, for Marx, surplus-value is the unpaid value of the worker's labour that creates a surplus-product, appropriated by the owner of the means of production (*CAI*, p. 344). But then Lacan (*SXVII*, 26.11.69, p. 20) proposes to "leave in abeyance" the analogy between *surplus-enjoyment and surplus-value*, which can be read as a symptom of the impossibility of translating a term from one theoretical framework into another.

## The Master's knowledge: lack and appropriation

For Lacan (*AP*, p. 98), in the first statute of the Master's discourse, knowledge is found in the slave since the master knows nothing, "he is a *boludo*". What operates from the discourse of the ancient master to that of the *modern master—the capitalist*—is something that has been modified in the space of knowledge by the intervention of philosophy, which makes possible the extraction and theft of the slave's knowledge—*a know-how*—to turn it into the *master's knowledge*, "a *theoretical knowledge*". Philosophy is, in this framework, a sort of "fabulatory enterprise in favor of the master", since he does not know anything but that "the thing goes" (*SXVII*, 26.11.69, p. 23). It is the philosophical discourse that animated and inspired the master with the desire for knowledge; unlike the slave, who knows many things and even knows what the master wants. Although, the master does not know it, because "otherwise he would not be a master" (*SXVII*, 17.12.69, p. 32). This is why *the master's desire is the desire of the Other*, it is the desire foreseen by the slave. In other words, the master is a discursive position that entails a hidden truth: that of appropriating the desire of the other. Similarly, the analyst becomes the cause of the analysand's desire and obtains knowledge—*analytic knowledge*—thanks to the philosophy that presses the slave's knowledge to obtain its transmission in the knowledge of the Master.

The discourse of the Master is, according to Lacan (*SXVII*, 20.05.70, p. 152), the discourse of truth. It begins with the predominance of the subject precisely because it tends to support itself only in that ultra-reduced myth of being identical to its own signifier: "*m'être à moi-m'ême*" (the term *m'être* is homonymous to *maître* which means "*master*", "*lord*", "*boss*"). The discourse of sciences, among which mathematics is paradigmatic, serves to reject mythical knowledge, "but at the same time, by excluding the latter it can no longer know anything except in the form of what we find under the species of the unconscious" (*SXVII*, 18.02.70, p. 91). The *knowledge of the master* is produced as completely autonomous from mythical knowledge; it is knowledge of science like mathematics that is based on laws distinct from *mythical knowledge*.

## Relevance of the term for feminist perspectives

For Lacan, that man imagines that he himself forms the woman, "is the most ancient figure of the infatuation of the *master/m'être*" (*SXVII*, 20.05.70, p. 152).

Feminist perspectives criticize the notion of the master/male as essential with respect to the woman, "defining her as pure alterity", raising the question: "Where does this submission come from in the woman?" (Beauvoir, 1949, p. 52). Teresa de Lauretis (1993) takes up this critique of exclusionary essentialism that "always works in favor of the oppressor and against the oppressed" and proposes to critically read feminism's postulate of an archetypal woman (pp. 75–76). This questioning has been radicalized and made more complex by Latin American, decolonial, and intersectional feminisms—referenced in black feminisms from the tracing of southern feminist genealogies,[5]—denouncing the class and race blindness of white hegemonic feminisms, since, in addition to gender oppression, poor and racialized women in the Third World and Global South are oppressed due to racial, sexual, and class belonging. In this sense, Angela Davis states, "the direct sexual exploitation of African women by their *white masters* was a constant feature of slavery" (Davis, 1981, p. 145).

## The white master, racial oppressor from the black and dissident feminisms

Aiming at the racial and geopolitical supremacy of the white heterosexual male master, black lesbian feminist Audre Lorde (1988) affirms that "the master's tools will never dismantle the master's house" and proposes to conduct a profound and structural change of the oppressions that are articulated with and overdetermined by themselves (p. 91). To this end, she postulates as an alternative, "Interdependence between women [as a] path to a freedom which allows the 'I' to be, not in order to be used, but in order to be creative". Moreover, she is against the overexploitation suffered by black women, who, as women, are required to educate men and, as black and third world women, "to educate white women"; which, according to Lorde, serves to keep "the oppressed occupied with the master's concerns" (Lorde, 1988, p. 92).

It should also be noted that black feminist bell hooks (2000), when proposing to consider feminism as an alternative to all forms of oppression, does not place the *male master* in the role of enemy, merely inverting the terms of the dialectic, but seeks to suppress any action and/or thought perpetuating oppressive patriarchal practices, since "feminism is for everyone". In the same vein, Paulo Freire (1970), eradicating the logic of domination and abolishing masters, not the mere reversal of roles, argues that "the authentic overcoming of the oppressors-oppressed contradiction does not lie in the fact that the oppressed of today became the new oppressors" (p. 58). In decolonial, black, Latin American studies and critical epistemologies from the South, developed mainly by feminisms, the term tyrannical master, understood as material and ideological oppression of which "we must become aware",[6] has a relevant status. And, just as in Lacan's reading of Marx, it established the notion of the master as a Subject-Centre supported by those oppressed by it.

## Notes

1 In the 7th century, the noun *herre* was more or less the equivalent of *dominus* (Grimm & Grimm, 1854, vol. 4, t. 2, pp. 1124 ff.).
2 Translation by the author.
3 The philosopher María Lugones (2012) radicalizes this formula for the case of colonized women—Indian females—as "the non-male of the non-human". Lugones starts from what she considers one of the fundamental dichotomies of modern coloniality: "the distinction between the human and the non-human" from which gender is only attributed to those who belong to the canon of the human, that is, to white subjectivities (p. 130).
4 For Tran duc Thao (1965), "the slave will reach effective liberation because he has discovered himself as an object and has been formed in his objective reality" (p. 37).
5 See Ciriza (2015).
6 See Fanon (1952).

## Further reading

Gordon, L. R. & Gordon, J. A. (2015). *Not Only the Master's Tools: African American Studies in Theory and Practice (Cultural Politics & the Promise of Democracy)*. London: Routledge.
Lordon, F. (2010). *Capitalisme, désir et servitude. Marx et Spinoza*. Paris: La Fabrique Éditions.
Wittig, M. (1992). Homo Sum. In: *The Straight Mind and other essays*. Boston: Beacon Press.

## References

Badiou, A. (2012). *The Adventure of French Philosophy*, B. Bosteels (Trans.). London: Verso, 2013.
Beauvoir, S. de. (1949). *El segundo sexo. Los hechos y los mitos*, A. Martorell (Trans.). Madrid: Cátedra, 2000.
Ciriza, A. (2015). Construir genealogías feministas desde el Sur: encrucijadas y tensiones. In: *Millcayac*, II(3): 83–104.
Davis, A. (1981). *Mujeres, raza y clase*, A. V. Mateos (Trans.). Madrid: Akal, 2005.
Di Pego, A. (2020). Derivas de la autoridad y del autoritarismo: el paterfamilias y la patria en el pensamiento de Hannah Arendt. In: *Resistances. Journal of the Philosophy of History*, 1(2): 29–41.
Duc Thao, T. (1965). *El materialismo de Hegel*. Buenos Aires: Siglo Veinte.
Fanon, F. (1952). *Black Skin, White Masks*, C. Lam (Trans.). London: Pluto, 1986.
Freire, P. (1970). *Pedagogía del oprimido*. J. Mellado (Trans.). Buenos Aires: Siglo XXI, 2005.
Grimm, J. & Grimm W. (1854). *Deutsches wörterbuch*. Munich: Deutscher Taschenbuch, 1984.
hooks, b. (2000). *Feminism is for Everybody. Passionate Politics*. Cambridge: South End.
Hegel, G. W. F. *The Phenomenology of Spirit*, T. Pinkard (Trans.). Cambridge: Cambridge University Press, 2018.
Kojève, A. (1942). *La noción de autoridad*. H. Cardoso (Trans.). Buenos Aires: Nueva Visión, 2004.

Kojève, A. (1982). *La dialéctica del amo y del esclavo en Hegel*. J. J. Sebreil (Trans.). Buenos Aires: Leviatán, 2006.

La Boétie, É. de (1576). *El discurso de la servidumbre voluntaria*. Buenos Aires: Terramar, 2008.

Lauretis, Teresa de. (1993). Sujetos excéntricos: la teoría feminista y la conciencia histórica. In: C. Cangiano & L. Dubois (Comps.) *De mujer a género* (pp. 73–163). Buenos Aires: Centro Editor de América Latina.

Lorde, A. (1988). Las herramientas del amo nunca desarmarán la casa del amo. In: Ch. Moraga & A. Castillo (Eds.) *Esta puente, mi espalda. Voces de mujeres tercermundistas en los Estados Unidos*. San Francisco: ISM Press.

Lugones, M. (2012). Subjetividad esclava, colonialidad de género, marginalidad y opresiones múltiples. In: *Pensando los feminismos en Bolivia* (pp. 129–140). La Paz: Conexión Fondo de Emancipaciones.

Chapter 15

# Materialism

*David Pavón-Cuéllar*

—Ara.: مادية —Chi.: 唯物論 —Fre.: *Matérialisme* —Ger.: *Materialismus* —Ita.: *Materialismo*. —Jap.: 唯物論 —Port.: *Materialismo* —Rus.: *Материализм* —Spa.: *Materialismo* —Tur.: *Materyalizm/maddecilik*

→ *Alienation*; *Labour/work*; *Money*; *Value*

## Lacan's materialism

Perhaps this entry should not exist. Lacan himself bluntly exclaimed that he "doesn't give a damn about materialism" (*je m'en fous du matérialisme*).[1] However, if one puts such an exclamation back in its context, it must be read as a complaint for having to "spend all the time explaining himself with the philosophers" (*SXXI*, 09.04.74). It seems that these philosophers, including many Marxists, were those who insisted on talking about materialism. This is how Lacan would have ended up claiming for himself a personal materialist position, his "very own materialism" (*mon matérialisme à moi*) (*SXXI*, 09.04.74). Such materialism was a fundamental piece of Lacan's way of approaching Marx, which perhaps justifies an entry like this.

Lacan adheres to Marx's materialist option. When he has to choose, the French psychoanalyst explicitly opts for Marx's "materialism" as opposed to the Hegelian idealist philosophy (*SVII*, 04.05.60, pp. 208–210). He also acknowledges that being a materialist is proper to "any sensible person like him or like Marx" (*LE*, p. 494). Recognizing this does not exclude that Lacanian materialism takes its distance from others.

As we will see in the following pages, Lacan particularly rejects materialist philosophies in which matter is conceived as a substance or as a substantial reality. Lacanian materialism is a materialism of the symbolic, of the signifier, in which there is still a place for the real and the imaginary. This materialism, being related to that of Marx, is presented as dialectical, and it places bodily materiality at the centre, giving rise to an ethics and a theory of truth.

DOI: 10.4324/9781003212096-15

## Critique of materialism: the material that is neither substantial nor real

Although materialistic, the Lacanian option is based on a radical problematization of materialism. One of the aspects by which Lacan problematizes materialism is its functioning as a philosophy, since "there is nothing more philosophical than materialism" (*SXX*, 20.02.73, p. 68). This is problematic from the perspective not only of Lacanian anti-philosophy, but of materialist anti-philosophy, especially that of Marxism, where philosophy is often synonymous with idealism and spiritualism.

The Marxist materialists, who seek to materially overcome philosophy by way of science or political praxis, are the most philosophical of philosophers in the eyes of Lacan. They are so because they believe in the substantial reality of the matter of their philosophical speculations. This belief makes Lacan attribute a "superstition" to them: that which "would designate in an ideality of matter the same impassive substance that was first put into the spirit" (*SXVI*, 04.12.68). The superstitious dogma of the spiritual substance is replicated in that of the material substance, a substance that exists only as an idea, as the ideality of matter. This philosophical dogma is idealist and not materialist.

In his early work Lacan already claims that "authentic materialism" abandons the "substantialist hypothesis" that gives rise to the "idea of matter" (*BRP*, pp. 73). This substantialism, characteristic of philosophy, is an extreme form of idealism because it idealizes even what underlies ideas, transmuting it into the idea of matter as substance. Lacan prefers getting rid of the philosophical notion of substance and bases his "materialism", as he himself continues to call it, on an insubstantial matter, on an "*insubstance*, the a-thing" (*insubstance, l'achose*), understood as "space where the creations of science unfold" (*SXVII*, 20.05.70, p. 159). Scientific work does not consist in discovering, but in creating in the insubstantiality, in the emptiness of matter, irreducible to any idea that philosophers may come up with.

Lacanian materialism excludes the classical philosophical idea of matter as a substantial correlate of ideas. It excludes it by recognizing that it is one more idea, as ideal or spiritual as the others, and that we can only accept its material transcendence with respect to ideas through a materialist "dogmatism" already denounced as such by Fichte (1797, pp. 120–129). Lacan continues denouncing this. He characterizes the materialists as "the only authentic believers", explaining that "their god is matter" (*SXVII*, 21.01.70, pp. 65–66), and describes a kind of Marxist "historical materialism" as "a resurgence of Bossuet's Providence" (*SXXI*, 09.04.74).

Just as the clergyman Jacques-Bénigne Bossuet (1681) confirmed divine intervention and its fight against evil in all moments of history, certain Marxists discovered in each historical event the confirmation of their ideas about class struggle and contradictions between the forces and relations of production. Both those Marxists of the twentieth century and the Catholic preacher of the seventeenth century unravelled in history something substantial that governed it, something that they judged as more real than history, something that was the real itself and that appeared as spiritual, for one, and as material, for the others. In the case of Marxists, this real was the same substantial thing that the superstition of materialism clung to.

Lacan harshly rejects materialism in which the real is substantiated as reality and "identified with matter" (*SXXIV*, 11.01.77). It is, for Lacan himself, the "materialism that has always been there, and that consists in kissing matter's rear in the name that it would be something more real than form" (*SXXI*, 09.04.74). This confusion between the real and the material, both conceived of as the same substantial reality, is a realist expression of the central substantialist error of the materialist philosophy criticized by Lacan. For him, as we know, neither the real nor the material are substantial. Furthermore, the real is neither material nor immaterial, whereas materiality, although it involves something of the real, is rather associated with the symbolic.

## The material in relation to the real, the symbolic, and the imaginary

Lacanian materialism is fundamentally a materialism of the symbolic order. It is in the signifier, in speech and in language, where materiality lies. The relationship of this materiality with the real and with the imaginary cannot be so easily established.

We have already seen that for Lacan the material is not the real. It should be added that the real, distinguishing itself from a substantial reality, corresponds to the impossible that has not yet been symbolized and that therefore causes the material to symbolize it to "accumulate" in the Other of language, conceived as a "reservoir of material" (*SXIV*, 10.05.67). The symbolic materiality of the signifier is treasured and displayed because of the constitutive impossibility of the real. No discourse can symbolize the real, making it possible and materializing it, without annulling it, since the real also excludes the symbolic, defining itself "by a kind of thought abolition of the symbolic material" (*SXVI*, 07.05.69). The real threatens the symbolic and resists any symbolization. For this reason, it cannot materialize, not because it is essentially immaterial, but rather because it is a kind of antimatter.

In contrast to the real, the imaginary has its own materiality. This materiality appears in Lacan, at least in the 1950s, as the raw material of the symbolic. The materialist thesis according to which "language is not immaterial, it is a subtle body, but it is a body", is based on the observation that "words are trapped in all the corporal images that captivate the subject; they can get a hysteric pregnant, identify with the object of the *Penisneid*, represent the urine flow of urethral ambition, or the retained excrement of greedy enjoyment" (*FFS*, p. 248). Similarly, "it is in the disaggregation of the imaginary unit that constitutes the self that the subject finds the signifying material of his symptoms" (*FT*, p. 355). Symbolic materiality comes from the imaginary.

Over time, although maintaining the assimilation of the material to the symbolic, Lacan will also conceive of materiality through the knotting of the registers of the real, the symbolic, and the imaginary. He will then explicitly affirm that the Borromean knot, which inextricably holds the three registers together, is "what in thought makes matter", then defining matter as "what breaks, what remains together and is flexible, what which is called a knot" (*SXXV*, 13.12.77). It is possible to conjecture, in order to maintain the consistency of Lacanian theory, that the materialist recognition of the inherent knotting of materiality requires the consideration of the symbolic material of signifiers, their imaginary raw material and their exclusion in the real. It would be necessary to tie together the three ideas to think about matter. The materiality would reside in the knot itself. As will be seen later, this nodal idea of matter is maintained in the Lacanian conception of symbolic materiality, especially in the definition of the material of the symptom as a knotting of signifiers.

## Marx and the Lacanian materialism of the symbolic

Although the imaginary and the real have a place in Lacanian materialism, it must be reiterated that it is a materialism of the symbolic. Being a materialist, for Lacan, "consists in accepting only material signs as existing" (*SXII*, 16.12.64). Lacanian materialism thus requires adherence to the symbolic materiality of the signifier, resisting the temptation of hermeneutic idealism, which attempts to understand signifiers by attributing an ideal meaning to them. Categorically rejecting this understanding, Lacan recommends not imagining what the words "mean", but concentrating on "what they say" (*SIII*, 23.11.55, p. 22). This way of proceeding is presented from the beginning as a "materialism of the elements in cause", of "the fully incarnated, materialized signifiers, which are the words that walk around" (*SIII*, 20.06.56, p. 289).

At first glance, Lacan's materialist option for the symbolic of the material word differs from Marx's materialist options for the existence that precedes consciousness, for practice as continuation of theory by other means, for the civil society that underlies the state, or for the economic basis of the ideological superstructure. In fact, scrutinizing the work of Marx, we discover in it a materialism of the symbolic equivalent to that of Lacan. This materialism can be appreciated first in *The German Ideology*, where Marx and Engels (*GI*), criticizing the young Hegelians of their time, bring the discussion to the field of language. The literal, material words are in the foreground of their materialist critique of ideas.

Before dealing with the discursive materiality of ideology, Marx and Engels depart from the following materialist premise: "language is practical consciousness, real consciousness, which also exists for other men" (*GI*, p. 44). Finally, after their critique, they can conclude, in the same sense, that "the immediate reality of thought is language" (*GI*, p. 446). These words elucidate the materialist method of Marx and Engels, who take the critique of ideology to the material domain of language because it is there that they locate the immediate reality of thought or the real substrate of ideas. Obviously the real and the reality here do not have the substantial meaning rejected by Lacan. It is simply the insubstantial materiality of words. Language thinks, as an Other, about the subject. The organ of thought is not the brain, but language. This is why Marx and Engels, like Lacan, prefer to focus on the immediacy of what the words say, what they think, rather than a detour to understand what they are supposed to mean.

The materialist rejection of understanding continues as Marx dabbles in history and economics. In his analysis of capitalism and the revolutions of the nineteenth century, Marx stays true to his materialism by describing and explaining what happens in its materiality, be it economic processes or historical circumstances, instead of trying to understand the profound significance of what he observes, the meaning attributable to history or economy, and the motivations or intentions of those involved. Marx's materialist interest is not in the ideal meaning of events, but in the events themselves treated as material signifiers, whether historic or economic.

In the case of economy, Marx's materialist privileging of the signifier instead of the signified translates into an emphasis on the economic sphere of value at the expense of the social reality of people and things. Marx realizes that capitalism is dominated and "propelled" not by "use-value", by the utility or intrinsic value of things and people, but by their "exchange-value" as commodities, its proper value, its abstract, extrinsic and relative economic value, summarized in money and converted into capital (*CAI*, pp. 247–257). This exchange-value reminds us of Lacan's signifier: it is something material, not understandable, although it can be explained, and it is what it is because of its relationship with other values or signifiers, especially that of life exploited as a labour force, and not because of itself or because of its relationship with a use-value, with a meaning. Furthermore, just as in Lacan, the meaning is subordinated to the signifier, so the use-value is subordinated to the exchange-value in Marx's description of capitalism.

In fact, exchange-value, which Lacan reconceptualises as "*jouissance* value", perverts use-value, reducing it to a pure "*jouissance* of value" (*SXIV*, 12.04.67). In capitalism, only the enjoyment of capital matters, its possession for the sake of possession, its accumulation, and prior to this its "valorisation", the production of a surplus-value, of a supplement of exchange-value (*CAI*, pp. 293–306). We are thus in a pure economy of the signifier, of value and of its enjoyment, of its production and its possession, to which meaning, that of society with its needs, is subordinated.

Lacan affirms categorically that "the so-called historical materialism does not make sense except precisely in perceiving that it does not depend on the social structure, since Marx himself affirms that it depends on the means of production" (*SXVI*, 08.01.69). It must be understood that for Marx these means are fundamentally "means of production of surplus value, means that create value, valorise value", and operate as "modes of existence of capital" (*CAI*, pp. 976–982). Even capital itself is "autonomous exchange value (money) as a process, as a process of valorisation" (*GR*, p. 232). We see that everything happens for Marx in the sphere of value of the signifier, not of the signified. This justifies that we attribute to him a materialism of the symbolic analogous to that of Lacan.

## Convergences with Stalin and with Marx and Engels: basis of language and dialectical materialism

The omission or underestimation of the symbolic order, of the signifier, of language and discourse, is for Lacan the main error of some currents of Marxism. The error manifests itself, for example, when a "gap" is left in the function of language in theory (*ST*, p. 745), supposing "the truth of materialism is dumb" (*ST*, p. 738), or when "materialists" do not understand why courtly love appeared in feudal times because they do not see that "it has its roots in the discourse of feudalism, of fidelity to the person" (*SXX*, 20.02.73, p. 69). The fact that the symbolic is the material basis, the determining foundation of a certain love relationship and other phenomena, would be unacceptable for many Marxists, but not for all.

Lacan refers in particular to Stalin, whom he credits for having understood, in his "materialism", that language is not "reducible to a superstructure (*FT*, p. 344). Certainly, Stalin (1950) categorically asserted that language "differs essentially from the superstructure" and "is not distinguished from the instruments of production" (pp. 2–5). Lacan comes very close to these ideas of the Soviet leader both when he sees in the symbolic a productive means, producer of enjoyment, and when he places it on a more infrastructural than superstructural level.

Confessing its proximity to Stalinist materialism, whose conception of language would be "far above logical neopositivism", the Lacanian theory of language is explicitly presented as a "materialist" theory (*RSF*, p. 112). Lacan rejects, also explicitly, the imputation of "pernicious idealist" against his person, since "the only danger of idealism" in a discourse like his would be medieval nominalism with its emphasis on the signifier (*SXVIII*, 20.01.71, p. 28). But this nominalism, by reducing the signifier to the name "that sticks on the real", would obviously be very far from the Lacanian conception of language as a material base and productive means, a conception that must be ascribed to "dialectical materialism" (*SXVIII*, 20.01.71, p. 28).

Lacan's adherence to dialectical materialism implies his proximity not only to Stalin, but to other Marxists and to Marx and Engels themselves, who also coincide with Lacanian materialism by putting the symbolic at the centre of their materialist perspective. In *The German Ideology*, before criticizing the discursive deployment of the ideas of the young Hegelians of their time, Marx and Engels justify their method by explaining that "from the start the spirit is afflicted with the curse of being burdened with matter, which here makes its appearance in the form of agitated layers of air, sounds, in short, of language" (*GI*, p. 44). Seemingly immaterial ideas are hopelessly contaminated by a material language.

This materialism of the symbolic, perfectly concordant with Lacan's, is also a masterful example of dialectical materialism. Marx and Engels state dialectically that the spirit is not identical to itself, being originally language in its materiality, with which there is no sharp difference between the material and the spiritual. If this distinction is not present, it is precisely because of the language that is involved in the spirit and it has a material composition that will later be emphasized by Lacan.

Lacanian materialism of the symbolic also proceeds dialectically by defining the signifier as "the matter that is transcended into language" (*RSF*, p. 112). By being transcended and being language, matter reveals itself as different from itself, but then the dividing boundary between matter and language disappears. The two elementary vectors of the materialist dialectic that we also find in the passage by Marx and Engels cited in the previous paragraph operate here: the inexistence of "rigid and fixed lines" and "the difference within identity" (Engels, 1883, pp. 443–447). The symbolic is the difference within the material identity, which excludes the existence of a *rigid and fixed line* between the material and the symbolic, as well as, consequently, between the material and the spiritual originally contaminated by the symbolic for Marx and Engels.

## *Moterialism* and *significantization*: the symbolic understood as the material

The symbolic is not only material, but *the* material transcending itself. It is to this essential and paradoxical materiality that Lacanian materialism of the symbolic points. The material of materialism is here the same as the symbol, the signifier, the word.

For Lacan, being a materialist is to concentrate on the word, on what is said, and not on the idea, not on what is supposedly meant by what is said. We understand then that Lacan has used the term "*mot*", which means "word" in French, to forge his untranslatable neologism "*moterialism*", which means something like "word-materialism" (*CG*, p. 13). The *wordtter* or *motter* is Lacan's matter, that which is transcended in language, that of the signifier with its material opacity, with the "irreducible materiality" of its structure (*RDL*, p. 551). This signifier does not correspond, like the signified, to a supposedly intelligible and transparent concept, to a supposed conscious idea, and it is for the same reason that it can serve as the foundation of the Lacanian theory of the unconscious.

Lacanian materialism of the symbolic not only puts the signifier in its materiality before the signified in its ideality, but also redefines the relationship between the two terms. Instead of a signification in which the signified governs the signifier that communicates it, we have a "*significantization*" where a signifier summons the other signifiers to which it refers, making them appear in the place of the signified by turning certain things into signifiers (*SV*, 05.03.58, p. 237). This process, which makes things "materialize as signifiers" (*SXVIII*, 01.13.71, p. 17), is an "intransitive materialization" that for Lacan sums up the very functioning of the unconscious (*RA*, p. 417). Materialization is intransitive, without an object, because the supposed meaning does not exist before materially sprouting as a signifier, before materializing by being *significantized*.

## Features of matter: language, uniqueness, knowledge, causality, symptom

Something must already be a signifier to have materiality. For Lacan, the material world is not a real world but, rather, it has a symbolic character. It is made of signifiers. These signifiers are the material things.

The matter of Lacanian materialism is the signifier, the symbolic, and not the ideal signified nor the real or substantial reference. This determines five characteristic features of the meaning of materiality in Lacan: its linguistic quality, its unique and indivisible character, its assumption of knowledge, its causal effectiveness, and its symptomatic truth.

In the first place, by being the signifier, matter is for Lacan what linguists work with, "the material that is in dictionaries, the lexicon, morphology also, in short, the object of their linguistics" (*SXXI*, 11.06.74). This does not mean that it is a "pure form" as linguists imagine it, since language material "is a content", but a content that it is not distinguished from the form (*SXVI*, 11.12.68). It is the symbolic origin of the form, the insubstantial that gives its formal characteristics to each thing, like the void around which the container is moulded.

Second, by being a unique void in each case, matter is each time "unique"; it is something "singular" that resists division, that "does not support partition", and therefore, if "we tear a letter into pieces, it continues to be the letter that it is" (*PL*, p. 16). It is not like mud, quarry, or oil. It is not a neutral, shapeless, indeterminate raw material. Its materiality does not simply consist in being extensive, in having a volume and occupying a space. Matter does not fill the void, but it is the void itself, its content, its structure that distinguishes it.

Third, by having a structure, matter implies a knowledge that appears as "supposed" in the "signifying material" (*SXXII*, 18.02.75). It is a knowledge whose "materiality" is in the signifier, a knowledge inherent to the symbolic, a knowledge that is more than what it "thinks it knows" (*SXXIV*, 16.11.76). It is, therefore, an unconscious knowledge that is indiscernible from the significance of the signifier, from its structure, from the very materiality of its matter, which is also not neutral for this reason.

Fourth, being not neutral, matter has effects, causal effectiveness. We can then speak of a "material cause" as Aristotle did, but granting full meaning to the concept, not as in Aristotle, since matter "for him was not a cause at all", but a "purely passive element" (*SXIII*, 08.12.65). This is not the case in Lacanian materialism, where there is a causality proper to symbolic materiality. The signifier, synonymous with matter, is here the "material cause of jouissance" (*SXX*, 19.12.72, p. 24). Lacan plays with the double meaning of the French verb "*causer*", which means both "speak" and "cause", to identify this material cause with the Freudian instance of the id that speaks and causes effects when speaking, since "it speaks and causes effects (*ça cause*), it even speaks and causes effects in a foolish way" (*SXXI*, 23.04.74). The matter of Lacanian materialism is Freud's id, that which does not stop speaking and causing effects, the signifier that is in the unconscious base and that from there both determines and disturbs the existence of the subject.

Fifth, as something determining and disturbing, matter is the very truth of existence: the truth that Lacan understands "materialistically" as "what is established in the signifying chain", what is revealed in the symptom, which "is made of the same paste from which the signifier is made" (*SQ*, p. 195). Lacan attributes to Marx the merit of having conceptualized the symptom as a revelation of the truth, but considers that psychoanalysis was needed for this concept to acquire a fully materialist meaning, not as a sign that represents the truth, but as the truth of the signifier itself, in its materiality. The Lacanian notion of the symptom is that of something purely material and without an ideal background: signifiers without meaning, "signifying matter", an intricate "knot of signifiers" (*TV*, p. 10). What is displayed in a material way in the symptomatic knot is the same that is revealed and has a purely symbolic character. It is not something real and substantial, but it is revealing and materially true, symbolically true.

## Materialism of the body in Lacanian conceptions of truth and ethics

The symptom is for Lacan what it was for Freud: a materially present truth, that of the id, that of the unconscious, that of the repressed that returns. This truth, in its Lacanian materialist sense, is presented as a unique and distinctive material of the subject, its materiality on which "the same is based" (*SXXIV*, 14.12.76). On the contrary, "everything that is not founded on matter is a scam (*escroquerie*)", constitutes "a lie" (*mensonge*), since "there is exchange, but not materiality itself" (*SXXIV*, 14.12.76). The material implication of a subject ensures that his word is a full, compromising, true word. There is no guarantee of truth without the material basis of existence.

Lacan situates the truth in a symbolic materiality, that of the signifier, which underlies the existence of the subject and is clearly distinguished from the real. This materialist notion of truth contrasts with the most influential notions cultivated in the Marxist tradition in Lacan's time: on the one hand, the positive one of official Marxism-Leninism, where the truth lies in a simple adequacy to objective material reality; on the other hand, the negative one of the Frankfurt School, where the truth can critically contradict the same objective material reality because it is confined in the speculative ideal sphere (Marcuse, 1941; Adorno, 1966). Lacan avoids the Frankfurtian philosophical idealism by giving a material basis to the truth, but this does not make him relapse into Soviet realist materialism, since he distinguishes this basis from objective reality and links it to the existence of the subject.

In the Lacanian materialist sense of the term, a word is true not because it corresponds to objective reality or because it contradicts and criticizes it, but because it involves speaking subjects, implying them because it is based on the matter of the signifier that distinguishes them. Subjects tell the truth when they imply and commit themselves in a symbolic way in their word, when they fill it, when they exist materially through it, when they put their bodies in what they say. These bodies, which are fundamental to Lacanian materialism, must be distinguished both from the organism and from the Cartesian *res extensa*. The corporeal materiality, once again, is neither real nor substantial, but symbolic and insubstantial.

The symbolic insubstantiality of the body in which Lacan thinks provoked the fact that its materiality was not recognized in the history of philosophy. Lacan refers to Democritus and the other atomists, for whom "a body did not seem materialistic enough" and for that reason they had to find "the atoms, and the entire apparatus, and the vision, the smell, and all what it entails" (*SXX*, 20.02.73, p. 71). It is closer than all this where the body of Lacanian materialism must be located. This body is nothing more than that with which one exists, experiences, enjoys. It is with it that the implication of subjects in their words can be assured. It is by betting it, delivering it as a certainty, that speakers guarantee that their words are true.

Truth has an existential, experiential price for the subject, a price that can only be paid with the body. We come here to another fundamental Lacanian materialist proposition: "there is no enjoyment other than the one of the body", or its equivalent: "there is only matter introduced into the field of knowledge" (*SXIV*, 31.05.67). These propositions, responding to the "demand for truth that exists in Freudianism", summarize the "ethical value of materialism" consisting of "refusing eternal joys and taking seriously what happens in our daily life" (*SXIV*, 31.05.67). It is not beyond where the true and the ethical are founded in Lacanian materialism; it is here, in the body that takes risks and always ends up losing itself.

The body that is at stake on the word is one of the expressions of Lacan's *objet (petit) a*. It is the price of the "matter of writing" where Lacan places his "personal materialism", which we referred to at the beginning (*SXXI*, 09.04.74). This materialism of the symbolic is also of the price of the symbolic, of the body in writing, of the "sexual relationship" in "poetry", which was what would have allowed Freud to found the psychoanalytic movement and Marx to "make a political movement" through what he wrote (*SXXIV*, 20.12.77).

If Marx and Freud were "poets" whose writings left traces in history, it was because they both materially put their bodies at stake on their word and thus demonstrated their truth, while verifying "historical materialism", which is "what is embodied in history" (*SXXIV*, 20.12.77). Thus, they deployed what psychoanalysis could return to Marxism: "a dialectical matter perhaps more conducive than the Party meat known for becoming the babysitter of history" (*RA*, p. 415). It is useless to accompany historical processes. It is necessary to incarnate in them, as Marx did in Marxism, through what we put the body into.

## Note

1 All translations were slightly modified by the author.

## Further reading

Eyers, T. (2011). Lacanian Materialism and the Question of the Real. Cosmos and History. In: *The Journal of Natural and Social Philosophy*, 7(1): 155–166.
Pavón Cuéllar, D. (2012). El manzano revolucionario de Gustave Flaubert y los ocho materialismo de Jacques Lacan. In: *Affectio Societatis*, 9(17): 10–20.
Sbriglia, R. & Žižek, S. (2020). *Subject Lessons: Hegel, Lacan, and the Future of Materialism*. Evanston: Northwestern University Press.

## References

Adorno, T. W. (1966). *Dialectique négative*. G. Coffin et al. (Trans.). Paris: Payot, 2003.
Bossuet, J. B. (1681). *Discours sur l'histoire universelle*. Paris: Flammarion, 1966.
Engels, F. (1883). Dialéctica de la naturaleza. In: *Obras filosóficas* (pp. 285–533). W. Roces (Trans.). Mexico: FCE, 1986.
Fichte, J. G. (1797). Introducciones a la teoría de la ciencia. In: Porrúa (Ed.). *El destino del hombre e Introducciones a la teoría de la ciencia* (pp. 115–181). Mexico: Porrúa.
Marcuse, H. (1941). *Razón y revolución*. J. Fombona (Trans.). Madrid: Alianza, 1999.
Stalin, I. (1950). *El marxismo y los problemas de la lingüística*. Pekín: Ediciones en Lenguas extranjeras, 1976.

# Chapter 16

# Money

*Pierre Bruno*

—Ara.: مال —Chi.: 金錢 / 交易 —Fre.: *Argent* —Ger.: *Geld* –Ita.: *Soldi* —Jap.: 貨幣 —Port.: *Dinheiro* —Rus.: *Деньги* —Spa.: *Dinero* —Tur.: *Para*

→ *Capitalism*; *Market*; *Surplus*-jouissance; *Value*

In a Marx through Lacan Vocabulary, money is undoubtedly one of the most suitable entries, not only to highlight specific parts of their work but also, by contrasting and not misinterpreting Freudo-Marxism, to produce and delineate an intelligent stereoscopic reading, capable of questioning what is often overlooked when these three giants are read individually.

## Money in Marx

Somewhat surprisingly, the concept "money" (*argent*) does not appear in the excellent *Dictionnaire critique du marxisme* published in 1982 in Paris, under the direction of Georges Labica. It is possible, nonetheless, to find "coin" (*monnaie*), and the inevitable question is if they are referring to the same thing. In *The Poverty of Philosophy*, we find a first distinction, namely that silver, a precious metal (*Silber*) has often been used as a currency (*Münze*). In *Capital*, the word "money" (*argent*) is used regularly to translate "*Geld*", especially when it is defined as "general equivalent". The term "coin" (*Münze*) is used, more rarely, only when it concerns the currency of a state or money as cash or monetary value. In English and in Spanish, a single word has acquired the monopoly of the translation of *Geld*: money, in English, and *dinero*, in Spanish. Finally, the German word *Wert* is translated in these three languages unequivocally: *valeur*, *value*, *valor*. We can simply emphasize that in French, *Mehrwert*, commonly translated as "*plus-value*" (surplus-value) is translated in Labica's dictionary as "*survaleur*".

This discrepancy (*décalage*), in French as well as in German, gives way, in the French translation of Maximilien Rubel, to a fluctuating hesitation: thus, in *Capital* (Books I, II, and III), "*Der Umlauf des Geldes*" is translated as "*cours de la monnaie*" (circulation of money),[1] then Die Münze as "*le numéraire ou les espèces*" (coins or pieces), "*Geld*" as "*La monnaie ou l'argent*", "*Weltgeld*" as

"*La monnaie universelle*" (world money), without reason or explanation for these choices. However, a more inflexible lexicology might have had the disadvantage of obscuring the complexity of the many sides of "*das Geld*". Thus, in *Capital* Marx (*CAI*, p. 81) writes: "Money necessarily crystallizes out of the process of exchange, in which different products of labour are in fact equated with each other, and thus converted into commodities". This metaphor of "crystallization" is reminiscent of the same metaphor that Stendhal uses in *De l'amour* (*On Love*) when speaking of the rising of the feeling of love. One can also find in Marx the expression "the thirst for gold" (*la soif de l'or*), to designate in a graphic way what is involved in hoarding (*thésaurisation*), or better still, a critique of mercantilism, which confuses wealth as accumulation and gold with the silver capital, which is a form of fetishism. In other words, Marx is very sensitive to this kind of quasi-geological bond which persists, once money, as a value-form, is born, and it retains its presence within nature in the form of a precious metal.

Now that the background has been established, it is appropriate to situate the implication of Marx's conception of money, from which he will derive the entire architecture of his critique of political economy, uncovering the secret of capitalist exploitation by means of a fundamental discovery: surplus-value. The core of this conception can be found in *Capital*, in Part 3 of the first chapter, entitled "The value-form, or exchange value" (*Die Wertform oder des Tauschwert*). We will carefully follow the process unfolding in four stages and going from the enunciation to the money-form.

### First step

Marx takes the commodity as his starting point and recalls that the commodity is such only through its double form, the use-value and the value-form. The use-value, that is, utility, is not particularly problematic. On the other hand, regarding the money-form (*Geldform*), Marx deems that it is necessary to provide its genesis or origin, which is a task never attempted by bourgeois economics. He dissects its origin as follows: in the first place, "the simple, isolated, or accidental form of value" (*CAI*, p. 139). Consider the equation "20 yards of linen= 1 coat". In this equation, 20 yards of linen is the relative value, and the coat functions as an equivalent form (*Äquivalentform*). Twenty yards of linen is nothing but useful material, but its value can only be expressed relatively in another commodity, a coat.

The two forms "are mutually exclusive". Let us examine the "relative form of value". On the one hand, it is the condensation of abstract human labour—"congealed quantities of human labour" (*CAI*, p. 141)—(without which it is not valuable) and, on the other hand, this condensation must take the form of an object different from the 20 yards of linen, namely, the coat. Thus, the garment is the "bearer of value" (*CAI*, p. 143). To summarize, the value of commodity A (20 yards of linen) thus expressed in the use-value of commodity B (coat), takes the form of relative value. It depends on the amount of labour required to produce commodity A and the amount of labour required to produce commodity B. The equation 20 yards of linen = 1 coat implies that the amount of labour or the same quantity of labour-time is identical on both sides of the equation. Of course, the respective quantities of labour of A and B can vary and modify the equation.

Let us turn now to the equivalent form: the amount of labour-time is determined independently of its value-form. Commodity A (relative form) is always expressed as a quantity of value, but commodity B (equivalent) does not express its own quantity of value, it only expresses the quantity of the value of commodity A. This distinction, where necessity does not impose itself spontaneously, is nonetheless what makes it possible not to see the expression of value as "merely a quantitative relation" (*CAI*, p. 148), as certain economists had mistakenly noted. The great Aristotle himself considers that two commodities as dissimilar as commodity A and commodity B cannot be commensurable. Aristotle's analysis of the concept of value fails because he was unable to see that what makes it possible to establish the equality of commodity A and B is nothing other than human labour (the question of the quantity of this labour is secondary).

Continuing his analysis, Marx then emphasizes the misunderstanding caused by the concept of "exchange-value". He even corrects his original definition of commodity that had been defined as a use-value and an exchange-value (*CAI*, p.153). Strictly speaking, a commodity is a use-value and a value, which comes from the fact that a commodity, when looked at in isolation, is a value and it becomes exchange-value only by entering an equation, a value-relation or an exchange relation, with a second commodity. Failing to recognize this point runs the risk of falling into the delusion of Mercantilists and the modern bagmen of free-trade. The former only pay attention to the equivalent form of the commodity (especially when under the form of "money" (*argent*)) and the latter are only interested in the quantitative side of the relative form of value. For them, accordingly, there exists no value nor magnitude of value anywhere except in its expression by means of the exchange relation (that is, "in the daily list of prices current on the Stock Exchange" (*CAI*, p. 153)).

### Second step: "The total or expanded form of value"

This is exhibited in a series of equations: 20 yards of linen (commodity A) = 1 coat (commodity B) = 10 lb. of tea (commodity C) = 2 ounces of gold (commodity D) = etc. The problem with this form is that the series of its terms does not have an end. There is then the need to proceed to the "general form of value".

### Third step: "The general form of value"

This is presented as follows:

1 coat =) 20 yards of linen
10 lb. of tea =) *idem*
2 ounces of gold =) *idem*

By this general form of value, commodities are for the first time, really brought into relation with each other as values, or permitted to appear to each other as exchange-values. At the same time, the whole world of commodities transforms the excluded commodities from this list into a universal equivalent, or better, it transforms any goods withdrawn from its list into a universal equivalent. Linen, coats, tea, an ounce of gold, can occupy this place. It is then enough to establish the gold commodity in this place to get to the fourth step.

### Fourth step: "The money form" (Forme monnaie ou argent)

The establishment of the gold commodity in this place of universal equivalent follows historical reasons. Thus, the origin of the money form as a universal equivalent from the simple commodity form is completed.

At best, this analysis can be confusing, at worst it seems to complicate matters unnecessarily. Without it, however, that which allows grasping human labour as the foundation of value, the discovery of surplus-value, would have been impossible. In fact, surplus-value rests on the preliminary position that labour-power, in the capitalist mode of production, has become a commodity. As a result, it becomes possible to underscore the excess value produced by the paid worker during his total working time, once the value of his labour power has been reproduced. This excess is the surplus-value. In *Value, Price, and Profit*, Marx provides a brilliant example:

> Take the example of our spinner. We have seen that, to daily reproduce his laboring power, he must daily reproduce a value of three shillings, which he will do by working six hours daily. But this does not disable him from working ten or twelve or more hours a day. But by paying the daily or weekly *value* of the spinner's laboring power the capitalist has acquired the right of using that laboring power during *the whole day or week*.
> 
> (*VPP*, p. 79)

It is no wonder, then, that the capitalist's laughter celebrates this perfectly legal fool's bargain.

On the other hand, without this analysis, it is impossible to bring to light what Marx calls "commodity fetishism" and correlatively, "money fetishism" (*fethichisme de l'argent*). What he denominates "fetishism", necessarily characterizing the phenomenal apprehension of the commodity, is due to the fact that "the definite social relation between men themselves" assumes here, for them, "the fantastic form of a relation between things" (*CAI*, p. 165). The impasse that makes the vulgar economy and the bourgeois economy on the basis of value in human labour renders this fetishism, which is analogous to a religious process, inseparable from this mode of production in which labour-power has become a commodity. It is already possible to note that, according to Freud, what produces the fetish is the impasse made upon castration, that is, a phallic substitute that contradicts castration, even when it has just been recognized.

We know that when Marx wrote *Capital*, financial capitalism was very far from being as developed as it is today in the 21st century. In *Un monde sans Wall Street?*, the French economist François Morin (2011) compares the money circulating in the financial economy and the money of the real economy. Of a total of transactions of 3688 trillion dollars (trillion = one thousand billion dollars), only 60 trillion (global sum of GDP) belong to the real economy (statistics of 2008). We can thus see, with a certain dismay, the monstrosity to which the fetishism of money can drive the capitalist mode of production, primarily through the functioning of the stock market, by the foreclosure of any apprehension of capitalist exploitation and, correlatively, any apprehension of the insatiable quest for obtaining the best amount of profit.

Before going in depth into the analysis of the status of money in Freud and Lacan, I want to mention a couple of matters: in Marx's style, money is often presented under a bifrontal allegory, Venus on one side and Caligula or Nero on the other. Moreover, for Marx the question of the price of the work or art was always puzzling (in spite of Picasso's reply to someone who had asked him why a single one of his drawings was worth a fortune).

Leon Walras was born less than 15 years after Marx, and he left his mark in the history of political economy while being completely opposed to Marx. Walras conceived of himself from the point of view of the consumer that desires and enjoys, and he defined the price of a commodity according to its scarcity. He thus claimed that a market balance regulated by what some desire and others offer— hence the impossibility of conceiving of a crisis due to overproduction, a point of view defended by Keynes. Walras, who generally introduced mathematization into political economy, also encouraged the emergence of a conception of money as a pure sign, as autonomous from the sphere of production.

## From Marx to Freud and Lacan

In the vocabularies of psychoanalysis in French, "money" (*argent*) has no citizenship right, except in an article on money and psychoanalysis that appeared in *L'Encyclopedia Universalis*. Those who scorn psychoanalysis would undoubtedly point out that psychoanalysts prefer to maintain as a taboo the question of the money that they earn by charging for the session and, for those who undergo analysis, the correlation between faecal retention and avarice is not very respectable.

Let us depart from Freud. We cannot say that Freud became rich by being a psychoanalyst. As for the price of the sessions, it followed the secular and spontaneous conception where the price was paid for the amount of work he had as a practising psychoanalyst. This did not prevent him from gathering financial assistance to pull the "Wolf Man" from his post-revolutionary misery, and he even encouraged the free sessions provided by the Berlin Psychoanalytic Institute. On 16 January 1898 he wrote a letter to Fliess where he says: "Happiness is the belated fulfillment of a prehistoric wish. For this reason, wealth brings so little happiness. Money was not a childhood wish" (Freud, 1898, p. 294). He discusses further childhood wishes in the essay *On the Transformation of Instincts, with Special Reference to Anal Erotism* (Freud, 1917, p. 128). This article refers to the relationship that Freud established between excrement, gifts, money, penis, and the child. There is a specific sentence that is of interest because it asserts that these five elements "in the unconscious are often treated as if they were equivalent and could replace one another freely". The term "equivalent" reminds us of the general form of value in Marx. It would be possible, then, to write the following: excrement = child = penis = gift = money. The difference in Freud is that if one were to look for a "universal equivalent" it would be the penis, or more precisely, the penis that might be lacking, that needs to be found. A network of relations, proven in the psychoanalytic clinic, is revealed by replacing this Freudian analysis, concerning the misfortunes of the drive in the configuration of the castration complex, and gives these equivalencies their specific meaning. Thus, in the analysis of Little Hans, it is not difficult to relate the *Lumpf* (*Lumpf machen* = to do the big commission) to Hans's desire to make his mother an imaginary child. Joyce's interest in Nora's dirty panties goes in the same direction. Concerning the penis envy (*penisneid*), which Freud will ignore as feminine at the end of the analysis, in this text it is made equivalent with the envy of a child, and so on. We cannot fail, then, if we claim the equivalence of penis to money, especially as a gift, to conclude that, both in terms of penis envy and in terms of money as a gift that is given or received, there is a structural *illegality*, that is, a circumvention of castration coupled with a transgression of the prohibition of incest.

This is further confirmed by Freud's discovery of fetishism: the absence of the penis in women is recognized and, at the same time, denied. The elective excitation aroused by a woman's pubic hair, or by her braids, that is supposed to cover the absence, bears a strange resemblance to the fetishization of silver and to that thirst for hoarding gold which, if we follow Weber, was a condition for the construction of capitalism, given Protestant ethics and the refusal to spend for the sake of luxury. To sum up, to separate money and value, as the unconscious mind does, is to subvert the law.

This conclusion should be retained, but it does not shed light on the relationship between law and money. *Notes Upon a Case of Obsessional Neurosis* (*Zwangsneurose*) sheds light on two sides of the status of money in the cure of the Rat Man, based on his debt. In the dream where Freud's daughter has "two patches of dung instead of eyes", we find the equivalence between shit and money. Freud provides us his "translation" of this dream: "he was marrying my daughter not for her 'beaux yeux' but for her money" (Freud, 1909, p. 200). In this sense, in this dream there is a transferential wish of incest: to marry the daughter of the "father". However, this dream exonerates Freud's analysand from the incestuous nature of this wish by positing money as a non-libidinal motive for the desired marriage. Similarly, the disambiguation between *Raten* (rats) and *Ratten* (*acompte*) entails a "rat money" (*monnaie-rats*), with which the Rat Man calculates the price of the sessions. This currency also has the function of paying off the Rat Man's debt to his father's place, and of Freud as his substitute.

Stressing these two sides of money is the best possible introduction to what Lacan was able to develop regarding money. Above all, Lacan admitted the revolutionary and true discovery of surplus-value by Marx, as well as what according to him was Marx's blind spot, namely that surplus-value (*Mehrwert*) is surplus enjoyment (*Mehrlust*). So, what was Marx's *misstep* (*bévue*)?

Lacan (*RSF*, p. 114) writes: "The object of psychoanalysis is not man; it is what he lacks—not an absolute lack, but the lack of an object. [...] It is not to scarce bread, but to cake that the Queen sent her peoples in time of famine". Such a statement could sound like water for Walras's mill, if psychoanalysts were not, from the outset, able to offer a reading that does not merely reduce money to a single symbolic value. If we follow this alternative reading, it is possible to begin with an exquisite expression of Pareto, the successor and pupil of Walras: ophelimity (*l'ophélimité*). Pareto begins with an incontestable observation (a drinker obtains less pleasure in the third glass of water than in the first) and deduces a law: the value of water decreases in proportion to its consumption. Walras's law of scarcity is related to this deduction. However, this axiom only takes into account the pleasure principle and, unlike Lacan's statement, he does not even suspect that the axiom can be contested considering the death drive. The death drive is, in Freud, how *jouissance* enters the scene, as he explicitly says when he mentions Barbara Low's article on the principle of Nirvana. Lacan is the one that elaborates and gives different names to the category of *jouissance*. One can also note that, having created the expression "surplus-enjoyment", and its ambiguity between "*plus*" (*jouissance*, it is over!) and "*plus de*" (*jouissance*, once again!), he translated it into German as *Mehrlust*, *Lust*, being both pleasure and enjoyment (although he could have used *Genuss*). With this translation, he inscribes pleasure as inseparable from the question of enjoyment, conforming to the second topic.

In *The Other Side of Psychoanalysis*, it is not with the glass of water that Lacan casts a spell, but with the vase of the Danaides, through which he presents what *jouissance* involves—water, which leaks as the vase is filled. Certainly, it is only an image, but it luminously evokes the insatiability of the vase, that is to say, a fundamental and major feature of the *jouissance* that Lacan remarks on as follows: "jouissance is the jar of the Danaides, and that once you have started, you never know where it will end. It begins with a tickle and ends in a blaze of petrol. That's always what jouissance is" (*SXVII*, 11.02.70, p. 72). Without a doubt, Marx also noted this deadly correlation between *jouissance* and super-ego when he referred to Juggernaut's chariot, under whose wheels the faithful of Vishnu were crushed, as emblematic of capital.

In other words, the more I consume, the more the gap grows between what would be the enjoyment of this consumption. Thus, the surplus enjoyment is the cause of desire which the capitalist mode of production makes its principle: the principle of extensive production. To the extent in which capitalist production, the cycle A–M–A', implies ever-enlarged consumption, if this production resulted in consumption capable of producing a *jouissance* that would slow it down by stopping it, the cycle would be limited. There is no possible satisfaction in Capitalist discourse. Lacan (*RA*) criticizes Marx on this precise point by asserting that the struggle aiming to redistribute surplus value "only induces the exploited to compete in principle in the exploitation, in order to defend their patent participation in the thirst of the lack-in-enjoyment". The core of this criticism lies in Lacan's thesis according to which "Whence the necessity of the surplus enjoyment (*plus-de-jouir*) for the mechanism to turn".[2] Marx did not see or did not want to see this hole (*trou*), and that is why Lacan can state that Marx's surplus value is his surplus enjoyment. This is not a symbolic hole, which one could easily fill by putting a book back in its place in a library, it is, rather, a real whole. However, the "real" of the hole is not ontological, as it can be in religions. The real is the trace of language, because language cannot signify itself or, again, because if language is put to the test of writing, it declares an impossibility to write—which is the same as that which would make the relationship between the sexes a relationship that can be symbolized. Even if this is a complex issue, it should be taken into consideration, otherwise we run the risk of disqualifying Lacan's foundation of the Freudian discovery.

What about money? Lacan certainly did not speak directly much about money. In *Seminar XVI*, Lacan (30.04.69) posits that the coin (*la monnaie*), as money (*argent*), is the fetish *par excellence*, and then he formulates the following question: "what value does it preserve when it is in a safe?" To which he replies with the outline of a question: "Is it not in its way, with respect to what constitutes the money, is it not an inside that is altogether outside, outside of what constitutes the essence of the money?" If money is a fetish, it can only mean one thing: it hides the foundation of its value in the same way that a woman's stockings, for example, hide the fact that she is castrated. Could we not deduce that the increasingly marked decoupling between the sphere of financial speculation and the sphere of material production can be explained by this fetish status embodied by money (*l'argent*)?

If so, can we assume that money stops being a fetish outside of the capitalist mode of production? In 1972, Lacan (*DDP*) proposed a *matheme* for the Capitalist discourse, which is characterized by, on the one hand, the inversion of the subject ($) and the master signifier ($S_1$), and on the other hand, by the abolition of the barrier of *jouissance*. Capitalist discourse is thus presented as a closed and endless circuit which allows for the idea that the *plus-de-jouir* (surplus enjoyment/object *a*) would be incessantly available to the subject ($). This is a beautiful illustration of "All capitalists". The consequence is the foreclosure, within discourse, of the "things of love". What does this mean? If love is what makes up for the impossibility of sexual intercourse, this foreclosure of love corresponds to a foreclosure of castration. Under these circumstances, the fetish status of money would then be unquestionable, to the point of becoming the crown of an enchanted empire, where credit *creates* money.

This change in the conception of money which has become the credo of liberal economics (despite Keynes's objections) is not, however, unstoppable, at least not any more than in fetishism the denial of castration can prevent castration from being recognized as a first logical step. In this regard, it is possible to conceive of and situate the function of money in the place of the Name-of-the-Father, and to conclude from this that it can have the value of a law for anyone dealing with it, in contrast to its original illegality that was first related to its equivalence with the missing penis. This double configuration is cohesive. The recognition of the symbolic lack of an imaginary object by a real agent, one of Lacan's main definitions of castration, unconditionally agrees with the substitution of money as the "imaginary object". In the same vein, for Lacan, accessing a number is often related with the effect of castration. What is the use of a number if not, primarily, to count money? Perhaps this clue will contribute to advance the open debate of the compatibility between socialism and the commercial world.

In the process of a cure, an analysand might forget to pay. With this forgetting, which is not a repression, he manifests, again without knowing it, that he would like to get out of the relationship characterized by the "debt-payment of the debt", which is the ordinary part of his treatment. This foreshadows the ending of the analysis, under the still insufficient mode of acting out. This prefiguration is in any case better than an economy of expenditure, such as the one Georges Bataille was considering when dealing with Marcel Mauss's work on the potlatch.

Translated from French by Christina Soto van der Plas

## Notes

1 In English, it is translated as "the circulation of money", "circulation (currency, *cours de la monnaie*)" (*CAI*, p. 210).
2 Translation by Jack W. Stone.

## Further reading

Goux, J. J. (1990). *Symbolic Economies: After Marx and Freud*. New York: Cornell University Press.
Klebanow, S., & Lowenkopf, E. (1991). *Money and Mind*. New York: Springer.
Kurnitzky, H. (1992). *La estructura libidinal del dinero: Una contribución a la teoría de la Femineidad*. Mexico: Siglo XXI.

## References

Freud, S. (1898). *The Complete Letters of Sigmund Freud to Wilhem Fliess 1887–1904*, J. Masson (Trans.). Cambridge: Harvard University Press, 1985.
Freud, S. (1909). Notes Upon a Case of Obsessional Neurosis. In: *The Standard Edition of the Complete Psychological Works of Sigmund Freud* (Vol. X, pp. 151–318), J. E. Strachey (Trans.). London: The Hogarth Press, 1981.
Freud, S. (1917). On the Transformation of Instincts, with Special Reference to Anal Erotism. In: *The Standard Edition of the Complete Psychological Works of Sigmund Freud* (Vol. XVII, pp. 125–134), J. E. Strachey (Trans.). London: The Hogarth Press, 1981.
Morin, F. (2011). *Un Monde Sans Wall Street?* Paris: Seuil.

# Chapter 17

# Politics

*Carlos Gómez Camarena and Edgar Miguel Juárez-Salazar*

—Ara.: سياسة —Chi.: 政治 —Fre.: *Politique* —Ger.: *Politik* —Ita.: *Politica*— Jap.: 政治 —Port.: *Política* —Rus.: *Политика* —Spa.: *Política* —Tur.: *Siyaset*

→ *Capitalism*; *Economy*; *Society*; *Superstructure*; *Value*

## Introduction: *Nous ne sommes rien, soyons [pas] tout!*

Politics, for Marx, entails a political critique of itself. The denial of politics through law, economy, psychologization, or any form of ideology is a political mode that is disguised as apolitical or neutral. Politics, for Marx, is showing how politics is denied. What is often denied is the antagonism of the class struggle in every system. Marx's contribution to politics is unveiling and explaining the subtle mechanisms of political economy, particularly the way in which the domination of one class by another is at stake in the sphere of production, the circulation and consumption of goods and services. At the heart of this machinery lies the socio-political mode of the mobilization of labour, which sheds light on Marx's surplus and Lacan's object *a*.

For Lacan the political core of politics is the opposite of politics. This is not unlike psychoanalysis, where politics is not exercising power. While politics exercises its power and dominion through identifications, the corruption of desire through the logic of the market—everything has a price—works by means of any metaphysical form (general, particular, of the sphere, of presence, of identity, etc.), and the direction of the treatment in psychoanalysis implies going against these identifications as well as underpinning and giving consistency to the unconscious desire through a praxis—and a theory—that goes against metaphysics. Lacan's contribution is considering *jouissance* as a political factor. Later on it will be equated to Marx's political economy, which will deepen the German's political analysis of micropolitics.

Marx and Lacan do not conceive of politics as agreement, diplomacy, or harmony, as Aristotle and Rousseau proposed. Instead, they are part of the political tradition where politics is seen as a conflict, the tradition of Machiavelli, Schmitt, and Hobbes—but avoiding the perspective of individualistic politics.

DOI: 10.4324/9781003212096-17

## Uses and political ruptures in Marx

It is often said that Marx's so-called "early period" is profoundly imaginary, idealistic or even utopic, instead of scientific. This is the period when he incisively criticizes Bruno Bauer and German idealism. It is also possible to read this period as fundamental for developing a critique of political economy and structuring a science based on it. This period of the early 19th century considers a return to the revolutionary Marxist spirit since, from our perspective, its critique of Hegel lays the foundation to radicalize politics through negativity. By criticizing Hegel, Marx manages to depart from his previous work, in its purest retroactive sense, allowing him to go from philosophy to economics in his later writings. Althusser (1969) would agree with us when we say that there lies his "dialectics" in a strictly "Hegelian sense"; with this and his "language of Feuerbach" Marx already inhabited "the objective contradiction" itself. If there is an originary political thinking in early Marx then this comes from a material language for "[the] whole development occurred in the words" and also from a "materialism" that has a Feuerbachian background, which is not necessarily equivocal but rather an antagonistic form of a conceptual evolution (p. 61). Here the importance of negativity, its persistence and the conception of language must be highlighted.

In *On the Jewish Question* Marx discusses the religious position and its collusion with the State, which is an organic relationship that masks the possibilities of emancipation of the people seen from the Jewish perspective that demands "civic rights". In other words, the state maintains a "secular contradiction" with "bourgeois" society and, because of this relationship "the emancipation of the state from religion is not the emancipation of the real man from religion" (*OJQ*, pp. 159–160). This implies a deep critique of the rights of, and the political relationships among, individuals. Marx will not abandon this critique in his late work bordering the so-called human rights and the civil binding of freedom. There are two routes: the first one can be seen in the political binding of the State and religion and, later on, the need to adapt to a bourgeois laicism lying at the zenith of the bourgeois organization of society.

This last discussion is pushed by Marx to the politics of human rights. For Marx, bourgeois freedom is not the "association of man", but rather it shows its "isolation" since he is "withdrawn into himself" in the realm of "private property" (*OJQ*, p. 162).[1] In criticizing the emancipators of the *bourgeois politics* of the State in the Declaration of Human Rights of 1793, Marx contests the "reduction" of the "political community" to a "means for maintaining these so-called rights of man" (*OJQ*, p. 164). From this perspective, politics in its non-communal and bourgeois adequation could already be conceived of as a means of circulation, that is, an exchange of legal terms as commodities that legitimize private, alienated, selfish, individualistic, and bourgeois law.

Legal violence that is reductive and isolating can be treated as violence of the structure, a violence legitimized by the State, and in Lacanian terms this could be phrased as material violence of the signifier. In his *Critique of Hegel's Philosophy of Right*, Marx states that "material force must be overthrown by material force" and, additionally, that theory can become a material force "capable of gripping the masses" manifesting *ad hominem*. In order to radicalize the masses, there is the need to use an unconscious materialist praxis that is not merely idealist, but rather that emerges from the contradiction of bourgeois man and of man itself. For Marx there is an emancipatory politics if there is at least an antagonistic critique of man, for within him lies the very "root of the matter" of political action (*CHP*, p. 182). It is noteworthy that despite having a certain idealistic touch, Marx does not cease to elaborate his critique from a materialist perspective. It is a *strange* materialism but it is free from the ideal of betting on bourgeois freedom.

Now, for the young radical Marx, politics as emancipation can only be possible by "the emancipation of the workers". By this he means not workers as individuals, but as an emancipation that "contains universal human emancipation" in contrast to the "servitude" that lies within "alienated work" and "private property" (*EPM*, p. 82). Thus capitalism as a system would lay the key elements of its own annihilation. The *derealization* of labour is alienated by labour towards other means of circulation. From its very origin, this idea suggests an option that does not lack alienation, but rather relies on a different distribution and mobilization of the world. The materialist critique questions the political antagonism of the forms of distribution, adequation, and symbolical alienation, and it is not merely a reflection of human consciousness. Marx departs from emancipation and the political division of rights, and not from an attempt to adjust or from false criticism. He begins with the negative aspects to question and subvert the positivity of bourgeois politics. This strategy stretches throughout his entire work and it is also *a method similar to that of Freud*, one that considers how the materiality of the unconscious emerges from a split and from the negativity that must be made politically positive in consciousness.

The clues that we take from the early Marx for our purposes are the following: (a) the criticism of human rights as a direct attack of the bourgeois organization, and (b) the derealization of the worker condensing his productive force as capital, which is ultimately his alienation. Both aspects are used here to analyse the later criticism of the political economy of the subjects' organization, their servility and exploitation and, in fact, their distribution as commodities in the capitalist economic and political system.

In continuity with the later Marx, it is crucial to think of politics as a political fabrication that centres on value. We may find a rupture that, retroactively, also implies a reworking, an epistemic cut that is vital for understanding the economic character of politics and capital's exercise of power. In the *Grundrisse*, Marx states that "exchange value presupposes population" but it is "a population producing [...] specific relations" (*GR*, p. 34). A politics that centres on exchange-value and the exploitation of abstract labour is a politics that focuses on process and circulation. Value is not the ultimate end but a kind of social relation overrun by discontent and fetishism.

People in political relations exchange values and make them circulate according to the needs of the economic system; therefore, they are produced and demanded by the system itself. There is a noteworthy parallelism between the change introduced by Marx and by Lacan: first it is about finding a structural causality in the surface phenomena so that political economy or *jouissance* can be introduced and thus create a retroactive change in qualitative terms.

In terms of the production of the political and social man both politics and economy are necessary entwined social processes that look for "'the anatomy' [of] civil society [which] has to be sought in political economy" since "the sum total of these relations of production constitutes the economic structure of society, the real foundation, on which arises a legal and political superstructure and to which correspond definite forms of social consciousness" (*CPE*, p. 11). This means that the Aristotelian political animal is also an economic animal that is produced and affected by the circulation of commodities and the difference between the use-value and exchange-value established in the world. The most interesting aspect of the political thought of the later Marx is the fact that the surplus is administered and mobilized. Since the first pages of *Capital*, Marx states that "labour is expressed in value", and "the measurement of labour by its duration is expressed in the magnitude of the value of the product" (*CAI*, p. 174). With this, Marx's political economy of capital goes beyond Ricardo and Smith's, by finding their mistake of not acknowledging exchange-value in labour, and thus linking politics to an economy centred on value and its mobilization. This is crucial for understanding the binding of economics and a political delimitation, as we will discuss. Some of these notions are transmitted to Lacan by Lévi-Strauss when he talks about "the individual myth of the neurotic" (*MIN*) or the unconscious structured as a language through exchanges.

In parallel, there are two decisive elements for the moving forward of Marx's theoretical development on political economy. The first is the administered surplus, since according to Marx "Capital did not invent surplus labour", it was already there in ancient Greece and the *"civis romanus"*. It was not until surplus labour "became a factor in a calculated and calculating system" that "the barbaric horrors of slavery" became "civilized horrors" due to "surplus labour" (*CAI*, p. 345). The second transcendental elements are manufacture and the division of labour. For Marx, "some crippling of body and mind is inseparable even from the division of labour in society as a whole" but it is not until "manufacture carries" that the social division of labour is enhanced and creates an "industrial pathology". This pathological manufacture is at the same time "progress" and "it appears as a more refined and civilized means of exploitation", which is when "Political economy, which first emerged as an independent science during the period of manufacture, is only able to view the social division of labour in terms of the division found in manufacture" (*CAI*, pp. 484–485). In conclusion, surplus and manufacture are milestones of the politics of Capital. This is then a political economy that emerges as pathological in itself because both surplus and manufacture carry with them discontent and suffering. Additionally, it is a politics that administers time and movement through accumulation (quantity) and exchange-value (circulation).[2]

This calculated regime produces a "relative surplus-value" that increases the "augmenting the self valorisation of capital – usually described as social wealth, 'wealth of nations', etc. – at the expense of the worker" (*CAI*, p. 486). The partial substitution of men by machines brought along the standardization of circulation in the originary forms of capitalist economy and, with that, a politics of men divided as machines according to a specific temporality. This disposition of labour and machines according to temporality creates what Marx calls the "principle of lessening" (*CAI*, p. 467). In other words, by dividing and organizing the social relations of production, capital distributes the administrative and positive disposition of a divided, functional, and sick worker. The conscious division creates, in parallel, accumulation and a politics that is aware of the exploitation of consciousness that, following Lacan, would be in itself a form affected by the constitutive division. Lastly, how could Lacan not be interested in Marx's thought since notions as crucial as surplus, domination, and discontent are reformulated? It is no surprise then that surplus and domination are related on a political level to circulation and the division of commodities.

## Mirror stage and master-slave dialectics

From the very beginning Lacan talks about the "other" and not the "self" (*AP*). The constitution of the "self" for the child depends on the image of the "other" (*MS*). There is no identity but rather imaginary identifications. This idea of the "self" is influenced by Kojève's reading (Lacan's teacher) of Hegel. It is a master and slave dialectic: two consciousnesses face one another, one of them—the slave—subjects himself because of a fear of dying, and the other—the master—who is not afraid, subjects the other. The paradox emerges later: the slave can work and also acquire consciousness, while the master cannot do either. These paradoxes are also paradoxes for the "self". Lacan tries to solve this problem—the paranoid knowledge, the identifications, the capture of the "self" in the mirror—, first by death (master-slave), then by a third party or horizontal identifications (game theory) and, finally, by a third party that is asymmetrical and is related to death: language. In order to overcome identifications and specular imaginary problems one has to alienate oneself through language.

## Collective logics, game theory, and horizontal identification

In 1945 Lacan publishes an interesting logical problem in his *écrit*, *Logical Time and the Assertion of Anticipated Certainty* (*LT*), where a prison warden will release one of the three prisoners that manages to solve the problem: there are three white disks and two black disks, each prisoner will have a disc on his back so that they cannot see what colour they have. The prisoner has to guess, without looking or being informed by another one, what colour the disc they have on their backs is. This problem has to be solved by logic only and not by probability, empirical test, or by guessing. Whoever solves the problem first will walk out the door and explain his conclusion through logic.

All the possibilities that result from the combination of the three white discs and the three black discs will not be explained here and we will focus instead on the more interesting problem: what happens when all three of them have a white disc on their back? The reader will have to read the *écrit* for further details. What matters is Lacan's logical solution. We will focus on the deconstruction of a syllogism by means of collective logic and the kind of subject that emerges. Indeed, there are three subjective modulations, that is to say, three ways in which the subject changes throughout three different moments in this text; each one coincides with a logical time and an intersubjective structure: (a) the impersonal subject of the instant of the glance, when it does not matter who knows that there are two black disks and three white disks, (b) the indefinite reciprocal subject of the time of understanding, when each subject knows what colour they might have regarding the position of the others or, to be more precise: what colour I have according to the perspective of the others as pure reciprocity; and, (c) the personal subject of the moment of concluding, characterized by the singularity that he claims to have a white disc, the one who asserts and enunciates after two scansions or stops, "mine is white".

Time, subjectivity, and knowledge are tackled by collective logics or, to put it in slightly different terms, by structural logics. This is the Lacanian attempt to formulate a science of the singular. Lacan makes a distinction between collectivity and class:

> *Tres faciunt collegium* [three make mass], as the adage goes, and the collectivity is already integrally represented in the form of the sophism, since the collectivity is defined as a group formed by the reciprocal relations of a definite number of individuals – unlike the generality, which is defined as a class abstractly including an indefinite number of individuals.
> (*LT*, p. 174)

*Collectivity* is the definite number of individuals formed by reciprocal relations (coins, prisoners) and not an indefinite abstract *class* without reciprocal relations, in other words: indefinite abstract non-dependent individuals. Lacan then moved from the classic Aristotelian syllogism (All men are mortal—major premise—; Socrates is a man —minor premise—; therefore, Socrates is mortal—conclusion—) to the collective expression of the assertion of the "personal subject" (*LT*, p. 174): (a) A man knows what a man is not (the instant of the glance); (b) Men recognize themselves among themselves as men (time of comprehending); and, (c) I declare myself to be a man for fear of being convinced by men that I am not a man (moment of concluding).

To summarize the argument: collective logic allows us to produce a subject that did not exist at the beginning of the logical movement and that is capable of assuming his own singularity, *but not without traversing collectivity*. "In this race to the truth one is but alone, although not all may get to the truth, still no one can get there but by means of the others" (*LT*, p. 173), says Lacan. We find the same logic at work on the *écrit The Number Thirteen and the Logical Form of Suspicion*, where Lacan presents another problem: there are 13 coins, seemingly alike, but one of them is "bad" because it differs in weight from the others, though it is not known whether it is heavier or lighter. Using a simple scale, the problem is this: finding out, in three weighings, which one is the odd piece. The solution implies two strategies that are called "tripartite rotation" and "three-and-one-position movements". The crucial point of this problem is that it is solved only if the uniformity of the object, in this case the coins, does not constitute a class—an indefinite number of individuals—but a collectivity—a reciprocal relation of a specific number of individuals. This time the singularity is asserted passing through the reciprocal relations of coins by means of the strategies of weighing: tripartite rotation and three-and-one-position. There is no singularity without collectivity, but conversely: it is impossible to produce singularity by means of an abstract general indefinite group logic. Lacan short-circuits the syllogism and derives singularity from collectivity. This anticipates what Lacan tries to think through the logics of alienation and separation in *Seminar XI* (27.05.64), where there is no subject without alienation to language. This goes against the classical liberal and psychological theories of subjectivity. If psychoanalysis tackles this matter on a "case by case" logic, it does it with a subject that belongs to a speaking community, that is to say, after being alienated from language and installed in discourse.

There is another twist in Lacan: he links what he called in these two last *écrits* "collective logics" to solve the problem of "vertical" identifications. In a relatively unknown *écrit* titled *English Psychiatry and the War* (*PAG*)—where he summarizes the five weeks of his own trip to London in 1945—Lacan comments on the article published in *The Lancet* journal titled "Intra-group Tensions in Therapy their Study as the Task of the Group" (Bion & Rickman, 1943) by the English psychiatrist and psychoanalyst Bion. At that time, Bion, Major Bion, was working with his former analyst Rickman for the Northfield Military Hospital. What impressed Lacan was that both of them directed a project that aimed to "readapt" injured soldiers, fighters affected by "the neurosis of war" and mad combatants considered misfits, dullards, or useless. To heal them, they implemented small groups *without leaders or chiefs*. Lacan is interested in comparing this pragmatic approach with the Freudian *Massenpsychologie*. In other words, what Lacan finds at work are lateral or horizontal identifications. Lacan uses there for the first time the term "a science of the singular", referring to Bion and Rickman's success, and he considers their role as crucial for England's victory over the Nazis. It is no secret that the same honours were also awarded to Turing, Morgenstein, and Von Neumann, who are all founders of game theory. Briefly, and following the Lacanian pun of "Linguistricks" (*linguisterie*), as Fink chooses to translate it (Fink, 1999, p. 15, fn. 6), in those three *écrits* Lacan opposes "sociologistricks" to the Aristotelian classical logic at work in the syllogism. He substitutes Freud's psychology of masses and classical logics with game theory, "collective logics", and horizontal identifications. This has enormous political consequences: we can think of the politics of diagnoses, mental health institutions, and psychoanalytic groups in a different way. Through these means, Lacan proposes the logic of the cartel through his invention of the School (*P9O*) as a solution to the impasses of the International Psychoanalytical Association (*SPT*).

## From the politics of an ostrich to the politics of a vampire

When we talk about politics and economy we are talking about binding, contingency, and antagonism. The political history of the world is the history of the struggle of antagonistic classes. However, Lacan introduces an analysis of a third party in discordance, a three-element politics. In his *Seminar on The Purloined Letter*, Lacan describes a politics structured by the enigma of the signifier. The first element is the blind gaze of the police and the King who never finds out. The second element is that someone realizes that the former "sees nothing believing to be covered what it hides" (the Queen), and the third element sees what is out in the open (the Minister and Dupin). In these three parties we could find a fundamental form of political distribution that can be translated to the key of the neurotic in capitalism: the relation between the King and the police in order to maintain the stability in the system, both closing their eyes and sticking their heads in the ground before the circulation of commodities and the traffic of the money signifier. That is to say, the neurotic subject being subjected to the state plan and the control of the police as a fundamental part of the State without flinching and omitting its place of enunciation. Secondly, the Queen (the State) that is supposed to be "invisible" since the neurotic has "his head stuck in the sand", and the third one, Dupin, the clever capitalist that "calmly plucks his rear" to the elusive ostrich (*PL*, p. 10). Here Lacan plays on the French words ostrich (*autruche*) and neighbour (*autruiche*) that presupposes that the ostrich's politics is also the politics of the neighbour, the same neighbour characterized by some differences in the bourgeois version inherited by religious thinking, and that Marx will call out in his own way when speaking of the bourgeois rights of men. The politics of the capitalist Dupin is the politics of the secret of the fetishism of commodities; the minister and him remain silent when facing everything that is evident and crystal clear; the metaphysical secret of commodities is the sense set in circulation that avoids the enigma of the signifier.

Interestingly, Freud (1914) in *Remembering, Repeating and Working Through* talks about the "ostrich-like policy" in relation to the patient's answer "adopted towards origins" of the disease, the discontent. Repeating and enjoying, the neurotic avoids knowing about the discontent that the politics in the capitalist distribution generates by prolonging this form of "repression" (p. 152). This repetitive and automatic politics is an Oedipal one preferring to self-mutilate or hide because of the horror of knowing and, at the same time, adhering to the politics of the vampire on a social level. On the contrary, by reworking, the subject avoids participating in the repetitive damnation of the exploitation of his death. There is a central knot that ties Marx and Freud and that is key for Lacan's reading. According to Marx in *Capital*, right before his known metaphor of the vampire he writes: "capital has one sole driving force [*Lebenstrieb*], the drive to valorize itself, to create surplus-value, to make its *constant* part, the means of production, absorb the greatest possible amount of surplus labour" (*CAI*, p. 342).[3] The politics of capital is in fact the politics of life by the exploitation of death but also the life drive of the capital exists through the political and economical exploitation of libido since, as Lacan showed, like Marx, this libidinal energy is a constant; more specifically, it is a "numerical constant" and its "life force" makes of what it consumes "a crude metaphor" (*TV*, p. 18). The ostrich politics leads to the politics of the vampire.

## Language, speech, and desire

The famous motto "the unconscious [...] is structured as a language" (*ST*, p. 737) means that the subject constitutes himself through the "Other" of language or of symbolical identifications. While the "self" is the result of imaginary identifications, the subject is a result of language. Lacan developed his theory during the fifties by means of linguistics, by differentiating *language* (*langue*) from *speech* (*parole*), and later introducing the logic of the signifier. All of these contributions have the same political idea: the subject does not speak but is spoken by the Other, he is constituted by the identifications that come from the Other. The direction of the treatment consists in disassembling both the imaginary and the symbolic identifications.

Lacan uses Bentham's theory of fictions in combination with his logic of the signifier, but gets rid of its eudemonism and messianism (Bettstrand, 2017, p. 58). In *Seminar VII* Lacan questions the ethics of psychoanalysis by revising philosophical perspectives on ethics and he reaches the conclusion that desire lies at the heart of the ethics of psychoanalysis. But this desire opposes politics, which has its foundation on postponing and corrupting desire:

> What is Alexander's proclamation when he arrived in Persepolis or Hitler's when he arrived in Paris? The preamble isn't important: "I have come to liberate you from this or that." The essential point is "Carry on working. Work must go on." Which, of course, means: "Let it be clear to everyone that this is on no account the moment to express the least surge of desire." The morality of power, of the service of goods, is as follows: "As far as desires are concerned, come back later. Make them wait".
>
> (*SVII*, 06.07.60, p. 315)

Here the "service of goods" implies eudemonistic ethics, but also the so-called "American way of life". Comfort is not a friend of desire but of the master and domination. This is the reason why Lacan considers happiness as a historical turning point in politics:

I would say that it is because, as Saint-Just says, happiness has become a political matter. It is because happiness has entered the political realm that the question of happiness is not susceptible to an Aristotelian solution, that the prerequisite is situated at the level of the needs of all men.

(*SVII*, 22.06.60, p. 292)

Since then, utilitarianism, the theory of the State, or Enlightenment itself all use happiness as a central and constant subject—that happiness should be brought from heaven to Earth. This is the same reproach that Lacan (*LD*) had concerning Marx's messianism. Lacan, through Bentham, suggests a kind of "utilitarianism of desire" (Cléro, 2008) where the desire is what is calculated and which does not participate in the logic of the market. This already makes libidinal devices and *jouissance* a political factor. Once again, psychoanalysis acts as the opposite of politics:

Enjoyment today effectively functions as a strange ethical duty: individuals feel guilty not for violating moral inhibitions by way of engaging in illicit pleasures, but for not being able to enjoy. In this situation, psychoanalysis is the only discourse in which you are allowed not to enjoy – not forbidden to enjoy, just relieved of the pressure to do so.

(Žižek, 2006, p. 104)

The tool with which psychoanalysis dismantles identifications and awakens desire is in fact love (of transference): "only love allows jouissance to condescend to desire" (*SX*, 13.03.63, p. 179). This is why love will be one of the key elements to read the political nucleus of psychoanalysis as the opposite of politics. This is present throughout Lacan's work, but also in the four discourses: "love is the sign that one is changing discourses" (*SXVII*, 09.12.72, p. 16). Love is no longer mere hypnosis or an imaginary illusion, it has an important role that makes it possible for the subject to transform the way in which he is being subjected to power and to modify the subject's constitutive alienation from imaginary and symbolic identifications—but never to be emancipated from them.

## The unconscious is politics

In 1967 Lacan praises the book *The Basic Neurosis* by Edward Bergler (1949) because of its talent and great analytical insight. Lacan pauses on Bergler's notion of masochism, particularly on the formulation of "being rejected" to invert it and say instead "make oneself be rejected". In fact, Bergler thinks that his formula is exclusively related to orality and the maternal dimension. It is the imago of the mother that nourishes, feeds, poisons, suffocates, etc. But Lacan thinks otherwise: one can vomit someone, something, or, more precisely, a system that imposes nourishment or any other object that has to be taken orally. Lacan starts to talk about the world situation, of a place in southeast Asia—probably Vietnam because of the geographic and political situation of the time—and refers to American imperialism, continuing to say the following (*SXIV,* 10.05.67):

> It is a matter of convincing people that they are quite wrong not to want to be admitted to the benefits of capitalism! They prefer to be rejected! [...] And specifically the following, for example, which will show us – which will show us no doubt, but today is not the day that I will even take the first steps in this direction – that if Freud wrote somewhere that "anatomy is destiny".

This is Freud's comment on Napoleon. Of course, it is an ironic comment since the French Emperor was rather short. It seems as if the very same thing could have been said by Napoleon himself, only with a slight difference—"geography is destiny" (Sous, 2017, p. 22). In any case, Freud meant another "geography", that is, the bodily geography as the anatomy to indicate that the erogenous zones are of great psychic importance. As a consequence, Lacan does not differentiate the psychic from the political and considers that "there is perhaps a moment, when people have come back to a sound perception of what Freud discovered for us, that it will be said – I am not even saying 'politics is the unconscious'", to finish with one of his most famous aphorisms: "but, quite simply, the unconscious is politics!" (*SXIV,* 10.05.67).

"The unconscious is politics" also implies that the subjects are related to others, to institutions, and to groups through libidinal devices, which is related to the four drives: the oral and the anal for Freud, and the invocatory and the scopic drive for Lacan. While the former are related to the demand of the Other, the latter bind together through a libidinal economy (that is to say, a political economy) of the desire of the Other (*SX,* 19.06.63). Jean-Louis Sous summarizes it as follows:

> one could say that the power area or areas that are often superimposed or localised, conceded or interpreted in a phallic way in the health institutions or schools of psychoanalysis, the parties, the corporations or administrations, the unions, in summary, all types of groups [...] would be equally impregnated with other oral or anal intensities: *making oneself* be controlled, surveilled, devoured, vomited, shat [...] would be the drives that would be found in the participants' encounter.
>
> (Sous, 2017, pp. 23–24)

There is no difference between sexuality and power, nor is there any difference between libidinal economy and political economy. From this perspective, Lacan's psychoanalysis is neither progressive nor reactionary: it shows a new element that must be considered in micropolitics and macropolitics, the libidinal political economy. It is then

> a battle of investments and counter-investments [...] [a subject that is subjected] to the pulsional regime of his subjection [and his micropolitical

agencies] as well as to his compliance or resistance modes (intimidation, discredit, resignation, blackmail, hiding in the closet [...]).

(Sous, 2017, pp. 27–28)

Thus Althusser's ideological interpretation (1970) is very limited from this perspective since it does not take into account the political economy of the libidinal devices. This represents a decisive change in Lacan's work. It is no longer just the Other that comes before us—that we are spoken by the Other. When the treasure of signifiers captures the subject it also ties him to work and subtracts a *jouissance*. In other words, once the subject is spoken, this provokes *jouissance*—which two years later Lacan will make equivalent to the surplus-*jouissance*. The crucial question here is where does this *jouissance* go and who makes use of it? Lacan has then a good reason to substitute the Freudian libido—an energetic and thermodynamic notion—by a notion from Marxist political economy (*SXVI*, 13.11.68). It is no longer about how "The unconscious is the Other's discourse" (*PL*, p. 10) but about how "the unconscious is politics", that is to say, the Other that captures us and makes us talk already has a dimension of political economy. In *Seminar XVI* Lacan argues: "From an Other to the other" must be read. Here, the other stands for the "object *a*" as surplus-*jouissance*.

## From libido to an economic libidinal politics

Much has been written about whether Marx's novelty lies in conceiving of surplus, originary accumulation, the class struggle, etc. Accordingly, the most incisive and fundamental criticism from Marx to Ricardo is that he forgot precisely about the abstract labour, "the dual character of the labour", and its relation to "value" (*CAI*, p. 174). This is crucial since it opens up a path according to Lacan's reading, an essentially Marxist reading based on the forms of labour and their measurement. If we consider abstract labour as one of Marx's most innovative proposals, we can relate it to Lacan's "unique invention": object *a*. Marx's discovery of abstract labour is central because this labour accumulates and is related socially and politically. Thus, what Lacan discovers thanks to value is not the surplus (of object *a*) but something more complex: the socio-political mode of labour's movement.

So Lacan's invention of object *a* must be understood not only as letter—as he forces Miller to say[4]—but as an algebraic notation which is a step closer to the real for Lacan. The argument goes as follows: if Marx formalizes the dual character of labour as force and abstraction, Lacan introduces an algebraic notation to what Freud formulates as a constant for the libido. Therefore, there is also a dual character of object *a* (as a constant and as notation). Freud formulates the libido as a constant in the partialized drive of abstraction and Lacan goes one step further—through the real as a crack in its formalization—introducing a notation. Consequently, the use of mathematics in Marx or Lacan should not be underestimated. What is more, Lacan's use of mathematics could reveal that Marx's argument of abstract labour and surplus is essentially mathematical—differential calculus—to the point that in his famous *Communist Manifesto* he states: "the bourgeoisie, therefore, produces, above all, is its own grave-diggers. Its fall and the victory of the proletariat are equally inevitable" (*MCP*, p. 496), which can only be the conclusion of a mathematical argument. When the relation between capital and labour *is written* with differential calculus, *this shows* the predicament that inhabits the whole of capitalism: crises are inherent to the capitalist system.[5]

## Four discourses and authority

After differentiating *language* (*langue*) from *speech* (*parole*), after the logic of the signifier, Lacan introduces his four discourses. As a response to a series of questions that Foucault formulates in his conference *What is an Author?* (1969), Lacan formulates his own series of questions that will become a research programme for *Seminar VIII*. A lot has been written about the four discourses since they are one of the most famous *mathemes*. Nevertheless, it is important to highlight an important aspect regarding politics: every discourse is a mode of exercising power. Thus, for Lacan the place of authority is more important than the form of power. If Lacan is relevant for political theory it is because he is a great theoretician of authority.

In contrast to his professor Kojève and to Weber—as well as to an old political German tradition—Lacan is affiliated to a long English tradition that considers power as a mode of authority, and not the other way around, which is the way the Germans consider it (Cléro, 2008, pp. 39–41). This tradition—Hobbes, Hume, Bentham, and even Austin—comes from the Latin term "author", which is at the same time a variation of "*augere*". In fact, the words "increase", "act", and "agent" come from this term. Is it by chance that on the upper and the left side of his quadripodes lies the agent-semblant?

Fictions and performative linguistics constitute crucial elements of this English tradition. Not without the signifier. But there is something else: Lacan shares with Foucault, who also analyses discourses, this tradition of authority. For both of them the power of pyramidal or vertical power is only another possible manifestation of a more diffuse, horizontal, and effective power, more phantasmatic than the illusion of sovereignty. When it comes to the relationship between authority and power, Lacan differs from Marx, but at the same time he further develops Marx's perspective.

More political consequences of other Lacanian concepts such as *sinthome*, *escabeau* (footstool), *parlêtre* (speakingbeing), or sexuation could be found, but all of them would amount to the same: psychoanalysis as the opposite of politics.

## Notes

1 See Jorge Alemán's (2012) statements on "Common : Solitude".
2 See more on the importance of time and space and their measurements in psychoanalysis in Samo Tomšič (2019), particularly chapters II (Measure of pleasure) and V (The labouring cogito).

3 Emphasis added.
4 Much has been said about the (disastrous) establishment of Lacan's seminars by Jacques-Alain Miller. There are plenty of references about it, we will not go further in that direction. The central question now concerns a small mistake: at the stenography—non-official transcript—of the seminar *On Anxiety* (*SX*, 09.01.63). Lacan speaks about the object *a* in terms of algebraic notation and *never* as a letter. For this discussion, see Allouch (2011).
5 "To write" and "to show" are two important Lacanian subjects. Both are complementary operations as an alternative to the Wittgensteinian impasse: "Whereof one cannot speak, thereof one must be silent". In Lacan it is still possible to write or to show what one cannot speak. This is a crucial point on the function of mathematics in Lacan. For more on the writing and showing function of mathematics in Lacan, see Duportail (2018) and Badiou (1998). Regarding Marx and his mathematical form of argumentation, see Damsma (2020).

## Further reading

Hoens, D. (2020). Jacques Lacan. In: Y. Stavrakakis (Ed.), *Routledge Handbook of Psychoanalytic Political Theory*. New York: Routledge, pp. 44–56.
Sous, J.-L. (2017). *Lacan et la politique. De la valeur*. Paris: Érès.
Tomšič, S. & Zevnik, A. (2016). *Jacques Lacan. Between Psychoanalysis and Politics*. New York: Routledge.
Zarka, Y. Ch. (Ed.) (2003). Jacques Lacan: Psychanalyse et Politique. In: *Cités* (pp. 1–191), 16.

## References

Alemán, J. (2012). Soledad: común. *Políticas en Lacan*. Madrid: Clave intelectual.
Allouch, J. (2011). La invención del objeto a. In: *Me cayó el veinte*, 1: 9–27.
Althusser, L. (1969). *For Marx*, B. Brewster (Trans.). London: Penguin.
Althusser, L. (1970). Ideology and Ideological State Apparatuses. In: *Lenin and Philosophy and Other Essays* (pp. 127–194), B. Brewster (Trans.). New York: Monthly Review Press, 2001.
Badiou, A. (1998). *Briefings on Existence*, N. Madarasz (Trans.). New York: SUNY University Press, 2006.
Bettstrand, W. (2017). *Psychoanalysis as a Science of Mirages: How Semblants, Fictions, Fantasies and Illusions Matter*. London: Borges University Press.
Bergler, E. (1949). *The Basic Neurosis*. New York: Grune & Stratton.
Bion, W. & Rickman, J. (1943). Intra-group Tensions in Therapy their Study as the Task Group. In: *The Lancet*, 242: 678–682.
Cléro, J.-P. (2008). *Dictionnaire Lacan*. Paris: Ellipses.
Damsma, D. (2020). *How Language Informs Mathematics*. Leiden: Brill.
Duportail, G.-F. (2018). *Wittgenstein et Lacan*. Paris: Hermann.
Fink, B. (1999). Translation of Seminar XX. In: J. Lacan (Ed.), *(1972–1973). The Seminar of Jacques Lacan. Book XX. Encore* (pp. vii–ix). New York: W.W. Norton & Company.
Freud, S. (1914). Remembering, Repeating and Working-Through. In: *The Standard Edition of the Complete Psychological Works of Sigmund Freud* (Vol. XII, pp. 145–156), J. E. Strachey (Trans.). London: Vintage, 2001.

Foucault, M. (1969). What is an Author? In: *Aesthetics, Method, and Epistemology* (pp. 205–222), R. Hurely (Trans.). New York: The New Press, 1998.
Tomšič, S. (2019). *The Labour of Enjoyment: Towards a Critique of Libidinal Economy*. Berlin: August Verlag.
Žižek, S. (2006). *How to Read Lacan*. New York: W. W. Norton & Norton Company.

# Chapter 18

# Proletarian/labourer/worker

*Silvia Lippi*

—Ara.: بروليتاري / عامل —Chi.: 無產階級/工人 —Fre.: *Prolétaire/ouvrier/travailleur* —Ger.: *Proletarisch/arbeiter* —Ita.: *Proletario/operaio/lavoratore* —Jap.: 労働者/プロレタリア —Port.: *Proletário/obreiro/trabalhador* —Rus.: *Рабочий /пролетарий* —Spa.: *Proletario/Obrero/Trabajador* —Tur.: *İşçi/ proleter*

→ *Communism*; *Labour/work*; *Master/tyrant*; *Slavery*

In Marx's work, the proletarian is the salaried worker forced to sell his labour power to live, whereas the "proletariat" is the social class, formed by all salaried workers opposed to the class of modern capitalists who own the capital and the means of production, that is, the "bourgeoisie". If the workers, in order to live in better conditions, demand higher wages, the owners, on the other hand, seek to increase their profits by employing labour at the lowest possible cost. A struggle arises from this opposition based on a *de facto* difference in interests, and this is what Marx (*CAI*, p. 96) names the "class struggle". The proletarian revolution, aiming to abolish disparities and reduce income inequalities by subverting the social and economic conditions of the working classes, is achievable, as Marx and Engels (*MCP*, p. 503) argue, through the collective action of the proletarians united against their oppressors.

How can the Marxist notion of "proletarian" be a contribution to psychoanalysis? And conversely, what does the psychoanalytic analysis of the concept, present in all of Lacan's work, contribute to Marxist theory? The question is the following: do the proletarian and the subject of the unconscious have something in common?

Although the Freudian discipline is often mistakenly considered a bourgeois practice, it is surprising to note the quantity of Marxist notions used by Lacan throughout his teaching. The term "proletarian", but also the term "worker" and "laborer" are present after the *Rome Discourse* (*FFS*) of 1953 and until the *Dissolution* (*SXXVII*) of 1980, thus becoming the faithful companions of major psychoanalytic concepts such as "subject", "truth", "knowledge", "symptom",[1] and "jouissance".[2]

DOI: 10.4324/9781003212096-18

The concept of "proletarian" comes up throughout Marx's writings: from the philosopher, still caught up in the Hegelian and anthropological paradigm (the "young Marx"), and the scientific, anti-humanist and truly materialist Marx (the "Marx of *Capital*"). On Lacan's side, we find the "proletarian" at the crossroads of the theory of the subject and of the truth of the first Lacan, and at that of the symptom and the *jouissance* of his last *écrits* and Seminars. In Marx, as in Lacan, the concept of "proletarian" does not signal the break between two antagonistic theories but rather, on the contrary, as we will see, it allows them to express their radical inseparability.

## From truth to symptom

In *Science and Truth*, Lacan introduces a problem dear to the Marxist tradition, that of the relationship between the (scientific) theory and the (revolutionary) action of the proletarian:

> In writing that "Marx's theory is omnipotent because it is true," Lenin says nothing of the enormity of the question his speech raises: If one assumes the truth of materialism in its two guises—dialectic and history, which are, in fact, one and the same—to be mute, how could theorizing this increase its power? To answer with proletarian consciousness and the action of Marxist politicos seems inadequate to me. The separation of powers is at least announced in Marxism, the truth as cause being distinguished from knowledge put into operation.
>
> (*ST*, p. 738)

Lacan is wondering about the place of Marxist theory within revolutionary action. We can also note that the articulation between theory and the act is also a central question for psychoanalysis: the analysand, like the proletarian, is traversed by the question of the relationship between knowledge, which makes it the object of its history, and its act insofar as it is a subject.[3] For Lacan,[4] the proletarian's awareness of his miserable condition does not guarantee anything: as for the analysand who realizes his discomfort, the unconscious is required to make the revolution. Thus, continues Lacan, it is the truth placed in the position of cause[5] which becomes operative, that is to say, the truth of the unconscious, the truth of the subjective division, which the symptom expresses (Freud spoke notably of the symptom as a compromise). It is in this sense that Lacan will say, much later, that Marx invented the symptom (*SXXVII*, 18.03.80): the proletarian complains of this symptom, and his strike will depart from there. Marxist theory cannot make the revolution on its own, it takes the proletarian truth that divides and tears apart capitalism. Lacan (*SXVI*, 12.02.69) specifies:

> [I]t is not any worse then to recall that what is at stake in Marxist theory, in so far as it concerns the truth, is what it states in effect. The fact that the truth of

capitalism is the proletariat. It is true. Only it is from that very thing that there emerges the series and the import of our remarks about what is involved in the function of the truth. It is that the revolutionary consequence of this truth, this truth from which Marxist theory starts, naturally it goes a little bit further since what it constructs the theory of, is precisely capitalism, the revolutionary consequence is that the theory starts in effect from this truth, namely, that the proletariat, is the truth of capitalism.

Thus, to convert the objective truth of Marxism into a practical truth of social transformation, something much stronger than a proletarian awareness is needed, that is, a symptom, which would express both the suffering of the body and the truth—its unconscious truth—of the divided subject: it expresses it but it does not know it, the symptom does not want to know anything about the truth, it simply wants to continue enjoying/suffering.

## The good use of the proletarian chains: the communist becoming

But what does the proletarian suffer from? What is its symptom? Marx and Engels (*MCP*) wrote that the worker is a mere appendage of the machine, and that "it is only the most simple, most monotonous, and most easily acquired knack, that is required of him". And as the repulsiveness of the work increases, the wage decreases (pp. 490–491). The proletarian is objectified by the capitalist system: privation (*EPM*, p. 73), dispossession [*dépouillement*] (*SXVII*, 17.12.69, p. 32), alienation,[6] exploitation (*SXV*, 07.02.68). If such is the condition of the proletarian *vis-à-vis* the capitalist, what is the condition of the analysand *vis-à-vis* its Other?

The analysand, like the proletarian, loses his marks, his primary attributions, his tracking system, his attitudes, his competence; he loses what he believed to be his position, his place, his identity (what he would like to be, what he would like to become, what he identifies with as an ego ideal). And, above all, he loses any prior knowledge, which makes him believe that he is going to become one thing or another.

The truth effect of the unconscious reveals a position that the analysand cannot sustain. The subject becomes a wandering element which loses all of the *possible* of its determination (you are not yet worthy of your mother's love, but one day you will be; you do not yet have the ideal man, but you are going to find him; you are not yet a great man, but you are going to become one), but on the other hand, it acquires the messianic *possibility*. But this new man[7] is not the proletarian liberated once and for all from his chains, as Marx and Engels believe, but the one who knows how to use them—although they are harmful!—to "attach themselves" to other proletarians, to unite with them to make a general strike (*FFS*, p. 236): "Working men of all countries, unite!",[8] acclaim Marx and Engels in their *Manifesto*.

The proletarian, like the subject in analysis, exploited by the Other (the capitalist Other and the parental and societal Other) lose everything, and this loss[9] corresponds to a particular—symptomatic—mode of *jouissance*: the analysand becomes the proletarian of the Other and sustains himself in the suffering which gives him his chains, in the symptom. For the proletarian, as for the analysand, the chains express the "necessary alienation" (*SXV*, 07.02.68),[10] which generates the formation of the symptom. It is these same chains of exploitation that become the chains of the unity of the revolted proletarians: communism thus becomes the symptom of capitalism.

The aim of the analysis is therefore to produce the communist who is in itself, that is to say, to manufacture a symptom that is *necessarily* formed,[11] given the alienated structure of each one. But the symptom is also a "deviation", "gap", "dissipation", in short, a *clinamen* (Lucrèce, 1998):[12] it is because of this "infinitesimal swerve"[13] that the painful chains join together and the proletarians can build a new social system: communism.[14] This deviation is always possible because of an unexpected encounter, of the order of "the aleatory and of contingency".[15] The unexpected encounter is the effect of a repulsion, and suddenly, the *clinamen* has come to represent a form of resistance and struggle or, according to Marx:

> Lucretius therefore is correct when he maintains that the declination breaks the fati foedera, and, since he applies this immediately to consciousness, it can be said of the atom that the declination is that something in its breast that can fight back and resist.
>
> (*DDE*, p. 49)

The contingent becomes necessary. The *clinamen* then takes the form of a necessity (communism) replacing another necessity (the chains). It is the revolution, where the symptom is both the growth and the effect.

The symptom produces the "subject-effect":[16] we go from the symptomatic particularity to the singularity of any act, which of course implies a certain amount of contingency, and which does not exclude anything other than the symptom, otherwise the knotting (like in the proletarian revolt) could go wrong. Lacan needs some luck to achieve the passage from the particularity of the symptom to the singularity of the act:

> it is worth getting the singular out, and it only happens with good luck, the kind of luck that still has rules. There is a way of tightening the singular, it is precisely through this particular, this particular that I am equating to the term symptom.
>
> (*PRF*)

The symptom is strangely attractive, a combination of chance and order, determinism and the unpredictable. It is the vector of a possible and productive imbalance, capable of breaking out of the metaphorical signifying chain, because it cannot be classified, and it cannot be defined. The symptom is therefore the key to any transformation operating from the subversive unity of the workers' movement.

One only becomes a communist through the unconscious; it is not enough for the proletarian to become aware of his condition of being exploited, he must be put in the position of truth-cause: what is the relationship between the truth of the subject of the unconscious, that is to say, the proletarian, and the symptom of the becoming communist? When the proletarian is proletarianized (that is, wounded by his chains), he sees it as something negative, he suffers and he complains about it, hence the *formation* of the symptom. The symptom is a *form*, or more precisely the *taking shape* [*prise de forme*], a bruise that takes shape on the body: it is the mark of the suffering of the proletarian caught in his chains, and this suffering manifests itself in the symptom. But the symptom is *formed* and *transformed*: the bruises on the body constantly change their shape and colour. If the suffering gradually decreases, the proletarian, who has become a communist, will not complain anymore, even if something from this suffering—the scars of his chains—will never fade away.

## Marxist knowledge and the blah-blah of the cure

When Lacan (*FFS*, p. 236) speaks of knowledge in relation to Marx, he is speaking about Marxist theory, exact, scientific, and "mathematical". And it is the truth-cause that allows for knowledge to hold onto the process. In other words, Marxist theory can have a hold on reality only if it is traversed by the subjective communist process, which from the point of view of the unconscious corresponds to the subjective division expressed in the enjoyment/suffering of the symptom. In other words, everything "said" [*dit*] (theory, history) becomes a "saying" [*dire*] ("true" word), if there is a symptom that sustains it (communism) (*LE*, p. 450).

The knowledge of theory becomes for psychoanalysis the discourse of the subject who seeks to analyze himself, who says things about himself. And this discourse is not merely blah-blah: Lacan (*SXIV*, 13.01.67, p. 58) speaks of *j'ouï-sens*, ("I hear meaning") *jouissance* that traverses the speech that is supposed to produce knowledge. If this knowledge has a hold on the process, it is not only because it produces a theoretical truth, but because it triggers a *jouissance*: hence Colette Soler's expression of "enjoyed-knowledge" [*savoir-joui*] (Soler, 2012, p. 46). On the side of Marxist theory, blah-blah works when it is caught up in the *jouissance* that it assigns to capitalism. This *jouissance* is not negotiable—therefore necessary—which means, as Marx thinks, that it is not possible to escape capitalism except by the means of capitalism. If it is true that *jouissance* is fixed, there is a process of transformation of the symptom: in an analysis this process leads to the formation of a "happy symptom",[17] in Marxism to the becoming of communism. The communist party is a big bruise: but does that old wound still hurt?

The blah-blah of the subject on the couch only makes sense if there is a symptom behind it, in the same way that the blah-blah of the Marxist theory only makes sense if the communist party is behind. If there is a link between the two, the blah-blah becomes knowledge: an enjoyed-knowledge [*savoir-joui*], of course! In this sense, it is a mistake to separate in the Lacanian teaching the theory of truth from that of knowledge:[18] the notion of the "proletarian" holds them together. The proletarian is at the same time the object of knowledge of Marxist theory, which says: "Workers, notice the objectivity of your condition as proletarians!", and the subject which results from the action of the truth as cause (the above-mentioned subject-effect).

Let us repeat that there is a regime of exactness in Marxist knowledge only if it is held by the symptom: Marxist theory takes hold on capitalism only if it is held in the process of formation and transformation of communists. Knowledge, then, presents its positive value in the same way as knowledge in an analysis ("if I am like that, it is because of what my mother did to me", etc.) which only counts if the subject is in the process of turning it into a symptom: the enjoyed-knowledge [*savoir-joui*] of the symptom is then linked to the *enjoy-meant* [*jouis-sens*].

There are therefore two different blah-blahs in a cure: there is a blah-blah that is not knowledge, because it is not correlated with the experience of a symptom in the process of being made (and this is where analysts sometimes get bored in their practice), and a blah-blah which is knowledge because there is a symptom (and this is where the analytic act acquires all its relevance). The subject is in the process of transforming the proletarian in him into a communist. The alienated subject leaves all his unhappy identifications, its complaints, etc., and becomes a communist (Marx's messianic subject): the disqualified entity accepts to build itself on the basis of this disidentification, this turmoil which becomes the communist organization. Neither the consciousness of the proletarian, nor the elaboration that the subject produces in analysis (where he says, for example, "my mother did this, my father did that") are forms of transmitting knowledge: the truth of the unconscious, nourished by fantasy,[19] which reveals itself here under its lying feature (*SXVI*, 12.02.69).

Linking knowledge and *jouissance*, or more precisely knowledge and the symptom, allows for formulating a theory of the articulation between consciousness and the unconscious, through the analysis of the proletarian, in his relation to the (unconscious) truth/lie and *jouissance* (of the symptom). Yes, consciousness enjoys! Because *jouissance* traverses consciousness,[20] and insofar as it remains fixed it changes its form through the symptom. "Change of satisfaction", says Colette Soler: for the communist, and for the subject at the end of the analysis.[21]

## The messianic symptom

The more dissatisfied the proletarian, the more likely he is to organize, to *form* and *transform* himself. But the history of capitalism did not respond to Marx, rather it sought to dissolve the proletarian dissatisfaction: if the proletarian is happy owning a TV, a car, a house, etc., he does not go on strike and loses its communist being. In the analytical framework, it is the hysteric who finds a man at all costs, the obsessive who saves a little more money, the bulimic who starts a diet. These are alienating satisfactions because the symptom does not manage to modify its form, whereas in the proletarian who becomes a communist, the satisfaction changes: the communist symptom is a prodigious formation, excessive in relation to capitalist logic, the structure of its singular alienation. In this form that takes hold there is something supernumerary that appears on top of it: the communists are monstrous, but at the same time they are necessary regarding capitalism. In communism there is a form that takes hold, while workers' discomfort has no form. At the beginning, something does not work: the truth is already there, the *jouissance* is already there, the proletarian is present, not so much as class consciousness, but as (unconscious) truth-cause or even as symptom, that is, the becoming communist—where communism indicates the active force of the organized proletarians. And the goal of an analysis, if we follow Lacan, is to become the communist of oneself, the communist of one's psychic system, as we have seen. All the different small manifestations of the negativity of the subject's discomfort, its anxiety, its inhibitions, the fact that it does not fit well ... well, it all gets organized, begins to take "one" form, like the proletarians who unite. And this symptom which is called communism becomes an ordinary symptom. It is an opening to the indeterminate, like a symptom that is yet to come, a messianic symptom.

The passage from the discontent to the symptom indicates the passage from the proletarian to the communist. A communist is not an individual who would like to keep the properties that characterize him as an individual (he is a man, French, a steel worker, etc.). If the proletarian succeeds in fabricating a symptom, he is still a proletarian, that is to say, totally undifferentiated, radically identical to all proletarians, who all go in the same direction, the becoming communist.

The symptom goes from "particular" (it is *my* suffering, *my* discontent) to becoming "singular", that is, indeterminate, undifferentiated, radically unspecified. The singular is something, but we do not know what it is. The proletarians are ordinary proletarians. The *sinthomé* subject is also arbitrary. The singular indicates the uncompromising *jouissance* assigned to the subject, which has neither place nor property in the structure. The singular, despite being determined, cannot be determined in the mode of particularization, cannot be put anywhere in the system; it cannot be found anywhere: the proletarian who assumes being a communist does not have a place in capitalist society. He explodes the structure. But ultimately, one also puts the communist party in its place, and this is how psychoanalysis becomes an endless process!

The end of the analysis implies an end of knowledge, but it is not the end of the symptom! Lacan will speak especially of an "identification with the symptom"[22] at the end of the analysis, where a symptom finally finds a place in the structure, while finding another way of relating with it. The proletarian should transform society and not just "be a party". Both Marx and Lacan wish for a *sinthomée* life [*une vie sinthomée*].

## Consequences

But did communism ultimately work or not? The communist party was not really a solution. In Marx's system there was a failure of the symptom. One can therefore qualify the problem of the history of communism as a failed symptom: the failure of a revolution is the failure of the symptom. Nevertheless, communism put an end to the First and Second World Wars and it allowed the creation of great social security institutions, transforming the world. In any case, one could hardly say that communism is a happy symptom, except if we consider that we are at the beginning of its history, that the times of transformation have not yet come to an end. Or that the process of the symptom has regressed, it has taken a wrong turn. Is there a single social symptom that is constantly happy?

Communism today does not even have a name nor plays a big role in most countries of the world. Or as in China, Korea, Vietnam, and Cuba, it presents itself as a form of dictatorship. But that is surely not the symptom of the proletariat that Marx speaks of: the general strike is always happy! Yes, because the revolutionary process is always happy! It is necessary to remember that for Marx communism is nothing other than the process of insurrection: the symptom is therefore a process of insurrection that psychoanalysis, unlike for example medicine, does not suffocate, but rather takes advantage of because, as we have seen, it is the symptom which gives the blah-blah of the analysis its status of knowledge. Marx favours the acceleration of the capitalist process. Good is not external to evil, it is the notion of dialectics itself, but it is possible to conceive of this theoretical conception from a structural point of view. In both cases, however, we have to deal with unstable systems.

For Lacan, the symptom was invented by Marx when speaking in particular of communists: the proletarians are the ones that have become communists, they are the truth and symptom of capitalism, that is to say, the proletarians united, and not the proletarians in the process of dispossession. The dispossession of the proletariat feeds the capitalist machine, it does not destroy it. Lacan affirms in *Dissolution*:

> I paid homage to Marx as the inventor of the symptom. This Marx is, however, the restorer of order, simply because he has reinspired among the proletariat the *dit-mension* (di-mention/mention of the said) of meaning. For that, it was enough for the proletariat to say it.
>
> (*SXXVII*, 18.03.80)

Marx is the inventor of the symptom, the founder of an order, and the one who reintroduced meaning [*sens*]. Here meaning [*sens*] indicates knowledge, and of course the meaning of history: the proletariat is the vector for building a classless society, a historical teleology, or even the truth of history.

The "*dit*" (said) of "*dit-mension*" (di-mention/mention of the said) and the "*dise*" of the proletarian indicates the relationship between the meaning (the said, *dit*) and the unconscious truth (*dise*) in knowledge,[23] which is produced by means of the symptom. The *dire* (the saying, conformed by "*dit*" and by possibly saying [*dise*]) must be held by the symptom; it wants to become knowledge or, more precisely, enjoyed-knowledge [*savoir-joui*]. There is of course the recognition of oneself as proletarian (the realization or awareness), but Marx reintroduces meaning because the proletariat is an unconscious process which must be reversed as a revolutionary dynamic. By naming things as they are, he necessarily reintroduces meaning, that is, a discourse designating a thing, an object: and there, the subject is lost anew. We are no longer in the immanent process of revolutionary action, but in the recognition of something that one can plan, organize, and instrumentalize.

Producing a Marxist theory has many order effects, and if one forgets that the saying it is part of the revolutionary process itself, and that it is not merely a representation that would fall nowhere on an evident truth. It is an act in and of itself. The *act* of saying it [*le dire*] matters more than the *fact* that it has been said [*que le fait de le dire*]. Once again, this sentence must be understood departing through the articulation of truth and knowledge. If we forget that there is the act of saying it [*l'acte de le dire*]—an enjoyed-knowledge [*savoir-joui*]—and that we only assert that the proletarian is the proletarian, not only do we separate the truth/falsehood of knowledge, but also the symptom's knowledge. Knowledge here is the only word coupled with a *jouissance* that leads to its transformation, that is, a "happy symptom", the bearer of a new satisfaction.

Translated from French by Christina Soto van der Plas

## Notes

1 From the point of view of psychoanalysis, even if the symptom generates suffering, it is not a sign of disease; it should not be eradicated or corrected (as medicine would do).
2 The term "*jouissance*", introduced by Lacan, designates suffering mixed with pleasure or the opposite. This experience is properly sexual, but it extends to other situations as well. *Jouissance* is linked to the traumatic structure of desire: it is in particular the *jouissance*/suffering of the trauma that the subject seeks to repeat through the symptom.
3 This question is addressed and deepened in the collective work edited by Lippi and Landman (2013).
4 Marx and Engels think exactly the opposite: "But they never cease, for a single instant, to instil into the working class the clearest possible recognition of the hostile antagonism between bourgeoisie and proletariat" (*MCP*, p. 519).
5 Which is certainly not the philosopher's truth. Alain Badiou (2018, pp. 135–136) writes: "In contrast, the love of truth is at the heart of the philosophical discourse. But—and it's here that Lacan's case against philosophy finds its main argument—the philosopher purports to love truth as *power* and not as impotence". That is, as a subjective division.
6 "The fact that labour is external to the worker, i.e., it does not belong to his essential being" (*EPM*, p. 74).
7 Marx speaks of a "complete re-winning of man" (*CHP*, p. 20). And in *RSI*, Lacan affirms: "the proletarian man realises the essence of man, and by being stripped of eve-

rything is charged with being the Messiah of the future. Such is the way in which Marx analyses the notion of symptom" (*SXXII*, 18.02.75).

8  This phrase of the *Manifesto* has made history: "Let the ruling classes tremble at a Communist revolution. The proletarians have nothing to lose but their chains. They have a world to win. Working men of all countries, unite!" (*MCP*, p. 519).

9  This loss is a "castrated *jouissance*" specific to the foundations of the unconscious, and therefore also of the symptom (Soler, 2012, p. 48).

10  Marx wrote in *The German Ideology*: "This '*estrangement*' ['*Entfremdung*'] (to use a term which will be comprehensible to the philosophers) can, of course, only be abolished given two *practical* premises. In order to become an 'unendurable' power, i.e., a power against which men can make a revolution, it must necessarily have rendered the great mass of humanity 'propertyless', and moreover in contradiction to an existing world of wealth and culture" (*GI*, p. 48).

11  For Lacan, the "necessary" never ceases to be written, it is the modal category of the formations of the unconscious and therefore of the symptom (*SXX*, 13.02.73, p. 59).

12  For a detailed analysis of the symptom as *clinamen*, see Lippi (2013).

13  "The clinamen is an infinitesimal *swerve*, 'as small as possible'; 'no one knows where, or when it occurs'" (Althusser, 2006, p. 169).

14  "Only within the community has each individual the means of cultivating his gifts in all directions" (*GI*, p. 78).

15  Althusser (2006) specifies: "[The materialism of the encounter] is opposed, as a wholly different mode of thought, to the various materialisms on record, including that widely ascribed to Marx, Engels, and Lenin, which, like every other materialism in the rationalist tradition, is a materialism of necessity ant teleology, that is to say, a transformed, disguised form of idealism" (pp. 167–168).

16  In his *Seminar XIV*, after mentioning the "production of proletarians", Lacan evokes "the status of the subject *qua* product" (01.03.67).

17  The expression "happy symptom" [*symptôme heureux*] comes notably from Colette Soler (2014, p. 102).

18  As does, among others, Soler (2012).

19  The fantasy is a scenario, constructed from defensive processes, which stages the fulfilment of an unconscious desire.

20  For Badiou, knowledge can be transmitted through the matheme, but for Colette Soler (2012) it is not possible: "knowledge is articulated, but the signifying element is not enough to constitute knowledge, *jouissance* must be added to it. Therein lies the distinction with information [...] the signifier is transmitted, but for *jouissance* it is more difficult [...] In other words, if knowledge is enjoyed, there is no didactics of knowledge that thinks, knowledge is the wall against which all pedagogy bumps into, be it professional or domestic. It is the barrier of transmission, it is the anti-matheme" (Soler, 2012, p. 46).

21  "[At the end of the analysis], This separation [from the Other, that is to say, from the subject-supposed-to-know, the analyst] conditions the fall of the mirage of truth, which is an epistemic benefit, but it is ultimately attested only by a specific affect, that corresponds to the end. This is the evidence that it is an end, because satisfaction has changed" (Soler, 2012, p. 51).

22  The phrase "identification with the symptom" is a hapax of Lacan which designates his last conception of the end of an analysis (*OSC*). For a very clear presentation of what I am defending here, but unfortunately reserved for insiders, see Soler (2014, pp. 99–106).

23  Recall the famous formula in "*L'étourdit*": "That one might be saying (*Qu'on dise*) remains forgotten behind what is said in what is heard" (*LE*).

## Further reading

Bruno, P. (2019). *Lacan and Marx: The Invention of the Symptom*. J. Holland (Trans.). London: Routledge.
McGowan, T. (2016). *Capitalism and Desire: The Psychic Cost of Free Markets*. New York: Columbia University Press.
Ryan, J. (2017). *Class and Psychoanalysis: Landscapes of Inequality*. London: Routledge.

## References

Althusser, L. (2006). The Underground Current of the Materialism of the Encounter. In: *Philosophy of the Encounter. Later Writings, 1978/1987* (pp. 163–207), G.M. Goshgarian (Trans.). New York: Verso.
Badiou, A. (2018). *Lacan. Anti-philosophy 3*, K. Reinhard & S. Spitzer (Trans.). New York: Columbia University Press.
Lippi, S. (2013). Sintomo, sinthome e clinamen: Joyce e la questione del determinismo in psicoanalisi. In: *Letter(a) – Joyce. Sinthomo, arte, follia* (pp. 110–126), n°3. Milan: Et al. Edizioni.
Lippi, S. & Landman, P. (2013). *Marx, Lacan: l'acte révolutionnaire et l'acte analytique*. Toulouse: Erès.
Lucrèce (1998). *De la nature/De rerum natura*. Paris: Flammarion.
Soler, C. (2012). L'énigme du savoir. In: *Le langage, l'inconscient, le reel* (pp. 37–51). Paris: Editions du Champ Lacanien.
Soler, C. (2014). *Lacan – The Unconscious Reinvented*, E. Faye & S. Schwartz (Trans.). London: Karnac.

Chapter 19

# Revolution

*Ricardo Espinoza Lolas*

—Ara.: ثورة —Chi.: 革命 —Fre.: *Révolution* —Ger.: *Revolution* —Ita.: *Rivoluzione* —Jap.: 革命 —Port.: *Revolução* —Rus.: *Революция* —Spa.: *Revolución* —Tur.: *Devrim*

→ *Communism*; *Freedom/liberty*; *Ideology*; *Materialism*

## Introduction

Let us try to think with Lacan and against Lacan (as well as with Hegel, Marx, Nietzsche, Lenin, and Žižek) about the only possible revolution: the one written in capital letters, the one that carries with it something new. Let us also try to reflect on, and perhaps against Lacan himself (and therefore against Žižek), Marx's revolution as the Revolution (with a capital letter), that is, the one of the proletariat trying to establish something new "despite" so much power and the Master that subdues us and takes us back to where we came from, a mere substitution of one Master for another Master (that is, the terrible circularity of the horrendous repetition). Let us try to think of a proletariat beyond this bourgeois trap, beyond Lacan, Kojève, and Žižek. Lacan is very clear and harsh regarding his anti-revolutionary vision where the revolution is written in lowercase letters. He considers the Russian Revolution as a totalitarian experiment that only gave more power to capitalism and also that May '68 was a "youthful-mass" shout for another Master that would subdue them (it was yet another revolution stuck in capitalism's web):

> If you had a bit of patience, and if you really wanted our impromptu to continue, I would tell you that, always, the revolutionary aspiration has only a single possible outcome-of ending up as the Master's discourse. This is what experience has proved. What you aspire to as revolutionaries is a master. You will get one.
>
> (*SXVII*, 03.12.69, p. 207)

In what follows we will not talk about this "revolution", but about the Revolution. We will not talk about the revolution that wants revolution, but about the

DOI: 10.4324/9781003212096-19

Revolution that liberates our desire. It liberates us from the capitalist chains and it opens the possibility of the WethOthers.[1]

"Revolution" is a damned "experience-concept" that nowadays hardly means anything and what it refers to is no longer possible. On the contrary, it only means more of the same: more subduing and the rendering of eternal capitalist domination. It also seems that what it refers to no longer "exists"; that to which this concept referred no longer exists (just like cassettes or telegrams). Let us not forget that as a damned experience-concept it became politically incorrect in the current, infantilized, prudish world of the ethical simulacra and capitalist "good manners" (we are told that speaking of Revolution in any way, especially in the unconscious is frowned upon because it is an open invitation to hatred and chaos, and can therefore generate violence against the system). So, why reflect yet again on an experience-concept that is fading, dissolving in a capitalist planet where it has been overcome? Why talk about Revolution in the Capitalist era? How does a Revolution not end up being yet another revolution and overcome Lacan's objection that Žižek reappropriated? Let us also not forget that if the concept of Revolution sounds very distant to us, it is even further away from young people. Many French or Latin American thinkers prefer to use the word "emancipation" instead, because they run the risk of being accused of being radicals or stale, of promoting violence and unruliness against the institution, particularly against the State. We do not want to say anything about the kind of revolution that is a mere circular determinism, a mere deadly repetition, nor of that revolution that goes back to the starting point, another Master as Lacan says. It does not make much sense to talk about such revolution nowadays with so many failed revolutions that have caused only more pain and serfdom: "It is not take that path because is a characteristic that all the same one must not forget in what are called revolutions, which is that this word is admirably chosen to mean, *returning to the starting point*" (*KIT*, 04.11.71, p. 7). We are not looking for another revolution that would only be a circular repetition of the same (against Heidegger), but for a Revolution that affirms life and creates something new in its repetition (Nietzsche as a revolutionary).

We cannot forget Hegel (Espinoza, 2016) when we talk about repetition (and Revolution) because he noticed before Freud that the idea of repetition is always linked to that which is worse (Hegel was the first analyst), although Hegel also has an affirmative dimension in his philosophy that allows us to see in his method an affirmation that enables and opens up the world (this is the Revolution with a capital letter that Lenin was looking for). That is why every revolution, even though it might not be a Revolution, will lead us to failure. Hegel's rarely quoted text, The Philosophy of History, lays the foundation for Marx, Benjamin, Lacan, Žižek, and many of the 20th- and 21st-century thinkers. In this important text, repetition (*Wiederholung*) talks about history itself, humanity, and the most important thing of all, which is that we never learn from history, or rather that we do so in a deceitful way. History repeats itself and what is contingent becomes necessary: "By repetition that which at first appeared merely a matter of chance and contingency becomes a real and ratified existence" (Hegel, 1837, p. 332).[2] Before Freud and psychoanalysis, Hegel can see very clearly by studying the Romans that repetition constitutes us historically. The decisive historical moments repeat themselves and thus repeat themselves to sink us deeper in life's mud, for we have not learnt anything from them. Repetition shows that in its beginning a historical moment was something merely accidental or, possibly, only to become a reality later on and establish itself as a need. This is precisely why revolution will always be a deadly and totalitarian repetition that perpetuates the logic of a higher moment or, in this case, the capitalist logic that becomes invulnerable.

Žižek says the following in *Pandemic!*: "Hegel wrote that the only thing we can learn from history is that we learn nothing from history, so I doubt the epidemic will make us any wiser" (Žižek, 2020, p. 3). What we learn from history is a repetition that becomes even more disastrous and then we learn nothing at all, for repetition brings deceit demonstrated by the arrival of Bonaparte's new emperor in 1851. The French and Europeans witnessed Napoleon's tragedy, but then the French repeated history and the most inept of Napoleon's nephews was brought to radical power so that France could become an imperial power once more. However, as is well known, Bonaparte was in fact a very limited man. This is the reason why the young Marx no longer knew what to expect from a revolutionary process. It is clear that the Hegel–Marx dictum establishes the following, which still holds a grain of truth nowadays: "Hegel remarks somewhere that all facts and personages of great importance in world history occur, as it were, twice. He forgot to add: the first time as tragedy, the second as farce" (*BLB*, p. 15).

Slavoj Žižek is constantly mentioning, in a provocative way and against classical leftists and against the theory of many activists, the following: "I often quote Walter Benjamin, who said: 'Every rise of fascism bears witness to a failed revolution.' This is perhaps more pertinent today than ever" (Žižek, 2013, p. 25). This means that we might no longer be in the era of thesis number eleven of Marx's *Theses on Feuerbach*. Our time is not one of transforming reality, of trying to achieve revolution for "everyone's" sake. Žižek emphasizes this quite notably and winds up "hurting" several thinkers in his interviews by being so blunt:

> Ah, Marx's stupid thesis number eleven: "Philosophers have done nothing but interpret the world in different ways, but what it is all about is about transforming it". I think Marx would say nowadays: In the 20th century we have been trying to change the world ever so eagerly. We don't know where we step. Is China capitalist or something new? I think China is setting a precedent of a new form of capitalist authoritarianism.
>
> (Žižek, 2018)

Žižek as well as Lacan-Kojève close the doors to the possibility of revolution. Therefore, is any revolutionary process nowadays even possible? Or is it only a kind of Kantian regulatory ideal of a certain Latin American leftist movement or of an impoverished, resentful, absurd, ideological, or fundamentalist mind? One of the abnormalities of the current system that has lasted several decades now and has been implemented worldwide (let us not forget that the entire capitalist system is an abnormality naturalized by extreme ideologization) is trying to resignify and disguise what takes place with neutral, proactive, "happy" signifiers, or "euphemisms". Lacan says it in a blunt way: "The principle of revolutionary agitation is nothing other than that there is a point where things are not liked" (*SXVI*, 04.06.69).

We do not want to delve into a speech that closes the political possibility of a revolution with a romantic perspective, which is something that Marx criticized in *The Eighteenth Brumaire of Louis Bonaparte*, and that is yet another game of power. This infantilized revolution is doomed to fail and so what is most necessary is the Revolution that opens and frees desire, which is the one that Marx was thinking about in the 19th century. This was Lenin's revolution in 1917 (although it later became an alternative machinery to capitalism). It is not about the "democracy that is yet to come", but rather about the "revolution that is yet to come", a revolution that stays open in its open affirmation of what happens to WethOthers (Cf. Espinoza, 2018, 2019). If this is not the case, Lacan would be inevitably right:

> This Master's discourse already has its letters of credit in the philosophical tradition. Nevertheless, in the way I am trying to uncover it, it takes on, here, a new light by virtue of the fact that in our day it so happens that it can be uncovered in a sort of purity –and this, through something that we experience directly, and at the level of politics. What I mean by this is that it embraces everything, even what thinks of itself as revolutionary, or more exactly as what is romantically called Revolution with a capital R. The Master's discourse accomplishes its own revolution in the other sense of doing a complete circle.
> 
> (*SXVII*, 18.02.70, p. 87)

Lacan was always close to Kojève's Hegel (let us not forget his famous course from 1933 to 1939). This means that he always thinks about reality from a closed dialectic where it articulates itself with its opposite and both are structured from power. As a result, history closes itself because the way out of this structural dialectic is another form of power that is always linked to Capitalism. It carries that which it wants to oppose within itself and so the only thing left is updating the capitalist power within the revolution.

Lacan is very clear about this:

> What is at stake in Marxist theory, in so far as it concerns the truth, is what it states in effect. The fact that the truth of capitalism is the proletariat. It is true. Only it is from that very thing that there emerges the series and the import of our remarks about what is involved in the function of the truth. It is that the revolutionary consequence of this truth, this truth from which Marxist theory

starts, naturally it goes a little bit further since what it constructs the theory of, is precisely capitalism.

(*SXVI*, 12.02.69)

This is the reason why this revolution is useless, but not everything is a closed dialectic as Kojève would suggest. The revolutionary subject WethOthers overcomes the structural problem of the proletariat and the bourgeoisie that are doomed to always go hand in hand. Lacan sees in the proletariat the same revolutionary-capitalist dialectic as Kojève:

> The proletariat, what does that mean? It means that labour is radicalised to the pure and simple level of merchandise; which of course means that this reduces the worker himself to the same measure. Only once the worker, because of the theory, learns to know of himself as that, one can say that through this step, he finds the paths of a status – call that what you will – of a savant. He is no longer a proletarian, as I might say an sich, he is no longer pure and simple truth, he is für sich; he is what is called class consciousness. And he can even at the same time become the class consciousness of the party in which people no longer speak the truth.
>
> (*SXVI*, 12.02.69)

It is possible to carry out a revolutionary process that will overcome Lacan's and also Kojève (as well as Žižek's) dictum. This is a process that is not in the old history books and that overcomes everyone's fear of change, that overcomes the closed dialectical structure, and that also rises up over that power as something that constitutes us, that locks us up and that, finally, chains us to the "enemy" that must be fought. Such fear originates in having to subject the body to the State's violent repression, a repression against the WethOthers that came to be. Revolution is possible nowadays. Lacan himself talks about a way to achieve Revolution with capital letters:

> Try not to lose the thread about what you are as effect of knowledge. You are split apart in the phantasy ($\$ \diamond a$). You are, however strange this may appear, the cause of yourself. Only there is no self. Rather there is a divided self. Entering onto this path is where the only true political revolution may flow from. Knowledge serves the master. I am coming back today to underline that knowledge is born from the slave.
>
> (*SXVI*, 25.06.69)

When knowledge originates in the slave it means that we are able to give way to something that will create a different form of organization. This WethOthers finally brings knowledge from the very roots and now these roots go through the socio-historical tissue of actual people and that no longer remain only in history books and the worn-out categories of philosophers. It is also not a matter of violence for violence's sake and a senseless "blood bath", which is what the people who administer power always say and that the media operates so that all social movements are quickly stigmatized as something "terrible" that betrays and goes against institutions. It is not about parties or movements or revolutionary people that want to destroy the system to establish power for themselves as a power articulated against its mortal enemy: capitalism. Lacan plays with this repeatedly in his work: "The irony of revolutions is that they engender a power that is all the more absolute in its exercise, not because it is more anonymous, as people say, but because it is reduced more completely to the words that signify it" (*FFS*, p. 234). This is also the case of the Podemos movement in Spain that is often stigmatized for wanting to destroy Spanish institutions. There are many other examples of this all over the world. Hence, the possibility of revolutionary processes exists nowadays in different places. To understand Revolution, it is crucial to reformulate the revolutionary subject. In that regard, both theory and praxis have failed in their diagnosis, in their concepts, and their activism, although it seemed to be quite clear who was the enemy to be subverted. We call this subject the WethOthers. But what is the WethOthers? It is an experience-concept that expresses a situated socio-historical tissue both in a material and a virtual way; the nihilist ideology of capitalism that shapes us in all possible ways: empirically, virtually, and unconsciously, which must be the fundamental ground to be conquered. This is why psychoanalysis, particularly that of Lacan, is so relevant. Is it possible nowadays to have a revolutionary WethOthers despite other impediments that un-articulate us? If it is the only revolutionary subject of our times (this is always the case, it is the sovereignty of the State of Exception), then no Revolution is possible and we are destined to remain adrift in the maze of so many revolutions (this was Nietzsche's criticism of the revolutionaries of his time). Lacan argued that existence was very complex because of the underdevelopment that was a condition for capitalism itself:

> I would even say more, what one notices, and what will be noticed more and more, is that underdevelopment is precisely the condition for capitalistic progress. From a certain angle, the October Revolution itself is a proof of it. But what must be seen, is that what we have to confront is an underdevelopment that is going to be more and more patent, more and more widespread. Only what in short is at stake, is that we should put the following to the test: if the key of the different problems that are going to propose themselves to us is not to put us at the level of this effect of capitalist articulation that I left in the shadows last year by simply giving you its root in the discourse of the Master.
> (*SXVIII*, 20.01.71)

Everything has turned into a territory that produces and distributes capital. Every territory is in some sort of dispute that implies daily battles (there is no operating ethic in these battles and all of us are their soldiers). This is especially the case of the unconscious for, as I mentioned before, it is radically required to be "the" capitalist sovereign spoils of war. The reason for this is that by winning this "battle" it is easier to win the "war" over capital, which is why psychoanalysis along with critical theory and feminism are of much help when it comes to analysing the situation. One could say that the lobbying by the Chinese, which may seem absurd, is crucial to prevent, even if only partially, the "naturalized" imperialism of America. China is constantly negotiating and offering good and efficiently priced products in the global market so that the potency of any revolutionary WethOthers has to be radically deactivated. If capitalism is also a logic of power, and therefore of knowledge, all of this knowledge will operate from the position of the Master:

> The interest, the only one, of the communist revolution, I am speaking about the Russian Revolution, is to have restored the functions of power. Only we see that it is not easy to hold onto, precisely because in the time when capitalism reigns, capitalism reigns because it is closely connected with this rise in the function of science. Only even this power, this camouflaged power, this secret and, it must also be said anarchic power, I mean divided against itself, and this without any doubt through its being clothed with this rise of science, it is as embarrassed as a fish on a bicycle now. Because all the same something is happening in the science quarter, something that transcends its capacity for mastery. So then what is necessary is that there at least a certain number of little heads that do not forget the fact that a certain permanent association of contestation with initiatives that are not controlled in the sense of revolution is vain. Well then, this again is what in the system, the capitalist system, can best serve it.
> (*SXVI*, 19.03.69)

Who we have become (all "too human") has been structured by the very production and distribution of capital that we ourselves are, be it as an "I" or an "us" (both are two sides of the same coin, and they are products of ideological European dialectical homogenization). This is the very same structural closure that subdues us to the capitalist maze. It is evident that we produce and distribute "ourselves" as products: the us from "here", from "there", the "good Europeans", the ones from the political centre, us the pure ones, us the nationalists, us the Westerners, us that know what is good for everybody, us that act in good faith, us the rational ones, us the originary people, us the "machos", us the feminists, etc. Lacan saw this very clearly:

> This is what, from time to time, Marx calls the economy, because these interests are, in capitalist society, entirely commercial. It's just that since the market is linked to the master signifier, nothing is resolved by denouncing it in this way. For the market is no less linked to this signifier after the socialist revolution.
> (*SXVII*, 11.03.70, p. 92)

We become mere and horrible merchandise and the world itself turns into a mere vulgar and horrible market. Also, truth becomes something that the Frankfurt

School was interested in understanding, which is a narcissistic recognition that generates more additional value and so accumulates every day in such a way that it doesn't ever seem to stop. Within this accumulation that becomes untouchable like Hegel's bad infinity, every human being perceives only his/her "self" as an "I" (the largest and most toxic European invention). An "I" that can do anything and that longs for infinity and struggles to the death for it. An "I" that "creates" Nature itself to make it work, as in the Latin American states, the common European market, the United States' "backyard", the British Commonwealth, the Chinese Asia Pacific region, etc. The modern European "I" (the anti-revolutionary *par excellence*) needs what can be dominated in order to dominate, and this is the only form of domination that it is capable of doing. This is how a dominator in the natural estate comes to be, not only in Latin America or Europe, but rather globally. In this natural estate everything is well established and any possible Revolution is uprooted from the very beginning. All positions are ontologically determined. There is nothing the master cannot see or that is not decided by him in the estate. The grand master is like a new god that has come to Earth in an Armageddon-like fashion. This is precisely the master that Lacan fears and experienced in May '68. Everything else is serfdom.

The "Revolution that is yet to come" articulates in a live manner a State with a WethOthers; State and Revolution is the State and WethOthers. What must be liberated by this movement is desire beyond a capitalist labyrinthian structure that is only death and deceit. Only as long as the State works with WethOthers to form a live and dynamic co-design can Revolution be understood not as a desire for revolution, that is, another simply failed revolution: another master and nothing else (this is what Lenin focused on in his book *State and Revolution* and what he tried to do during the October Revolution of 1917). But if Revolution, in this logic of permanent co-design with the State, invites us to believe in freedom and thus to liberate desire, then Revolution is possible. It is not about wanting revolution, but about the fact that the "Revolution that is yet to come" in this living State, in co-design, allows us to liberate desire from the capitalist chains. This is the challenge. Lacan points to this very precisely: "it is the freedom to desire that is a new factor, not because it has inspired a revolution – people have always fought and died for a desire– but because this revolution wants its struggle to be for the freedom of desire" (*KS*, p. 662).

A Revolution is what lets the Capitalist maze dissolve and, as a consequence, allows for something new to open, which needs to be built by everyone, a construction that will always be in an individual, social, and historical movement, and which will also allow for the possibility of Revolution risking failure.

Translated from Spanish by Carla Tirado-Morttiz

## Notes

1 This is a Spanish neologism that consist in writing "*Nosotros*" (We) with a capital "O" (NosOtros = We-Others). We propose the English translation as "WethOthers" (We-Others/With-Others.) (Note from the editors).

2 Hegel's text is extremely insightful when explaining the need to choose an emperor after the Roman revolution failed, which rendered the revolutionary possible: "But it became immediately manifest that only a *single* will could guide the Roman State, and now the Romans were compelled to adopt that opinion; since in all periods of the world a political revolution is sanctioned in men's opinions, when it repeats itself. Thus Napoleon was twice defeated, and the Bourbons twice expelled. By repetition that which at first appeared merely a matter of chance and contingency becomes a real and ratified existence" (Hegel, 1837, p. 332).

## Further reading

Alemán, J. (2019). *Capitalismo: crimen perfecto o emancipación*. Madrid: NED.
Laclau, E. (1990). *New Reflections on The Revolution of Our Time*. London: Verso.
Parker, I. (2011). *Lacanian Psychoanalysis: Revolutions in Subjectivity*. London: Routledge.

## References

Espinoza, R. (2016). *Hegel y las nuevas lógicas del mundo y del estado*. Madrid: Akal.
Espinoza, R. (2018). *Capitalismo y empresa. Hacia una revolución del nosotros*. Santiago: Libros Pascal.
Espinoza, R. (2019). *NosOtros. Manual para disolver el capitalismo*. Madrid: Morata.
Hegel, G.W.F. (1837). *The Philosophy of History*, J. Sibree (Trans.). New York: Prometheus Books, 1991.
Žižek, S. (2013). *Demanding the Impossible*. Cambridge: Polity Press.
Žižek, S. (2018). Entrevista a Slavoj Žižek por Darío Prieto. *Diario El Mundo*. 15 May 2018.
Žižek, S. (2020). *Pandemic! COVID-19. Shakes the World*. New York: OR Books.

# Chapter 20

# Segregation

Jorge Alemán and Carlos Gómez Camarena

—Ara.: فصل —Chi.: 種族隔離 —Fre.: *Ségrégation* —Ger.: *Ausgrenzung* — Ita.: *Segregazione* —Jap.: 分離 —Port.: *Segregação* —Rus.: *Сегрегация* — Spa.: *Segregación* —Tur.: *Ayrım*

→ *Ideology*; *Politics*, *Proletarian*; *Surplus*-jouissance

## Introduction

The etymological root of segregation comes from the Greek term *grex* or *grego*, which refers to the herd and is contained in words such as congregate, disaggregate, and, of course, segregate. Much less obvious is the explanation of how one segregates in the attempt to live in community. This is a recurring theme both in Lacan's thought and in Marx's philosophy.

Lacan's citations of this term—or racism—can be divided into three groups: (1) science; (2) the institutions clarified through the University discourse; and (3) the invention of the School. With respect to Marx's work, segregation is a social and particularly geographical (urban and international) effect of the relations of exploitation. Exploitation and segregation are mutually implicated. In this sense, segregation is not only an effect of exploitation, but also something necessary for the reproduction of the capitalist system. Regarding this last point, the discussion about whether language is part of the infrastructure or the superstructure of the capitalist system is crucial, since for Marx, segregation is "always already" the capitalist system itself, where the system is its own infrastructure–superstructure relationship. For Lacan, segregation is an effect of discourse. In this case, the central question lies in the social bond and the regimes of the so-called University discourse, Capitalist discourse, and in the existence of a scientific discourse. On the other hand, in Marx, the crucial concepts are those of "tendency of the rate of profit to fall", "division of labor", and that of the "reserve army of labor".

## On the side of Marx

Marxism is a path of internationalization against imperialism and the headless capitalist will that segregates the workforce while exploiting it. Marx was very clear about this international dimension. He was concerned that ethnic prejudices put the unity of the working class at risk. On 23 November 1862, he wrote the following for the Austrian newspaper *Die Presse* about the elections in the United States:

> The Irishman sees in the Negro a dangerous competitor. The efficient farmers in Indiana and Ohio hate the Negro second only to the slave-owner. For them he is the symbol of slavery and the debasement of the working class, and the Democratic press threatens them daily with an inundation of their territories by the "nigger".
>
> (*TER*, p. 264)

Almost two years later, when Marx drew up the General Rules of the First International, he noted the following: "all societies and individuals adhering to it will acknowledge truth, justice, and morality as the basis of their conduct toward each other and toward all men, without regard to color, creed, or nationality" (*PRW*). Sixteen years later, when he drew up the Program of the French Workers' Party, Marx declared that "the emancipation of the productive class is that of all human beings without distinction of sex or race" (*PPO*, p. 376). All these matters are important, since one of the crucial issues—both for Lacan and for Marx—is the following question: what type of social organization is compatible and transmits in a better way the most radical aspect at stake in psychoanalysis and in the Marxist proposal? Communism has as its central purpose, for example, the elimination of classes and the most fundamental socio-economic differences in society, not only between workers but also peasants, producers of all kinds, men, women, and people of all nations and races. The core question lies in the best form of social organization to achieve such purposes.

For Marx, it is evident that capitalism produces social segregation through its economic mechanisms, and that ideology naturalizes these inequalities and discriminations by race, gender, and class. Racism and segregation are structurally determined problems. The sharpening of this tendency is demonstrated by the emergence of the Nation-State, national identities, and progress. Nazism is the most complete example of this logic.

In Chapter I of the first volume of Capital (*CAI*) Marx articulates the negative effects of the division of labour—a central concept for the structural analysis of segregation. These effects are individualization, the brutalization of the process of work, the need to exchange money in the market, and the concentration of the means of production in the hands of a few. In terms of segregation, the division of labour imposes a classification of labour. Quantifying and classifying is the most important task for the proper functioning of this division of labour. The economist David Ricardo was the first to theorize this international division, considering that in the world market, each country would dedicate itself to producing the goods with which they obtained the best benefit. For this, it was important to consider the costs of raw materials, the wages of each country, and, above all, the prices of the international market. This would explain why one country would devote itself to producing wine, another meat, and another corn. With the international division of labour and the international market, competition, a virtue recognized by Adam Smith as well as Ricardo, increases.

What escaped them in this theorization was precisely political economy: in production, exchange, and consumption; what is at stake is power and domination. Ultimately, the capitalist system via the free international market will produce walls and barriers so that labour does not circulate freely. This is not so for merchandise. In this way, the working class would be stratified in the dominant countries and in the peripheries. Such stratification and classification would divide countries from each other, but also divide countries internally into regions and zones. This would explain why there are more and more walls, barriers, and visas between countries, but also between the city and the countryside, or even between the centres and the peripheries of large cities. Segregation in Marx is structural but appears as a phenomenon of time and space (Harvey, 2001). The other two concepts related to "segregation" are those of the "reserve army" and the "decreasing trend of the rate of profit".

Competition is the capitalist's main motive for increasing productivity. However, as Marx shows mathematically in the third part of the third volume of *Capital* (*CAIII*), in this same movement there is a tendency for profit to decrease. In an attempt to neutralize this tendency, the capitalist increases the rate of exploitation, lowers wages, decreases constant capital, and initiates international trade. In the long run this trend is inexorable. But there is another solution: export the exploitation to other regions or countries and import the goods from elsewhere. This begins in the city—producing belts of poverty—and ends in other regions or countries where labour is cheaper, laws are laxer, and raw materials are cheaper. To keep the wages of the labour force low, it is necessary that there be structural unemployment, named by Marx as the "reserve army" in Chapter 1 of the first volume (*CAI*). A worker will accept low wages because the other option is unemployment—an unemployed person would be willing to take a job with worse conditions. For this same reason, natural and artificial borders ensure that these conditions are maintained. It is not a minor detail that hatred of the immigrant is stoked precisely by denouncing (falsely) those who supposedly take jobs from natives.

In regions and countries where working conditions are worse, it is necessary to have more authoritarian governments, more repressive methods, justifying narratives of injustices, and, of course, psychologists to better manage the workforce in psychic terms—but also to deploy segregation theories and practices based on identity, development, pathology, and other distinctions between normality and deviance. That is, in more "developed" countries, the police will monitor the borders and the psychologists will also monitor the good spirits of the population in terms of mental health—also justifying why the immigrant, the madman, and the deviant are individually responsible for their misfortune. From this perspective, medicalization and psychiatrization—with the help of science—are already segregating regimes in themselves. Lacan will call this "Discourse" (*SXVII*).

In other words, capitalism must exclude and keep at a distance the labour force that it exploits and deprives. The capitalist system must take advantage of natural borders, create artificial walls and a whole time-space apparatus to divide worlds. The prosperous and luxurious world—where surplus-value is consumed—must distance itself from the miserable worlds where that same surplus-value is produced. Before it was the city; today it is the country. The greater the distance, the less risk of riots and the more profitable the exploitation. Ideologically, segregation, discrimination, and distance are defended by the (far) right. Thus, the logic of capitalism lies in neutralizing the downward trend of profit and ensuring a reserve army that keeps wages low. Capitalism needs to create a segregated exterior in which the conditions of accumulation of the surplus-value that will be consumed in the so-called "Global North" or "first world" are ensured.

## What Lacan says

### Freud and the psychology of the masses

Taking the term "mass psychology" (*Massenpsychologie*) from Gustave Le Bon (1895) and articulating it to the meta-psychological novelty of the "analysis of the ego" based on narcissism, Freud makes a bridge between the two apparently heterogeneous dimensions of the collective and the individual. Freud makes an analysis of two artificial masses—the Church and the Army—introducing a structure of identification that gravitates around three concepts: the ideal, identification, and love as a libidinal bond. The central mechanism of *Massenpsychologie* is the identification with the "unary trait" (*einziger Zug*) of a person who is not the object of sexual instincts and who is recognized as important to a group. With this he begins a dialectic between an object and the ideal of the ego. This deals with what Freud calls "the formula for the libidinal constitution of groups" (Freud, 1921, p. 120), which is articulated through love and hypnosis. The antecedent to such libidinal constitution is found in *Totem and Taboo* (1913) in the idea of "horde". There are two important issues to keep in mind: the mass is articulated in the constitution of the ego, and that such constitution, in turn, is the effect of a relationship between the ideal ego and the ego ideal—via identification and whose cement is the libido. In this sense, the two examples of the masses used by Freud, the Church and the Army, segregate. This segregation is constitutive of the ego, something that Freud will later call "narcissism of minor differences" (Freud, 1918, p. 199; 1929, p. 114): a mechanism by which the smallest detail is sought to distinguish oneself from someone else in order to segregate. Lacan knows this very well and that is why he affirms that there is no "I know only one single origin of brotherhood" other than "segregation", to end by saying "they discover they are brothers, one wonders in the name of what segregation" (*SXVII*, pp. 132–133).

In the constitution of the ego and of narcissism in the ideal, we find the psychic spring of the masses and segregation. This is the "bad news" that psychoanalysis always brings with it. This should be understood when Lacan states that "there is no need for this ideology for a racism to be constituted" (*SXVIII*, 20.01.71) and that the "unary trait" (*einziger Zug*) also implies a *plus-de-jouissance*: "the tiny surplus enjoying of Hitler, that went no further perhaps than his mustache, this was enough to crystalize people who had nothing mystical about them [...] that involves in terms of questioning of surplus enjoying in its form of surplus value" (*SXVIII*, 20.01.71). In sum, for Lacan the constitution of the subject implies identification but also enjoyment; for this reason, no type of ideological-political articulation is necessary. Lacan investigates more about the identification and psychology of the masses by making a double movement: (1) distinguishing the ideal ego from the ego ideal: the symbolic identification of the imaginary identification, and (2) exploring forms of identification that are horizontal and manage to escape the mirror stage and the dialectic of master and slave. The second point is related to game theory and the invention of the "cartel" in the School.

### The structural segregation of the subject

Within the symbolic, there are symbolic identifications and the constitution of the subject, not only of the ego, as an effect of language. This is marked by segregation, responding to the famous phrase "the unconscious is structured like a language" (*ST*, p. 737). On this point, Lacan follows Kant's work: the definitive idea that when a thought comes into the world, it always explicitly or implicitly segregates, whether that thinker wants it to or not. Thought segregates a mandate. There is no thought that is declined, finally, by a mandate. For example: "Know yourself" (Socrates), "Become who you are" (Pindar), "Get away from physics and go towards my idea of good" (Plato), "Know your limit and do not overflow it" (from Delphi to Aristotle), "Be more than a man, prepare the abode of the superman" (Nietzsche), "Return to being after having denied it" (Hegel), "Be happy, configure yourself according to the order of world events" (Wittgenstein), or "Prepare properly for the 'auspicious event'" (Heidegger). There is no thinker who, in one way or another, does not end up segregating a mandate, a master signifier. It is of fundamental importance in Kant to investigate the formal structure of these mandates. That is why, for Lacan, the subject does not think but is thought of by language, is spoken of by language. Language produces segregations. We should note this, because this position is opposed to critical theories based on the cognitive or that centre the self.

The constitution of the subject takes Lacan to the question of the "lack in being" (*manque à être*), an expression used at least 20 times throughout his work. Subjects are constituted from symbolic and imaginary identifications but never definitively, and for this reason the "lack in being" is also inherent in subjectivity. It is the "flipside" of being, or what Lacan calls *desêtre*, the "un-being" or "dis-being", a term also mentioned at least 15 times by Lacan. He even goes so far as to speak of "passions of being" (*SI*, 30.06.54, p. 273; *DTP*, p. 524) in the sense of articulations of the imaginary and the symbolic which give themselves a consistency of being that counteracts the lack in being. These three passions are love, hatred, and ignorance. We will put aside ignorance in this work and focus briefly on love and hatred. These two passions lead us to a third form of segregation—already mentioned in relation to Hitler—that is an effect of structuring the subject: enjoyment. Enjoyment is another (failed) strategy to give consistency to being, feeding both the consumption of objects to give oneself a being as well as the hatred for those who we consider—in terms of our fantasy—to have taken away the enjoyment that we need. It is important to mention with respect to this matter that the *plus-de-jouissance* is the strategy of wanting to regain the lost enjoyment. In the *plus-de-jouissance* lies one of the secrets of capitalism that Lacan clarifies through Pascal's wager (*SXVI*, 13.10.68; 15.01.69).

Later, Lacan problematizes the relationship between hatred and enjoyment—as a response to the lack in being—as one of the mechanisms of racism and segregation of the Other. For Lacan, the enjoyment that symbolizes the body of the Other does not become a sign of love, which is why we could infer that love does not reach the point of enjoyment of the Other (*SXX*, 21.11.72, p. 4). Lacan sees hatred as being in a more appropriate position to address the being of enjoyment that exists in the Other. Every universal statement that had value as an ultimate foundation finally achieves, as a result, a new type of segregation, a hatred, in short, for that which is not included in the universal statement. It is for this reason that racism or segregation receive their strength from the hatred that can be heard, the hatred directed at the being, which shows how little can be expected from the different modalities to a call to love between men (*SXX*, 10.04.73, pp. 90–91). From this angle—from the hatred that reaches the being of enjoyment in a truer way than love—it can be noted that the loving praise is directed at the clothing of the Other, clothing that can be one's own body and that is how the insult seems to be aimed more directly at one's being. This explains the presence of pseudo-insults in the loving vocabulary of lovers.

This has consequences in the way of conceiving of the modern State and its relationship with democracy. As is well known, there are authors who consider that—unlike the Totalitarian State that is always sustained by a founding Myth—the specificity of the modern Democratic State is its support based in a rational, transmissible story, mediated by the free play of institutions (Lefort, 1981). The famous passage from myth to a narrative as described by Plato, that unfolds and transforms it until it dissolves, in a certain way fails to take into account what psychoanalysis teaches: that no structure, however symbolic, manages to reduce and suppress imaginary inertias which try to impose an identity at the cost of segregation. The unconscious always reveals what the myth houses in its essence. It is not just the configuration of an epic feat, since this is only a modality of that which tries to suture the fracture, the split that prevents the fullness of the origin.[1] For this reason, no society, however democratic it may be, is spared from imagining that those who "represent" the law, "enjoy an extra benefit", that in the exercise of the law there are not only pure procedures but also the accumulation of an "enjoyment" that has been stolen from its citizens. Hatred as a fantasy of the theft of lost enjoyment—which never existed in the first place—is currently exploited both by neoliberalism against the Welfare State (as hatred of democracy or the defence of the public and the commons) and by the extreme right against immigrants, the poor, and minorities (Pavón-Cuéllar, 2020).

Lacan goes beyond Freud: that the subject is an effect of language and that enjoyment is put into play—as an attempt to recover its lack in being—are two aspects that deepen how segregation is constitutive of the subject. However, enjoyment is not exclusive to segregation; it instead accentuates racism. It is for this reason that philosophers such as Adorno (1951) and Benjamin (1969) made a great theoretical effort when trying to incorporate Freud into the field of historical materialism, in particular problematizing the field of ideology that was previously considered a field reduced to conscious cogitation. It is the same movement that Althusser (1993) operated to update Marxism. Identifications, voluntary servitudes, economics—and its libidinal devices—and segregative effects must be taken into account as part of critical theory and militancy without being confined to the irrational.

The fact that segregation and racism are inherent in Lacan's constitution of the subject should not be confused with a psychologizing explanation. That is, in terms of a deep, individual, inner mentality. Horkheimer affirms that, "the liberal conception of history is fundamentally psychological" (1932, p. 115). Furthermore, Lacan warns us against this psychologization by pointing out that "One is simply helpless against the attraction of diversifying the forms of the concentration camp: psychologizing ideology is one of them" (*RSF*, p. 109). Other authors such as Ian Parker (2011), Jan de Vos (2013), or David Pavón-Cuéllar (2017) have also warned us of this risk, in turn avoiding it through a close relationship between Marx and Lacan. When it comes to the imaginary, symbolic, or real aspects of otherness, the constitution of the subject is diagonal to the distinction between individual and society. The term that Lacan used for this is "inmixion" (*IMX*, p. 186), which refers to the effect when two substances are mixed and thus become indistinguishable.[2]

In this sense, that segregation is constitutive of the subject does not mean that this is the nature of the human being—Lacan would agree with Marx on this point. The constitution of the subject is not natural or cultural, but *structural*. The imaginary and symbolic identifications of the structural need for the constitution of the subject are historical. The form is constitutive—not innate or natural—and the content is historical. This must be taken into account to analyze politics and the clinic.

## Science and segregation

Lacan—with the same orientation as Heidegger—captures the historical moment of modern science by demonstrating the emergence of nihilism at a certain moment, a time period that makes everything interchangeable, equivalent, evaluable, and calculable. In his meditations, Lacan goes further. When studying the way in which science is an "ideology of the suppression of the subject" (*RA*, p. 437), he opens different epochal considerations about the direct effects, typical of the homogenization carried out by the *discourse of science*. Namely, these are: the increase in racist hatred, which always considers the Other either as an underdeveloped enjoyment or as the bearer of an excess of malignant enjoyment. For this reason, Lacan captures in the concentration camp the vanishing point of contemporary societies. While there was a time in Lacan's teaching where science was similar to Hysterical discourse—due to its capacity to produce knowledge with the truth hidden from the subject—Lacan later anticipates a new torsion of science where knowledge is tied to the drive, recognizing the new growing impasses of civilization.

The unleashing of technology and its imbrication with the capitalist market constitutes a "refusal of castration". The Capitalist discourse performs a circular movement (*DDP*, p. 48), where the Will manages to reunite the subject with the enjoyment of the object, without the limits or the symbolic distance that castration imposes. The signs of this disappearance were anticipated by Lacan in various ways: homogenization procedures, disintegration of the concept of experience, disappearance of memory, decline of the paternal imago, increase in racism, globalization of the gaze—object *a* as gaze.

Object *a* is not in front of the subject of representation, it is not an object of the world as ontology would want, but it is an object that, within the subject, causes its division. Object *a* is indebted to an experience, its place is an unprecedented object, as well as its operations. For this reason, in *The Logic of the Phantom*, Lacan speaks of the object *a* as the *Dasein* of psychoanalysis (*SXIV*, 16.11.66). If Heidegger had faced what *being* implies of slag and sacrifice, he would have recognized the true essential fact found in the technical unfolding in the age of science: segregation. As Lacan recalls in *Encore* (*SXX*, 10.04.73, p. 90), hatred is directed at being, and it is the attempt to standardize scientific discourse that provides the conditions for this segregation under the cruellest form of human sacrifice (*SXI*, 24.06.64, p. 275). In this sense, the discourse of science is the precursor of "the rearranging of social groupings by science and, notably, of the universalization science introduces into them" (*P9O*, p. 257). The fact that there are institutions that feed on these sacrifices is what forces psychoanalysts to reflect on what kind of collective instance they should promote in order to transmit the analytical discourse, which promotes other conditions for the experience of being. This explains why one of the places where the term "segregation" has more weight is the *Proposition of 9 October 1967 on the Psychoanalyst of the School*.

In the beginning, Lacan seems to assimilate science to the discourse of Hysteria (*SXVII*, 10.06.70, p. 176), and at certain times to the discourse of the University (*SXVII*, 13.05.70, pp. 148–149). At other times the phrase "discourse of science" is equivalent to the discourse of Capitalism, to the point of saying that science is born from the function of the subject, which is made possible by the discourse of the Master (*SXVII*, 10.12.69, p. 23). When it comes to the last position, Lacan takes a Heideggerian stance, even creating neologisms inspired by the German philosopher, such as the "alethosphere", a kind of atmosphere populated by "lathousies" created in and by Capitalist discourse (*SXVII*, 20.05.70, pp. 161–163). It is possible to distinguish in Lacan's work the concepts of science as a *discourse* from *science in and of itself*. While the first is almost assimilable to the "Capitalist discourse" and very similar to what is usually called "technoscience" (Mumford, 1934), the second implies a historical-epistemological rupture. This last aspect can be found in *Science and Truth*, where Lacan draws on Alexandre Koyré's conception of science, whom he calls "my guide" (*ST*, p. 727). Indeed, as several of his commentators have already pointed out—Alenka Zupančič (2017), Jean-Claude Milner (1995), or Samo Tomšič (2019)—science for Lacan produced a change in the status of knowledge, in such a way that religion, art, and philosophy were forever transformed in modernity. In this sense, it is about being aware of the response of analytical discourse to science as discourse, but also about how psychoanalysis is born on the horizon of science (as such): "What I must stress here is that I claim to pave the way for the scientific position of psychoanalysis by analyzing in what way it is already implied at the very heart of the psychoanalytic discovery" (*SQ*, p. 194). In any case, scientific discourse—which reproduces segregation—and science are two different things for Lacan: "the analytic discourse is not a scientific discourse, but rather a discourse of which the material is provided by science, which is quite different" (*SXIX*, 19.04.72, p. 122).

Regarding science as such, that is, modern science, Lacan considers it to be the native soil of psychoanalysis. Therefore, the emphasis in science lies not so much in the technological impact —social, political, libidinal or economic—but in a qualitative change in knowledge and in the introduction of a new subject: the divided subject. "Psychoanalysis has played a role in the direction of modern subjectivity, and it cannot sustain this role without aligning it with the movement in modern science that elucidates it" (*FFS*, p. 284), so that modernity would be marked by this change in knowledge and by the introduction of the subject in that knowledge. For this reason, the practice of psychoanalysis "implies no other subject than that of science" (*ST*, p. 733). The introduction of the subject into knowledge as the specificity of modernity is marked by the reduction of the subject to an eye in Panofksy (*SXI*, 11.01.64; *SXIII*, 04.05.66) or to the formula of a matrix of significant combinations in game theory or in set theory (*ST*, p. 730). Modern science is the reduction of knowledge to a combinatorial game of letters (Newton's invention) and an effect of the mathematization of the universe that empties it of its content (as in Galileo and Descartes), transforming "the closed world" into an "infinite universe" (Koyré, 1957). The modern subject, on the other hand, is also stripped of all content—via mathematization—and in turn is the product of doubt and certainty (introduced by Descartes) as decentred, between two foci of an ellipse, as in Kepler (*SXX*, 01.16.73, p. 43). Psychoanalysis is contemporary to science and in turn a response to that change in the status of knowledge. This conception of science is similar to that of Mao Tse-Tung, for whom one of the best sources of ideas is scientific experimentation (1963, p. 168) or that of Lenin, who pointed out that Taylorism, like all capitalist progress, is a refined mix between brutal bourgeois exploitation and the best scientific developments (1918, p. 259). In both interpretations of science—as a subject of modern knowledge or as a discourse—there is a possible effect of segregation. Lacan takes these two ways of thinking about science seriously—as a discourse and as a change in knowledge—in order to think about his School.

### Institutions and university knowledge: the difference between segregation and the death camp

The term "segregation" in Jacques Lacan's teaching appears early, in the context of psychiatric institutions of English psychiatry and the war in 1947 (*PAG*), institutions that segregate *dullards*. Twenty years later, Lacan has not changed his position, picking up the word "segregation" when he founds his School and writes the so-called "four discourses". Most of these references are concentrated between 1967 and 1971 in his Seminars *XVI* (05.02.69), *XVII* (11.03.70) and especially the *XIX* (04.11.71; 06.01.72). Segregation is associated with the universalization of university knowledge as well as with psychiatric, psychological, or psychoanalytic institutions that assimilate scientific knowledge to university bureaucratic discourse or to the "common markets" promoted by Capitalist discourse (*P9O*, p. 257).

For example, in 1967, making some notes on psychoses in children, he affirmed that each social structure is the result of the progress of science, warning that this will have a segregating effect in psychiatry (*APE*, p. 362). In 1971 he was invited to return to the Saint-Anne hospital to give a series of talks entitled "The Knowledge of the Psychoanalyst", where he reminded his audience of mostly psychiatrists that psychiatry itself participates in the segregation of mental illness:

> For anyone who dwells here within these [...] walls of the clinical asylum, it would be as well to know that what situates and defines the psychiatrist as such is his situation in relation to these walls, these walls whereby secularism has created, on the inside, an exclusion of madness and of what madness means.
>
> (*PAM*, p. 89)

In 1970, in the preface to Anika Lemaire's thesis on his own work, Lacan locates segregation as an effect of discourse, specifically that of the University:

> The segregation of psychiatry in the Faculty of Medicine, where the university structure displays its affinities with the managerial system. This segregation is supported by the fact that psychiatry itself performs the office of social segregation. The result is that psychiatry designates a spare room on the strength of the University's liberal funds, those who have a right to this

lodging being repressed into the ghetto which was once, and with some reason, known as the asylum.

(*PTH*, p. VIII)

Segregation, a product of University discourse, is found in the present field of psychiatry and is motivated more by politics than by practice, the core of the social bond of University discourse. However, Lacan wonders if the psychoanalyst does not inhabit that same discursive rationality since he has a natural antipathy for "academic discourse". He responds that this is not the case; however, this position "is translated into institutions conveying secondary benefits". For this reason, Lacan must think of the invention of the School as another form of bonding between psychoanalysts.

Lacan warns psychiatrists that segregation will spread: "in four or five years' time, we are going to be swamped by problems of segregation, which will be labeled or excoriated with the term racism" (*PAM*, p. 31). In this same conference he mentions Foucault (*PAM*, p. 7), for whom the foundation of the Enlightenment lies in the subject of reason—and for that same reason those who are affected by madness cannot share this same space. Indeed, the social contract and the universal subject of rights are situated in reason, so that segregation is based on the universality of reason and the exclusion of non-reason. When the subject is deprived of reason—when it is crazy—it loses the main attribute of itself as a subject. Lacan interrogates psychiatrists, since they inhabit the places where modern segregation is (re)produced in the field of madness, hence it is necessary to interpret their discursive place and understand the position of the psychiatrist through their speeches and the work of Michel Foucault.[3] If any community to be constituted must segregate, Lacan affirms that science outlines this segregation to the "second power" through "the science of the social" (*RDT*, p. 183).

Lacan's warning is not only about institutions and psychiatric knowledge. It also envisions a change in capitalism: "The segregation of mental illness, namely something that is other, that is yoked to a certain discourse, the one I've been pinpointing as the discourse of the Master" which according to Lacan has mutated throughout history into "the discourse of the Capitalist, of which we wouldn't have had the faintest idea had Marx not set himself to completing it, to giving it its subject, the proletariat". What is particular about this transformation of the master's discourse into a Capitalist discourse is the rejection of the symbolic (*Verwerfung*), that is, the rejection of castration. Lacan ends by saying: "Any order, any discourse that aligns itself with capitalism, sweeps to one side what we may simply call, my fine friends, matters of love. You see my friends, it's a mere nothing" (*PAM*, pp. 90–91).[4]

Today, after these Lacanian foresights, it is possible to revisit the current landscape and verify the various havoc wreaked by Capitalist discourse. In this landscape, there are capricious children, who are nevertheless captured very early on by distinct and rigid evaluation protocols, according to which they will be diagnosed and have their skills examined. Silenced children with diagnoses, almost *accused* of having disorders. Adolescents censored and consumed by cyberspace, also accused of things like Oppositional Defiant Disorder (ODD), always with a segregating logic.⁵

A final footnote by Lacan, certainly enigmatic, about the difference between the Soviet Union and the United States, leaves us thinking about the relationship between University discourse and science: "Naturally, the refusal of segregation is basic to the concentration camp" (*PTH*, p. xv). And the footnote is about how the universalization of the subject of science—the one who is the precursor or at least the enabler of the concentration camp according to Lacan (*P9O*, p. 588)—opens the door to discrimination. However, the concentration camp does not discriminate any more: it concentrates, standardizes, reduces, eradicates differences. The central characteristic of the concentration camp is indifference. Currently there are tens of millions of people in the world who live in these conditions: refugees and displaced persons in waiting areas, transit areas, detention centres, migrant cities, etc. And this is the solution that capitalism has, to maintain a distance from, contain, and reject what cannot be accounted for: humans as organic matter, as industrial waste.⁶

## *Psychoanalytic School: base of operations for discomfort*

"It is impossible to free oneself from the constitutive segregation of this ethnic group with the considerations of Marx, and even less with those of Sartre", Lacan points out when referring to the Jews, offering us some indications against segregation in his School (*P9O*, pp. 588–589). Sartre in his book *Anti-Semite and Jew* (1944), frames self-segregation based on his idea of man as a being "in situation", while Marx in his 1843 book *On the Jewish Question* (*OJQ*) shows that the term "Jew" is a social exception that passes from the religious register to political segregation. Lacan summons two philosophers to warn of the risks of any psychoanalytic grouping: self-segregation and becoming an exception.

In 1956, Lacan (*SPT*) made a diagnosis of the situation with the *International Psychoanalytical Association* (IPA), looking for a way to reform it from within. For this, he focuses on the diagnosis of four elements: the ethics of psychoanalysis, the bond between analysts, the conception of the end of analysis, and the teaching of psychoanalysis. The result is disappointing because the IPA turns out to meet all the requirements to be a *Massenpsychologie*, not so different from the Church and the Army: a pyramid structure and identification with the leader. Years later he was expelled—segregated—from this institution.

If segregation is structural as an effect of discourse and inherent in the constitution of the subject, Lacan will seek solutions in the structural design of a new form of social bond where psychoanalysts and people interested in psychoanalysis could work without the religious and hypnotic effects of the psychology of the masses. Can thought establish a social bond that, while finding its universal legitimacy, does not lead to segregating results? Would psychoanalysis, in its attempt to unravel the secret of the object of enjoyment, have a historical opportunity to intervene in this problem? These questions indicate the relevance of psychoanalysis to the issues that arise in our time and that are crucial for Lacan.

A solution to this problem was outlined as early as 1945 through game theory in *Logical Time* (*TL*) and *Number Thirteen* (*N13*), but also in the group work developed by Bion and Rickman, where specific tasks were performed and there was no leader (*PAG*). The idea of the cartel, the empty space, and the lateral identifications have their antecedents here. The *School* also has its origin in the Hellenistic schools—Epicureanism, Cynicism, and Stoicism—which at the time sought a solution to the problem of the transmission of knowledge via the social bond—a way of life—that was compatible with that same knowledge. This happened in the midst of the moral and social crisis in Greece: "It is to be taken in the sense in which in ancient times it meant certain places of refuge, indeed bases of operation against what might already be called the discontents of civilization" (*FA*, p. 103). For example, while the analysis in the IPA ended in identification with the analyst, in the case of the French School it was "a desire to obtain absolute difference" (*SXI*, 24.06.64, p. 276). The semi-anonymous magazine *Silicet* as a way of coping with the "litter-publication" (*poubelleication*),[7] the cartel, the matheme, and the device of *the pass*—a way to consider if there was analysis and where the analyst is not the guarantee, dismissing all identification—these are some of the inventions associated with the School. "I hereby found—as alone as I have always been in my relation to the psychoanalytic cause—the *École Française de Psychanalyse*" (*FA*, p. 96), says Lacan to make clear that each member of the School is alone also in relation to the cause, that is, regarding the void of the analyst's desire.

In this sense, there is a politics that is not only identification with the master signifier. It is precisely in the opposition between politics and psychoanalysis as opposite principles that the most political imprint of psychoanalysis lies. This is the answer to the segregation that Lacan invents through the School. This is also the interest in a different principle of doing politics. Beyond the political procedures in their nature of management, administration, and their legal logic, the exceptional moments of history are energized by the irruption of the singular Solitude of the subject embodied in the emergence of the Common. As in a Moebius band, the "Common : Solitude" (Alemán, 2013, p. 51) and its unlimited space is materially specified in the manner of a historical turn, of a sequence that alters the interpretation of the past, where the inert weight of the identifications, the "for all" of the master's speech is crossed diagonally by the "Solitude : Common". The "Solitude : Common" is the matrix of sovereignty in the people, and not those of identifications that collectivize them. Put another way, it is about the People or a grouping still without a name, willing at a later time to participate in a new collective logic.

This solution is also a response to the problematic and senseless command of "love one's neighbor" (Freud, 1929, p. 109; *SVII*, 03.23.60, p. 179), of a will that is captured neither by the identifications of the ideal ego, nor by the deadly circuit of the super-ego. It would then be about loving the irreducible and heterogeneous enjoyment of otherness, an Otherness that also inhabits me and is the *extimate*. For Lacan, it is about loving the *evil jouissance* that the other and I have in common (*SVII*, 20.03.60, p. 186). This is another form of "Common : Solitude".

## Lacan with Marx and Marx with Lacan: segregation, neoliberalism and the extreme right

Reading Marx with Lacan and vice versa, we find a pincer logic: while capitalism is a will for accounting, exploitation, and accumulation, and neo-fascism embodied in far-right politics, via segregation there is as a political project to create visas, walls, borders, seas, and trenches: "The discriminatory capital ensures inequality in the interior while the segregating ultra-right is in charge of maintaining the difference abroad" (Pavón-Cuéllar, 2020, p. 34). Neoliberal capitalism puts a price on everything, and the political extreme right does the dirty work of discriminating and propping up a vertical structure. While the first makes any classification possible, the second makes it vertical. Capital circulates freely, labour does not: behind the supposed brotherhood of the international markets lies the crouching lion of bourgeois identity, nationalism.

In its eagerness to quantify everything, the capitalist system works as a headless force. Lacan calls Pascal the "master" and "pioneer of capitalism" for this reason (*SXVI*, 06.25.69). In this will for calculation, the capitalist system dissolves qualitative differences and reinscribes them in quantitative inequalities; that is, in exchange values since it is only about objects, services, and human goods circulating in the system. Segregation excludes, diminishes, devalues, and inferiorizes. What cannot be discriminated against is then segregated. This is precisely the function of the far right and neo-fascism. Additionally, it is the function of the multiplication of identities and diagnoses. It is a biopolitics of disposable and precarious lives. In this sense, the expressions "human capital" and "self-entrepreneur" are notable: the first because, while trying to give dignity, it takes it away; the second for the clarity of self-exploitation or voluntary servitude to Capital. Coaching, counselling, or self-diagnosis makes subjects feel depressed or guilty for their misfortunes by not being able to increase their self-esteem—their self-worth, one could say. One could even think of a quasi-Marxist formula Se–M–Se' (Self-esteem–Merchandise–Increased Self-esteem). In this sense, that which does not enter into the computation of capital, that part of living labour that cannot become quantifiable and accumulative dead labour, must be segregated, even self-segregated. Self-esteem already implies quantifying and regulating the irregular. That is why the will to quantify and accumulate—typical of self-esteem and social networks—must be distinguished from desire. All of self-esteem and every attempt at valorisation takes a toll on desire.

To counteract the decreasing trend of the rate of profit, it is necessary to maintain a closed space and an exterior. For the development of the capitalist system, the underdevelopment that this same system produces is a necessary condition.

For this same reason, it is important to remember that for Lacan "underdevelopment is not archaic", but is precisely "what is produced by the extension of the capitalist kingdom". Furthermore, it is "the condition of capitalist progress" (*SXVIII*, 20.01.71). Thus, it is not a matter of development—behind the first world is the third—but rather a logical matter—the underdeveloped world is an effect of the developed world and is closely linked to it.

Now, what is revealing in the concept of "enjoyment" is that for the extreme right and neo-fascism it has a double aspect: on the one hand, the fantasy that the marginalized is the one who deprives them of their enjoyment is sustained; on the other, more secretly, the enjoyment must be that of possessing the object and simultaneously depriving others of it. One's secret and most characteristic enjoyment is to deprive others of any good while one imagines—projects—that it is others who prevent it. This is how the preference for meritocracy is understood, which focuses more on maintaining privileges than on extending rights. In fact, privilege is confused with rights: the only right is privilege ... which one must keep for oneself. But, as Pavón-Cuéllar points out, we must excuse them because it is not only about their enjoyment but rather the enjoyment of capital (2020, p. 36). In the end it is about gaining a *plus-de-jouissance* and then sacrificing it to the dark gods of Capital. Thus, it should be understood that "there is only one social symptom: each individual is actually a proletarian" (*TT*, p. 94).

The effect of such a logic of neo-fascist and far-right enjoyment is the reduction of all symbolic resources, or what Lacan himself has called "in reserve" (*P9O*, p. 237). It can be said that there is a neoliberalist contempt for all tradition and a deep hatred on the extreme right of what Lacan calls *lalangue* (*thelanguage*) as an accumulation of mistakes that persist in a language (*LE*, p. 490).

A revolutionary project with the potential to be emancipatory or subversive would imply a mobilization of the sedimentation of "knowledge in reserve" or *lalangue*. This mobilization is what Lacan calls *Sinthome* (*SXXIII*) and it functions either as an anchoring point or as a way to decipher the present with the past. It is for this reason that one of the most important questions at the beginning of the 21st century is whether it is possible to privatize or modify *lalangue*, since it would be the "point of sovereignty" in psychoanalysis: "Lalangue is irreducible to merchandise [...] the day that the language and capital are the same, the crime would be perfect" (Alemán, 2013, pp. 36–37). In addition to sovereignty, *lalangue* may well be the most fundamental of the "commons" that Negri and Hardt (2009) speak of. Very little has been discussed on this point in the clinic. The (re)reading of Marx through Lacan with the term segregation takes on all its relevance since every contemporary symptom is basically a social symptom or, as Samo Tomšič argues, "every demand for the cure always-already contains a demand for a change in the social structure" (2019, p. 187), or that this suffering "always-already enunciates a certain truth of the socioeconomic condition" (2019, p. 17).

Translated from Spanish by Carla Tirado-Morttiz

## Notes

1 This is precisely the function of the myth for Lacan: "the attempt to give an epic form to what is operative through the structure" (*TV*, p. 34).
2 In the discussion at the end of George Poulet's lecture in the Symposium called "The Structuralist Controversy" in 1966, Lacan explains what is at stake in the term "inmixion", also announcing the title of his paper bearing this concept (which is never mentioned in the conference itself!): "I am thinking of the word 'in-mixing' [*inmiction*]. I think that the first time I introduced this word was precisely in respect to subjects. Subjects (even the *Natural History* of Buffon was not so 'natural' as that, may I add) are not as isolated as we think. But, on the other hand, they are not collective. They have a certain structural form, precisely 'inmixing'" (Poulet, 1966, p. 44).
3 Foucault (1961), see also Foucault (1947–1975).
4 Translation slightly modified by authors.
5 See Stavchansky (2015).
6 For a line of thought that takes on the philosophical challenge of turning human waste into a work of art through a political, scientific, loving, or artistic subjectivation, see Badiou (2018).
7 Drawing inspiration from James Joyce's use of "litter" and "letter", Lacan created the neologism "*poubellication*", which sounds both like "publication" and also "litteration".

## Further reading

Hook, D. (2012). *A Critical Psychology of the Postcolonial. The Mind of Apartheid.* London: Psychology Press.
Khan, A. (2018). Lacan and Race. In: A. Mukherjee (Ed.), *After Lacan. Literature, Theory, and Psychoanalysis in the Twenty-First Century* (pp. 148–164). Cambridge: Cambridge University Press.
Pavón-Cuellar, D. (2020). El giro del neoliberalismo al neofascismo: universalización y segregación en el sistema capitalista. In: *Desde el Jardín de Freud*, 20:19–38.
Jenkins, D. & Leroy J. (Eds.) (2020). *Histories of Racial Capitalism*. New York: Columbia University Press.

## References

Adorno, T. (1951). *Minima Moralia. Reflections on a Damaged Life*. E. F. Jephcott (Trans.). London: Verso, 2006.
Alemán, J. (2013). *Conjeturas sobre una izquierda lacaniana*. Buenos Aires: Grama.
Althusser, L. (1993). *Écrits sur la psychanalyse: Freud et Lacan*. Paris: Stock/IMEC.
Badiou, A. (2018). *L'immanence des vérités. L'être et l'événement 3*. Paris: Seuil.
Benjamin, W. (1969). *Illuminations: Essays and Reflections*. H. Zohn (Trans.). New York: Schocken.
De Vos, J. (2013). *Psychologization and the Subject of Late Modernity*. New York: Palgrave Macmillan.
Freud, S. (1913). Totem and Taboo. In: *The Standard Edition of the Complete Psychological Works of Sigmund Freud* (Vol. XII, pp. 1–161), J. E. Strachey (Trans.). London: Vintage, 2001.

Freud, S. (1918). The Taboo of Virginity. In: *The Standard Edition of the Complete Psychological Works of Sigmund Freud* (Vol. XI, pp. 191–208), J. E. Strachey (Trans.). London: Vintage, 2001.

Freud, S. (1921). Group Psychology and the Analysis of the Ego. In: *The Standard Edition of the Complete Psychological Works of Sigmund Freud* (Vol. XVIII, pp. 1–144), J. E. Strachey (Trans.). London: Vintage, 2001.

Freud, S. (1929). Civilization and its Discontents. In: *The Standard Edition of the Complete Psychological Works of Sigmund Freud* (Vol. XXI, pp. 57–146), J. E. Strachey (Trans.). London: Vintage, 2001.

Foucault, M. (1947–1975). *Society Must be Defended*. R. Swver (Trans.). New York: Picador, 2003.

Foucault, M. (1961). *Madness and Civilization. A History of Insanity in the Age of Reason.* R. Howard (Trans.). New York: Vintage Books, 1988.

Harvey, D. (2001). *Spaces of Capital: Towards a Critical Geography*. New York: Routledge.

Horkheimer, M. (1932). *Between Philosophy and Social Science*, F. Hunter (Trans.). Cambridge: MIT Press, 1993.

Koyré, A. (1957). *From the Closed World to the Infinite Universe*. Baltimore: Johns Hopkins Press.

Le Bon, G. (1895). *The Crowd. A Study of the Popular Mind.* New York: Dover, 2001.

Lefort, C. (1981). *The Political Forms of Modern Society*. London: Polity Press, 1986.

Lenin, V. I. (1918). The Immediate Tasks of the Soviet Government. In: *Lenin Collected Works*, C. Dutt (Trans.) (Vol. XXVII, pp. 235–278). Moscow: Progress Publishers, 1965.

Milner, J.-C. (1995). *A Search for Clarity: Science and Philosophy in Lacan's Oeuvre.* E. Pluth (Trans.). Evanston: Northwestern University Press, 2020.

Mumford, L. (1934). *Technics and Civilization.* London: Routledge & Kegan Paul PLC.

Negri, A. and Hardt, M. (2009). *Commonwealth*. Cambridge: Harvard University Press.

Parker, I. (2011). *Lacanian Psychoanalysis. Revolutions in Subjectivity.* London: Routledge.

Pavón-Cuéllar, D. (2017). *Marxism and Psychoanalysis. In or against Psychology?* London: Routledge.

Pavón-Cuéllar, D. (2020). El giro del neoliberalismo al neofascismo: universalización y segregación en el sistema capitalista. In: *Desde el jardín de Freud*, 20: 19–38.

Poulet, G. (1966). Criticism and the Experience of Interiority. In: R. Macksey & E. Donato (Ed.), *The languages of Criticism and the Sciences of Man: The Structuralist Controversy* (pp. 56–88). Baltimore: Johns Hopkins Press, 1970.

Sartre, J.-P. (1944). *Anti-Semite and Jew. An Exploration of the Etiology of Hate*, G. J. Becker (Trans.). New York: Schocken Books, 1995.

Stavchansky, L. (2015). *Autismo y cuerpo. El lenguaje en los trazos de la perfección.* Mexico: Paradiso editores.

Tse-Tung, M. (1963). Where Do Correct Ideas Come From? In: *On Practice and Contradiction.* (pp. 167–168). London: Verso, 2007.

Tomšič, S. (2019). *The Labour of Enjoyment.* Berlin: August Verlag.

Zupančič, A. (2017). *What is Sex?* Cambridge: MIT Press.

# Chapter 21

# Slavery

*Juan Pablo Lucchelli and Todd McGowan*

—Ara.: عبودية —Chi.: 奴隷制 —Fre.: *Esclavage* —Ger.: *Sklaverei* —Ita.: *Schiavitù* —Jap.: 奴隷制度 —Port.: *Escravidão* —Rus.: *Рабство* —Spa.: *Esclavitud* —Tur.: *Kölecilik*

→ *Ideology*; *Imperialism*; *Master/tyrant*; *Proletarian*

## Introduction: love in the dialectic of master and slave

To make sense of Lacan's deployment of any Hegelian concept, one must always look to Alexandre Kojève. Nowhere is this truer than when Lacan takes up the dialectic of the master and slave. Understanding how Lacan theorizes slavery requires taking stock of Kojève's unique influence on Lacan's thought. The very fact that Lacan uses the French terms *maître* and *eslave* for Hegel's *Herr* and *Knecht* indicates, simply on the level of language, the debt to Kojève rather than Hegel, since these are Kojève's inexact translations of Hegel's terms. Lacan frequented Kojève's famous introductory course on Hegel in the 1930s, where he picked up Kojève's version of Hegel. In order to understand how Lacan makes sense of the position of the slave and slavery, we must examine what Lacan calls the metaphor of love, which is realized through the dialectic of Hegel's master and slave. In this way, we will see the clinical and theoretical use of the concept of slavery in Lacan's work.

## Not Marx, but Plato's *Symposium*: a riddle from Kojève

It is pretty curious that while in Lacan the notion of "master" owes a lot to Marx's notion of work, especially in its differentiation from the "ancient master" (*SVIII*, 23.11.60, pp. 21–27), the notion of slavery likely comes from Alexander Kojève. To arrive at how Lacan theorizes slavery, we must take an unanticipated detour through Plato, specifically through Plato's dialogue *The Symposium*, a dialogue about love. In his seminar on *The Transference*, Lacan interprets this major work by reading the different speeches of the six characters who take the floor in different turns, according to an order established by the same characters at the beginning of the dialogue. When it comes to dealing with the most celebrated speech,

DOI: 10.4324/9781003212096-21

that of Aristophanes, Lacan pauses to address Aristophanes's hiccup that interrupts the dialogue and shifts the order of the speeches. Lacan considers the hiccup, even more than any of the speeches, the point of inflection of the dialogue.

Lacan theorizes the hiccup as the irruption of life in the dialogue, the introduction of the body, which arrives in the form of a disorder that raises the desire for another form of approach to Eros, quite differently from that of previous speeches. The reversal that the hiccup portends echoes the reversal that occurs in the master–slave dialectic. Just as the slave ends up in the privileged position relative to the master, the hiccup reveals the revenge of the body on the mind. As the dialogue nears its conclusion, Alcibiades intervenes and disrupts the proceedings. His arrival provides the occasion for him to proclaim his love for Socrates, but it is also his body that makes itself felt through the physicality of his presence. He comes in drunk and speaks without restraint, failing to respect the established order of speeches. The hiccup of Aristophanes follows the same logic as Alcibiades's interruption. Both events bypass logos and put a wrench in the order of the speeches. As a result of the case of hiccups, Eryximachus must speak on behalf of Aristophanes, so that his speech will last "the time of a hiccup".

The hiccup is the nodal point of Lacan's intervention (Plato, 1951, p. 184bc). It not only provides the key to interpreting *The Symposium* but plays the crucial role for his theorization of the slave. One must understand Lacan's conceptualization of slavery through the encounter with the hiccup and its toppling of the order of things. But he might not have stopped on this point had it not been for a conversation that he had with Kojève. In his seminar, Lacan recounts having spoken with Alexandre Kojève about Plato's *Symposium*. What does Kojève say about *The Symposium*? When he speaks with Lacan about it, he declares, according to Lacan's recounting, that he does not remember much of the dialogue because "he had not reread it". But even as Kojève claims not to have reread Plato's text, he manages to let slip an enigmatic remark that utterly conditions Lacan's own interpretation. He tells Lacan, "In any case, you will never interpret *The Symposium* if you don't know why Aristophanes had the hiccups". As he reads the text, Lacan remains focused on this enigma and advances the hypothesis, like so many other commentators, that if Aristophanes had hiccups, it is because he was writhing with laughter.

But why is the pretext of hiccups necessary in the dialogue? According to some, this episode functions as Plato's revenge on Aristophanes. By imposing hiccups on him, he shames him, just as the comic poet did by giving farts to Socrates in *The Clouds*. One might say that Plato silences the comic poet, reducing him to pure animality—like an animal, deprived of speech. The dialogue is full of inversions—the inversion of bodily noises (from the fart to the hiccup), the inversion of the order of speech (Eryximachus speaks instead of Aristophanes), and even the inversion of the usual roles of real, historical characters (serious Socrates becomes comic in *The Clouds* while comic Aristophanes becomes serious at *The Symposium*).

Despite giving Aristophanes the hiccups and thereby displacing him in the order, Plato gives him the decisive speech of the dialogue, the one that has aroused more commentary than any other. In this speech, Aristophanes develops the myth of a self-satisfied humanity divided by the gods. This myth serves to inaugurate a new stage of the dialogue, in which Socrates will invoke Diotima and thereby articulate a new theory of love. The round being imagined by Aristophanes functions as a necessary preamble to this new conception of Eros. The shift that occurs when Eryximachus speaks in the place of Aristophanes anticipates the way that Diotima will speak in the place of Socrates in the final speech. This change of place, this permutation, is a key element of what Lacan will call the "metaphor of love", which will lead ultimately to an understanding of slavery.

## The dialectical metaphor of love: the key for Lacan's concept of slave

In reading Plato's *Symposium*, Lacan describes what he calls the metaphor of love, namely the passage from one subjective state to another. Through the metaphor of love, one transitions from the state of the beloved to the state of the lover. This metaphor designates the subjective change of the one who falls in love, which necessarily implies that the one who does not love—and therefore does not undergo this subjective change—is necessarily in the position of being a beloved.

This is apparent in the case of Alcibiades, who not only praises Socrates but also reproaches him for having bewitched him, for having provoked in him a state of love. Lacan seems to have a very clear position: "Alcibiades here makes a feminine scene for Socrates". It is curious that Lacan puts in close relation the feminine position and that of love as an active agent of desire. Here we are far from the feminine figure who makes herself desired, who is simply a passive object. On the contrary, it is she who desires and who has the active role, which is what Lacan stipulates in particular with regard to the role of Penia.

When one returns love to the lover, one is no longer an *erómenos*. In other words, when Lacan asserts that Alcibiades occupies a feminine position, he is not feminine in the way that this traditionally understood—not the *erómenos* or the beloved. In the metaphor of love, it is the passage from one state to another that is decisive and that makes one love, rather than a position that is fixed forever. The metaphor of love involves a change. It is a becoming and in no way a definitive, acquired status.

For Lacan, love is this passage, characterized by the feeling of the lack of the other (or the beloved) from one subjective position to another: one passes from being loved to being a lover. This is the fundamental paradox of love according to *The Symposium*: when one loves, one is no longer an *erómenos*, for one recognizes oneself as *erómenos* and, what's more, one manifests oneself to another with the aim of being recognized by this other who is supposed to embody what the lover lacks. In this sense, the metaphor of love isolated by Lacan follows as closely as possible the Platonic definition of Eros: when he experiences lack, he desires, and when this lack is satisfied, the desire is extinguished. It is thus necessary to speak of metaphor because it implies at least two terms, one referring to the other and not a single isolated term. But this tension between two terms will bring us back to the dialectic of master and slave.

## Replying to Kojève

To continue in the direction inaugurated by Kojève's riddle, which gives particular importance to hiccups, we would like to move forward with the verification of the following hypothesis: in the *The Symposium*, it is the inversion of roles and, therefore, the setting of a new role in the dialogue's dialectical relationship, as an inversion of the places of enunciation between the different characters, which is key for interpreting the dialogue—and it is also the key to the priority of the slave over the master in Lacan's thought. This dialectical reversal begins with the hiccups. Alcibiades takes over, drunk, what Aristophanes (the real one, the one who had to keep silent because of the hiccups) could not formulate against Socrates. Alcibiades's entry inverts the rules given by Eryximachus: he will speak before Socrates, in the same way that the hiccups made the doctor speak before Aristophanes. Thus, Alcibiades plays, in the first part of his speech, the role of a character of *The Clouds*. In a broader way, hiccups give rise to changes in the place of enunciation that end up inverting the roles.

This is, in our view, the importance of inversions and our answer to Kojève's riddle. The equivalence would be the following: *the master is to the beloved what the slave is to the lover*, with the tension that this connection implies, particularly regarding the existence of two metaphors of love.

## The first metaphor of love

Let us return to the metaphor of love. It only applies to the *erómenos*, the beloved, the rich, like Poros, when s/he becomes the lover, experiencing the lack produced by the experience of love. Metaphor is in itself a process of changing and contradictory nature, that is to say, a dialectical process. Lacan's explanation of the subjective change mentioned, as well as the two figures involved, namely the beloved and the lover, brings us face to face with a particular functioning of the links that connect these two figures. On the one hand, we have the lover's becoming of the *erómenos*, that is to say the metaphor of love proper, and on the other hand, we also have another process that is capable of provoking the metaphor. Indeed, let us specify that at this stage it is as if Lacan were adding yet another state, that of the *erastés*, of the lover who begins to have a precise idea of love by the fact of having lived it. This position could be that of the one who loves the truth, namely the philosopher. In a third stage (the first two are first that of the beloved and then that of the beloved who has become a lover), therefore, one will undoubtedly become a malicious *erastés*, who knows something about love and who, in this way, is not completely deluded as to the nature of love. For, in fact, if one suffers because of love, one can only do so inasmuch as one has left one's role as *erómenos*, as Alcibiades does: it is from this suffering, from this lack, that Lacan conceives the metaphor of love. It is only the *erómenoi* who suffer from love when they are no longer *erómenoi*, that is to say, from the moment when they wake up to love and desire, by which we mean: when they recognize themselves as desiring, as *erastés*.

This is how the metaphor of love should be understood: a first metaphor of love, isolated by Lacan, according to which the beloved becomes a lover, which is, for example, the case of Alcibiades. We thus find ourselves faced with a paradox, similar to that of Penia, described by Plato, and her desire to emerge from her state of poverty, except that Penia's paradox shows a second stage in the evolution of desire. In order to become rich, one must first have been poor: conversely, one could say that in order to become an *erastés* (Penia), one must first have been an *erómenos* (Poros). Didn't Pausanias tell us at *The Symposium* enough about the *erastés*, at least enough for us to get an idea about their nature? What does he say? He compares him to the experience of a slave. In the dialogue, Pausanias says,

> This is indeed the rule with us: just as there was, in the case of lovers, no flattery on their part in accepting to be, in an unimaginable slave, the slaves of their beloved ones, and there was nothing to blame there either, so, on the other side too, there remains only one voluntary slavery that is not to be blamed, and it is the one who has the merit for the object. We believe that, if a man is willing to serve another, in the hope of perfecting himself by his own means in some science or in some part of virtue, this servitude is not shameful and is not called adulation.
>
> (Plato, 1951, p. 184bc)

Pausanias expresses a paradox: that of voluntary slavery. The allusion here is to Étienne de la Boétie and his *Discours de la servitude volontaire*.

## The second metaphor of love

Is there another kind of voluntary slavery of which Socrates is an example? Jacques-Alain Miller (1991) isolates a second metaphor of love, following on from the one described by Lacan, a hypothesis that we will take very seriously. At what point does this second metaphor occur? At the moment when an *erastés*—here Socrates, because he knows what love is, because it has already been a scrap of a man in its turn, because it has been an initiated—loved beyond its *erómenos*, it becomes desiring beyond any object of desire. Socrates is an *erastés* who desires something else; *he is a slave but he has no master*. And it is through this desire for something else, for a beyond of all loved and all objects within his reach, that he becomes himself an *erómenos*, that he becomes desirable, a movement by which his usual *erómenos* (Alcibiades, for example) can eventually become desiring—or a slave.

It is Alcibiades who utters this second metaphor of love, in which the *erómenos* becomes the lover, so he becomes the *erastés*: "the young man is at half mast by being the lover, whereas he plays the role of the beloved instead of that of the love" (Plato, 1951, p. 184bc, 222b). It is this knowledge that would make Socrates the beneficiary of a kind of aura and even an *agalma* of knowledge. Lacan, for his part, defines such a subjective position in the following way:

> Coming back here to our own terms, we can say that the dialectical definition of love, as developed by Diotima, meets what we have tried to define as the metonymic function in desire. This is what we are talking about in his discourse—something that is beyond all objects, that is in the passage of a certain aim and a certain relation [to] desire […]. [It is] a perspective without limits […]. In short, the further the subject takes his aim, the more he has the right to love himself, if one may say so, in his ideal self. The more he desires, the more he himself becomes desirable.
> 
> (*SVIII*, 25.01.61, p. 128)

Socrates metaphorically becomes desirable through his unrestrained desire. Although he does not function as a master, he nonetheless produces a slave to love in the figure of Alcibiades.

## From love to slavery

Most interpreters of Hegel see Kojève's reading as extremely one-sided, as focusing obsessively on the dialectic of the master and the slave (cf. Žižek, 2012). This dialectic, this short passage from *The Phenomenology of Spirit*, becomes the matrix through which Kojève understands the entirety of the Hegelian project. The influence of Kojève on Lacan implies that Lacan himself also shares his one-sidedness, as Lacan himself sometimes admits. For instance, in his first seminar, Lacan proclaims, "at every turn, I take my bearings from the master-slave dialectic, and I re-explain it" (*SI*, 09.06.54, p. 222). Lacan's conscious invocations of Hegel are almost always invocations of Kojève's specific interpretation of Hegel.

Kojève's riddle of the hiccups signifies that a new type of dialectic emerges in Plato's dialogue. But to Kojève there is no other dialectic than that of the master and the slave. To apply this dialectic to the moment of the hiccups, we must see that, first, there must be a change of place and thus a change in the place of enunciation: Eryximachus will speak in place of Aristophanes, Diotima will do so in place of Socrates, Alcibiades will do the same in turn, just before Socrates. Secondly, the dialogue will introduce a fiction: Aristophanes is not the real historical Aristophanes, Diotima probably never existed, and the two stories told—the one about the round being and the one about the birth of Eros—would be nothing but fables invented by

Plato. Thirdly, the relationship between the beloved/lover pair will be modified in the sense already indicated by the two metaphors of love. Finally, this asymmetrical and paradoxical relationship inaugurated by the subjective change of the metaphors of love resembles in certain points the master–slave dialectic. The dialectic of the master and the slave provides the answer to the riddle of the hiccups.

If the interpretation we have given of Kojève's riddle is relevant, then it gives rise to a kind of equivalence between the Lacanian metaphor of love and Hegel's master–slave dialectic, reread by Kojève in his course on Hegel. This would also imply that Lacan was inspired by Kojève, but not only because of the already mentioned riddle: the Kojèvian trace remains indelible in Lacan from the beginning and until the end of his work.

Indeed, from the start of his seminar on *The Transference*, at the beginning of the session of November 30, Lacan intends to present transference as the product of a dialectic modeled on Kojève's interpretation of the master and the slave (Kojève, 1947). At the beginning of the session, Lacan says, "Last time we ended with the positions of ερᾳστής (*erastés*) and ερώμενος (*erómenos*), the lover and the beloved, the dialectic in the *Symposium* allowing us to present them as the basis, crux, or essential articulation of the problem of love". Lacan thus thinks of love as a becoming, as a transformation, a turning point, a modification in the subject. He goes even further when he stipulates that love owes everything to transference and not the other way around: "The problem of love interests us in so far as it will enable us to understand what is happening in the transfer –and to some extent, because of the transfer" (*SVIII*, 30.11.60, p. 36). The transference causes, in a certain sense, love, explains it, and this through a dialectical turning point due to a subjective change.

The pair involved here is that of the beloved and the lover, according to a type of loving relationship, which Lacan had formulated in this way a few years earlier in his seminar on *The Object Relation*: love is giving what one does not have. The lover is "the subject of desire", the beloved for his part "is the only one to have something" (*SIV*, 16.01.57, p. 128). Except that what s/he has, the beloved, is not what causes the lover's desire: the question of the relationship between desire and what s/he sets herself/himself before has already led us to the notion of desire as a desire for something else. If things present themselves in this way, it is because in no case will the lover be able to find what s/he desires in the beloved. The relationship will remain asymmetrical and unsatisfied as such. We could also say that if the relationship becomes satisfactory between the two protagonists, then the dialectical relationship between the two, the relationship opened by the change, by the metaphor, becomes closed or flattened.

This asymmetry may remind us of the master–slave dialectic, but only at certain points: there would thus be points of convergence and points of divergence between the two models. The main point of convergence between the Platonic metaphor of love and the Hegelian dialectic of the master and the slave lies in the matrix idea of a reversal or inversion of places, which immediately engages the meaning of dialectic in each of the two authors. For Lacan, in Plato, the general schema of this movement of inversion resides, as we have said, in the metaphor of love: the passage from *erómenos* to *erastés* (a passage that implies the transformation of the beloved into a lover, from the one who has to the one who does not and who desires). This is an inversion that, in the Platonic thought, presupposes a certain number of *underlying inversions* which are in a certain way its conditions of existence.

In Hegel, the general scheme of this dialectical process consists in the *progressive inversion of statuses*: what we could respectively call a becoming-master for the slave and a becoming-slave for the master (Hegel, 1807, B, IV, A). But precisely because it is dialectical and therefore presupposes the test of a mediation, this dialectical process is not resolved in the relationship of two subjects or two consciousnesses (which is similar to the Lacanian idea of transference as a kind of objection to intersubjectivity), but involves at least three terms that are like the motors of the dialectic: the fear of death, the desire for recognition, the relationship to nature. Consequently, the understanding of this process of inversion in Hegel returns us to what precedes and conditions the moment of the relation of mastery and servitude, namely the moment of the struggle to the death where the two consciousnesses face each other, while desires, having a certainty of themselves by the recognition of the other, raise the latter to the category of truth.

The master is the one who, wanting to be recognized as a subject (which supposes denying his natural existence), prefers freedom to life and is therefore able to brave the fear of death. And, conversely, the slave is the one who surrendered and renounced freedom in the name of his attachment to life. Hegel emphasizes—and this is a decisive point—that it is therefore in relation to death ("the absolute master") that he submits himself, even more so than to the other consciousness. In both cases, however, it is a failure or incompleteness of the process of recognition. Hegel states from the outset that the pure concept of recognition presupposes reciprocity, which is lacking in the described process. The slave recognizes the other but is not recognized, while the other, the master, is recognized but by a human whom he does not recognize as a human (a subject who remains stuck as a thing or object).

Beyond the general proximity of these two inversion schemes, which are thus found respectively in *The Symposium* and the *Phenomenology of the Spirit*, it would be necessary to establish a deeper underground kinship or affinity, which is due to two essential elements. First of all, it would seem that both the Platonic and the Hegelian texts obey the same conception of the relation to the Other in that they appeal to a transcendental relation, which is not limited to the immediate and specular Other, as Lacan would call it (in this sense, for both authors, there would be an "objection to intersubjectivity", as Lacan specifies); with this consequence that in both texts the same necessity emerges, which is that of recourse to a form of mediation. In *The Symposium*, this involves what Plato elsewhere calls a conversion of the gaze that allows or enables one to detach oneself from one's primary attachment to the immediacy of the sensible experience in order to access the plane of the intelligible. And in Hegel's case, it passes through the experience of work and *Bildung* which, because it forbids the slave access to immediate *jouissance* and maintains him in a restrained desire, allows the beginning of a liberating process. In both cases, the same reversal of the conception of the relationship to the other occurs: in Plato, via the passage of a conception of the control where it is so to speak the *erómenos* which dominates the *erastés* to the conception according to which the true domination proceeds from the departure of a domination exerted on oneself (in accordance with the ideal of *sôphrosunê*) which will be the practical basis of the second metaphor of the love.

But a second point of convergence can be established between the two texts, which is due to the fact that they present a deep proximity on the question of the desire envisaged in its essence or in its truth. At the same time as the relation to the other is criticized each time, it is also a certain conception of desire as a relation to the immediacy of pleasure or filling, to which *The Symposium*, like the figure of mastery and servitude, opposes a completely different conception of desire, no longer referring to consumption or possession, but to research and a form of creation. In other words: a desire no longer based on consumption, but on production and access to what is not immediately there—an essentially productive desire. Socrates shows that one can access this desire only through dialectical ascent (access to the order of truth), and which Hegel links to the idea, also dialectical but in another sense, that it is because the slave is forced to restrain his desire that he is led to form (*bilden*) a world.

## Lover and beloved, master and slave

The lover, as we pointed out in Pausanias's speech, is a slave. But let's make this clear: *he is a slave to desire and not to his beloved*. He is caught in the trap of love, and the *erómenos* only comes on top of it. This subjective position becomes clearer when read against the second metaphor of love, in which the lover sets himself as the horizon of desire this "other thing", this desire which cannot be satisfied by any *erómenos* and of which the famous Socratic *sôphrosunê* could be one of the forms (the other, derived from it, would be the analyst's desire). The lover, classically a man older than his *erómenos*, with more experience and even wealth than him, is a dominator, but also and paradoxically a slave of desire. In the *Phaedrus* dialogue, Plato states,

> He who dominates desire, and who is the slave of desire, will seek to morally belittle his friend, for fear of appearing inferior to him [...] If we now consider the influence of the lover on the condition and fortune of the beloved, we see that he wishes it as devoid as possible of any friendship that might divert him from their love, or of any property that might make him independent of it [...] The lover loves his beloved as wolves love lambs.
> (Plato, 2005, p. 241bc, 239d–241d)

In this description of the lover, it is clear that being a slave to his passion does not prevent him from exercising domination over the beloved. On the contrary, slavery is a necessary condition of domination, as if the split Hegelian self-awareness reaches here an apogee.

But another element also counts: that of mediation, in the sense that the beloved is only a simple means for the passion to be fulfilled. Thus, the lover's passion for love will later find other *erómenoi* over whom to dominate. This does not escape Plato in the *Phaedrus*, so that the *erómenos* will seek in vain that his former lover remains faithful to the amorous promises of the past (Plato, 2005, p. 241bc). The reversal occurs at the expense of the beloved, who thus becomes a lover in spite of himself, especially when he is duped by an older lover. We take the liberty of quoting extensively the authors of *De Kojève à Hegel* (Jarczyk & Labarrière, 1996, p. 79):

> Two co-necessary moments structure this complex situation of the servant. One is turned towards the master, but in reality goes further than him [cf. seminar on *The Transference*: the horizon of erastés goes beyond the simple *erómenos*]: it is expressed as the banal fear of the one who lives in submission - this fear being however only the translation of a fundamental anguish, the one that found its origin, at the end of the fight, in the sudden awareness of a possible loss of life [the *erómenos* loses his status of *erómenos* = cf. Alcibiades's praise of Socrates]. We now understand it: the choice of non-autonomy that the servant made at that time – and which made him a servant – proceeds from the lucid consideration of one of the conditions of all true autonomy, namely mere subsistence in being [let us take this in the Lacanian sense, namely of being and not of having : the *erómenos* is the one who believes he has something, like Poros in *The Symposium*—whereas Penia is servitude personified, in his autonomy], as it comes under what one might call the "principle of reality" [the said principle implies that one can lose one's place as an *erómenos*]. It is in this sense that the servant prevails over the master: he escapes the alternative of autonomy and non-autonomy, of switching from one to the other, choosing the latter to preserve the essence of the former.

Let's take up this line again. "One is turned towards the master, but in reality goes further than him". This indicates as well that the slave aims at the master but, beyond him, at nature and death, the latter being the famous absolute master. His chosen instability obeys a forced choice that has as its horizon a desired stability (autonomy) and he makes this choice of instability and dependence in order to preserve life. This comparison, i.e., the relationship between the slave and the desiring, can be problematic, especially with regard to an unambiguous definition of the slave. Indeed, the two metaphors of love implied by Lacan in *Seminar VIII* suggest that there would be at least two different statuses of the lover, i.e., the slave, according to our comparison: (1) the slave who loves his beloved, of which Alcibiades is the prototype, except that it implies a kind of failure, of straying as to the true object of love; (2) the slave who loves beyond his beloved, of which Socrates seems to be the most accomplished form. The slave thus fulfils a dual definition that contains within it the essence of Lacan's advances in his reading of *The Symposium*, as well as in the appropriation he makes of it in his conception of the analyst's desire. This second form of erasure would reveal a desire that does without any recognition because it does not have an object made to its measure and because it is above all a desire that is not a desire of.

## Further reading

Clemens, J. (2014). The Field and Function of the Slave in the Écrits. In: L. Chiesa (Ed.), *Lacan and Philosophy. The New Generation* (pp. 193–202). Melbourne: Re-Press.

Lucchelli, J. P. (2012). *Métaphores de l'amour, lecture lacanienne du banquet de platon*. Rennes: Presses Universitaires de Rennes.

Strauss, L. (1959). *On Plato's Symposium*, S. Bernadette (Trans). Chicago: The University of Chicago Press, 2001.

## References

Hegel, G. W. F. (1807). *Phenomenology of Spirit*, M. Inwood (Trans.). New York: Oxford University Press, 1977.

Jarczyk, G. & Labarrière, P.-J. (1996). *De Kojève à Hegel: cent cinquante ans de pensée hégélienne en France*. Paris: Albin Michel.

Kojève, A. (1947). *Introduction to the Reading of Hegel*, J. Nichols (Trans.). Ithaca: Cornell University Press, 1969.

Miller, J.-A. (1991). Les deux métaphores de l'amour. In: *La cause freudienne*, 18: 217–222.

Plato (1951). *The Symposium*, W. Hamilton (Trans.). London: Penguin.

Plato (2005). *Phaedrus*, C. Rowe (Trans.). London: Penguin.

Žižek, S. (2012). *Less than Nothing. Hegel and the Shadow of Dialectical Materialism*. London: Verso.

# Chapter 22

# Society

*Edgar Miguel Juárez-Salazar*

—Ara.: مجتمع —Chi.: 社會 —Fre.: *Société* —Ger.: *Gesellschaft* —Ita.: *Società* —Jap.: 社会 —Port.: *Sociedade* —Rus.: *Общество* —Spa.: *Sociedad* —Tur.: *Toplum*

→ *Alienation*; *Economy*; *Politics*; *Surplus*-jouissance; *Uneasiness*

## Introduction

Society is a concomitant and oblique concept in Lacan's theory. Although it can be found throughout his teaching, it is not included as a main term. It could be considered as a notion that hinges on and connects other relevant concepts in his proposal, such as family, signifier, structure, or culture. On the other hand, in Marx's intellectual work, society is a key idea to understand Marxian anthropology, which focuses on individual social origins and labour flow in a historically determinate society. However, both authors present society as a mythical, original, structured, structuring, exchangeable, and degraded condition. The homology between Marx and Lacan around the notion of society resides in an accurate critique of the organization and distribution of the surplus as pillar of the conformation of societies. Both Marx and Lacan explore bourgeois-capitalist society, since within this society there is a policy of surplus accumulation and a systematic regulation of the surplus- enjoyment and surplus-value. Furthermore, Lacan's well-known phrase about the impossibility of the sexual relationship would allow us to suppose, in parallel, the impossibility of the social relationship, since both are sustained in the void produced by the effect of the inscription of the signifier.

## Early approaches to society

In Lacan's early writings, we can find significant elements that revolve around the concept of society. It is important to highlight that these initial approaches are very close to the concrete-materialist psychology explored by the Marxist philosopher Georges Politzer. In his doctoral thesis, Lacan studied society related to the subject's personality along three important paths. First, he mapped a "biographical development" focused on "*Erlebnis*" as a concept of Freudian influence. Second, as

DOI: 10.4324/9781003212096-22

an "understanding of the self" defined "objectively as vital attitudes and dialectical progress" and transformed "by the subject through more or less 'ideal' images of himself". Finally, he defined it as a "certain tension of social relations", "objectively" established by "the pragmatic autonomy of the behavior and the social bonds of ethical participation" and realized in the subject through "the representative *value* by which he feels affected face-to-face by others" (*DPP*, p. 43).[1]

From these three structural pathways, Lacan attempts to trace human personality. It is relevant to consider his outlook on the second point mentioned above in order to begin our analysis. Lacan underlines, in a footnote, the "diversity" of personality types. He observed its "artificiality" where "happy personal fulfillment is characterized by the regularity and human significance of personal development, the coherence of their ideals, behaviors and progress". In contrast, an "unhappy" form is "produced by the opposite conditions". Nevertheless, these two perspectives are linked in terms of *worth*. Lacan identifies an "economic point of view" that "plays a primary role in psychological science" (*DPP*, p. 43).

Therefore, Lacan's perspective associates the ideals with a pragmatic economy, built between society's ideals, bonds, and subjects. This structural and economic approach is not limited to profit or waste, instead there is a dialectical link in which happiness and unhappiness coexist as *worth* in constant circulation. Thus, this first Lacanian proposal is similar to Marx's theory in *The Economic and Philosophic Manuscripts of 1844*. In a critique of Adam Smith, Marx argued that "the goal of the economic system is the unhappiness of society" given that "the wealthiest state of society leads to this suffering of the majority" (*EPM*, pp. 24–25). As evidenced by the proposals of both Marx and Lacan, society and its discontents can only be understood in logical terms, in other words, if there is wealth in a normal society then the misery of subnormal people is imperative. As a consequence, for the prosperity of private interest, it is essential to produce discontent in the majority.

Lacan then develops an analogy to support the previous idea. He suggests, "the economy of the pathological seems to be traced over the structure of the normal". The "coherence" of that "economy" lies in the "structure" itself (*DPP*, p. 56). Therefore, the pathological condition is a reflex of the normalized structure, and at the same time a needed part of human consciousness resulting from social tension. This engenders a pathological social circuit that flows between subnormal consciousness and normal life and possesses a dialectical and material exchange as a result of structural forces. This circuit then condenses and represents the subject's concrete, material, and social reality. Duplicity and contradiction create social tensions through a normalized path. Marx and Engels, in their own way, conceived of something very similar to Lacan's viewpoints. They wrote in *The German Ideology* that "the phantoms formed in the brains of men are also, necessarily, sublimates of their material life-process, which is empirically verifiable and bound to material premises" (*GI*, p. 36). Even if Lacan does not directly suggest an exploration of the material conditions of existence, he does emphasize the concrete, vital, and material conditions in the subject.

To summarize this point, the materiality of social tension is caused by the material practices in the subject's life as a social being and not as an essentiality organic or biological subject. Although *Erlebnis* is introduced as an interior experience, it is also damaged by the traumatic exteriority formed in the limits of the social being. Lacan states, in parallel, that "a human being" as an "organism" has "total vital reactions". These "reactions derive their meaning in terms of the social environment that in animal-human development plays a primary role". That is to say, the "vital social functions", from the "human community" perspective, have "direct relationships of understanding". In the "subject's representation", these associations are "polarized between the subjective ideal of the self (*moi*) and the social judgment of the others" (*DPP*, p. 247). For Lacan, the subject's personality is based in the structural effect of the relationship between beings, because this effect condenses the reality of the human experience by means of the subjective eclipse of the self as conscious fantasy.

In *Beyond the "Reality Principle"*, a critical text for psychology as a field of the imaginary, Lacan uses a foundation in materialism to describe a double "relationship" between "man" and "nature" knotted on links of "properties of identificatory thought". Moreover, these bonds are established through "the use of instruments or artificial tools". Beyond social institutions and language, Lacan observes that the essence of "social groups" is based in the primary form of exploitation of "man" by "his semblable". Thus, exploitative relationships modify nature and consequently, it is in this "anthropomorphism" that "the myth of nature" is based (*BRP*, p. 70). The Lacanian proposal, at this point, is invaluable to understand that any human relationship between men depends on their identifications and the artificial products of their work as men. Likewise, psychism, as supposed imperative rationality, is an artificial creation. It is produced by the exploitation of the human work force. Lacan, emphatically and closely resembling Marx's thought, referred to the "subversion of nature" as essentially, "the *hominization* of the planet: the 'nature' of man is its relationship to man" (*BRP*, p. 71).[2]

The previous paragraph brings us once again to Marxist theory. For him, "all production is an appropriation of nature by the individual within and through a definite form of society". Psychism is thus a property that can only be obtained through an external social bond. This bond is productive and self-determinate because there is an exchangeable product within the social relationship of production. In Marx's theory, it is impossible to imagine a "society" that does not appropriate anything: "appropriation which does not make something into property is a *contradictio in subjecto*" (*GR*, p. 21). Every society has its own mode of psychic production and its original, primitive forms to produce man. The supposed universal laws of psychism, as a positive, individual, and cognitive invention, are put into doubt because of the relationship between production and property. This relationship originated in early man's communal organizations which eventually became the modern economic distributions, invented by the unjust appropriation of private property and the bourgeoisie.

Marx had already found the material and indeterminate realization of nature at the antithesis between Democritus and Epicurus. This antagonism is concentrated in Democritus's sceptic subjective passion about "the way in which the relationship between the atom and the world that is apparent to the senses is determined". In contrast, Epicurus had a dogmatic and objective passion about the "objective appearance" of the world (*DDE*, pp. 39–40). Both Marx and Lacan take a materialistic stance when interpreting the world. For Marx, the world implies nature transformed by labour and an objective world in which man and nature are a singular unit in themselves. Lacan explains homologically the subjective determination of psychism by the social exterior in line with the structuralist model. In both ideas, the authors critique and formulate a radical opposition to illusory harmony between the interior and the exterior world, proposing a human transindividual dimension. Lacan (*SVII*, 10.02.60, p. 139) later invents the neologism of *extimacy*, "the intimate exteriority", to further explain this difference. The theoretical ties between the two authors undoubtably occur in part because of Freud's metapsychological discovery of the *drive*.[3] It was Freud (1905, 1915) who proposed this new intermediate element that lies between the symbolic exterior reality and imaginary interior perception. As a result, the drive's aleatory work is to destabilize the mythical adaptation of the social and individual establishment. Interestingly enough, in the supposed and perhaps apocryphal letter from Marx to Freud, the German philosopher suggested to his "young friend" that there was a pressing need to build a "critical metapsychology" that would "cling to the entrails of alienated work and abandon the restricted horizon of the individual in order to realize their unsuspected potentialities". Thereby, Marx continues, "in the life of modern societies we can see what is not, what occurs is founded in a powerful process that appears at the backs of consciousness". Marx ended his words of advice by reminding Freud that "the critical and materialistic science" had already "anticipated" all psychological scopes that he proposed (*CAF*, p. 15). If the letter is true, then a certain indeterminacy between the unconscious and the political is left open.

## Family as a social group, imaginary servitude, and utilitarianism

First of all, it is necessary to explore the familial institution as another parallel route to early Lacanian reflections about society. For Lacan "culture introduces a new dimension into social reality and into psychic life. This dimension specifies the human family, as well as the rest of man, as social phenomena" (*CF*, p. 23). Lacan suggests that this cultural condition serves to underpin a "concrete psychology" and to understand many psychic events in light of the power relations and hierarchies that are produced by the family structure. Due to cultural inscription, other processes of social domination and cultural-social relationships are also registered. However, Lacan openly critiques the universalist idea that there is a biological or natural link between the individual and the social being within a family organization. That is where familial complexes appear as cultural effects. His argument focuses on the "continuity" and the limits that "family establishes" which is the "causality of mental order" (*CF*, p. 25). The familial institution is a constituted group, and it has used principles of authority and social rules throughout human history. Despite this, the family is a model, a continuation of the social mental order beyond biological conditions, that it transmits and delineates by culture. For this reason, the family is also a social product, due to a culture that has modified its core organization by social exchanges and sexual commerce.

Moreover, Lacan, using a Durkheimian approach, highlights a split between "marriage" and "family", since "marriage" is a political and civil contract that produces a new association called the "conjugal family", where the social functions create different mechanisms of civil relationships (*CF*, p. 27). Thus, a new delimited family appears, reduced to a husband, a wife, and their children. In terms of this structure, social and political means establish an interior and private space of the family. In psychoses, neuroses, and perversion, the familial complexes are generated as an intimate cutout of the external social life, a split that provokes social division between cultural subjects. Among Lacanian complexes, it is possible to extract an economic link between objects—like *imagos*—and ideals. Lacan talks about this "reduction" of the "family" as a problem of "social progress". Because this organization utilizes a "biological group" as an imperative to build the societies in which "economic concentration" and "political catastrophes" are "suffered" (*CF*, p. 60).

Marx and Engels proposed that the family in modern societies can only be established as a concrete reality through the division of labour and its economic structure. However, the bourgeois society "has torn away from the family its sentimental veil, and has reduced the family relationship to a mere money relationship" (*MCP*, p. 487). The family as a group would sustain exploitative social relationships among its members. Even if Lacan is not referring explicitly to money, it is possible to see how there is an exterior economic market situated and organized in social progress. In this structural market, there are many strategies to maintain a social channelling based on the "matrimonial demands" that produce psychological discontents within the conjugal family. Last but not least, Marx and Engels mention

> the bourgeois clap-trap about the family and education, about the hallowed co-relation of parent and child, becomes all the more disgusting, the more, by the action of modern industry, all family ties among the proletarians are torn asunder and their children transformed into simple articles of commerce and instruments of labour.
>
> (*MCP*, p. 502)

In bourgeois modern social life, proletarian women and children are nothing more than the tools to reproduce domination over the working class and, as such, they are equally exploited. The conjugal family perfectly supports and reproduces class domination.

Lacan describes "the historical enterprise of society" as a place which has nothing more than a "utilitarian function". But, to clarify its effects, Lacan suggests seeing "the function of misrecognition that characterizes the ego in all the defensive structures" seeking to understand "the passions of the city" (*MS*, p. 80). These civil passions are important to distinguish in Lacanian psychoanalysis as the force created by the knot of an *imaginary servitude* that constitutes the social subject crossed by social (civil) repressions and virtual *imagos*.[4] Meanwhile, Marx had already considered the utilitarianism condition, and in his theory this consideration is more incisive and forceful. Regarding the circulation of commodities, and phenomena in capitalist society and its way of life, we can find "the paradise of human rights". The human is like an exiled and bourgeois fruit, given that Adam and Eve, along with their children Cain and Abel, are the original social group and find themselves face-to-face with "liberty, equality, property and Bentham!". Bentham, as the founder of the philosophy of utilitarianism, takes on great relevance within bourgeois society and its organic relationships: groups or collectives, in which the family is included. The social beings that intervene in these acts of collectivity do so "because each looks only to his own advantage". In the bourgeois family, "the only force bringing them together, and putting them into relation with each other, is the selfishness, the gain and the private interest of each person" (*CAI*, p. 280).[5]

Marx and Lacan also converge in their critical frameworks set up against the humanist conception of bourgeois society. They grounded their radical and critical position on the social ideals in which society develops. Thus, in Lacan's words, "the ideals of humanism dissolve into the utilitarianism of the group". For Lacan, this utilitarian humanism "expresses both the revolt of the exploited and the guilty conscience of the exploiters, to whom the notion of punishment has become equally unbearable" and this produces an "ideological antinomy reflects, here as elsewhere, a social malaise" (*FPC*, p. 112). Lacan never forgets the Benthamian proposal; he will even return to Bentham's approaches in *Seminar XX*. Lacan will reaffirm Bentham's theory of fictions that places "fictions" at the level of "language" and its materiality because we can only understand "fictions" from their "use-value" (*SXX*, 21.11.72, p. 3). Based upon this, we can talk about the utilitarian progress as a producer of discontents and imaginary servitude in societies praising the principles of liberty, equality, and fraternity.

## Society as a signifier and structure: towards a world of the social machine

When Lacan was focusing on structuralism, we find many instances where society comes up as a concept. During this time, Lacan was deeply influenced by structural anthropologists Marcel Mauss and Claude Lévi-Strauss. At the same time, he moved away from anthropological humanism and repeatedly criticized it. Following both Mauss and Lévi-Strauss, Lacan argues that "the structures of society are symbolic" (*FPC*, p. 108). We can pinpoint, from the fifties onwards, how Lacan develops a more specific exploration of his approaches to imaginary and symbolic identifications across the social spectrum. Moreover, he developed a framework on paternal function, where he elaborates Oedipal drama sublimation. From a Freudian point of view, Lacan (*S0*) declares that "sublimation" is a "socialization of the instincts" that is formulated through the myth and the structure of the symbol. For Lacan, on the one hand, the myth born from the Oedipus complex "linked" the subject to "a fundamental symbolic value". On the other hand, "the myth" is "donated" as a "discursive formula", which is the key that orders the soul's life and the subject's social uneasiness (*MIN*, pp. 14–15).

This order is a function of social relations that subsist by the effects of the symbolic structure. Furthermore, the myth grants the subject a partial truth, that she/he experiences as the complete reality. This also positivizes the subject's reality, supported by his neurosis. The myth manages the subject's life through a discourse that is inserted by means of the symbolic figure of the father. Indeed, we are not talking about a virile, powerful, or strong father. On the contrary, we are speaking here of a "lacking and humiliated father" that does not have any "normalizing" value; his value is instead "pathogenic" (*MIN*, p. 45). The structural force of culture is not in the father; it is essentially in the symbolic structure that gives him an opportunity to transmit a structuring metaphor. Hence, society is founded as a cultural degradation because the father's function is reduced to its pathogenic effectiveness of transmission. This metaphorized *communication* resides in social illness that lives in a positive mode of cultural-symbolic and imaginary distribution from ideals and illusionary *imagos*. The relationship between the subject and his "*imagos*" is, in itself, the first "alienation" and "identification" with the mythological social life that emerges from "social conditions of the human *Umwelt*" (*PPC*, p. 148). With this last point, Lacan draws upon the Hegelian perspective on desire and its recognition as one of the pillars by which society would sustain a dialectic, produced by the subject's imaginary and symbolic identification with its fellow subjects and its structure.

In *The Function and Field of Speech and Language in Psychoanalysis*, Lacan analyses "the unconscious" as "that part of concrete discourse *qua* transindividual, which is not at the subject's disposal in re-establishing the continuity of his conscious discourse" (*FFS*, p. 214). It is not an overstatement to say that the unconscious produces a discourse with the same key and the same transindividual characters in consciousness, due to the cultural forces articulated in the form of the signifier and the transindividual oppression of signification. In this period of Lacan's thought, culture and language pre-exist in the subject, because they stand before nature like a kind of denaturalization as a consequence of culture. However, Lacan added that "culture assigns" to the subjects a few "social services related to language", and these services blur and reproduce "the complex structures of civilization" (*FFS*, p. 232). Here is where these structures install the significance of subjective reality and where the subject is identified and resists, as Freud (1930) pointed out in *Civilization and Its Discontents*.

Therefore, Lacan questions and transforms the classic distinction between nature and culture thanks to the potency of the contra nature and the *moteriality* of the signifier.[6] This entails a strong distinction between "society grounded in language" and "an animal society". In the first of these, "exchange" is its most important "characteristic" and moreover, it has "other foundations" beyond "needs (even if it satisfies them)". Thus, the society of speaking beings is a society devised as a signifier that represents its social exchanges: in other words, from what is given, and at the same time, from what is traded by an inter-signifier tie. That is to say, "what has been called the gift as total social fact" (*FT*, p. 346). If society is an organized signifier only in its exchanges, then it is something totally different from culture. As a result, Lacan proposes "a ternary conception of the human condition: nature, society, and culture" (*IL*, p. 414). In this division, the dualistic perspective between nature and culture is completely displaced to make way for the centrality of signifying structure produced by culture, the Other's place as discourse. According to Lacan, society is nothing more than a signifier that, as such, "signifies nothing" and for that, it is "more indestructible". On "the modern idea of nation", the signifier is a fundamental pillar of population distribution and not of the population as such. It is possible thus to question the notion of society from the signifier's force inasmuch as being itself is a unique signifier, thus making it a true "signifier"; a deceptive signifier that arbitrarily represents an absence whose shape "has entered our social reality like the prow of a ship, like a ploughshare" (*SIII*, 11.04.56, pp. 185–186).

Given that society is a signifier and is distinguished from nature and culture, its economic circulation is then also a mode of repetition into the symbolic structure as the machinery of the social relations of production. It is a blade of a ploughshare that works on the *real* of nature. The signifier's insertion into human nature entails knowledge and this creates the social (signifying) relationships of production based on the perversion of man's needs. In line with political economy, Marx also taught us that "the tendency of Capital" is "the transformation of what was previously superfluous into what is necessary, as a historically created necessity". Thus, "needs created by production itself, social needs, needs which are themselves the offspring of social production and intercourse, are posited as necessary" (*GR*, pp. 451–452). In the Lacanian notion of society, the passage from *polis* to *civitas* is consolidated thanks to the hierarchical order of State's institutions. In Marx's theory, society can only be understood as an essential antagonism between the exploited and the exploiters, between proletarians and the owners of the means of production. In other words, society has always been a perforated whole, split by its signifying operation.

On the other hand, society is a signifier that structures reality and the social order by functioning like a machine. It goes from being a fictionalized structure to a machine that produces fictions and reality, as the structuring function of society resides in the force that moves the machine of signification associated with a signifier of a social nature. In that way, the social nature of man, for Marx and Engels, cannot be reduced to the machine's operativity. By contrast, "machinery and money", other indestructible signifiers, are "destructive forces" that, in the capitalist social relations of production, prevent the exploited class from "enjoying its advantages" (*GI*, p. 52). In accordance with Marx and Engels, Lacan (*SII*, 08.12.54, p. 47) wrote that "the machine is the structure detached from the activity of the subject" and "the symbolic world is the world of the machine", thus "the most complicated machines are made only with words". It is the machinery that tries to make man into nothing more than a repetitive mechanical production and subsequently a commodity. By his "speech", man is "first and foremost that object of exchange" and in constant labour that is made visible by the movement of his money, or in commodified working life. Even so, according to the Freudian discovery elucidated by Lacan, the brain is man's modern thinking machine, a "dream machine", that through the work of dreams produces speech and enjoyment. For Lacan, society is also a signifying structure that produces and makes the gears of social order work, but in effect a machine needs to be "fed" and "maintained" because "they tend to wear out" (*SII*, 12.01.55, pp. 75–76).[7] As a result, the structuring function of society is a degraded form of the productive and cultural life of the social being. The unconscious drive in life is not a machine and it does not function as such either, but it is required to function as a machine insofar as it is repressed and condemned to be enjoyed in the field of knowledge.

## From culture to brothel: degradation, entropy, and enjoyment

This section follows an analysis of the social function of cultural ideals as a set through which the signifying machine has instituted an externally determined social order. Lacan references Marx's *Capital* when he describes "the relations between values are defined as signifying relations, and all subjectivity, and possibly even that of fetishization, comes to be inscribed within this signifying dialectic" (*SVI*, 15.04.59, p. 313). Thus, we talk about the dialectic of desire focused on fetishized relations of a signifying effort where culture produces damaged subjectivities. Lacan affirms that "as soon as man arrives somewhere, he builds a prison and a brothel—that is, the places where desire truly is—and he waits for something, a better world, a future world" (*SV*, 15.01.58, p. 161). It is through desire linked to the signifier that the subject can enjoy himself in this imprisoned brothel called the world.

For Lacan (*SV*, 05.03.58, p. 248), "we live" in a "brothel" as "society cannot be defined in any other way than as a more or less advanced state of the degradation of culture", that is, the daily space of perversion. In other words, the subject in society finds enjoyment in the advanced degradation of culture. This approach is similar to Marx's theory when he defines "activity and *enjoyment*" as "social" elements in their "mode of existence", as both are methods of "social bonding". This condition is antagonistic to "community *enjoyment*", because it is opposed to the enjoyment of civil or bourgeois society (*EPM*, p. 104).⁸ According to Marx, "private property" and its social "process of transformation" means that "the workers have been turned into proletarians and their means of labour into capital" (*CAI*, p. 928). Capitalist societies, subsequently, alienate the worker's labour and exploit it, repeating its modes of extraction and exploitation to produce private and not collective capital, thereby private society is imposed on social communism. Likewise, in Lacan's theory the "public thing" adheres to the private world because it takes the shape of a "social body", inevitably increasing the "swelling and excess" of "abusive wealth" and reproducing an obstinate and repetitive condition of enjoyment (*SXIII*, 19.01.66).⁹

On the other hand, Lacan describes "the relationship between culture and society as a relationship of entropy, inasmuch as what passes over from culture into society always includes a disintegrating function". He adds: "What presents itself in society as culture and which has thus entered, in various guises, into a certain number of stable conditions, which are also latent, that determine the circuits of exchanges", thus it "establishes a movement or dialectic in society that leaves open there the same gap as the one in which we situate the function of desire". Hence, desire is *always-already* dialectic and produces movement within the social realm, a sign of exchange with some degree of social "perversion" within the culture and that finally finds its way out in "sublimation" (*SVI*, 01.07.59, pp. 483–484). Entropy, as a physical phenomenon, generates disorder, chance, propagation, combinatoriality, and loss as effects. Consequently, we could suggest that in the social energy system of desire, the more entropy that exists between culture and society, the more liberation of sublimated or perverse energy there will be. There is no possibility of a return to an inert or homeostatic state, and what is more, a propensity for degradation persists in the social system in itself. Lacan (*SXVII*, 14.01.70, pp. 48–50) will later say that, "knowledge at work produces an entropy" and this is nothing other than the effect of "*jouissance*", the "*mehrlust*" as surplus, more exactly a "surplus-jouissance" that gives way to the "negative". Marx concurrently saw "usefulness" of the "unproductive functions" that makes a capitalist "society" not "pay" for "surplus labour", instead placing it in "positive" circulation by a "negative restriction on the valorisation of his capital", thus constantly producing a profit (*CAII*, p. 210).

Therefore, the idea of the purely positive perfection of closed and irreversible machines and economic systems is clearly naive. A greater disorder, minimal expression of energy, concentrates the perverse actions of the subjects in an *indestructible* signifier, society, thus determining and perpetuating an impregnable social order. Marx demonstrates in *The Poverty of Philosophy* that, "machinery is merely a productive force" and, at the same time, "the modern workshop, which is based on the application of machinery, is a social production relation, an economic category" (*PP*, p. 183). Thus, we could suggest that when speaking of desire in its function as social machinery in Lacan, a political and libidinal economy of desire is manifested. This desire's economy dialectically works for the ordering and perverse reproduction of social life that brings together subjects in a circuit of *enjoyable machines*. Culture is degraded by society because it sets a signifying order of desire. According to Lacan (*SXVII*, 14.01.70, p. 49), this is an "apparatus of enjoyment [*jouissance*]" that puts into motion the signifying social machinery that emerges in and reproduces the social relations of production and circulation of money and commodities as articulated by Marx.

At the same time, the dialectic of desire leads to the process of sublimation as a response, based on the social ideals enshrined in the progress of civilization. Ideals that Lacan (*SVII*, 23.12.59, p. 78) identifies in the first instance are those glorified in the ten Judeo-Christian commandments, their cultural ordering and their subsequent reworking to the legal horizon of the modern State. But their acceptance is not limited to being observed and fulfilled; on the contrary, it is found in their transgression since "societies prosper as a result of the transgression of these maxims" and modern society only can be operable through non-compliance with the laws. We can thus observe that it is the first identification with ideals that institutes the repressive-transgressive design in modern capitalist societies. Due to this, Lacan considers that "ideals are society's slaves" (*PU*, p. 705). Likewise, Marx determined, the transformation of "religion" as "the spirit of civil society" is a producer of "egoism" and "it has become the expression of man's *separation* from his *community*" as an "essence of difference". In sum, the man in bourgeois-civil society is socially isolated and divided into "a public man and a private man" where the communal culture has been left to the mercy of the provisions of bourgeois-civil society. There is a difference "between the *living individual* and the citizen" that is produced based on the ideals that build off the rights of man in bourgeois society (*OJQ*, pp. 154–155).

## If there is no sexual relationship, then there is no social relationship

According to Lacan, the "social structure" in "capitalism" is dominated by "accumulation of capital" that resides in knowledge's function of the "Cartesian subject". This function is also an "accumulation of knowledge" (*SXII*, 09.06.65). Both accumulations are similar and dominant in the social spectrum and that is where the subject emerges, between the symbolic exchanges that organize the social whole. In Lacan's words, it is in "modern structuralism" where we can pinpoint the relevance of aleatory mechanisms of "alliance" in which social functioning is organized "at the level therefore of the signifier" by reproducing the "exchange" (*SXI*, 29.04.64, p. 150). It is then possible to talk about a society that is different from its natural environment and from the conditions essential to biological inheritance thanks to the action of the signifier as a key figure in social exchanges.

This last Lacanian proposal inevitably leads us to the concept of civil society in the works of Marx and Engels. They suggest that "civil society embraces the whole material intercourse of individuals within a definite stage of the development of productive forces. It embraces the whole commercial and industrial life of a given stage and, insofar, transcends the state and the nation" (*GI*, p. 89). In both

Marx's and Lacan's theories, material (and signifier) exchange establishes the emergence of a society that will depend on the dominant modes of production. In capitalist modes of production, this necessarily entails a sharpening of the enjoyable relationships from the inscription of "the Other" on the bodies in this economic system. Moreover, as Lacan (*SXIII*, 20.04.66) observes, both "Socrates" and "Freud" did not write "social critique", since they both knew that every social organization "was situated" in the middle of an "economic problem", more specifically, the economic problem of "the relations between desire and enjoyment" rather than in the social relations themselves. Lacan discovers, from a structuralist reading of Socrates, Marx, and Freud, the ambiguous implication of sexuality as a failure in the symbolic system of culture to establish order and control over all forms of socialization. If Marx's sixth thesis on Feuerbach is correct in saying: "the essence of man is no abstraction inherent in each single individual. In its reality it is the ensemble of the social relations", then we can determine that the essence of the social being resides in the economic relations between desire, enjoyment, and its renouncement (*TOF*, p. 4).

The sexual act involves castration so that societies can function structurally as machines whose oil is the renouncement of enjoyment. This first renouncement of enjoyment in order to enter the dialectic of desire produces a surplus of enjoyment, a *plus de jouissance*, which is mobilized by the society of masters. However, in sexuality, as a problematic as forced choice, a founding prohibition appears first. Based in Freud's work, Lacan places this prohibition in the "homosexual" clan of brothers of the primordial horde. This would be the "starting point" of any "social bond" due to the creation of a specific bond by the "interdiction of enjoyment" (*SXIII*, 08.06.66).[10] The improvement of societies can only be recognized to the extent that they make commercial use of the surplus-enjoyment produced by the impossibility of a sexual relationship, of an absolute enjoyment. Marx already spoke about a "refinement of society" that "impoverishes the worker and reduces him to a machine" (*EPM*, p. 26). According to Lacan, it could be said that bourgeois society, in its refined enjoyments and division of labour, produces isolated and administered pleasured machines within the excess of surplus-enjoyment homologous to Marxian surplus-value. Society, as Lacan (*SXVII*, 11.03.70, pp. 114–115) observed, is founded on "segregation" and is situated from the beginning in "brotherhood" as a utilitarian and institutional fiction. This is the regulatory body of the surpluses of enjoyment through discourse and whose "articulation" as support resides in "social relationships" (*SXVI*, 26.02.69).

In *Seminar XIX*, Lacan (17.05.72, p. 160) describes the "sexual relationship" as something different from a "form of exploitation". Conversely, it is because of "exploitation" that subjects organize themselves sexually and socially. In this way, submission to exploitation would affirm the circulation of knowledge to try and hide the impossible relationship between subjects through their fantasies. The force of the signifier also shows the fracturing of the subject to access the full meaning. Because of this, Lacan's well-known slogan, *there is no sexual relationship*, highlights that there is an impossible sense of relationship due to the impossibility of taking the form of *au-sens*. It is this absence of sense that also makes it conceivable for the labour force to come to oppose the pleasured capitalization of those who control the means of production and commodification. There is no sexual relationship because of the structural split that fragments in itself all possibility of a relationship; there is no social relationship since reality shows the relational impossibility of the perfect crime in capitalist exploitation, since it jumbles the coordinates of knowledge and signification.

In Lacan and Marx, there would be, in short, a homology in communism founded by labour, the communal clan, and the homosexual society that is disturbed by the original impasse of the heterosexual relationship. In other words, there is no sexual relationship, specifically heterosexual relationship, since commerce and exchange at the level of the signifier is inscribed in it. Homosexuality would represent a resistant and symptomatic modality to a society that is fancifully constructed in the illusion of universal completeness. Both Marx and Lacan find in society, and in bourgeois society specifically, values of use and exchange between men and women and not a stability that is differentiated by biological and anatomical laws. If there is no sexual relationship, then there is no social relationship due to the impossibility of filling the foundational void of castration. It is an eternal sentence of not being able to obtain the impossible mythical *jouissance*, since it was exchanged for a universal signifier, such as the signifier of society, which has been traversed by a master signifier from the beginning. Finally, both Marx and Lacan find the social problem in the surplus and in the circuit that distributes it. Not surprisingly, Marx (*EPM*, p. 24) stated flatly: "the surplus would have to die".

## Notes

1 Emphasis added.
2 Lacan's emphasis.
3 See Dahmer (1983, p. 152).
4 See Flower-MacCannel (2016) on "human society defined as a commerce of images" (p. 76).
5 See Jameson (1981, p. 47).
6 Lacan refers to this concept as "*moterialisme*", a play on words of *mot*, French for word, and *materialisme*, French for materialism (*CG*, p. 13).
7 For an extensive discussion on Lacan's machine world, see Pavón-Cuéllar (2010).
8 The translation was modified; the original German edition of Marx's Manuscripts (*Ökonomisch-philosophische Manuskripte aus dem Jahre 1844*), says: "*Die Tätigkeit und der Genuß*". We can translate *Genuß* as enjoyment. The German verb *Genißen* frequently is used to translate Lacanian *jouissance*. In the English version reviewed the word used is "consumption". On the other hand, we also must distinguish the ambiguity between bourgeois society and civil society because both terms have been translated from German "*Bürgerliche Gesellschaft*" so it is possible to find a similarity between them. This would clarify that only bourgeois-civil society enjoys in terms of being something different from the community.
9 See Tomšič (2019).
10 Freud (1921) had also detected the elemental link in the relationship between the common and work in his *Group Psychology and the Analysis of the Ego*: "[The] sublimated homosexual love for other men, which springs from work in common" (p. 103). Transl. modified.

## Further reading

Laclau, E. (1990). *New Reflexions on the Revolution of Our Time*. London: Verso.
Neill, C. (2011). *Lacanian Ethics and the Assumption of Subjectivity*. London: Palgrave.
Zafiropoulos, M. (2001). *Lacan et les sciences sociales. Le déclin du père (1938–1953)*. Paris: PUF.

## References

Dahmer, H. (1983). *Libido y sociedad. Estudios sobre Freud y la izquierda freudiana*, F. Blanco (Trans.). México: Siglo XXI.
Flower-MacCannel, J. (2016). Lacan's Imaginary: A Practical Guide. In: *Between Psychoanalysis and Politics*, Jacques Lacan (Ed.). (pp. 72–85). London: Routledge.
Freud, S. (1905). Three Essays on the Theory of Sexuality. In: *Standard Edition of the Complete Psychological Works of Sigmund Freud* (Vol. VII, pp. 123–243), J. E. Strachey (Trans.). London: The Hogarth Press, 1981.
Freud, S. (1915). Instincts and their Vicissitudes. In: *Standard Edition of the Complete Psychological Works of Sigmund Freud* (Vol. XIV, pp. 109–140), J. E. Strachey (Trans.). London: The Hogarth Press, 1981.
Freud, S. (1921). Group Psychology and the Analysis of the Ego. In: *Standard Edition of the Complete Psychological Works of Sigmund Freud* (Vol. XVIII, pp. 65–144), J. E. Strachey (Trans.). London: The Hogarth Press, 1981.
Freud, S. (1930). Civilization and its Discontents. In: *Standard Edition of the Complete Psychological Works of Sigmund Freud* (Vol. XXI, pp. 57–146), J. E. Strachey (Trans.). London: The Hogarth Press, 1981.
Jameson, F. (1981). *The Political Unconscious. Narrative as a Socially Symbolic Act*. London: Routledge, 2002.
Pavón-Cuéllar, D. (2010). La conception lacanienne de la société, entre désagrégation névrotique et protestation homosexuelle. In: *Oxymoron*, 1: 1–11.
Tomšič, S. (2019). *The Labour of Enjoyment: Towards a Critique of Libidinal Economy*. Berlin: August Verlag.

# Chapter 23

# Superstructure

*Daniela Danelinck and Mariano Nicolás Campos*

—Ara.: بنية فوقية —Chi.: 超結構 —Fre.: *Superstructure* —Ger.: *Überbau* –Ita.: *Sovrastruttura* —Jap.: 上部構造 —Port.: *Superestrutura* —Rus.: *Надстройка* —Spa.: *Superestructura* —Tur.: *Üstyapı*

→ *Alienation*; *Economy*; *Ideology*; *Politics*; *Society*

## Überbau in Marx

The term "superstructure" (*Überbau*), which literally refers to a construction over the floor—which is why it can also be translated as "building"—comes from Marx's famous architectonic metaphor in the prologue of the 1859 *Zur Kritik der politischen Ökonomie*. In order to explain his conclusions from his studies in the 1840s, when he had to overcome the Hegelian concepts of civil society and State, Marx states the following:

> In the social production which men carry on they enter into definite relations that are indispensable and independent of their will; these relations of production correspond to a definite stage of development of their material powers of production. The sum total of these relations of production constitutes the economic structure [*Struktur*] of society - the real foundation, on which rise legal and political superstructures [*Überbau*] and to which correspond definite forms of social consciousness. The mode of production in material life determines the general character of the social, political, and spiritual processes of life. It is not the consciousness [*Bewußtsein*] of men that determines their existence [*Sein*], but, on the contrary, their social existence determines their consciousness.
>
> (*CPE*, p. 11)

The building metaphor comes in handy for Marx to introduce the difference between two different levels, one buried and conflictive whose modification implies upsetting the entire building, and the other superficial and conscious, where the conflict is resolved by "the legal, political, religious, aesthetic, or philosophic – in short, ideological – forms in which men become conscious of this conflict and fight it out" (*CPE*, p.12). Thus, the superstructure refers to the legal and political level—including all the social institutions that represent them—as well as the most diverse ideologies that are often characterized as the spiritual or cultural life and that are in contrast with the material aspect of the foundation. From what can be inferred from the prologue, natural science is not an element of the superstructure (although this was very much debated in Marxism). Regarding the relationship that mediates the foundation and the superstructure, which Marx does not develop any further, it was not until later on that it was deciphered by the Marxist tradition from three statements: the superstructure is determined by the foundation, the superstructure has relative autonomy, and the superstructure reacts on the foundation (De Lara, p. 1109).[1]

It is important to highlight, for further analysis, that the *Struktur* is the blind spot of the superstructure for reasons that are not entirely clear but are indeed suggested by the reference to the *Ideologie*, which has a negative connotation of mystifying the foundation. Although Marx is talking about the means of production in general, the first Marxist generations—Friedrich Engels, Franz Mehring, Georg Plejanov, Antonio Labriola, Karl Kautsky, among others—applied these terms to the capitalist system in order to decipher the bourgeois ideology as covering exploitation (even authors such as Maurice Godelier will say that the metaphor is *only* applied to capitalism).

## *Superstructure* in Lacan

If we turn to Lacan's work, the only reference to the superstructure, in the sense in which it was developed by Marxism, appears in *Seminar XVI*, when he questions the relationship of determination that mediates the social relations of production and the ideological sphere:

> People begin by saying that philosophies for example throughout the centuries were only ideologies, namely, the reflection of the superstructure, of the dominant classes. So then the question is settled. They are of no interest. You have to aim elsewhere. Not at all! People continue to fight against ideologies qua ideologies. They are there for that. It is completely true that there have always been, naturally, dominating or enjoying classes, or the two, and that they had their philosophers. They were there to be abused in their place. That is what is done, namely, people follow orders. In fact, it is not at all correct, is that not so, it is not at all correct! Kant is not the representative of the dominant class of his epoch.
>
> (*SXVI*, 19.03.69)

Lacan bases his definitions on *Zur Kritik* when he defines ideologies as "the reflection of the superstructure, of the dominant classes", but particularly on Lenin who in *Materialism and Empirio-Criticism* of 1909 defends the theory of consciousness as a reflection of reality (thus solving the ambiguity of the German verb "*bedingen*", which means causing, determining, or conditioning). Refusing to include Kant in this system is another way of saying that Lacan does not take part in what Raymond Williams called "the mechanical materialism" of orthodox Marxism (Williams, 1977).

Outside mechanical materialism, Lacan faces what Louis Althusser (1965) had called, just a few years earlier, "the problem, basic today, of the superstructures" (p. 114). Antonio Gramsci in his *Prison Notebooks* written between 1929 and 1935 had tackled this with the statement: "structures and superstructures form an 'historical bloc'", which means that "the complex, contradictory and discordant ensemble of the superstructures is the reflection of the ensemble of the social relations of production" (1971, p. 366). In 1962, on the path of Gramsci's "beautiful totality" (Althusser, 2018, p. 33), Althusser (1965) stated in *Contradiction and Overdetermination* that the economic structure determines the superstructure but it is also overdetermined by the multiple instances of the superstructure. Therefore, Lacan's comment in the late 1960s should be read less as a critique of Marx's theory than as a way of placing himself on the road paved by Gramsci and followed by Althusser.

Except for the reference of 1968, when the social revolt plays an important role, there is a constant reappropriation of the building metaphor in the rest of the Lacanian use of the term "super-structure" that is used for diverse means and where that which works as "basis" changes according to the addressed subject. Thus, in *Motives of Paranoiac Crime: The Crime of the Papin Sisters*, the paranoid intellectualization is catalogued as superstructural because it "is justifying and negating the criminal drive" (*MDP*, p. 26). In *Family Complexes in the Formation of the Individual*, it is stated that "obsessional thinking" belongs to the same architectonic level, "mystify anxiety" (*CF*, p. 75); and in *Intervention to the first World Congress of Psychiatry*, the ego is declared a citizen of the same superstructure because, just like Marx's *Bewußtsein*, it does not recognize "social alienation".[2] It is noteworthy that whenever Lacan uses the term "superstructure" in an affirmative or acritical manner he maintains the double pejorative meaning that Marx gave it, that is, its superficial and mystifying character, but he rejects the Marxist determinism.

In the fifties, the term "superstructure" is used to describe a narrow notion of discourse, intellectuality, and rationalization. As for the first, in *Seminar III*, Lacan reminds the audience that "the very foundation of the order of discourse" demands the rejection of "its status as superstructure, its relationship of pure and simple reference to reality, its having the character of signs, and the equivalence that is supposed to exist between naming and the world of objects" (*SIII*, 08.02.56, p. 136). As for the second, it has the purpose of maintaining "some sense of proportion when it comes to the sweeping notion of intellectualisation which has been wielded here, there and everywhere with its somehow pejorative tone". Lacan states the following in *Seminar IV*:

> I mean that it ought to teach us to realise that something which on first blush might present as being situated in the intellectual domain clearly holds an

importance that simple and sweeping opposition between intellectual and the affective could never account for. We are called *childhood theories,* or the child's activity of *research* concerning sexual reality, correspond to a necessity that is quite different from what we label – unduly, but it has to be recognised as a kind of diffuse notion – as the superstructural character activity which is more or less implicitly admitted in what it might be termed *the font of belief with which common consciousness aligns.*

(*SIV*, 27.03.57, pp. 243–244)

Two years later, in *Seminar VI*, Lacan goes back to the same association of common sense between superstructure and rationalization when he states that "long before psychoanalysis, psychologists had already noticed the superstructural, rationalized, and rationalizing nature of the reasons the subject gives" (*SVI*, 11.03.59, p. 255).[3] From this perspective, the superstructure refers to "the myriad different, self-contradictory, and inconsistent reasons the subject gives" (*SVI*, 11.03.59, p. 254).[4] All in all, we can conclude that since the fifties the discourse, rationality, and intellectuality are only "superstructural" for Lacan from the point of view of belief and common sense (*la conscience commune*), where he includes psychology.

## "Stalin's Theorem"

The different Lacanian discussions deserve an independent analysis, starting with *The Freudian Thing* of 1955 and Lacan's first reference to "Stalin's Theorem" that brings into question the place of language in the architectural metaphor.[5] The attempt to create a philosophy of language based on Marxist principles and, specifically, in relation to the foundation and superstructure metaphor is, incidentally, not new. It goes back to the Soviet era when Voloshinov's *Marxism and Philosophy of Language* of 1929 stated that "individual consciousness is not the architect of the ideological superstructure but only a tenant of the social building of ideological signs" (1929, p. 13).[6] That being said, Stalin's position is better explained by the juncture than by the general problems of linguistics.[7]

Lacan's source is a statement that Stalin gave in 1950 in order to answer some young comrades' question: Is it true that language is a superstructure on the base?, to which he answers: "No, it is not true" (*ICM*, p.147). The question reproduces a certain conjunctural urgency for the opposite answer implied the need to eliminate Russian as a bourgeois language and substitute it by a new proletarian language, according to the new foundation created by communism. As it can be seen in *The Instance of the Letter*, Lacan is perfectly aware of this backdrop:

> Recall that discussion about the need for a new language in communist society really did take place, and that Stalin, much to the relief of those who lent credence to his philosophy, put an end to it as follows: language is not a super-structure.

(*IL*, p. 414, fn. 6)

Also in *Responses to Students of Philosophy* of 1966, Lacan goes back to the theorem to highlight another local aspect of Stalin's statement, which is that of his opposition to Nikolai Yakovlevich Marr's theory who, in Stalin's words, was the one who "introduced into linguistics the incorrect, non-Marxist formula that language is a superstructure, and got himself into a muddle and put linguistics into a muddle" (Stalin, 1950, p. 178). Regarding this, Lacan draws on not only the superiority of the understanding of "language" in relation to Marxism, but also to logical neopositivism (*RSF*, p. 111). Lastly, in a 1967 conference he adds that Stalin would agree with Heidegger on his statement saying that "In language man dwells" (*POE*, p. 27). However, the explanation does not solve the place of language in the foundation-superstructure system but rather sends it to a different universe, that of Heidegger's theory of language.

## The foundation-superstructure relation

As we mentioned before, Lacan uses the term "superstructure" quite early on to talk about the complex musings of obsessive thinking, the castles in the air that the paranoid personality fabricates based on a foundation that remains hidden, disfigured, and mystified in the representational content. This pejorative meaning of the term remains stable in Lacan's later teachings and it also remains linked to "the empty word" phenomena and the imaginary capture of meaning. Still in *Radiophonie*, on the verge of his last teaching, he answers in the following manner a question that evoked the word "revolution" in its formulation:

> Your question is going to tickle the hopes, tinted to make me fear, inspired by our epoch's devolved sense for the word: revolution. One could mark its passage to a superegoistic function in politics, to the role of an ideal in the career of thought. Let us note that it is Freud, not I, who brings into play here those resonances from which only the structural cut can separate the imaginary as "superstructure".
>
> (*RA*, p. 420)

But while the characterization of the superstructure remains stable, Lacan has difficulties fixing that which would act as a material or real foundation in his own psychoanalytic theory. If in the work he did in the thirties and forties the foundation goes from "the criminal drive" to the libido (*CF*, *BRP*) or sexuality (*ICM*), in the fifties Lacan acknowledges only language as the material foundation of discourse. *The Freudian Thing* and *The Instance of the Letter* are two writings where Lacan ties up the Marxist problem of the relations between foundation and superstructure to his own theory of language because, like for Marx, the building metaphor allows him to introduce a difference between the two levels, in this case two levels within language: on the one hand, the level of communication and meaning, "the connections characteristic of the signifier, and of the magnitude of their function in generating the signified (*IL*, p. 415); and, on the other, the instance of the letter in the unconscious, where "letter" is the "material medium [*support*] that concrete discourse borrows from language" (*IL*, p. 413), something that makes the signifier structure "essentially localized" (*IL*, p. 418).

From this moment on, Lacan embarks on a journey in his teachings that 15 years later takes him to his great propositions of *Lituraterre* (*LTE*) and the creation of a discourse theory that can logically articulate two levels or heterogenous dimensions of language: representation—of meaning—and production—of *jouissance* (Tomšič, 2015, pp. 204–208). During this long period of time Lacan devoted great effort to the formalization of an impossible relation between two levels or heterogenous aspects, and that is where the development of the *vel* of alienation, the discourse *matheme*, and topology patiently await the time for their reception by a new generation of Marxist theoreticians, as necessary theoretical inputs to reanimate the old problem of the foundation/superstructure relation.

Translated from Spanish by Carla Tirado-Morttiz

## Notes

1 The term "*Überbau*", which also appears in *The German Ideology*, rarely appears in the mature work of Marx.
2 "Thus the ego, trustee [syndic] of the most mobile functions by which man adapts to reality, reveals itself to us as a power of illusion or even deception; it is that it is a superstructure engaged in social alienation" (*ICM*, p. 129).
3 Slightly modified translation.
4 Slightly modified translation.
5 The signifier "Stalin's Theorem" belongs to Jean-Claude Milner (1995), who formulates it as follows in *L'œuvre claire*: "Language is immune to major cuts (or in political language), language is immune to revolutions" (p. 52).
6 The authorship problem of the texts from the so-called Bakhtin's Circle in which V. N. Voloshinov, P. N. Medvedev, and I. Kanaev participate is still subject to revision.
7 See Stalin (1950).

## Further reading

Larrain, J. (1991). Base and Superstructure. In: T. Bottomore (Ed.), *A Dictionary of Marxist Thought* (pp. 45–48). Wiltshire: Blackwell Publishers, 2001.
Mounin, G. (1976). Marxismo y Lingüística. In: *La lingüística del siglo XX* (pp. 235–261). Madrid: Gredos.
Szemerenyi, O. (1986). *Direcciones de la lingüística moderna*. M. Martínez (Trans.). Madrid: Gredos.
Williams, R. (1977). *Marxism and Literature*. New York: Oxford University Press.

## References

Althusser, L. (1965). *For Marx*, B. Brewster (Trans.). London: Verso, 2005.
Althusser, L. (2018). *What is to Be Done?*, M. Goshgarian (Trans.). London: Polity Press, 2020.

De Lara, Ph. (1999). Superstructure. In: G. Labica & G. Bensussan (Eds.), *Dictionnaire critique du marxisme* (pp. 1106–1111). Paris: PUF.
Gramsci, A. (1971). *Selections from the Prison Notebooks*, Q. Hoare & G. N. Smith (Trans.). New York: International Publishers, 1992.
Lenin, V. I. (1909). *Materialism and empirio-criticism*. London: Wellred Books, 2021.
Milner, J.C. (1995). *A Search for Clarity: Science and Philosophy in Lacan's Oeuvre*, E. Pluth (Trans.). Chicago: Northwestern University Press, 2020.
Stalin, I. (1950). *Marxism and Problems of Linguistics*. Moscow: Foreign Languages Publishing House.
Stalin, J. (1950). A propos du marxisme en linguistique I, (Pravda, 20.06.50). In: L.-J. Calvet (Ed.), *Marxisme et linguistique* (pp. 147–179). Paris: Payot, 1977.
Tomšič, S. (2015), *The Capitalist Unconscious*. London: Verso.
Voloshinov, V. N. (1929). *Marxism and the Philosophy of Language*, L. Matejka & I. R. Titunik (Trans.). Cambridge: Harvard University Press, 1973.

# Chapter 24

# Surplus-*jouissance*

*Nadia Bou-Ali*

—Ara.: فائض المتعة - فائض القيمة —Chi.: 附加享受-附加值 —Fre.: *Plus-de-jouir* —Ger.: *Mehrlust* —Ita.: *Plusgodere* —Jap.: 剰余享楽－剰余価値 —Port.: *Ganho de prazer* —Rus.: *Прибавочная стоимость* —Spa.: *Plus-de-goce* —Tur.: *Zevk – Artı/k Değer*

→*Labour*; *Market*; *Proletarian*; *Value*

Surplus-*jouissance* is a fundamental concept for Jacques Lacan and has a singular function for the constitution of unconscious mechanisms. It is a crucial concept for understanding the relationship between psychoanalysis and politics. Surplus-*jouissance* is related to signification, discourse, and repetition in modernity. The concept of *jouissance* that Lacan develops is based on Freud's analysis of pleasure in his meta-psychological works (*Beyond the Pleasure Principle* and *Civilization and its Discontents*). Freud argued that pleasure cannot be understood in terms of a homeostatic principle, as a release of "instinctual" pressures and demand. Pleasure does not result from the satisfaction of needs, but from an accidental stimulation that is experienced at the site of satisfaction of "need" (the oral, anal, scopic, etc.) (Freud, 1920, 1930). The satisfaction of needs produces an accidental by-product, pleasure, which is experienced in the absence of the object of satisfaction. The impossibility of pleasure marks subjects with a "beyond of pleasure" (*Mehrlust*). Freud singles out two mechanisms through which pleasure functions: (a) pleasure is derived from contrast, from stumbling upon an object of satisfaction which is always a re-found object (an object that has always been lost); (b) pleasure is derived in repetition, no object can satisfy a desire yet the status of object of satisfaction is maintained for the subject in their desire. Freud's most notable example of the emergence of "pleasure beyond pleasure" is the child at the breast: although the demand for the breast is initially a demand for the satiation of hunger, the child experiences at the oral orifice (the mouth) an excitation that is no longer attached to the object-breast but which becomes an incessant demand for satisfaction. The cry of hunger transforms into a demand for satisfaction beyond the object-breast and is directed at the Other. Through this example we can see that Freud places the subject within a dialectic of desire before even coming into speech.

DOI: 10.4324/9781003212096-24

For Freud, primal repression, the negativity implicit in desire, is constitutive of the unconscious. Desires are by default always already repressed and what emerges from that repression is pleasure. There is something about repression, about renunciation that produces an excess element—or a surplus in economic terms—i.e., the repressed element is a negation which is affirmed. This expelled element, the excess, is thereby sought outside the subject and is a fundamental component of fantasy which in turn structures our experience of reality. Freud's "reality principle" dictates that all pleasure will be "found-again" pleasure in "outside reality": to refind an object is to convince oneself that it is already "out there". Affirmation and negation then produce three different things: the pleasure principle, the reality principle, and the place of their difference, the unconscious.

In this way, Freud argued that pleasure is derived from a contrast, an impossibility of satisfaction. Psychoanalysis would be the study of how this impossibility (pleasure in unpleasure) marks the subject through language, in both body and speech. Symptoms emerge from repression and they are evidence of how subjects suffer in regimes of pleasure that they have been unconsciously locked into. Pleasure beyond pleasure, Freud (1930) argues, is the "quantum of energy" or the libido that drives civilization, and sublimation or repression is "a conspicuous feature of cultural development" (p. 95). Freud proposed that the neurosis of modern civilization is symptomatic of the human condition, which is troubled by desire and negativity. He singles out neurosis as the symptom of modernity: what characterizes neurosis is a fundamental ignorance towards libidinal functions. Neurosis (obsessive compulsions, hysteria) is a symptom that covers up the "non-rapport" in which subjectivity finds itself; it is a way of coping with the unbearable excess of life itself.

Freud (1921) argued in *The Ego and Group Psychology* that social formations are characterized by libidinal functions. The libido is characterized by negativity (loss of pleasure for the gain of pleasure) and excess, which drives a process of repetition. Society is not simply a collective of individuals but of relations of identification that bind it together and that also carry the possibility of its dissolution. In *Group Psychology*, Freud uses for the first time a graph or a *matheme* to represent the relationship between individuals, the leader, and the group. In his analysis, Freud argues—against Le Bon's distinction between individual and group and against group psychologists who claim that group formations are regressive—that the individual and the collective both stem from the same structure of identification. Both are the result of an unconscious primary process or structure of identification. Individuals are retroactively constituted through the introjection of an ideal-ego, and the group is constituted through the projection of an ego-ideal that has to be assumed to exist outside the individual. The libidinal lack of distinction (between inside and outside) is what generates both exteriority and interiority (*Innenwelt* and *Umwelt*). Love is what Freud calls the "libidinal binding" that occurs in identification processes: love is crucially a sublimation of aggression: it is the transformation of the desire to put one's self in the place of another in mechanisms of identification. In other words, the desire to *be* an Other conflicts with the desire to *have* an other. This conflict is displaced or cathected in a symptom which develops in the place of this irresolvable antagonism.

Lacan restated this problem of the split between the *Ich* and *Ideal-Ich* (*The Four Fundamental Concepts of Psychoanalysis*) as what "is in you more than you". Sociality is then not a regression to primitive instincts (as group psychologists would claim) but is based on the mobilization of unconscious mechanisms that work through libidinal binding: group formations (like the army and the church) mobilize unconscious mechanisms politically. Freud's political theory (or Freud's account of the political, the group, the collective) proposes that mechanisms of identification are not individual: the individual is nothing but the knot of social ties (Dolar, 2008, p. 17). Thus, both society and the individual in Freud's account emerge from the negativity implicit in the process of identification: there is an implicit impossibility in social unification, and from this impossibility are generated imaginary unities. The leader or master signifier is an accidental point at which a group of "egos" project their fantasy. This implies that the basis of a social bond is always open to disruption and instability. Freud suggests that the source of this disruption is the drive (a surplus element, an excess, a derailment): while Eros, or Love, is the force of libidinal binding there is a "murderous underside" (Dolar, 2008, p. 22) to love which threatens it constantly with dissolution. Every libidinal binding (love which represses aggression towards the other) is threatened by compulsions (return of the repressed) from within.

Lacan argues that Marx shares Freud's account of conflict and antagonism (or non-relation) as the core impasse of sociality and that both Marx and Freud perceive society as a site of conflict and antagonism (a correlation that Althusser also signals, 1993, p. 229). This non-relation is foreclosed through regimes of enjoyment and characterized by a logic of repetition, which is in turn sustained by knowledge, *savoir*. For Lacan, Marx and Freud both uncovered the "truth" of the non-relation: they uncover that the truth is always half-said or that there is a discourse that is unsaid in all saying, i.e., that there is a difference between an utterance and a statement, and this difference has material implications. While Freud asks "How can we know without knowing?", Marx asks "How is capitalist society structured around actions that are bereft of knowledge?" In other words, how is that we act (in social relations built around commodity exchange) unconsciously? Lacan's formulations of discourse, or the different logics of a social link, will bring together Marx and Freud: the social relation is driven by an unconscious knowledge and this knowledge reveals itself in repetition through the logic of surplus or excess.

Marx (*CAI*) argues that labour power is a source of capitalist accumulation only once it takes the form of surplus-value, when it is valorized as a commodity. This surplus-value is what drives capitalist accumulation and mediates social relations, both objective and subjective. The logic of excess in capitalist society is the source of the valorisation of value, it both structures social relations (relations of imaginary identification) and gains an autonomous status (symbolic value that appears as autonomous from imaginary identifications). Surplus-value constitutes the mechanism of the compulsion of capital to repeat its circuit of gaining profit. For Marx, value is always already surplus-value: labour as a commodity is unconsciously a source of value. There is no value inherent in labour power itself: even if we consider it as an expenditure of energy, it is a loss, an expenditure that is entropic by nature, and it is only in capitalist society that it has come to be counted as surplus. Alenka Zupančič argues that "capital makes waste count". It is in this sense that labour is a source of value that does not know itself as such. This unconscious knowledge has to be discursively assumed in the social (non) relation. Elaborating on Marx, Lacan calls labour a "knowledge that does not know itself" (*SXVII*, 17.12.69, p. 30).

Lacan maintains that there is an unconscious element that operates in discourse, or the social link: this element is knowledge (or labour power for Marx), and enjoyment is what characterizes this unconscious knowledge. Freud's "drive" [*Trieb*] is what Lacan will later call "surplus-enjoyment". Lacan also renames Freud's process of identification the "unary trait". Lacan argues that the "knowledge" which originates in processes of identification is an imaginary knowledge that does not know itself and is motivated by *jouissance*. It is what grounds the social link or discourse. *Thanatos* compels *Eros*: knowledge is on the side of the death drive and not instinct. Discourse is structured around an entropy, a *jouissance*, which Lacan compares to the Jar of Danaides: a bottomless pit which churns out an endless repetition of surplus-*jouissance*. This *jouissance*-cum-knowledge is related to the death drive (and not instinct):

> knowledge is what brings life to a halt at a certain limit on the path of *jouissance*. For the path towards death—this is what is at issue, it's a discourse about masochism—the path towards death is nothing other than what is called *jouissance*.
> (*SXVII*, 26.11.69, p. 18)

Lacan makes a crucial distinction here however, between *jouissance* and castration, arguing that *jouissance* is what emerges from the loss of castration, from the appearance of a whole that we call *I* whose unifying image represents the subject with a loss. Lacan's theory of the drive is too complicated to recount here; however, it is crucial to distinguish between drive (*jouissance*) and signification.

In *Seminar II*—one of his earliest and richest seminars—Lacan proposes that Freud introduces the notion of information, or "the signifying chain", as that which emerges through repetition. Lacan reads Freud's *Beyond the Pleasure Principle* as an explanation of the need for repetition that goes against the logic of adaptation and biology. The crucial point here is not simply that man is a dis-adapted animal, but that the need for repetition is different from the logic of adaptation, and *jouissance*—which compels the need for repetition—is beyond biological death. As Lacan puts it: "pleasure principle is concrete dissolution of the corpse" (19.01.55, p. 80). He adds: "life is only caught up in the piecemeal, decomposed" (p. 90). This state of "caught-upness" of life in its own decomposition through repetition, in *jouissance*, excretes a system of "information", a chain of signification, that corresponds to the Real. Life is concerned solely with dying, with its own decomposition: "life doesn't want to be healed", "life is a detour", "ex-sisting life" (*SII*, 18.05.55, p. 233). The example that Lacan gives is adapted from the "wisdom" of a gambler: life is nothing but a throw of dice. However, this doesn't mean that life is always left to chance, entirely contingent, open to possibility. Rather, Lacan insists that the game of dice is always a game of loaded dice: "the very notion of probability and chance presupposes the introduction of the Symbolic into the Real" (*SII*, 30.03.55, p. 182). The symbolic, which involves the introduction of desire through speech, is structured like a machine. However, signifiers are not exhausted by the symbolic, they are collateral to it but not saturated by it. If life is a play of loaded dice, the odds are that desire will always fail its object, and the signifier calls it even, but there is always another throw of dice.

This brings us back to the relationship between knowledge and enjoyment insofar as the former sustains the imaginary idea of a whole. The first example that Lacan gives of unconscious knowledge that supports the social link and discourse is that of the slave's labour (*SXVII*, 17.12.69, p. 30): the slave's labour [*savoir faire*] operates invisibly to sustain the discourse of the Master ($S_1$). In other words, the slave works for the Master's knowledge and enjoyment. The Master is the "subject supposed to know" *how* it is that the slave is put to work, and all the Master has to do is to give a sign, an order, or a command to get them to work. Knowledge in turn is what guarantees the Master's discourse: it serves as a battery of signifiers that ensue after $S_1$. This "knowledge" is the "other side of psychoanalysis": what psychoanalysis seeks to question or de-base.

Lacan represents discourse using a formalization with four positions: agent (top left), truth (bottom left), other (top right), and product (bottom right). In *Seminar XVII*, he outlines a theory of four discourses: the discourse of the Master; the discourse of the Hysteric; the discourse of the Analyst; and the discourse of the University. The discourses are represented by four clockwise permutations of the four positions (Schema 4).

Despite the differences between the four discourses, they are all driven equally but in different ways by a desire for knowledge (*savoir*). Knowledge, for Lacan, is the "Other's jouissance". Knowledge (*savoir*) is what sustains a chain of signification or a "signifying battery" (*SXVII*, 26.11.69, pp. 12–13).

In the theory of four discourses, Lacan argues that the function of analysis or the discourse of the Analyst is to create a separation between the subject of knowledge (subject of *jouissance*) and the subject of the signifier. Psychoanalysis proposes that speech in the analytic context is different from everyday speech: the signifiers that present themselves in free association create a "desire for knowledge" or a "desire for the Other's enjoyment" (*SXVII*, 26.11.69, p. 23) that weaves a chain of signification retroactively in search of a new $S_1$. Discourse or the social link, which the discourse of analysis lays bare, is already structured around a

Discourse of the Master

$$S_1 \longrightarrow S_2$$
$$\frac{\phantom{S_1}}{\$} \times \frac{\phantom{S_2}}{a}$$

Discourse of the University

$$S_2 \longrightarrow a$$
$$\frac{\phantom{S_2}}{S_1} \times \frac{\phantom{a}}{\$}$$

Discourse of the Hysteric

$$\$ \longrightarrow S_1$$
$$\frac{\phantom{\$}}{a} \times \frac{\phantom{S_1}}{S_2}$$

Discourse of the Analyst

$$a \longrightarrow \$$$
$$\frac{\phantom{a}}{S_2} \times \frac{\phantom{\$}}{S_1}$$

*Schema 4* The four discourses. Source: Schemas adapted from Lacan (*DDP*, p. 40).

fundamental disjunction between $S_1$ and $S_2$. Lacan argues that $S_1$ and $S_2$ are linked together through *savoir* and not *connaissance*, knowledge and not representation. However, this knowledge is not a "knowledge that is known" (*SXVII*, 26.11.69, p. 23). In the Master's discourse, labour constitutes this unconscious knowledge. In the University discourse (or the modified Master's discourse, as Lacan calls it), knowledge becomes enjoyment, i.e., the workers are not only dispossessed of their *savoir faire*, they are also restituted for their dispossession with enjoyment or *jouissance* by the Other's enjoyment and surplus-enjoyment. This means that in the University discourse, which coincides with the development of capitalism, the enjoyment of the Other is constantly affirmed and the non-existence of the Other disavowed. The dominant element in the University discourse is $S_2$. $S_2$ is the element that occupies a place which orders the discourse: it is a mutation of the discourse of the Master, whose dominant element is $S_1$ or the law. Lacan elaborates two other structures of discourse, the Hysteric's and the Analyst's. In the Hysteric's, the symptom (or barred $) is the dominant element, while in the Analyst's discourse, *a* or surplus is the dominant in discourse. All the discourses, besides that of the Analyst, are motivated by knowledge: the Master steals the knowledge of the worker, the University restitutes *jouissance* in the place of knowledge, and the Hysteric demands or fabricates a "desire to know" out of the impasses of the non-relation, thereby revealing that the Master does not know and that truth lies in the symptom. In all the discourses, $S_1$, the master signifier, makes the Other emerge as a field and $S_2$ acts as the "trojan horse of the Big Other" (*SXVII*, 17.12.69, p. 33). $S_2$ "populates the stomach of the Big Other" and carries a knowledge "that is not known". $S_2$ provides the Other with a battery of signification. $S_2$ is used interchangeably by Lacan to mean both knowledge and enjoyment, with the understanding that *jouissance* marks the subject in their body and speech: this marking by *jouissance* is not transgressive (as the law would be for instance); rather, it is excessive, characterized as a "wearing away", or as an "effect of entropy" (*SXVII*, 14.01.70, p. 50). Most importantly, surplus-*jouissance* is always an effect of the group that acts within the subject and on them.

In the Master's discourse, $S_2$ is the slave's labour; in the University's, $S_2$ is in the position of the Master; in the Hysteric's, $S_2$ is relentlessly questioned: where does the desire to know come from? It is only in the discourse of the Analyst that $S_2$ takes the position of truth, which would mean the annulment of *jouissance* that is necessary for a new $S_1$ to come forth and institute a discourse of a different sort. Psychoanalysis reformulates the hysteric's question—Hegel being Lacan's example of the hysteric *par excellence*—"where does the desire to know come from?" into "how is it that we know without knowing?" Lacan argues that this separation between truth and knowledge is what he shares with both Marx and Freud (*SXVII*, 17.12.69, p. 37). Both recognized that truth is always what is half-said and that the status of truth is foreclosed in discourse: it is always masked in the pursuit of a knowledge in enjoyment, a surplus of enjoyment, which proceeds by the claim that something has been lost and must be recovered. This foreclosure is the foreclosure of castration *through* loss.

Marx, Freud, and Lacan question the wasting or wearing away, the surplus generated by entropy. Some scholars have argued that the relation between them is one of homology (Tomšič, 2015). Homology implies a materialist consequence: if the analyses of Freud and Marx's are true, then so is Lacan's, but if they are both false then there is still an implication of truth in Lacan. The homological relation is premised on a shared account of structural negativity in the social relation, a negativity that can and must be thought against its reification in theory. There are multiple critiques of homology as a relation and these critiques effectively question the ontological status of negativity in psychoanalysis and Marx. There is an ongoing but unresolved debate in Lacanian psychoanalytic theory with regard to theorizing negativity: a bifurcation exists between Adrian Johnston and Lorenzo Chiesa on the one hand; and Alenka Zupančič, Mladen Dolar, and Slavoj Žižek on the other.

Briefly put, the Real in Lacanian parlance is not an ontological determination; it cannot be thought without the Kantian destitution of metaphysical ontology. Yet it is irreducible to Kantian transcendental philosophy and more akin to the Hegelian account of the immanent materiality of the symbolic order itself. The early Lacan resorted to cybernetics, rather than Hegel, to argue for a non-transcendental account of the symbolic. Lacan invoked the machine against the transcendence of the symbolic. His claim that between Freud and Hegel lies the machine can be understood in these terms: beyond Freud's apparent dualism (of instinct and drive), Lacan offers an account of the symbolic according to which it is not an a priori regulating principle of life: the imaginary ego in the human has an alienating function, while the symbolic introduces the function of separation. Alienation and separation are the premises for understanding the *matheme* or formula of fantasy. While for Hegel the subject and the other are somewhat equal in the struggle for recognition, for Lacan the subject in its confrontation with the other drops out of the picture. The mirror stage is the story of the disappearance or *aphanisis* of the subject, i.e., the ego or the imaginary identification that captures the subject comes in the place of a non-existing subject. In other words, the subject only retroactively emerges when faced with an imaginary identification, an Other from small other to Big Other. The oft-repeated joke used by the Slovenian school to articulate this type of subjectivity is the one about a request for coffee without milk from a waiter who retorts that they don't have coffee without milk, but only coffee without cream. This "with-without" status of the subject implies that there is no subjectivity prior to the Other, and that the encounter with the Other only affirms the subject as an "empty set": there is no subject without the Other, but no subject with Other; the Other is with-without the subject. The subject is without or has no being, and only appears in the field of the Other. What comes back to the subject is not really its image (the image is de-formative, as Lacan argues in the *Mirror Stage*) but a signifier, a sign that comes back "to petrify the subject in the same movement by which it calls the subject to function, to speak, the subject" (*SXI*, 27.05.64, p. 207).

Signification captures the labouring subject and entraps it in a dialectic that is pre-linguistic, and that persists after the entry into language. The chain of signifiers constitutes discourse, or the social link, and is the place where the subject's conduct and actions are inscribed. The inscription into a social relation, into sociality, is only possible through the disavowal of negativity, of the non-rapport or alienation, which characterizes subjectivity. The subject is then caught up in discourse "that which is a structure without speech" (*SXVII*, 26.11.69, pp. 12–13). *Jouissance* has the singular function of keeping a discourse together and soldering it, while surplus-*jouissance* is produced by discourse. Although the concept of *jouissance* emerges in Lacan's early lectures—*Formations of the Unconscious (SV)*—and surplus-*jouissance* in his later seminars (*Seminar XVI* and onwards), Lacan maintained from the outset that "jouissance is already surplus-jouissance" (*SXVII*, 26.11.69, p. 19).

The intervention of the symbolic, of language, is a moment when the subject becomes immersed in everyday speech, or empty speech; immersed in the materiality of language. It is here that the first signifier is inaugurated, the Ego-ideal or $S_1$ of signification. What Lacan calls the "unary trait", or the trait of one-ness, puts into effect an $S_2$, a chain of signification. Ultimately, alienation is the forced choice of the subject through which he comes to be subject without being, present only in the field of the other. Lacan will then argue that the Other is also lacking; that lack presents itself in the field of the subject and the other:

> the desire of the Other is apprehended in the subject in that which does not work, in the lacks of the discourse of the Other, the child's *why* reveal not so much an avidity for the reason of things, as a testing of the adult, a *Why are you telling me this?* ever-resuscitated from its base, which is the enigma of the adult's desire.
> 
> (*SXI*, 27.05.64, p. 214)

The subject asks the Other: can you lose me? The subject devotes themselves to the enjoyment of the Other, desire is always the desire of the Other. This desire is what constitutes fantasy and commodity fetishism is the reigning fantasy that organizes social relations in capitalist society.

The use value of labour for Marx (the *savoir* of the worker) is a fantasy that is retroactively assumed in making that loss of labour count, or in turning entropy into surplus. Value marks the fantasy of capitalist society: surplus-value is the object-cause of the social link organized around the exchange of labour as a commodity. Lacan will claim that the logic of surplus-value is knowledge at work, a specific articulation of signification, and that work is nothing but signifiers at work (*SXVII*, 14.01.70, p. 50). The principle of exchange value in capitalist society is a contingency turned into necessity: surplus-*jouissance* is enjoyment taken from the subject and given to the Other; it is the Other's enjoyment. In Lacan's theory of discourse there is a "recognition of the discursive dimension of enjoyment" (Zupančič, 2006, p. 155). In capitalist society, a shift in discourse occurs:

> we are no longer dealing with the form of repetition characteristic of the Master's discourse. Instead, we have an endless movement where the otherness linked to the surplus (enjoyment) is smoothly and constantly reintegrated into the mass of capital, which needs this constant differentiation and reappropriation of the differential as a condition of its increasing power.
>
> (Zupančič, 2006, p. 170)

This shift is premised on the counting of surplus as enjoyment.

While Freud had maintained a number of designations for *jouissance* such as joy, ecstasy, libido, sexual satisfaction, sexual pleasure, and pleasure, Lacan unified Freud's various designations into the concept of *jouissance* as that which is "always of the order of tension, of forcing, of expenditure, even of exploit. *Jouissance* is undoubtedly there at the point where pain begins to appear" (*PEM*). This pleasure in pain is excessive and not transgressive: for Lacan (1969–1970) it is akin to a "squandering" and is characterized by being an excess element. Furthermore, *jouissance* for Lacan is always already a "loss of sexual jouissance" and a loss of castration. The object-cause of desire, or *objet petit a*, opens up a "gap/hole" or a "lack in jouissance" (*SXVII*, 26.11.69, p. 19); a lack in knowledge. In other words, the *objet a*, which is the main effect of the discourse of analysis, puts *jouissance* into question because *jouissance* makes it appear that there are verifiable objects of desire which are posited as stand-ins for the object of the drive.

*Jouissance* is derived from the verb *jouir* and it is used by Lacan in different forms: *jouissance* and *joui-sens*. These different designations distinguish between enjoyment experienced in the body and an enjoyment that is without a body. Lacan argues in *Seminar XVII* that surplus-*jouissance* as imitation (semblance) is the glue that holds together modern capitalist society. Enjoyment characterizes discourse *tout-court*; it is the inherent impossibility of pleasure that characterizes desire and the drive. However, in capitalist society where the Master's discourse morphs into that of the University, enjoyment is emptied of the impossibility that underlines it: now there is an injunction to enjoy, a command to overcome the impossibility inherent to enjoyment—which is the inner limit of pleasure. Late capitalism promises that the impossible is no longer possible, that nothing is impossible. The impasse of late capitalism is that of an enjoying Other; value enjoys on our behalf, surplus-*jouissance* is a singular universal. Our *jouissance* doubles that of structure: *jouissance* is doubled in surplus-*jouissance*.

## Further reading

McGowan, T. (2004). *The End of Dissatisfaction? Jacques Lacan and the Emerging Society of Enjoyment*. Albany: SUNY Press.
Miller, J-A. (2000). Paradigms of Jouissance. In: *Lacanian Ink*, 17: 10–14.
Žižek, S. (2008). *For They Know Not What They Do: Enjoyment as a Political Factor*. London: Verso.

## References

Althusser, L. (1993). Sur Marx et Freud. In: *Ecrits sur la psychanalyse*. Paris: STOCK/IMEC.
Dolar, M. (2008). Freud and the Political. *Unbound-Harvard Journal of the Legal Left*, 4(15): 14–29.
Freud, S. (1920). Beyond the Pleasure Principle. In: *Standard Edition of the Complete Psychological Works of Sigmund Freud* (Vol. XVIII, pp. 1–64), J. E. Strachey (Trans.). London: The Hogarth Press, 1981.
Freud, S. (1921). Group Psychology and the Analysis of the Ego. In: *Standard Edition of the Complete Psychological Works of Sigmund Freud* (Vol. XVIII, pp. 65–144), J. E. Strachey (Trans.). London: The Hogarth Press, 1981.
Freud, S. (1930). Civilization and its Discontents. In: *Standard Edition of the Complete Psychological Works of Sigmund Freud* (Vol. XXI, pp. 57–146), J. E. Strachey (Trans.). London: The Hogarth Press, 1981.
Tomšič, S. (2015). *The Capitalist Unconscious*. London: Verso.
Zupančič, A. (2006). Surplus Enjoyment as Surplus Jouissance. In: J. Clemens & R. Grigg (Eds.), *Jacques Lacan and the Other Side of Psychoanalysis* (pp. 155–178). Durham: Duke University Press.

# Chapter 25

# Uneasiness/discontent/unhappiness

*Nadir Lara Junior*

—Ara.: ارتباك —Chi: 不適 —Fre.: *Malaise.* —Ger.: *Unbehagen.* —Ita.: *Malessere.*
—Jap.: 不安 —Port.: *Mal-estar* —Rus.: *Недовольство.* —Spa.: *Malestar.* —Tur.: *Huzursuzluk.*
→ *Capitalism; Consumption; Ideology; Politics; Society*

Sigmund Freud used the concept "uneasiness" in the title of his work *Das Unbehagen in der Kultur*, written in 1930. Jacques Lacan proposed his understanding of the term based on Freud's work. In French, it is written "*malaise*"; in Portuguese, it is written "*mal-estar*", and in Spanish, "*malestar*".

## Lacan's comments on *Das Unbehagen in der Kultur*

"Civilisation, you know, does not get rid of any discontent, as Freud remarked, quite the contrary, *Unbehagen*, the not being at ease, but anyway it has a precious aspect to it" (*PAM*, 04.11.71). Lacan uses the above sentence in the context of the Saint Anne hospital, where ignorance about the care of the mentally ill was the norm until Henri Ey got to be the "civilizer of such ignorance". Lacan points out that Freud writes "*Unbehagen*" (uneasiness), not only "not-well-being", and society does not spare us the feeling of such uneasiness, like the uneasiness that came from the ignorance towards the mentally ill.

Lacan questions knowledge and non-knowledge, as well as their relation with the psychoanalyst's knowledge. When referring to the idea of Freudian resistance, he says that the latter ultimately becomes "not wanting to know". In this sense, "uneasiness in culture" is a revolution proposed by Freud that brings about a subversion of both the function and the structure of knowledge. That is why this Freudian scheme is part of the Copernican revolution, which turns around man's comprehension of his own world, the space where he lives. Lacan states that the "I", the ego, is the knowledge that is known, and what psychoanalysis brings as something new is showing that this knowledge is not known by itself. In addition, such knowledge that is not known is structured like a language. Therefore, this not-known knowledge operates at an unconscious level.

Lacan recovers Freud's *Beyond the Pleasure Principle* and says that the fundamental pleasure is directly related to the death drive. Pleasure responds to death! "Because the dimension of enjoyment for the body is the dimension of the descent towards death". Therefore, surplus-enjoyment is the production of displeasure for mere pleasure and death. In this sense, Lacan says that in *Das Unbehagen in der Kultur* Freud argues for a "beyond" the pleasure principle, and also "if not that very probably well beyond the repression described as social, there ought to be – he writes it textually – an organic repression" (*SXIX*, 04.11.71). Sexuality is at the core of everything that happens in the unconscious. There is no sexual relationship. For the speaking being, pleasure is not limited to copulation, since the latter is a religious matter. And enjoyment (*jouissance*) is not limited to the sexual act, "the only enjoyment is to die" (*SXIX*, 04.11.71). Hence, the psychoanalyst's knowledge is in a place that is entirely different from the death drive and in opposition to uneasiness. This knowledge consists of knowing one's place in relation to the analysand in order to be able to sustain knowledge as a semblace.

In *Seminar XIX*, Lacan says that in Plato's *Symposium* there is a certain degree of sexual frenzy, whose parallel can be found in the Master's discourse, which produces symbolic castration: "From Socrates onwards, this knowledge of *jouissance* was only to survive on the fringes of civilization, not without thereby feeling what Freud discreetly calls *its discontents*" (*SXIX*, 10.05.72, p. 148).[1] Thus, uneasiness is a concentrated form of enjoyment (*jouissance*) which is an effect of the symbolic castration. It is represented by the "object *a*" in the algebraic scheme of the Master's discourse. Underdevelopment propagates as a condition of capitalist progress. The more a society develops, the more underdevelopment proliferates.

## Uneasiness and psychoanalysis

When he was delimiting the structure of the French School of Psychoanalysis, Lacan (*FA*, p. 97) established a few vital pillars for the formation of psychoanalysts. For him, the school must stand upright in the Freudian field in order to restore "the cutting edge of his discovery" and, in this way, denounce deviations and concessions in its praxis that may harm the use of psychoanalysis in its formative process:

> Namely for a labor, I have said as much – which in the field opened up by Freud restores the cutting edge of his truth – which brings the original praxis he instituted under the name of psychoanalysis back to the duty incumbent upon it in our world – which, through an assiduous critique, denounces the deviations and compromises blunting its progress while degrading its use.
>
> (*LD*, p. 129)

For this purpose, Lacan points out that the dimension of criticism and self-criticism of the analytical practice within the school, the dialogue with other sciences, and the respect for the ethics of psychoanalysis become important strategies for psychoanalysis to go back to Freud, and to respect the movement of the time in which it came about.

Freud's name should not be used to confront Marx's name considering the differences between them. Lacan tells us that "Marxism fails to account for an increasingly immoderate and insane power insofar as politics is concerned". However, psychoanalysis could contribute with its analysis exposing the contradictions of such "political madness". Lacan reaffirms that, in the Freudian field, his understanding of the term "school" is opposed to cultural uneasiness. In its field, what is of value is the critique and the basis of experience resulting eventually in a kind of lifestyle that functions as a key of the psychoanalyst's formation (*FA*, p. 104).

In *Seminar XIII*, Lacan comments on texts by André Green, Claude Conté, and Charles Melman (22.12.65). The authors discuss the psychoanalytic cure departing from the psychoanalyst's speech (word—*parole*). In this context, the above-mentioned authors state that, in the process of the cure, the analyst's speech could remove the analysand's bodily and somatic sensations of uneasiness. Something in the process of transference of the analytic experience operates in such a way that the analyst's speech (which is in the position of object *a*) disarticulates the feeling of uneasiness.

In *Seminar XXI*, Lacan also presents us with some key figures that have discussed the analytic experience, not as a norm, but as a form of developing analysis. To explain analysis as a process, he defines the unconscious as a structured knowledge that requires a connection between signifiers, and later defines it as a form of inconsistent knowledge. For this reason, unlike what biology states, "life has nothing natural about it" (11.06.74), and analysis allows the subject to elaborate his unconscious knowledge.

In this sense, it is the analyst's position that allows us to operate in the state of free-floating attention during the analysis. It allows the analysand to elaborate his/her own thought and, at the same time, the analyst can be thinking something completely different. The interval between these two moments is when an interpretation can be produced. In the free-floating attention stage the analyst listens to everything "through" what the patient is saying, and this allows the analyst to be wary of where his/her thoughts come from, that is, his/her own semiotics, emerging from the former existence of *lalangue*:

> [I]t [semiotics] comes from nothing other than the ek-sistence of *lalangue*. *Lalangue* ek-sists elsewhere than in what he believes to be his world. *Lalangue* has the same parasitic quality as phallic enjoyment, with respect to all other enjoyments. And it is what determines as parasitic in the Real what is involved in unconscious knowledge.
>
> (*SXXI*, 11.06.74)[2]

Lacan describes that the phallic enjoyment (*jouissance*), referring to the penis, becomes a kind of privileged enjoyment within society. Meanwhile, the analytic experience demonstrates that the phallic logic is characterized by the privilege, if we may say so, of the sexual meaning. This was Freud's initial idea when proposing his theory. However, Freud realized in *Civilisation and its Discontents* "that meaning is only sexual because meaning is substituted precisely for the sexual which is lacking" (*SXXI*, 11.06.74). Meaning does not reflect the sexual, but rather substitutes the sexual. The function of *lalangue* is to "semioticize" all scattered and confused feelings. This function allows words to be preached in all senses, and that is the reason why *lalangue* is key in the analytic process.

## Uneasiness: aggressiveness, violence, and crime

Lacan's goal in his presentation *Aggressiveness in Psychoanalysis* is to show how the concept of aggressiveness can be considered and applied scientifically. The death instinct lies at the core of the notion of aggressiveness. Aggressiveness is constituted and manifests itself as a subjective experience. The analytic experience helps us understand aggressiveness. In the analytic experience, we can read the symbolic meaning of the symptom and, in changing from the imaginary axis to the symbolic, the subject becomes less defensive and its fundamental fantasies become manifest. Therefore, in this relationship, the subject recreates something of its everyday subjectivity. Aggressiveness becomes part of the ego and of everyday social relations. Therefore, aggressiveness takes on an important role both in the constitution of modern neurosis and also in the uneasiness of civilization.

Lacan highlights Darwin's study on the law of natural selection over living beings where aggressiveness appears as something natural in the sphere of animal human nature. However, he also highlights that Hegel, when presenting the master–slave dialectic, goes back to human ontology where aggressiveness becomes part of subjectivity. It is, then, constitutive of the "I" and is socially organized in culture.

> From the conflict between Master and Slave, he deduced the entire subjective and objective progress of our history, revealing in its crises the syntheses represented by the highest forms of the status of the person in the West, from the Stoic to the Christian, and even to the future citizen of the Universal State
> (*AP*, p. 98)

In this way, Lacan affirms that Darwin's ideas are different from those of Hegel's dialectics, where the master imposes his logic of death where the fulfilment of desire goes through the work and desire of the other, namely, the slave. The Master exploits the slave and their relationship allows us to see that aggressiveness is not natural, like a pure animal instinct, but rather that when the master subjects another master tyrannically he extracts value from the work of the exploited.

Lacan emphasizes that the ego's self-preservation drive "willingly gives way before the temptation to dominate space, and above all the extent to which the fear of death, the 'absolute Master'" (*AP*, p. 100). In the attempt to dominate space there is a subjective tension where the uneasiness in culture is displaced as anxiety and develops in a temporal dimension. At the crossroads of this subjective tension is where Lacan claims that Freud located the death drive. Therefore, in modern society this results in a subject that can never feel at ease: "It is a self-punishing neurosis, with hysterical/hypochondriacal symptoms of its functional inhibitions, psychasthenic forms of its derealizations of other people and of the world, and its social consequences of failure and crime" (*AP*, p. 101).

This modern subject combines aggressiveness, violence, and crime as elements capable of producing uneasiness in culture. In *A Theoretical Introduction to the Functions of Psychoanalysis in Criminology*, Lacan puts forward the argument that psychoanalysis in the area of criminology will help elucidate the doubts regarding the notion of responsibility of the modern subject. These scintillating points of the subject that are to be elucidated are related to the uneasiness in culture which "lays bare the articulation of culture and nature". However, psychoanalysis does not give us an account of the entire sociological context nor of all the mechanisms that push our society towards uneasiness (*FPC*, p. 104).

In the modern subject, super-ego introduces itself as a regulatory instance, but one that also organizes the human being in its totemic relationship to law and crime. Therefore, in a society characterized by utilitarian ideals and determined to remain in the capitalist mode of production, the idea of punishment is substantially transformed because the ideals of humanism subject themselves to the utilitarianism of the group. And this idea of punishment is then treated as a humanitarianism, whose power norms take advantage of "the revolt of the exploited and the guilty conscience of the exploiters, to whom the notion of punishment has become equally unbearable" (*FPC*, p. 112). This is also a reflection of social uneasiness, that is, the tension between the exploited and the exploiters that functions as the basis for the social uneasiness, reflected as well in the production of violence, which is often not recorded in the criminal analyses for the enforcement of punishment.

## Uneasiness: the exploitation of a few over others

When Lacan presents the logical origins of the surplus-enjoyment he directly mentions the Hegelian master–slave dialectic: "The speaking being believes he is two, namely that, as they say, he is master of himself" (*SXVI*, 11.06.69). The first belief refers to the being seeking the ideal—the mere prestige of becoming *one with the slave*. The second goes back to the ethical level—the slave functions as the master's ego-Ideal (the body that obeys), since the Master makes sure that the slave is a body that obeys. The slave asks the master for what he needs, hence there is an exploitation of the person over the person.

Lacan takes into account that the exploitation of the person over the person is found at the ethical level in a society that takes as its point of departure the exploitation of some over others while attempting to find prestige and produce wealth. The product of this social ethic is the culture's uneasiness. And if we follow this logic in our society, there is always someone acting as the master to dominate people, namely: "this procedure of the 1 that is equal to 1, of the game of mastery, the Trojan horse absorbs more and more into its belly, and that costs more and more. That is the discontent of civilisation" (*SXVI*, 11.06.69).

Lacan goes back to Hegel to present the master as "one", meaning, as one under whose domain the slaves can be found. Lacan rescues the image of the Trojan horse: the horse represents the one that bears many men in its stomach in order to dominate another master and, thus, to obtain more slaves and wealth. Therefore, the uneasiness in culture follows the logic of the domination of one person over another. In the game of one against one, the master is pulled against the master in a battle searching for the prestige of becoming one with the slave. Liberal society recovers its enjoyment from the exploitation of labour, that is, enjoyment lies in the body. Repetitive obsession at work produces surplus-enjoyment. Lacan is referring to our society when he says: "You have your body, it belongs to you. Only you can dispose of it so that it finds itself in the frying pan" (*SXVI*, 11.06.69). This subject is working "freely" in favour of capital.

In the logic of the capitalist mode of production the labour of the worker becomes a commodity with use-value, in other words, a thing that will serve to fulfil needs, in this case the capitalist that contracts the worker to produce. In this way, the labour-power remains separate from the mode of production. For this reason, the labour orders the worker to use its physical and mental force to accomplish the process of transforming nature into products. The subject modifies nature and also modifies his/her body to better perform the tasks for the chain of production. However, in capitalism, the subject acquires "freedom" to sell its own body for capital. Its body is a product with a certain exchange-value for money and in this operation money is treated as a symbolic and imaginary representation of the capital. Marx argues:

> Our capitalist has two objectives: in the first place, he wants to produce a use-value which has exchange-value, [...]; and secondly, he wants to produce a commodity greater in value than the sum of the values of the commodities used to produce it, namely the means of production and the labour-power he purchased with his good money on the open market.
>
> (*CAI*, p. 293)

Lacan (*SXVII*, 18.02.70, pp. 88–101) goes back to Hegel to remind us that the master finds his truth in someone else's work, in the slave who loses his/her body and from whom the master accumulates his enjoyment. On the other hand, Lacan tells us, from psychoanalytic experience, that the master is castrated, and this is the repressed truth from its origin. As can be seen in the *matheme* of the Master's discourse, the bar makes sure that the truth is not revealed to the other—$S$ in the position of truth (18.02.70, p. 92). Work, in this case, functions as that which sustains the obstruction of the truth in the relationship between the master/employer and the slave/worker.

The Master's discourse is not mythical, because it is supported by the scientific discourse. That is why it functions under the logic that there is something true and something false, which greatly excludes knowledge produced by the unconscious, as it does not fit into this kind of scientific knowledge, which deals with truth as a game of values. Psychoanalysis works with unconscious knowledge, therefore it rejects this kind of scientific knowledge, precisely because it demonstrates the exploitative logic of society under the aegis of the master.

Unlike mathematical logic, in which A, for instance, has a meaning in itself so that it can operate in an equation, signifier $S$ can signify anything except itsself, precisely because it needs to be linked to a chain of signifiers, since its self-reference is produced as a relationship effect.

> Here, at this crossroads, we state that what psychoanalysis enables us to conceptualize is nothing other than this, which is in line with what Marxism has opened up, namely that discourse is bound up with the interests of the subject. This is what, from time to time, Marx calls the economy, because these interests are, in capitalist society, entirely commercial. It's just that since the market is linked to the master signifier, nothing is resolved by denouncing it in this way. For the market is no less linked to this signifier after the socialist revolution.
>
> (*SXVII*, 18.02.70, p. 92)

The discourse of the Hysteric reveals the relationship between the discourse of the Master and enjoyment (*jouissance*) since the hysteric is not a slave (*SXVII*, 17.12.69, pp. 32–33). She goes on some kind of strike and does not hand in her knowledge, but rather asks for the Master's knowledge. In the same vein, the hysteric reveals the truth that he is castrated when she does not place herself as the object of his desire by showing that she does not feel represented by his knowledge.

Lacan goes back to Freud to say that, in a dream analysis, the dream represents not only a present desire of the subject, but finds its foundation in a childhood desire. Lacan relates the master's function to capitalism given that his desire to accumulate capital stems back from a childhood desire, from the immaturity of excluding other forms of enjoyment and sticking only to surplus-enjoyment.

Lacan questions how much "one can play at doubling surplus enjoyment or nothing with eternal life" (*SXVII*, 18.02.70, p. 100), because what is at stake is the performance of the super-ego where, for instance, God becomes an invested object, an object *a,* the object cause of desire. In this sense, Lacan returns to Freud in order to tell us that:

> Yes, this recourse to the myth of Oedipus is really quite sensational. It is worth making the effort to elaborate this. And I was thinking of getting you today to appreciate what is outrageous in the fact that Freud, for example, in the last of the *New Introductory Lectures on Psychoanalysis*, should think he had cut the question of the rejection of religion off from any acceptable horizon, should think that psychoanalysis has played a decisive role in this, and should believe that it was the end of the matter when he has told us that the support of religion is nothing other than this father whom the child has recourse to in its childhood, and who he knows is all loving, that he anticipates, forestalls what may manifest itself within him as malaise.
>
> (*SXVII*, 18.02.70, p. 100)

Lacan, based on Freud, will show that the father is castrated from the outset, because, in Freudian theory, the primordial father is assassinated by his children, and then ends up being loved by them. Thus, this father figure is inscribed in the phallus which is equivalent to the master's phallus. In *Seminar XVIII*, Lacan tells us that surplus-enjoyment is at stake in the Master's discourse. The phallus is the signifier of surplus-enjoyment. There is no sexual relationship because enjoyment is possible with a semblant. Phallus is the name of the father and, in this vein, "the woman is precisely in this relation, this relationship, for man, the moment of truth" (20.01.71). On the contrary, man suffers from uneasiness as he sustains the enjoyment and the semblant. And in this way, he operates in the discursive logic of surplus-enjoyment. Woman has greater freedom regarding the semblant; man, on the other hand, obtains nothing. That is the reason why in *Seminar XVII*, Lacan affirms that the Hysteric's discourse runs counter to this phallocentric logic.

## Uneasiness produced by the Master's discourse

If, on the one hand, the discourse of the Master appears to be unambiguous, it is because it covers up the subject's division. On the other hand, psychoanalysis puts forward the argument that the subject is not unambiguous but, rather, it is divided/castrated ($). In the Master's discourse *matheme*, the divided subject ($) can be found in the position of truth, which, conversely, is precisely hidden by the bar so that this castrated master does not become visible in the discursive operation.

> What have I said, in effect, about any possible saying [*dire*] in the place of truth? The truth, I have been saying, can only be stated via a half-saying [*mi-dire*], and I have given you a model for it in the enigma. For this is how it is always presented to us, and certainly not in the form of a question. The enigma is something that presses us for a response in the name of a mortal danger. Truth is a question, as has been known for a long time, only for the administrators. "What is truth?" We know by whom that was, on one good occasion, eminently pronounced.
>
> (*SXVII*, 11.03.70, p. 103)

In the Master's discourse, truth, as a half-saying, takes advantage of the condition of the divided subject (*Spaltung*) in order to cover itself rather than entirely displaying itself. In the University discourse (*SXVII*, 10.12.69, p. 20), $S_1$ is located in the position of truth, that is, truth as master-signifier, because it operates by organizing how the Master's discourse is implemented, and science becomes its strategy *par excellence* to formalize its goal. $S_1$ in the position of truth becomes the subject's duty to not cease knowing and continue seeking even more knowledge. And, in this position, the scholar takes a student and makes him/her produce something (theses, dissertations, etc.); Lacan uses the term "astudied" to refer to students taken as object *a* (*SXVII*, 11.03.70, p. 105).

By calling the supposed subject of science into question, Lacan tells us that the uneasiness of the "astudied" lies precisely in the fact that they are summoned to be subjects of science. Science takes these people as humus and renders them available for the discourse of the Master which, conversely, takes them as slaves ($S_2$) and imposes the duty: Always work more! Produce surplus-enjoyment! Thus, Lacan (*RA*) argues that Marx helps our society to understand the fundamental concept of surplus-value, which is shown to be the cause of the capitalist's desire. He also states that Freud could guess this operation in unconscious terms, which Lacan will call surplus-enjoyment. In this sense, the only thing that Freud and Marx have in common was that they considered a certain number of facts as symptoms.

In this way, the capitalist produces a use-value (a merchandise) with exchange-value (selling products). In this process the capitalist needs to have money to buy raw material and to pay the production and cost of labour. In addition, the capitalist aims to recover the invested value and also gain some surplus-value. The surplus-value is produced from labour-power which the worker does not get paid for. "The rate of surplus-value is therefore an exact expression for the degree of exploitation of labour-power by capital, or of the worker by the capitalist" (*CAI*, p. 326). In this capitalist operation there is always accumulated work which is the result of a previous process that adds to the labour in the manufacturing of the product. The perfection of the products makes us ignore the previous work added to the product. Then one is under the impression that the products are the true owners of capital. The worker puts his/her labour under the capitalist domain. As Marx shows,

> he creates surplus-value which, for the capitalist, has all the charms of something created out of nothing. [...] What distinguishes the various economic formations of society, the distinction between for example a society based on slave labour and a society based on wage-labour – is the form in which this surplus labour is in each case extorted from the immediate producer, the worker.
>
> (*CAI*, p. 325)

Uneasiness resides in the fact that the subject is exploited in the capitalist system and it produces surplus-value. Freud also hints that the unconscious also operates in this uneasiness and produces surplus-enjoyment. Surplus-enjoyment, in the capitalist society, functions as the truth of work, thus propelling the movement of the signifying chain.

Lastly, Lacan (*SXVII*, 11.03.70, p. 102) claims that "Or rather analysis draws its importance from the fact that the truth of the Master's discourse is masked", that is, the discourse of psychoanalysis questions the truth of the capitalist Master's discourse. In other words, it wonders about the capitalist master being a castrated subject who takes the other of its relationship and makes him work in order to maintain its status quo. The discourse of psychoanalysis cannot agree with the capitalist system, precisely because it should not stir up uneasiness in culture.

## Notes

1 Lacan's emphasis.
2 Transl. modified.

## Further reading

Cabas, A. G. (2019). *Marx com Lacan. A ideologia Alemã*. Curitiba: Lummer.
Pavón-Cuéllar, D. (2017). *Marxism and Psychoanalysis In or against Psychology?* London: Routledge.
Stavrakakis, Y. (1999). *Lacan and the Political*. London: Routledge.

Chapter 26

# Value

*Jean-Pierre Cléro*

—Ara.: قيمة —Chi.: 價值 —Fre.: *Valeur* —Ger.: *Wert* —Ita.: *Valore* —Jap.: 価値 —Port.: *Valor* —Rus.: Стоимость —Spa.: *Valor* —Tur.: *Değer*

→ *Capitalism*; *Economy*; *Market*; *Politics*; *Surplus*-jouissance

Even if it appears that Lacan brilliantly linked the concept of the Marxist surplus-value and the surplus-enjoyment (*plus-de-jouir*) that he developed for psychoanalysis, this link is far from being an immediate and totally original occurrence. It is necessary to reorient this discovery, which seemed inevitable, even if an insightful and legitimately recognized researcher such as Albert O. Hirschman (1977) strangely missed it. In Hirschman's unforgotten and suggestive book, *The Passions and the Interests*—whose subtitle, *Political Arguments for Capitalism Before its Triumph*, seems very important for our inquiry—the author emphasized the gradual substitution, in the classical era, of the power of explaining human phenomena, for an interest that is usually related with the passions, but never completely replaces it. Hirschman adeptly shows that the discourse on passions came to terms with the discourse on interest, even though the latter seemed to dominate and appeared to speak the real, whereas the first one only spoke about its interpretation or its fiction. It is possible to suspect that, within the RSI system, which was developed very early within the first sessions of the Seminar, and was never questioned again, Lacan had all the means to formalize this idea. Hirschman did not have a serious and in-depth reading of utilitarianism, and specifically of its main founder, Bentham, and Lacan, on the other hand, was very keen on noticing his importance from the beginning. It is not the right time to question if Hirschman, who wrote his book more than a decade after the work we are going to analyze, has an excuse for ignoring the notion of *utility*. Instead, in the last chapter of Bentham's (1843) *Pannomial Fragments*, we will retrace the missing link that will allow Lacan to construct a powerful homology—the word he tackles on the lesson from 27.11.68—[1] between the "surplus-value" of the economists in the wake of Marx, and the "surplus-enjoyment" of psychoanalysis. Lacan immediately saw the advantage of the theory of fictions, while he trusted others to explore the Panopticon as if it were the essential component of Bentham's work, while the most important part resided elsewhere.

Those who believed they could substitute the interest for the game of passions, even though they would have admitted there was a "passional" residue from the operation, did not see the ensuing link—and it is remarkable that Bentham uses arithmetic or algebraic "mathemes" to express it. Bentham was not the first to notice—Maupertuis (1751),[2] who was a fine mathematician, had already observed that when experimenting with what happens affectively when winning or losing the same amount of money, by varying the magnitude of this sum in relation to the initial capital, the noted effects can appear to be "really" symmetrical, except in the affective level: there is more pain in losing a sum of money than there is happiness in winning it, even if the absolute value of the amount is the same. And Bentham tells us the reason: if a sum is won, this sum returns to the starting capital to which it is added while, if it is lost, the sum must be paid from the same starting capital from which the sum is subtracted. That is to say, $\Delta S / (S + \Delta S)$ is always smaller than $\Delta S / (S - \Delta S)$. We notice, with this very simple *matheme*, that there is no symmetrical effect of the addition or withdrawal of $\Delta S$. However, economically speaking, the symmetry seems to be necessary. Such notation might only have an anecdotal importance, but this has significant consequences for Bentham's conception and for Lacan, who does not quote these texts but rather presupposes them whenever he is dealing with passions.

There is no need to establish an opposition between what happens in economics and what happens in the domain of passions, even if the logic of goods and services is not that of passions: the logic of goods and services must always be reread as a logic of passions, and the logic of passions must also be capable of being transposed in economic terms, so that, in the same way that Adam Smith said that texts of law were the true treatises of the passions,[3] we can say that it is possible to read the economic treatises, like those of Smith, Ricardo, and Malthus, as treatises on passions; conversely, it is also possible to read the treatises on passions like economic treatises. It is therefore not a matter of absorbing, with or without remainder, the passional within the economic or of rendering the passional in economic terms: it is a matter of articulating them in the same equations, in the same mathematical expressions, reading them separately, albeit in a radical conjunction.

Departing from Aristotle's second book of *Rhetoric*, Lacan began making an interpretation that can only be described like that of the projective geometry of Girard Desargues. Then, the topology of Desargues turned out to be too geometric for his project, and thus Bentham's scheme began to function in an underlying way. The theory of value developed by Marx, which will interest Lacan for his research from the end of the 1960s—the first allusions to Marx, from this point of view, go back to November of 1968—and the beginning of the 1970s, which continue until the end of the Seminar, cannot ignore utility, conceived within the framework of a theory of fictions, and it cannot focus on interest by itself as separated from passions.

Lacan's work begins here. His *mathemes*, which are even in this field more algebraic than those of his predecessors, find their archaic foundations in the *Pannomion* but, to complete the task, the outline of the "calculation" found in Bentham is no longer enough, even if from the 1950s to the 1980s no one understood the interest of Bentham's link better than Lacan. Lacan's own contribution consists in bringing together two apparently heterogeneous sources, of which, if taken separately, he is neither the inventor nor the pioneer. The *first* lies in the functioning of pleasure, which both in its individual and collective evolution, tends to take less and less pleasure in its immediate fulfilment, without delaying what is likely to satisfy us, and at the same time takes more and more pleasure in organizing the very conditions of its fulfilment, of a desired pleasure that is imagined to be greater, but whose fulfilment is postponed. Surprisingly, one of the laws of pleasure is its destiny to return, to reverse itself. Instead of seizing pleasure as soon as it passes, the task is to obtain greater pleasure, but it is only possible if we work for this potential pleasure, while no longer having the illusion of fulfilling it, so we end up assimilating it to its production, which is immediately its opposite. The *second* entails considering the surplus-value, a notion derived from Marx's work.[4] Capital is obtained by purchasing commodities with added value, obtained only by making people work, so that whoever can buy this labour power sells it under the form of a modified commodity of higher value, which will be sold at market price; because the *entrepreneur* (business owner) is not the only one selling the manufactured products. What matters is to sell them at the best possible price so that the added labour is not paid to the worker at the price of the value he has added to the commodity to commercialize it. Lacan's ability lies in having understood that there was a certain identity between the two outlined processes: the affective process of the indefinitely postponed pleasure and the surplus-value that is constantly added to capital so that its operation always begins again.

It should be emphasized again that this is a quasi-identity and not merely an analogy (*SXVI*, 13.11.68):

> It is more than probable, and for a good reason which is that we have, for that, introduced the surplus enjoying. That one can consider that this absolutization of the market is only a condition so that surplus value can appear in discourse. There was therefore required this thing that can with difficulty be separated from the development of certain effects of language, namely, the absolutisation of the market to the point that it encompasses labour itself, for surplus value to be defined in the fact that in paying with money or not, with money because we are in the market, for labour, its true price, as the function of exchange value is defined in the market, there is an unpaid value in what appears as the fruit of labour, in a use value, in what is the true price of this fruit. This unpaid labour, even though paid in a correct fashion with respect to the consistency of the market, this, in the functioning of the capitalist subject, this unpaid labour is the surplus value. It is the fruit of the means of articulation that constitutes the Capitalistic discourse from capitalist logic.

Freud was not the first one to discover that *jouissance* is essentially masochistic, always postponing the fulfilment of pleasure:

> This is where the function of the lost object originates in Freudian discourse. And there is really no need to remind you that it is explicitly around masochism, conceived only in the dimension of the search for this ruinous *jouissance*, that Freud's entire text revolves.
> (*SXVII*, 14.01.70, p. 46)

Hegel (1807), and before him Hume, also knew it: pleasure deviates from itself by turning towards elaborating what constitutes its conditions, and by repeating the same operation. There is no reason why one consumes more pleasure than the pleasure one has produced for the sake of turning away from another pleasure. From postponed pleasure to postponed pleasure, the subject no longer enjoys anything. He turns away from life and glides towards realizing a desire of death (*désir de mort*). Lacan correctly underlines the interest of Freud's analysis of the death instinct (*l'instinct de mort*):[5] —almost *instinctively*, which is not well chosen, because there is a human fabrication in question and it is by no means natural—and he particularly highlights the repetitive nature of the process: and in the repetition, pleasure and even enjoyment is lost: "in repetition itself there is a reduction in *jouissance*" (*SXVII*, 14.01.1970, p. 46). It must be specified that *to repeat does not mean to do exactly the same thing*, but to resume the same operation along with what allowed us to modify the situation the first time, then a second time, and so on. The process of postponing is reiterated and becomes the law of pleasure itself, its sombre law.[6]

Regarding the indefinite production of surplus-value by capital and its relentless accumulation, many economists have identified and recognized their causes in labour. Hume notes how difficult it is to transform all professions into merchants of their own labour power. They obtain the least enjoyment possible from what they produce and save to the point of being greedy of what they would always rather return to the circuit of production.[7] However, he thinks that there is no other economic system capable of producing wealth and that, even if it appears directly contrary and hostile to human nature, human nature will nevertheless owe its deliverance to it, and will modify itself as a consequence of this necessary scansion: to work not to consume more, but rather to work more to become always richer, that is, in a function of greed that is the same as that of the merchants (*marchands*). The thinker of pleasure becomes the apologue of work. It is important to understand how this is an inversion that goes even further than the one that Rousseau articulates when he explains what gave rise to agriculture: instead of eating the seed I have in my hands, I sow it so that it multiplies itself a few months later, provided that I renounce nomadism and settle down, transforming the land I occupy into a property, accepting a system for defending it, etc. Now it is a matter of postponing pleasure by enjoying it phantasmatically and symbolically by relying on money to represent both the pleasure I do not obtain, and that I am supposed to find multiplied at the end of a process that distracts me from any living accomplishment other than work. A mad machine began acting on my behalf, dispossessing me, not of the right to enjoy what could be pleasurable, but of every opportunity to do so, and anxiety takes its place.

Lacan identifies the scheme of the functioning of affectivity—composed of pleasure and displeasure—with that of production, circulation, consumption, goods, and services. And, like Bentham and Maupertuis, he states it in mathematical terms. However, where Bentham's discourse was only concerned about a $\Delta S$ that was added or subtracted from an $S$ sum, as well as the double reading of the two isolated and not well-developed relationships we have cited, the Lacanian discourse will be based on processes that are indefinitely reiterated and whose consequences allow a mathematical expression of a certain breadth. Lacan's favourite scheme for expressing both surplus-enjoyment and surplus-value is the Fibonacci sequence, which he begins to employ on 22 January 1969; and then he names it the following week, on 9 January 1969. Neither Marx nor the economists who preceded him, nor the theorists of passions were aware of its relevance and pertinence.

We obtain a Fibonacci series by taking each of its terms such that they are the sum of the two preceding ones, starting with 0 and 1. The sequence of numbers is the following:

1 1 2 3 5 8 13 21 ...

This is a Fibonacci sequence. We can generalize it by noting it as follows:

$U_0 = 1$ ; $U_1 = 1$ ; ... ; $U_n = U_{n-1} + U_{n-2}$

As such, it captures very well a certain kind of accumulation or agglutination that comes from earlier terms. This kind of capitalist accumulation takes place according to this model, provided that, however, there is an exceptional surplus-value, which has nothing in common with the surplus-value that is commonly and empirically gained on the market. The scheme, however, is valuable if it is considered abstractly as the basis for the capitalist affair under ideal conditions where he has no competitors in the market: having competitors always reduces the margin of capital growth, instead of increasing it or stabilizing it on a given value. Up to a point, the scheme might also be capable of expressing the sequence of pleasures as long as they are considered as pleasures that renounce themselves for the sake of an even greater pleasure, whose "realization" or fulfilment is just as uncertain as the renounced pleasures.

Lacan, however, goes much further than tracing an analogy between the affective system and the economic system and he is not satisfied with Bentham's double reading of the series with his variations on $\Delta S/S$. Lacan wants to write and formalize this double reading, instead of allowing it to be loose, and he then obtains a double sequence of Fibonacci numbers. There is a discrepancy (*decalage*) between the first terms of the sequence and the second ones, but they are nevertheless arranged in such a way that the terms relate to one another. Through this system, Lacan's intention is to tie the capitalist system of surplus-value with the affective system of pleasure-displeasure that has become that of *jouissance*, which is not equivalent to pleasure—one can find *jouissance* in that which is the opposite of pleasure. Hence, it is possible to write:

1 2 3 5 8 13 21 34 55 ...

and:

2 3 5 8 13 21 34 55 ...

Superimpose these two series, and then, instead of considering only one relation, such as Bentham did ($\Delta S/S$, with its two variations, $\Delta S/(S+\Delta S)$ and $\Delta S/(S-\Delta S)$, according to that, having the sum S, we have won or lost one of its fragments denoted $\Delta S$), Lacan can rightly examine an infinite amount of them, especially in their relation to one another:

1/2 2/3 5/8 8/13 13/21 21/34 34/55 ...

Thus, the $\Delta S/S$, with its two variations, $\Delta S/(S+\Delta S)$ and $\Delta S/(S-\Delta S)$, which was the limit of what Bentham considered, is replaced here by a sequence which has as its property, when we divide 3 by 2, 8 by 5, 13 by 8, etc., tends to – as the numerators are gradually larger – towards the same number, $(1 + \sqrt{5})/2 = 1,618033988...$ One should not be surprised by the fact that this number is the so-called golden ratio or golden mean,[8] since it can be demonstrated. However, what matters here is that there is a fast stabilization, and then a quasi-stability of the relations thus ordered in the series, that is to say, those that are placed in relation to one another. What is of interest in Marx, for Lacan, is not only that with the S sum we can make the sum (S+$\Delta S$) if one wins—whether in *Mehrwert* or in *Lustgewinn*—and (S−$\Delta S$) if one loses, and then compare [$\Delta S/(S+\Delta S)$] to [$\Delta S/(S-\Delta S)$], but rather to understand, with more clarity and to a greater extent, how is it that with S one can make S+$\Delta S$ = S', which becomes S'+$\Delta S$', which becomes S'', etc. This mechanism [($\Delta S/S$) → ($\Delta S'/S'$) → ($\Delta S''/S''$) → etc.] is the one that links subjects to each another, and that makes some of them rich, others impoverished and destroys others, without anyone seemingly able to do anything about it. This is what is of interest for Lacan, even more than the singularity of the terms he brings into play. It is important to notice that we can hold on to the propositions of the *Pannomion*—and, moreover, that the Fibonacci sequence is analyzed both in the sense of being additive (the capitalist gain), and subtractive (which could suggest a loss)—but it is less what happens with regard to a relationship than the sequence of its wrapping (*enveloppements*) what Lacan is interested in following. Even though there is a discrepancy (*décalage*) between the cause of surplus-enjoyment and the cause of surplus-value, they uphold the same real that Lacan writes about: it is more than an "affective" reading of economic phenomena or an economic reading of affective phenomena. Their knot (*noeud*) is tied in the same place. Lacan expressed this in different ways. Through this discrepancy (*décalage*) he intends to provide the added value the meaning of a "*mémorial du plus-de-jouir* (memorial to surplus-enjoyment)". And, moreover, this equivalent of the surplus-enjoyment is considered to be "homogeneous" to surplus-value (*SXVII*, 11.02.70, p. 81). Lacan went a step beyond Bentham, and he encourages us, by restoring the notion of affect that he had previously despised at the beginning of his Seminar,[9] to understand *Capital* as a sort of treatise on the passions, while giving us a hypothesis about work as it is alienated when assimilated as a commodity.

However, what is not clear in Lacan's brilliant analysis is the relationship of Fibonacci's mathematics with the real or with empiricism. If, as Lacan said, mathematics is the real (*SXX*, 20.03.73, p. 93), and the unconscious is of their order (*SXXV*, 10.01.78), then they articulate and organize the functioning of things better than any other experience for which they provide a reason. But Lacan is too great a practising clinician to accept this dangerous proposal and to not to give enough space for experience. Mathematics seems only to provide a useful scheme for describing what happens both in economics and in affects, without there being any ground for claiming that it is an explanation. Hume and Bentham clearly supported this last thesis (Hume, 1748, p. 28). Lacan, however, hesitates more on this key issue, which somewhat taints his remarkable discovery. At the end of the 1960s and at the beginning of the 1970s, other authors, like E. Coumet, were able to demonstrate the extent to which Pascal's mathematics—underlying both the wager and the problem of the division of the stakes—were linked to an already dominant liberalism.

There is more to say about this equivocal point. Lacan tried to demonstrate that his theory of the object *a* was in agreement with the mathematization of the presentation of the matrix of the Fibonacci sequence, 1/ (1+a). The problem is the equivocal nature of the term "object *a*", even if we stay within the context of the late 1960s and early 1970s. The object *a*, which began signifying the other, as opposed to the Other, the remainder of which is the result of a symbolization when it is measured against the real, ends up signifying the excess of *jouissance*, which has no other use value than that of continuing to produce the conditions of imaginary pleasures that wrap (*s'enveloppent*) each other and will never be realized. But is there a coherence in the different uses of the term object *a*? Interestingly, Lacan is so concerned about saying the same thing, that several decades later, he sometimes poignantly suggests that the *a* could signify the increasing number of workers bound to making the surplus-value with a labour that will never be paid to them.

> Namely, if you wish, the number of slaves at stake. […] is from the *a* that I called the *surplus enjoying* in so far as it is what is sought in the slavery of

the other as such [...] It is in the fact, for the master, of having *the disposition of the body of the other*, without being able to do anything more about what is involved in his enjoyment, that there resides the function of the surplus enjoying.

The link of *a* with the disposition of the body of the other allows us to see

the body's rate, if I can express myself in this way, of what in this dialectic passes into exploitation, this rate of the body participates as they say in the same style, of the logically prior rate of the *surplus enjoying*. Whether 5 + 3a can come or not come to possess, as they say, 3 + 2a, it nevertheless remains that 3 had all the same its 2a, these 2a that are inherited from 2, from the still earlier stage. The body, the body idealised and purified of enjoyment, calls for the sacrifice of the body.

(*SXVI*, 04.06.69)

Lacan went quite far in this direction in trying to explain racism as different from the idealization of race. If, as Lacan diagnosed at the beginning of the 1970s, the underdevelopment of many parts of the world is "the condition for the progression of capitalism", then

whoever is a little bit interested in what may happen would do well to tell himself that every form of racism, in so far as a surplus enjoying is very well capable of supporting it, is now what is on the agenda. This is what is in store for us in the years to come.

(*SXVIII*, 13.01.71)

As one of the possible interpretations, it is both unexpected and interesting to see how Lacan inserts racism in the link between surplus-value and surplus-enjoyment.

Nothing prevents us from putting forward a metaphysical interpretation of the discrepancy or gap (*décalage*) that we have identified between the sequence or the series of surplus-value and that of surplus-enjoyment. In *Le pur et l'impur*, Jankélévitch (1960, pp. 42–43; 52–53; 60–62) shows how the soul cohabits with the body precisely by emphasizing this discrepancy. However, as it can be now understood, this is neither Marx's point of view nor Lacan's. Undoubtedly, Lacan thinks that the "counterpoint" that Jankélévitch mentions is more effective in the form of arithmetic and algebra than in the discourse of the University or the metaphorical discourse of the "pure" and the "impure". But if this metaphysical reading is still possible, it is because even if mathematics have become more refined from Hume to Bentham, from Bentham to Marx, and from Marx to Lacan, they still remain at the threshold of calculations: they do not have the consistency that game theory already had acquired at the time in which Lacan was writing, and it is not known to which units this applies nor what these displaced double series refer to. Lacan seems to be thinking of large units, going along the line of what utilitarianism has become today, as seen, for example, in T. Mulgan.

Translated from French by Christina Soto van der Plas

## Notes

1 "This surplus enjoying appeared, in my last talk, in function of a homology with respect to the Marxist surplus value. Homology, clearly means –and I underlined it– that the relation is not one of analogy. It is indeed the same thing that is at stake. It is a matter of the same stuff in so far as what is at stake is the scissors' mark of discourse" (*SXVI*, 27.11.68).
2 See especially the first two chapters.
3 Adam Smith (2002): "Systems of positive law, therefore, though they deserve the greatest authority, are the records of the sentiments of mankind in different ages and nations" (p. 403).
4 See Marx (*VPP*) and Marx (*CAI*), Chapters: The Production of Absolute Surplus-Value, The Production of Relative Surplus-Value, and The Transformation of Surplus-Value into Capital.
5 "Enjoyment would tend, Freud tells us when he tries to elaborate what is at first only articulated metaphorically, to lower the threshold necessary for the maintenance of life. This threshold that the pleasure principle itself defines as an infimum, namely, the lowest of the heights, the lowest tension necessary for maintaining this. But one can fall still lower, and that is where pain begins and can only be exalted, if really this movement, as we are told, tends towards death. In other words, behind the affirmation of a phenomenon that we can hold to be linked to a certain context of practice, namely, the unconscious, it is a phylum of a completely different nature that Freud opens up with this beyond" (*SXVI*, 13.11.68). "The coherence given of the mortal point, then conceived without Freud underlining it, as a characteristic of life but in truth, what people do not think of is, in effect, the fact that we confuse what is non-life, and which is far, my word, from not stirring up the eternal silence of the infinite spaces that dazed Descartes. […] What is called the inanimate world is not dead. Death is a point, is designated as a terminal point, a point at the term of what? Of the enjoyment of life" (*SXVIII*, 13.01.71).
6 "What necessitates repetition is *jouissance*, a term specifically referred to. It is because there is a search for *jouissance* as repetition that the following is produced, which is in play at this stage of the Freudian breakthrough what interests us qua repetition, and which is registered with a dialectic of *jouissance*, is properly speaking what goes against life. It is at the level of repetition that Freud sees himself constrained, in some way, by virtue of the very structure of discourse, to spell out the death instinct […] It means that repetition is not only a function of the cycles that life consists of a cycle that embraces the disappearance of this life as such, which is the return of the inanimate. […] As everything in the facts, in clinical experience indicates to us, repetition is based on the return of *jouissance*. And what, in this connection, is well spelled out by Freud himself is that, in this very repetition, something is produced that is a defect, a failure" (*SXVII*, 14.01.70, pp. 45–46).
7 David Hume (1758), in *Essays: Moral, Political and Literary*: "The man who has nothing to do short of one pleasure to another: "Give him a more harmless way of employing his mind or body, he is satisfied and feels no longer that insatiable thirst after pleasure. But if the employment you give him be lucrative, especially if the profit be attached to every particular exertion of industry, he has gain so often in his eye, that he acquires, by degrees, a passion for it, and knows no such pleasure as that of seeing the daily increase of his fortune. And this is the reason why trade increases frugality, and

why, among merchants, there is the same overplus of misers above prodigals, as among the possessors of land there is the contrary. Commerce increases industry, by conveying it readily from one member of the state to another, and allowing none of it to perish or become useless. It increases frugality, by giving occupation to men, and employing them in the arts of gain, which soon engage their affection, and remove all relish for pleasure and expense" (p. 309).

8 As Descartes (1684) in *Rules for the Direction of the Mind* says: "Those who attribute wonderful and mysterious properties to numbers do just that. They would surely not believe so firmly in sheer nonsense, if they did not think that number is something distinct from things numbered" (p. 61).

9 However ambiguous it might be, since affect remains an effect of discourse, this rehabilitation is clear in its response—it is truly very free, on 13 May 1970—to a public which reproaches him for not taking affects into account. He mentions anxiety as a fundamental affect. However, the "lived" side—*Stimmung* or *tune*—of affect is dismissed. Returning, eight days later on his declaration of 13 May 1970, Lacan affirms: "In effect, from the perspective of this discourse, there is only one affect, which is, namely, the product of the speaking being's capture in a discourse, where this discourse determines its status as object" (*SXVII*, 20.05.70, p. 175).

## Further reading

Landman, P. & Lippi, S. (2013). *Marx, Lacan: L'acte révolutionnaire et l'acte analytique*. Toulouse Érès.

Özselçuk, C. & Madra Y. (2010). Enjoyment as an Economic Factor. Reading Marx with Lacan. In: *Subjectivity*, 3: 323–347.

Pavón-Cuéllar, D. (2013). *Lacan, lecteur de Marx*. Rouen: Université de Rouen.

## References

Bentham, J. (1843). Pannomion. In: J. Bowring & W. Tait (Eds.), *The Works of Jeremy Bentham* (Vol. III, pp. 224–230). Bristol: Thoemmes Press, 1995.

Coumet, E. (1970). La théorie du hasard est-elle née par hasard? In: *Annales, Économies, Sociétés, Civilisation*, 25e année, mai-juin 1970, n° 3.

Descartes, R. (1684). *The Philosophical Writings of Descartes: Volume 1.*, J. Cottingham, et al. (Trans.). Cambridge: Cambridge University Press, 1984.

Hegel, G. W. F. (1807). *Phenomenology of Spirit*. New York: Oxford University Press, 1977.

Hirschman, A. O. (1977). *The Passions and the Interests: Political Arguments for Capitalism Before Its Triumph*. Princeton: Princeton University Press, 2013.

Hume, D. (1748). *An Enquiry Concerning Human Understanding*, T. L. Beauchamp (Ed.). Oxford: Clarendon Press, 2006.

Hume, D. (1758). *Essays: Moral, Political and Literary*. New York: Cosimo, 2006.

Jankélévitch, V. (1960). *Le pur et l'impur*. Paris: Flammarion.

Koshy, Th. (2001). *Fibonacci and Lucas Numbers with Applications*, Vol. I, Texte électronique, Hoboken, NJ: Wiley, 2018.

Maupertuis, P. L. M. de. (1751). *Essai de philosophie morale*. Berlin: Luzac Fils.

Smith, A. (2002). *The Theory of Moral Sentiments*, K. Haakonssen (Ed.). Cambridge: Cambridge University Press.

# Annex I. Transliterations

## Challenges of translating into Arabic
*Abdallah El Ayach*

### Subject

The term "subject" has been given multiple translations in the Arabic language which can broadly be categorized as logical/grammatical and ontological. Translators of Aristotelian philosophy, premodern philosophers Al-Farabi and Averroes, used the terms 'المحمول عليه' (*mahmūl ʿalayh*) and 'موضوع' (*mawdūʿ*) to designate the subject of a predicate ('المحمول', *mahmūl*). The latter terms for subject corresponded to the Greek word "ὑποκείμενον" (hupokeimenon), for they denote the meaning "that which lies under" (in Latin, *subjectum*). Notably, the grammatical form of the word 'المحمول عليه' (*mahmūl ʿalayh*) implies that a predication ('الحمل', *al-himil*) has been done onto a thing for it to be a subject. For that reason, the modern philosopher Moussa Wehbeh, translating Kant's *Critique of Pure Reason*, chose to reformulate the word into 'حاملة' (*hāmila*) which grammatically grants agency to the subject as a doer ('فاعل', *fāʿil*). After Wehbeh, modern Arabic philosophy employed the word 'حاملة' (*hāmila*) to mean the logical subject of a predicate, and 'موضوع' (*mawdūʿ*) to mean "subject matter" (*Gegenstand*).

In order to distinguish the subject at the logical order from the human subject, Arab thinkers in modernity chose the word 'الذات' (*al-dhāt*) to mean human subject. This term ('الذات', *al-dhāt*) was used by the premodern philosophers Al-Farabi and Averroes to designate both Aristotelean substance and essence. Averroes also argued that the most adequate use of the word 'الذات' (*al-dhāt*), with the definite article 'ال' (*al*), denotes the primary substances which are also termed 'جوهر' (*jawhar*). Adding the term 'ذات' (*dhāt*) without the definite article 'ال' (*al*) to the term "thing" ('شيء', *shayʾ*), as indicated by Al-Farabi, was used to mean "the thing itself" and "in-itself". It is worth noting that Averroes did not take the individual human to be the subject of thought, nor did subjectivity, in its modern conception, play a role in Averroes's thinking about the intellect. The only indication of subjectivity found in Averroes's writing resulted from a translation error performed by his Latin translator.

The modern use of 'الذات' (*al-dhāt*) to mean "human subject" did not prove to be problematic in the wake of Cartesian philosophy, for the Cartesian subject is a thinking thing (*res cogitans*). Descartes's subject was immediately a substance. Therefore, transposing 'الذات' (*al-dhāt*) to imply a "human subject" allowed the term to remain in close affinity to its original use implying substance. The term 'موضوع' (*mawdū'*) also witnessed a displacement to mean, within the paradigm of consciousness, "the object of a subject", making 'ذات - موضوع' (*dhāt – mawdū'*) the chosen translation of the "subject–object" relation. Moreover, the term 'الذات' (*al-dhāt*) was also employed to mean "the self", while keeping its original use as in-itself and for-itself when speaking of a "thing". What resulted was the use of 'الذات' (*al-dhāt*) to mean interchangeably "the self" (*Selbst*) and "the subject" (*Subjekt*), obfuscating any possible productive conceptual distinction.

The subject–object distinction, the conflation of self and subject, and the implication of substance in the use of the term 'الذات' (*al-dhāt*) do not allow for grasping the psychoanalytic problem of the Lacanian subject. For Lacan there is an excess crucial to the logic of subjectivity not accounted for when the subject is understood as the subject of an object. Moreover, the term 'الذات' (*al-dhāt*) indicates that we are speaking of a reified thing, entity, or substance. Implying in Arabic that subject is also immediately substance through the name 'الذات' (*al-dhāt*) does not allow the full grasp of the problem of modernity as theorized by Hegel. The name 'الذات' (*al-dhāt*) obfuscates the problem of mediation in the process of subject becoming subject. More so, such meaning and use of the term stands at a great distance from the notion of the psychoanalytic subject. The Lacanian relational subject cannot be substantialized nor does it designate a substrate. Moreover, the conflation between subject and self in the use of the term 'الذات' (*al-dhāt*) does not posit the psychoanalytic problem of the self being always already an-other. This distinction must also be present in the language itself. For these reasons, the use of the word 'الذات' (*al-dhāt*) in Arabic to denote the word "subject", in the psychoanalytic sense, prevents the Arabic language from speaking the problem of psychoanalysis specifically, and theorizing the problem of modernity (in a Hegelian sense) more generally. The crucial problem for psychoanalysis in Arabic becomes: if the language in question cannot speak of the problem of psychoanalysis how can it allow an understanding of the unconscious inscribed within it?

What appears as an impasse, produced by the repetitive act of translation, is actually an opportunity. It is an occasion to reformulate the problem of the subject of psychoanalysis within the Arabic language while keeping ourselves in close affinity to Lacan's formulation of the problem of the subject within language. As Lacan formalizes the subject in language, as the subject of the signifier, we find ourselves facing this opportunity and grappling with the language (linguistics) of the subject. The term 'هو' (*huwa*) in the Arabic language is used as the pronoun "him". It designates and signifies an implicit referent that is not present explicitly. In addition to its use as a pronoun, 'هو' (*huwa*) was also used by premodern philosophers to translate the Greek term 'ἐστιν' (*estin*, in English, "is"). The ontological meaning that 'هو' (*huwa*) took allowed premodern philosophers to derive the term 'هُوية' (*huwiyya*) to mean "being". The derived term 'هُوِيَّة' (*huwiyya*) more precisely indicated "the mode of being of a thing". In line with this linguistic formulation and the ontological understanding of identity, premodern philosophers designated the term 'الهو هو' (*al-huwa – huwa*) to mean identity (*idem* in Latin) and oneness. It must be noted that in modern philosophy the term 'هُوِيَّة' (*hawiyya*) became conventionally used to mean subjective "identity". Arab Heideggerian thinkers have occasionally designated 'الهُو' (*al-huwa*) to be "self", in order to theorize in Arabic, following Ricoeur, the problem of self as selfhood (*ipse*) and sameness (*idem*). Nevertheless, this problem is better captured in the term 'الذات' (*al-dhāt*) which both implies self and sameness.

Following Lacan's insistence on the linguistic formalization of the subject of psychoanalysis, the productive opportunity is to use in Arabic 'الهُو' (*al-huwa*) as a noun to mean "the subject". In this regard 'الهُو' (al-*huwa*) is a noun that is derived from the pronoun 'هو' (*huwa*) designating the implicit referent, which in turn has roots in the use of the letter 'ه' (*h*) that refers something to another. This formalization allows for 'الهُو' (al-*huwa*) to signify the implicit subject. Moreover, such use would deontologize identity, where 'الهو هو' (al-*huwa – huwa*) would explicitly indicate that identity is a process of identification which always entails a doubling of the subject. Such a translation could prove to be productive for both the Arabic language and the problem of psychoanalysis in Arabic. One example is deriving a word for subject that means "a subject to another" (subject to the law, or subject to the sovereign). French thinkers, such as Lacan, have taken the identity of the problem of subjectivity with the problem of subjection to be crucial to their thinking. In Arabic there is no word for subject in the sense of subjection, "a subject to another"; it usually takes various independent translations depending on the context. Designating 'الهُو' (*al-huwa*) as the subject allows us the opportunity to coherently produce a term for "a subject to another" that is derived directly from language, 'الهو لغيره' (*al-huwa li-ghayrihi*). Lastly, this exercise opens the following question regarding the philosophical projects underlying the act of translation in Arabic: how are we to transpose the materialist project inscribed in Lacanian psychoanalysis and Marxism without struggling within language with the Heideggerian fundamental-ontology project dominating translations of philosophy in the Arabic language?

## Challenges of translating into Chinese
### Tzuchien Tho

### *Plus-de-jouissance* 附加享受

The French verb "jouir" and its substantive "jouissance" is hard to translate in any language. It differs from "*plaire*" or "*se plaire*", and "*plaisir*". Hence "enjoyment" and "pleasure" is used, in English, to translate them. However, in standard Chinese there are no words to distinguish between these two French terms just as the difference between enjoyment and pleasure is minimal in English. Of course the introduction of the Marxist notion of "surplus" [*plus*] further complicates the issue. 附加享受 means literally "added enjoyment/pleasure" and takes its form from the standard translation of "surplus value" or the more common term "added value" 附加值. The key word here is 享 and can express both inner and external enjoyment. It can mean the partaking of something that is in one's own domain or the reception of something as a gift. The additional 受 has the same topological ambiguity. It can refer to the accepting or enduring of some external action as well as the feeling of something internal to the domain.

## Superstructure

The transliteration of "superstructure" as 超結構 combines the notion of prefix "super-" and "structure". Whatever is "super" is beyond. Yet, the "super" can also topologically be interpreted as the highest part of something, though not beyond it. This ambiguity is preserved in scientific domains and engineering where the terms 超結構 (super- or trans-structure) and 上部結構 (upper structure) are both used in different fields. Marxists tend to use 超結構.

## Value

The whole question here is the difference between value and profit. 價值 transliterates "value" in the most generic sense. It is generally used in a normative way, referring to "values" in the moral or cultural sense. The ambiguity of the moral and economic notion of the term "value" or "profit" is captured by the Chinese transliteration.

## Challenges of translating into Japanese
### *Hidemoto Makise*

### *Plus-de-jouissance* 剰余享楽

People describes one's age at death as "享年", using the word "享" of "享楽 (*jouissance*)" in Japan. Because the word "享" includes the meaning of being given something, receiving something, the word "享年" allows people to imagine the length of time that the dead have "been given", "received" their life from heaven. In this way of using words, we are not "living" beings, but "being given life" or "receiving life" beings. It seems interesting to find the connection between this and what Lacan conceptualized with the word "享楽 (*jouissance*)", or primitive life as an imperfect form of subjective life.

## Communism コミュニズム

"Communism" has been translated as "共産主義" until now in Japan. The "communism" that Marx aimed at was not something like the former Soviet Union that nationalized the wealth of society and the means of production, but a society based on the common. In other words, it is an equal and sustainable steady-state economic society in which everyone shares and autonomously manages so that the wealth of society does not appear as a product. I translated "communism" as "コミュニズム" to emphasize this point.

## Wealth 富

"Wealth" in Japanese is the word that makes us imagine goods that can be measured with money, such as money and real estate. "Wealth" that Marx refers to, however, also includes the fact that something is abundant, such as the abundance of clean air and water. Although it cannot be measured with money, what each person needs to live affluently is the "wealth" of society.

## Value 価値

"Value" in Japanese includes personal importance such as memories and affection. The "value" based on the labour theory of value mentioned by Marx, however, is determined by how much working time was required to produce the product.

## Work 労働

When thinking about "work" in Japan, we cannot forget the idiom "The man who will not work shall not eat". This work ethic encourages people to overwork, and more and more people commit suicide or suffer from depression. Theoretical development of Marx-Lacan will reconstitute the structural problems behind such problems and bring about new ways of working and living possibilities for the subject.

## Further reading

Kazushige, Shingu. (2019). Le saint homme-sinthome jouit - d'une autre façon que du discours capitaliste. In: *Iichiko quarterly intercultural*. Winter, 37–56.
Kohei, Saito. (2020). *Hitoshinsei no "Shihonron"*. Tokyo: Shueisha.

# Challenges of translating into Russian
## Maria Melnikova and Sergey Sirotkin

### Capitalism, communism, ideology

The concepts of Latin origin, for the most part, were integrated into the Russian language in the same form as into other European languages (for example, "capitalism [капитализм]", "communism [коммунизм]", "ideology [идеология]"). There are no difficulties in conveying these concepts.

### Uneasiness

"Uneasiness" can be translated as "недовольство". At least that is how the term is often rendered in the title of Freud's book *"Das Unbehagen in der Kultur"* (English: *"Civilization and Its Discontents"*). However, the English "uneasiness" is closer to another Russian notion: "беспокойство [disquiet]", "озабоченность [concern]".

### Freedom

"Freedom (Liberty)" is translated as "свобода (вольность)". At the same time, it should be noted that the concept of "freedom" does not fully cover the Russian concept of "воля (will)". Freedom is thought of as the absence of restrictions and will as an expression of desire. "Воля (will)" is etymologically closer to the German "wollen", "Wahl". It is also worth noting such a historical reality as the liberation from serfdom (19th century): "дать вольную (to give freedom)", "дать волю (to give free rein)".

### Master–tyrant

"Master–tyrant" is translated as "господин – тиран". Here, however, it should be noted that in the Russian language there is the word "мастер (master-hand)", which is not equivalent to the concept "господин (master)", but means "умелец (craftsman)", "тот, кто достиг значительных умений (one who has achieved significant skills)".

### Economy

"Economy" is translated as "экономика", in the sense of the economic activity of society, relations in the production system. Likewise, it is in the psychoanalytic sense of mental economics. At the same time, a different form is used in the

Russian language, the word "экономия (economy)" as "бережливость (thrift)", "выгода при бережливом использовании (profit with lean use)".

### Labour/work

"Work" often means "работа". In Russian, the term "work" is used in a procedural sense, as an action as well as a result of an action. It is used to describe human actions, as well as work in physics, the work of the mental apparatus in psychoanalysis, etc. Etymologically, the word "работа (work)" is associated with the words "раб (slave)", "рабство (slavery)". In addition, in the Russian language there is the concept "труд (labour)", which is generally synonymous with the concept "работа (work)". However, the word "труд (labour)" expresses an ethically more significant action. It is precisely the term "труд" that is used in Marx's translations ("the eternal natural condition of human life" (Marx, Engels. Collected Works. Vol. 23, p. 195). In this context, most likely, it should be transferred as "труд".

## Challenges of translating into Turkish
### Sanem Guvenc

### Alienation

Alienation is translated into Turkish as *yabancılaşma*; but the literal translation would read, "to become estranged". Even though, in alignment with its English/French counterpart, *yabancılaşma* does include the connotation of a foreign land, the word embodies *yaban*, which means "wild", whose immediate reference is to rural countryside. *Yaban-cı* would mean "strange-r", but the literal translation could also be heard as "an ally of the wild", "the one who is with the wild", or "wildling"; although these are not common usages. One usage that might be of interest would be "*yabana atmak*", in its literal translation "to throw out into the wild", which is a phrase that means undermining someone's thoughts, arguments, or words, rendering them non-sensical. On the other hand, *yaban* is also situated in the horror figure, *gulyabani*, the ghoul of the wild. The ghoul of the wild belongs to the desert and to transitory spaces seizing wanderers or travellers. But within Turkish literature, this figure could haunt those who are wandering around deserted houses or abandoned buildings. Therefore, in addition to indicating a land that is far away, *yaban* could also find us next door in a derelict building. But more importantly, in addition to its actual spatial designations, *yaban*'s topological implications mark the abandoned, the deserted, putting it in contact with the uncanny.

*Yabancılaşma*'s connection to the wild, wilderness, and the desert highlights the concept's relevance to topology, drawing attention to a comment Lacan made in *Seminar XI* that has been noted by Eric Laurent and Bruce Fink, but that has not yet been explored closely. Chapter 16 begins with Lacan arguing that science of the unconscious must start from the notion that "unconscious is structured like a language", and that this accounts for the fact that the constitution of the subject is topological. Lacan does not stop there and after constructing the subject within the locus of the Other, or the chain of signifiers, he grounds the structure of the signifier in the "function of the cut" he argues to be the "topological function of the rim", which reappears only a few pages later when he reformulates the *losange* as the functioning rim, the artifice that supports the topology. Already in the chapter, on more than one occasion, the Other is designated as a field—another spatial concept—and the subject of the unconscious is said to occupy an "indeterminate place".

On the one hand, the "rim process" or the "circular process" already suggest that alienation and separation be considered together, making all such readings topological even if they are not formulated as such. Yet, it would be worth speculating on how, thinking the combination of these two concepts topologically would change their potential reinterpretation, not only as a theoretical pursuit, but in clinical work as well. On the other hand, these spatial and topological references prompt the question as to whether or not it is possible to read the *vel*, the forced choice of either money or life that Lacan provides as an example, as a forced choice concerning spaces, or one that underlines non-space(s). At this point Georg Simmel could become an unexpected ally for Lacan. The concept of "the stranger" (*fremden*), the figure, who, according to Simmel points to the one who comes today and stays tomorrow, is the potential wanderer, and even though it refers to individuals, it is predominantly a spatial concept: the stranger makes the group boundaries act as spatial borders. The position of the stranger as a member of the group and yet outside of it, or, to put it in connection with another Lacanian concept, the *extimacy* of the stranger, complicates the notion of proximity marking the non-linear positioning of the stranger as being both far and near at the same time.

A similar topological reading could also be suggested for Marx's usage of alienation. In *Economic and Philosophical Manuscripts of 1844*, Marx uses alienation (*Entäusserung*) together with its sister concept, estrangement (*Entfremdung*). What is more interesting, after discussing how the object that the worker produced has become alien and hostile to him, an alien object, Marx makes the following comment:

> The alienation of the worker in his product means not only that his labor becomes an object, *an external existence*, but that *it exists outside him*, independently, as something alien to him, and that it becomes a power on its own confronting him.

If one wants to pursue the topological connotations of alienation, one possible reading would be to conceptualize the object as both a marker and a maker of the outside, of what is external to the subject, highlighting on the one hand that the commodities are the emblems of the *extimate*, and on the other that the outside is not a spatially present entity, but something that is constructed.

## *Plus-de-jouissance*/Surplus-value

In the latest Turkish translations of Lacan, *jouissance* is kept as it is. However, before, for instance in *Television*, *jouissance* is translated as *zevk*, i.e., pleasure. However, that translation might not be accurate considering that *jouissance* is not just pleasure but embodies suffering: in the words of Jacques-Alain Miller, Lacan's own rendering of Freud's death drive. *Zevk* does not embody the semantic multiplicity that *jouir* has in French, including to come, and property to be enjoyed. However, *zevk* embodies the meaning of "taste", both in the sense of enjoying food, but also taste with regard to music or arts or house decoration, etc., and could be seen as echoing Pierre Bourdieu's *cultural capital*, which speaks to its class character. What this might mean for *jouissance* would be interesting to contemplate, especially considering its connections with *extimacy*, particularly in Jacques-Alain Miller's *Extimate Enemies*.

# Annex II. What is a *matheme*? Four discourses and mathematics in Lacan

*Daniela Danelinck and Carlos Gómez Camarena*

Lacan maintained a love affair with mathematics throughout his intellectual life and from the starting point of his teaching in the Rome Discourse he strove to place psychoanalysis in the field of formal sciences: "This is the problem of the foundations that must assure our discipline its place among the sciences: a problem of formalization, which, it must be admitted, has gotten off to a very bad start" (*FFS*, p. 235). Already in *Seminar I* Lacan defines mathematics as formalization and invention, as a writing of new signs that enables new thoughts:

> Follow the history of a science like mathematics. For centuries it stagnated on problems which are now transparent to ten-year old children. And yet these were powerful minds which pondered them. We were stuck on the solution to equations of the second degree for ten centuries too many. The Greeks could have solved it, since they found out cleverer things concerning the problems of maxima and minima. Mathematical progress is not progress in the power of thought of the human being. It comes good the day some man thinks of inventing a sign like this, $\sqrt{\phantom{x}}$, or like that, $\int$. That's what mathematics is.
> (*SI*, pp. 274–275)

However, within Lacan's vast work it is possible to distinguish at least five different uses or presentation modes of mathematics, the *matheme* being only one of them: formalizations, diagrammatic thinking, numericity, fragmentary mathematical objects, and *mathème* (Gómez, 2018). The term "matheme" appears for the first time on 10 November 1971 (*PAM*, p. 53) in Lacan's oeuvre. Nonetheless, every time Lacan says "my little algebra" or "my little letters" he is referring to the *matheme*, he mentions these expressions at least five times throughout his seminars and *écrits*. The terms "mytheme"—minimal unit of the myth—from Lévi-Strauss, who in turn appropriates this use from "phoneme" or "semanteme"—minimal units of sound or meaning in linguistics, resonate in "matheme". "I have introduced [it] as an algorithm; and it is no accident that it breaks the phonemic element constituted by the signifying unit right down to its literal atom" (*SSD*, p. 691). As Jean-Claude Milner would later formulate in *L'œuvre claire* (1995), a *matheme* is an "atom of knowledge", such that it guarantees a complete transmission of psychoanalytic theory. Lacan's invention of *mathemes* concerns then a specific use of mathematics where formalization has as its aim the transmission of psychoanalytic theory.

In line with the above, a *matheme* stands in Lacanian theory for *the minimal unit of transmission of an impasse*. This is a specific use of mathematics in Lacan: the *matheme* localizes an impossibility or impasse. For this reason, the so-called "matheme of discourse(s)", invented by Lacan in 1969, does not represent a reality, but a discursive deadlock. In the writing of the formula the "little rotating quadrupeds", as Lacan calls them (*SXVII*, 26.11.69, p. 17; 17.06.70, p. 180), the vectors that connect the elements and the places, indicate that the discourses are "broken" or founded on a "weak logic". Each one of them point to an impossibility: it is impossible to govern (master), to educate (university), to desire (hysteria) and to analyse/cure (analyst) (*SXVII*, 10.06.70, pp. 165–173).

Lacan refers in 1972 to a "tetrahedral matheme of these discourses" based on the operations of the Klein Group (*PAM*, p. 65). There, he presents the graph—a vectorized graph—that is the basis of the four discourses. This explains the vectors of the four discourses, but also the absence of the downside vector, which points out the impossibility of each one of them. In the four edges of this Klein Group there are four positions, and each position could be occupied by one of the four terms (Figure AII.1).

These are quadrupeds, and like all *mathemes* in Lacan, they are designed to run counter to transference. They are a sort of device against any obscurantism, mysticism, or initiatory experience of transmission. Transmission, especially philosophical transmission, is always impregnated with (transference) love. The matheme is an antidote for this. In addition, the *matheme* is a scientific attempt of transmission as long the mathematical letters strip out any metaphor, meaning, or content. *Matheme* is not a language—ruled by syntax or language "inertia"—but an algebraic notation—letters as function or mathematical operations. Then, formalization, based on syntax, is different from mathematization, founded on functions and operations. Here it is important to distance mathematics from language, since "language betrays the truth" and "literal meaning [is] against figurative meaning" (*SX*, 08.05.63, p. 215). "The algebraic notation has precisely the purpose of giving us a pure identity marker [...] it can only leave the function of the signifier itself outside of any signification", concludes Lacan (*SX*, 09.01.63, p. 86). Lacan is here implicitly setting the "linguistic turn" against mathematics. This is the starting point of Badiou's philosophical project (1988) and the main objection of "Speculative Realism" to the linguistic turn (Bryant, 2011). In this sense, the "four discourses" are discourses "without speech" (*SXVII*, 26.11.69, p. 12).

The *matheme* provides accuracy for reading as long as it is not sustained by meaning. Emptying any content—images, metaphors, meaning—the *matheme* allows not only operations and functions, but a rigorous reading since algebraization entails univocity. At least the letter in the *matheme* reduces readings and has no equivocity of languages: "the matheme is not bilingual" (*CDJ*) because "it is

# TERMS

$\$$ = Subject, Symptom

$a$ = Surplus Jouissance, Object a

$S_1$ = Master signifier, Power

$S_2$ = Knowledge, rest of signifiers

# POSITIONS

| Agent | Other |
|---|---|
| semblant | labour |
| Truth | Production reminder |

*Figure AII.1* Terms and positions. Source: Figure adapted and produced from Lacan (*DDP*, p. 40).

designed to allow for a hundred and one different readings, a multiplicity that is acceptable as long as what is said about it remains grounded in its algebra" (*SSD*, p. 691). Let us recall that the algebraic letter allows for several contents, but not all, since the algorithm follows certain rules of functions and operations. At the same time, the *matheme* in Lacan allows for a certain amount of equivocity: "The un-teachable I made into a matheme by assuring it from the fixion of true opinion, fixion written with an x, but not without the resources of equivocation" (*LE*, p. 483); if not, it would be only under the heel of the Master's discourse regime: "the principle of discourse insofar as acting the master is to think of oneself as univocal" (*SXVII*, 11.03.70, p. 103).

The most obvious and classic way in which the *matheme* of the four discourses has been read is from the point of view of Lacan's "return to Freud". Within Lacanian psychoanalysis, prominent theorists like Jacques-Alain Miller, Eric Laurent, and Colette Soler agree that the *matheme* of discourse(s), in particular the *matheme* of the Master's discourse, is an algebraic writing of Freud's discovery. However, as we have indicated, the *matheme* of discourse(s) supports multiple readings. Another quite widespread way of reading the formula of the Master's discourse is with the lens of the Hegelian master and slave dialectic as Kojève reconstructed it in his seminar (Klepec, 2016; Dolar, 2006; Huson, 2006). Lacan himself seems to support these readings by maintaining that "you have been able to see, on the upper line of the structure of the Master's discourse, a fundamental relationship, which is, to state quickly, the one that forms the link between master [$S_1$] and slave [$S_2$]" (*SXVII*, 11.03.70, p. 107). The important thing to underline here is that Lacan's *matheme* formalized the Hegelian dialectic at the exact point of its impasse, "to perceive where the Hegelian construction gapes, remains gaping, and has been closed up in a forced way" (*SXVII*, 14.01.70, p. 51). In a way, Marx demonstrates that capitalism is its own gravedigger, reasoning through differential calculus—showing a mathematical impasse.

Lacan finds in the Hegelian discourse the best expression of the Master's discourse *from the point of view of the master*, enunciated from the place of the dominant agency. But Hegel's discourse, continues Lacan in *Seminar XVII*, "seem to have been definitively refuted by discoveries made by Marx" (11.02.70, p. 79). From this point of view, it is only possible to read the *matheme* of the Master's discourse starting from the Hegelian dialectic of the master and the slave (formalized on the upper level), if we incorporate Marx's critique (formalized on the bottom level). There the symptom ($) and surplus-value (*a*) are written, the two great inventions that Lacan attributes to Marx. In the place of truth (bottom left) the symptom of the capitalist mode of production is written as something that can only be half said in the place of the Other.[1] In the place of production (lower right) the surplus-value is written, the object cause of bourgeois society, the object that is both a loss and an excess.[2]

In May 1972 Lacan proposed for the first and only time a "fifth discourse" (*DDP*), the Capitalist discourse, which alters the order of the elements and fundamentally modifies the vectors. What is crucial on the orientation of vectors resides on the inversion of the left vector, which is now upside down producing a short-circuit avoiding the connection between the two terms on the upper side and perpetuating an interminable movement of capital following a circuit of vectors. (*PAM*, p. 60) (Schema 5 and Schema 6).

Since there is no relationship between the upper terms, there is no social bond. This is the reason why Alemán claims that the Capitalist discourse is not a discourse but rather a device (2013, p. 143).

Finally, the four discourses are also, for Lacan, a way of coping with the impasses between enunciation and the enunciated (statements). Psychoanalysis is a practice attempting to treat the real through the symbolic (*SXI*, 15.01.64, p. 6). This is why Lacan in his conferences in the United States writes the discourse of the analyst in this form (*CNA*, pp. 59–60) (Schema 7).

Annex II. What is a *matheme*? 289

Discourse of the Master

$$\frac{S_1}{\$} \rightarrow \frac{S_2}{a}$$

Discourse of the University

$$\frac{S_2}{S_1} \rightarrow \frac{a}{\$}$$

Discourse of the Hysteric

$$\frac{\$}{a} \rightarrow \frac{S_1}{S_2}$$

Discourse of the Analyst

$$\frac{a}{S_2} \rightarrow \frac{\$}{S_1}$$

Discourse of the Capitalist

$$\frac{\$}{S_1} \quad \frac{S_2}{a}$$

**Schema 5** The Capitalist discourse among other discourses. Source: Schemas adapted from Lacan (*DDP*, p. 40).

## Discourse of the Capitalist

$$\frac{\$}{S_1} \quad \frac{S_2}{a}$$

**Schema 6** The Capitalist discourse. Source: Schema adapted from Lacan (*DDP*, p. 40).

## DISCOURSE OF THE ANALYST

| Silence | What is enounced |
| --- | --- |
| Half-say of truth | What is not said |

**Schema 7** The Analyst discourse—with words. Source: Schema adapted from Lacan (*CNA*, p. 28).

## Notes

1 Samo Tomšič (2015, 2019) has convincingly argued that the hidden truth in Lacan's discourse of the master is the Marxian concept of "labour power", insofar as it is something that only achieves a partial representation in the market ($S_2$) when it is exchanged for its exchange value.
2 Daniela Danelinck (2018) has shown this same displacement in the University discourse, which also enables a Marxian reading where the emphasis shifts from production to exchange.

## Further reading

Cléro, J.-P. (2012). Les mathématiques, c'est le réel. In: *Essaim* 28: 17–27.
Mathews, P. (2020). Lacan the Mathematical Charlatan. In: *Lacan the Charlatan* (pp. 69–101). London: Palgrave.
Ricci, A. (2018). The Mathematics of Marx. In: *Lettera Matematica* 6(4): 221–225.

## References

Alemán, J. (2013). *Conjeturas sobre una Izquierda Lacaniana*. Buenos Aires: Grama.
Badiou, A. (1988). *Being and Event*, O. Feltham (Trans.). London: Bloomsbury, 2017.
Bryant, L. *et al* (Eds.) (2011). *The Speculative Turn: Continental Materialism and Realism*. Melbourne: re.press.
Danelinck, D. (2018). *Debería darte vergüenza. Ensayo sobre álgebra lacaniana*. Buenos Aires: Heterónimos.
Dolar, M. (2006). Hegel as the Other Side of Psychoanalysis. In: Clemens, J. and R. Grigg (Eds.), *Jacques Lacan and the Other Side of Psychoanalysis: Reflections on Seminar XVII* (pp. 129–154). New York: Duke University Press.
Gómez-Camarena, C. (2018). *Poème et mathème dans la clinique psychanalytique*. Paris: Université Paris Sorbonne Cité.
Huson, T. (2006). Truth and Contradiction. Reading Hegel with Lacan. In: Žižek, S. (Ed.), *Lacan: The Silent Partners* (pp. 56–78). London: Verso.
Klepec, P. (2016). On the Mastery in the Four Discourses. In: Tomšič, S. & Zevnik, A. (Eds.), *Jacques Lacan. Between Psychoanalysis and Politics* (pp. 115–130). London: Routledge.
Milner, J.-C. (1995). *A Search for Clarity: Science and Philosophy in Lacan's Oeuvre*, E. Pluth (Trans.). Chicago: Northwestern University Press, 2020.
Tomšič, S. (2015). *The Capitalist Unconscious: Marx and Lacan*. London: Verso.
Tomšič, S. (2019). *The Labour of Enjoyment. Towards a Critique of Libidinal Economy*. Berlin: August Verlag.

# Index

Page references in *italics* indicate figures.
Page numbers followed by 'n' refer to notes.

absolutization 37, 116–121, 130
Adorno, T. W. 203
Alemán, J. xxviii, xxxvii, 16, 20, 23, 288
alienation 1–14; and automatism 17, 21; and communism 45; and economy/*oikonomia* 64, 67; and freedom/liberty 76; and ideology 98–100; and imperialism 108; and market 126, 128, 132; and politics 164, 168, 171; and proletarian/labourer/worker 179, 180, 183; and society 231; and superstructure 241, 244; and surplus-*jouissance* 252–253; translation of 282–283
Althusser, L. xxvi, 6, 14, 16, 18, 56, 65, 68, 86, 92–93, 100, 163, 173, 203, 241
analysis xxvi; and alienation 2; and bourgeoisie 23, 25; and communism 45–46, 50; and consumption 61; and economy/*oikonomia* 63, 65, 70; and freedom/liberty 74, 82; and history 85–86, 88, 90, 92, 94; and imperialism 102, 104; and labour/work 117, 122; and master/tyrant 135; and materialism 146; and money 155–158, 161; and politics 162, 169; and proletarian/labourer/worker 177, 180–184; and segregation 198, 200, 208–209; and society 233; and superstructure 242; and surplus-*jouissance* 246–247, 250, 254; and uneasiness/discontent/unhappiness 258, 262; and value 269, 272
Analyst's discourse *see* discourse of the Analyst
animal 136, 165, 215, 227, 249, 259

animality 215
antagonism: and alienation 3; and capitalism 43; and communism 52; and politics 162–164, 169; and proletarian/labourer/worker 178; and society 228, 232–233; and surplus-*jouissance* 248
anti-communism 46, 52
anti-humanist 98, 178
anti-philosophy 23, 143
anxiety 9, 20–21, 183, 260, 270
appearance 11, 40, 65, 83n2, 97, 99, 107, 131, 147, 249
*Arbeit* 110, 113, 114, 122n2; *arbeitgeber* 135; *Arbeitsanforderung* 123n12; *Arbeitskraft* 115; *Durcharbeiten* 117; *Mehrarbeit* 116; *Traumarbeit* 122; *Witzarbeit* 123n9
Aristotle 83n1, 123n3, 135, 149, 155, 162
Augustine 9
automatism xxx, 16–22

Badiou, A. xxxvii, 80, 86, 286
Balibar, É. 7, 96
Bataille, G. 161
benefits 43, 50, 58, 60–61, 67, 198
Benjamin, W. 189–190, 203
Bentham, J. 50, 66, 171, 174, 230, 266–268, 270–273
Bergler, E. 171
Bianchi, P. 41
*Bildung* 221
Bion, W. 168, 209
biopolitics 70, 210
body: and alienation 4, 8–9; and automatism 17; and bourgeoisie 27; and capitalism

37; and consumption 57–58, 60–61; and economy/*oikonomia* 64, 69; and labour/work 113, 115–119, 121; and master/tyrant 137; and materialism 150–151; and proletarian/labourer/worker 179, 181; and revolution 192; and segregation 202; and slavery 215; and society 234, 236; and surplus-*jouissance* 247, 251, 254; and uneasiness/discontent/unhappiness 257, 260–261; and value 273
Bossuet, J.-B. 143
bourgeoisie 23–29; and alienation 1, 3, 6; and communism 49, 52; and consumption 58, 60; and economy/*oikonomia* 66–68, 71; and market 128; and master/tyrant 136; and money 154, 156; and politics 163–164, 169, 174; and proletarian/labourer/worker 177; and revolution 188, 192; and segregation 206, 210; and society 225, 227, 229–230, 234–237; and superstructure 240, 242
bureaucracy 38, 43, 108
bureaucratic 48, 206

capital: and alienation 4, 5; and automatism 16; and bourgeoisie 24, 29; and capitalism 35, 39, 40, 42; and consumption 57, 58; and economy/*oikonomia* 69; and labour/work 117, 118, 121; and market 126, 132; and master/tyrant 137; and materialism 146, 147; and money 154, 159; and politics 164, 165, 166, 170, 174; and proletarian/labourer/worker 177; and revolution 193, 194; and segregation 199, 210; and society 234; and surplus-*jouissance* 249; and uneasiness/discontent/unhappiness 261, 262, 264; and value 267, 268, 269, 270
capitalism 31–44; and consumption 55, 58–59; and economy/*oikonomia* 64, 70–71; and imperialism 104–106; and labour/work 111, 118, 120–122; and market 127, 130, 132; and materialism 146; and money 157–158; and politics 164, 169, 174; and proletarian/labourer/worker 178, 180–184, 188; and revolution 191, 193–194; and segregation 198, 200, 202, 204, 207–208, 210; and society 235; and surplus-*jouissance* 251, 255; translation of 281;

and uneasiness/discontent/unhappiness 261–262
Capitalist discourse 288, *289*; and automatism 16–22; and bourgeoisie 28; and capitalism 31, 37, *40*, 40–44; and economy/*oikonomia* 64, 69–70; and imperialism 104; and market 131; and money 160; and segregation 197, 204–207
Cassin, B. xxx, xxxi, xxxiv, 75
castration: and capitalism 33, 36–37, 42; and money 156, 158, 160–161; and segregation 204, 207; and society 236–237; and surplus-*jouissance* 249, 252, 254; and uneasiness/discontent/unhappiness 257, 261–263, 265
citizen 235, 241, 259
citizenship 157
civilization: and alienation 2; and automatism 20; and bourgeoisie 27–28; and ideology 98; and segregation 204; and society 235; and surplus-*jouissance* 247; and uneasiness/discontent/unhappiness 259
civil society 83n1, 145, 165, 235, 237n8, 239
class: and bourgeoisie 24, 25, 27, 29; and capitalism 42–43; and communism 45–46, 52; and market 128; and master/tyrant 136–137, 139; and materialism 143; and politics 162, 167–168, 173; and proletarian/labourer/worker 177; and segregation 198–199; and society 229, 230, 233
class consciousness 34, 183
clinical: and alienation 9; and automatism 18, 21; and consumption 56, 58; and economy/*oikonomia* 71; and freedom/liberty 78; and slavery 214
colonialism 58, 60, 105–106; post-colonialism 102
commerce 24, 130, 161, 229, 235–237
commodity/commodities: and alienation 4, 6; and automatism 20–21; and capitalism 32, 37, 42, 43; and communism 50; and consumption 55–58, 61; and economy/*oikonomia* 66–67, 70–71; and ideology 99; and labour/work 115; and market 127, 130–131; and materialism 146; and money 154–157; and politics 163–166, 169; and society 230, 233, 235; and surplus-*jouissance* 248–249, 254; and

uneasiness/discontent/unhappiness 261; and value 268, 272
communism xxx, 45–53; and alienation 5; and freedom/liberty 80; and proletarian/labourer/worker 180–181, 183–184; and segregation 198; and society 234, 237; and superstructure 242; translation of 280, 281
communists: and alienation 5; and economy/*oikonomia* 71; and proletarian/labourer/worker 179–184
competition 104, 199
compulsion 68, 70, 111, 247–249
conflict: and communism 49, 51; and history 87; and labour/work 111–112, 119; and market 128; and politics 162; and superstructure 239–240; and surplus-*jouissance* 248
*connaissance* 251
consciousness: and communism 49; and ideology 97–98; and labour/work 112–113; and master/tyrant 135–136; and materialism 145; and politics 164, 166; and proletarian/labourer/worker 182; and slavery 221; and society 226, 231; and superstructure 240
consumption xxx, 55–61; and automatism 22; and bourgeoisie 28; and economy/*oikonomia* 67, 70; and labour/work 115, 119–122; and market 128; and money 159; and politics 162; and segregation 199, 202; and slavery 222; and value 270
contingency xxi, 169, 180, 189, 196, 254
contradiction 3, 5, 40, 52, 119, 120, 139, 163, 164, 186n10, 226, 241
Coumet, E. 272
crises 21, 174, 259
critique/critical theory: and alienation 1–4, 6–7, 9, 14; and automatism 17; and bourgeoisie 25–26, 28; and capitalism 31–32, 35–37, 44; and communism 45, 51; and economy/*oikonomia* 63–70; and history 87; and ideology 97–101; and imperialism 108; and labour/work 110–111, 113–115, 118–119, 121; and market 126, 128; and master/tyrant 137, 139; and materialism 143–146; and money 154; and politics 162–164; and revolution 194; and segregation 201, 203; and society 225–226, 228, 230; and superstructure 241; and uneasiness/discontent/unhappiness 258

culture: and communism 45–46, 52; and consumption 56; and history 85; and society 225, 228–229, 231–236; and uneasiness/discontent/unhappiness 259–261, 265

*Dasein* 204
Davis, A. 139
death: and automatism 22; and communism 46, 50; and freedom/liberty 78; and master/tyrant 135–137; and money 159; and politics 166, 169, 170; and revolution 195; and segregation 206; and slavery 221, 223; and surplus-*jouissance* 249; and uneasiness/discontent/unhappiness 257, 259–260; and value 269
death drive 159, 249, 257, 260, 284
decolonial 139
decolonialism xxxvii
dehumanization 17
Dejours, C. 21
Deleuze, G. 55
democracy 191, 202, 203
Democritus 151, 228
deprivation 41, 58, 66, 120, 207
Descartes, R. 8, 28, 79, 119, 151, 205, 235, 277
desire: and alienation 9, 12–13; and automatism 16, 18, 20–21; and bourgeoisie 25; and capitalism 33–34, 38, 41, 43; and consumption 59; and economy/*oikonomia* 65–66; and freedom/liberty 78, 82; and history 94; and imperialism 105; and labour/work 110–112, 116; and market 126–127; and master/tyrant 135–136, 138; and money 157–159; and politics 162, 170–172; and revolution 189, 191, 195; and segregation 209–210; and slavery 215–222, 224; and society 231, 233–236; and surplus-*jouissance* 246–248, 250–254; and uneasiness/discontent/unhappiness 259, 262, 264; and value 269
de Vos, J. 203
dialectic: and bourgeoisie 24; and capitalism 34; and economy/*oikonomia* 67; and freedom/liberty 77, 80, 82; and history 92; and master/tyrant 134, 136–137, 139; and materialism 148; and politics 166; and proletarian/labourer/

worker 184; and revolution 191–192; and segregation 200–201; and slavery 214–215, 217, 219–221; and society 231, 233–236; and surplus-*jouissance* 246, 253; and uneasiness/discontent/ unhappiness 259, 260
dictatorship 184
disappearance xxix, 11, 204, 252, 274n6
discontent *see* uneasiness/discontent/ unhappiness
discourse of the Analyst 19, 44, 250–252, *251*
discourse of the Capitalist *see* Capitalist discourse
discourse of the Hysteric 43–44, 204, 250–252, *251*, 262–263
discourse of the Master: and automatism 20; and capitalism 37–41, *38*, 43; and economy/*oikonomia* 69–70; and imperialism 104; and market 130–131; and master/tyrant 138; and surplus-*jouissance* 250–252, *251*, 254; and uneasiness/discontent/unhappiness 257, 261–265
discourse of the University: and bourgeoisie 27; and capitalism *38*, 38–41, 43–44; and economy/*oikonomia* 70; and ideology 101; and imperialism 108; and market 131; and segregation 197, 204, 206–208; and surplus-*jouissance* 250–252, *251*, 254; and uneasiness/ discontent/unhappiness 262, 264; and value 273
discourses, four 285–289, *289*; and automatism 16, 20; and capitalism 37, 39; and consumption 55; and economy/*oikonomia* 64, 69–70; and imperialism 103; and market 126, 129, 132; and politics 171, 174; and segregation 206; and surplus-*jouissance* 250, *251*
dispossession 39, 103, 179, 184, 251
dissatisfaction 37, 116, 121, 182
division: and alienation 3; and automatism 17; and consumption 56; and economy/*oikonomia* 63, 66–67; and ideology 97–98; and imperialism 105; and labour/work 115; and market 126, 128, 131; and materialism 149; and politics 164–165, 166; and proletarian/labourer/worker 178, 181; and segregation 197–199, 204; and society 229, 232, 236; and uneasiness/ discontent/unhappiness 263; and value 272
Dolar, M. 252
drive: and capitalism 41, 43; and communism 52; and economy/*oikonomia* 66–67, 70; and labour/work 111–119, 121; and money 157–158; and politics 170, 172–173; and segregation 204; and society 228, 233; and surplus-*jouissance* 248, 249, 254; and uneasiness/discontent/ unhappiness 257, 260

economy/*oikonomia* xl, 63–71; and alienation 1, 3, 4; and bourgeoisie 25–31; and capitalism 32, 35–37, 45; and communism 50; and consumption 59–60; and imperialism 104; and labour/ work 111, 114, 116, 118–119, 122; and market 128, 133; and materialism 146; and money 154, 156–157, 161–162; and politics 163–166, 169, 172–173; and revolution 194; and segregation 199; and society 226; translation of 281–282; and uneasiness/discontent/unhappiness 232–234
ecosocial 46
education xxxv, 2, 19, 39, 229
ego: and alienation 9–10; and communism 52; and economy/*oikonomia* 64–65, 67; and segregation 200–201, 209; super-ego 159, 210, 260, 262; and superstructure 241; and surplus-*jouissance* 247, 252–253; and uneasiness/discontent/unhappiness 256, 259–260
Einstein, A. 49
emancipation 41, 68, 106, 163, 164, 189, 198
Engels, F. 3, 6–7, 13, 24–25, 29, 48, 66, 97–98, 136, 145–148, 177, 179, 226, 229, 233, 235, 240; *see also* Marx, Karl, (and Friedrich Engels)
enjoyment: and alienation 9, 12–13; and capitalism 32–33, 36–37, 41–43; and consumption 55, 57, 60–61; and economy/*oikonomia* 70; and imperialism 104; and labour/work 114, 116, 118–122; and market 126, 128–129; and master/tyrant 137–138; and materialism 144, 146–147; and money

159–160; and proletarian/labourer/
worker 181; and segregation 201–204,
209–211; and society 225, 233–236;
and surplus-*jouissance* 248, 249–255;
translation of 279; and uneasiness/
discontent/unhappiness 257, 259–266;
and value 269–270, 272–273
*Entäusserung* 2, 4, 283
*Entfremdung* 2, 3, 186n10, 283
entrepreneurs 28, 268
entropy: and capitalism 33; and
economy/*oikonomia* 71; and labour/
work 118, 120–121; and society
233–234; and surplus-*jouissance* 249,
252, 254
Epicurus 228
exchange: and capitalism 34, 39;
and consumption 55–61; and
economy/*oikonomia* 65, 70–71; and
labour/work 115; and market 127–128,
130–132; and master/tyrant 137; and
materialism 146–147, 150; and money
154–156; and politics 163–165; and
segregation 198–199, 210; and society
226, 232–237; and surplus-*jouissance*
254; and uneasiness/discontent/
unhappiness 261; and value 268
exploitation: and alienation 5; and
capitalism 32, 39, 41–42; and
communism 46; and consumption
57–58, 61; and economy/*oikonomia* 66;
and ideology 98; and labour/work 111,
122; and master/tyrant 139; and money
154, 157, 160; and politics 164–166,
169–170; and proletarian/labourer/
worker 179–180; and segregation 197,
199–200, 206, 210; and society 227,
234, 236–237; and superstructure 240;
and uneasiness/discontent/unhappiness
260–261, 264
*extimacy/extimate* 69, 100, 210, 228,
283–284

Fanon, F. xxxvii
fantasy 10, 25, 40, 69, 94, 113, 126, 131,
132, 182, 186n19, 202, 203, 211, 247,
248, 252, 254
Federici, S. xxxvii, 58
feminism xxxvii, 82, 127, 138–139, 194
fetishism: and alienation 7; and capitalism
35; and economy/*oikonomia* 66, 70;
and ideology 98–100; and money 154,

156–158, 160; and politics 164, 169;
and surplus-*jouissance* 254
feudalism 24, 68, 134, 136, 147
Feuerbach 3, 5, 91, 100, 163, 236
Fichte, J. G. 8, 143
fiction: and consumption 59; and
economy/*oikonomia* 66–67; and history
87, 93, 94; and politics 170, 174; and
slavery 219; and society 230, 232, 236;
and value 266–267
Fink, B. 70, 168, 282
First International 47, 198
Foucault, M. 26, 55, 174, 207
freedom/liberty 74–82; and bourgeoisie
25–29; and capitalism 34; and
economy/*oikonomia* 64, 67, 69; and
master/tyrant 139; and politics 163–164;
and revolution 195; and slavery 221;
and society 230; translation of 281;
and uneasiness/discontent/unhappiness
261, 263
Freire, P. 139
Freud, S. xxvii, xxix, xxxii, xl, 10, 32,
34, 36, 49–51, 53, 55, 60, 63–65, 70,
85–94, 98, 110–116, 118–119, 150–151,
156–159, 164, 168–173, 178, 189–190,
200, 203, 228, 232, 236, 243, 246–249,
252, 254, 256–260, 262–264, 269, 281,
284, 287–288
Freudianism xxvii, 28, 31, 36, 52,
64–65, 85–90, 110–116, 119, 122,
127–128, 150–151, 153, 158, 160, 168,
173, 177, 225, 231, 233, 256–258,
263, 269
Freudo-Marxism xxvii, 1, 49, 86, 153

gaze 42–43, 59, 169, 204, 221
*Gesellschaft* 237n8
Gramsci, A. xxxvi, 241

Hardt, M. 211
Hegel, G. W. F. 2–3, 5, 7–8, 55, 74–80,
91, 94, 134–136, 163, 166, 188–189,
190–191, 195, 201, 214, 219–222, 252,
259, 261, 269, 277, 288
Hegelianism xxxvii, 4, 8, 34, 38, 49, 52,
64, 82, 97–98, 100, 136, 142, 145, 147,
163, 178, 214, 219–221, 223, 231, 239,
252, 260, 277, 288
hegemonic xxxvi, 139
hegemony 86
Hirschman, A. O. 266

history 85–94; and bourgeoisie 24; and communism 46–48; and ideology 97–98, 100; and imperialism 107–108; and master/tyrant 136–137; and materialism 143–144, 146, 151; and politics 169; and proletarian/labourer/worker 184; and revolution 189–191
homosexuality 237
hooks, b. 139
Horkheimer, M. 203
human rights *see* rights
Hume, D. 174, 269, 272–273
Hysteric 35, 43, 144, 182, 250–252, 262; discourse of the Hysteric 43, 250, 262; Hysteric discourse 43

idealism 99, 100, 128, 143, 145, 147, 150, 163, 186n15
identification: and alienation 9, 12; and automatism 17; and ideology 100; and imperialism 105–106; and market 127–128; and politics 166–169; and proletarian/labourer/worker 183; and segregation 200–201, 208–209; and society 231, 235; and surplus-*jouissance* 247–249, 252–253; translation of 278
ideology 96–101; and alienation 6; and automatism 18; and bourgeoisie 24, 26, 29; and economy/*oikonomia* 71; and market 128; and materialism 145–146; and politics 162; and revolution 193; and segregation 198, 201, 203; and superstructure 240; translation of 281
illusion: and bourgeoisie 25, 28; and capitalism 35; and communism 49–51; and ideology 98, 100; and politics 171, 174; and society 237; and value 268
imaginary 75–76; and alienation 9–12; and economy/*oikonomia* 64–66, 71; and freedom/liberty 74; and ideology 96, 100; and market 127; and master/tyrant 137; and materialism 142, 144–145; and money 161; and politics 163, 166, 170–171; and segregation 201–203; and society 227–228, 230–231; and superstructure 243; and surplus-*jouissance* 248–250, 252–253; and uneasiness/discontent/unhappiness 259, 261; and value 272
imperialism 102–108, 172, 194, 197
impossibility 20, 41, 49, 68–70, 104, 113, 116, 120, 121, 138, 144, 157, 160, 225, 236, 237, 246–248, 254, 255, 286

impossible xxvii, xxxvii, 2, 10, 18, 32, 37, 41, 43, 45, 46, 57, 68, 69, 118, 144, 156, 168, 208, 227, 236, 237, 244, 255, 286
institutions: and automatism 21; and bourgeoisie 26; and capitalism 35; and communism 47–49, 51–52; and politics 169, 172; and proletarian/labourer/worker 184; and revolution 189, 193; and segregation 197, 202, 204, 206–208; and society 227–229, 232; and superstructure 240

Jankélévitch, V. 273
Johnston, A. 252
*jouissance*: and automatism 18–19; and bourgeoisie 25, 27, 28; and capitalism 32–33, 34–35, 38, 41–44; and consumption 56; and economy/*oikonomia* 64, 66–69; and freedom/liberty 74, 82; and imperialism 104; and labour/work 114; and market 126–130, 133; and master/tyrant 137–138; and money 159–160; and politics 162, 165, 171, 173; and proletarian/labourer/worker 177–178, 180–183, 185; and segregation 210; and slavery 221; and society 234, 237; and superstructure 244; translation of 278–279, 284; and uneasiness/discontent/unhappiness 257, 259, 262; and value 269, 271–272; *see also* surplus-*jouissance*

Kant (kantian) 190, 201, 240, 241, 252
Klein, M. 81, 87
knowledge: and alienation 2, 6; and automatism 21; and bourgeoisie 24, 26; and capitalism 38–39, 43–44; and communism 47; and consumption 58; and economy/*oikonomia* 69–70; and freedom/liberty 76; and history 85–86, 93; and ideology 97–98; and imperialism 102–103, 108; and labour/work 112, 120; and market 126, 131–132; and master/tyrant 138; and materialism 149; and politics 166–167; and proletarian/labourer/worker 177–179, 181–185; and revolution 192, 194; and segregation 204–207, 209, 211; and slavery 219; and society 232, 235–237; and surplus-*jouissance* 248–252, 254; and uneasiness/discontent/unhappiness 256–258, 262

Kojève, A. 8, 52, 107, 134–136, 166, 174, 188, 190–192, 214–215, 217, 219–220, 288
Koyré, A. 205
*Kultur* 256, 257, 281

La Boétie, É. de 135
labourer *see* proletarian/labourer/worker
labour/work 110–122; and alienation 3–6; and automatism 17, 19; and capitalism 32, 37, 40, 42–43; and consumption 56–58; and economy/*oikonomia* 68, 70–71; and history 92; and ideology 97–99; and market 126, 128–131; and master/tyrant 138; and materialism 146; and money 154–156; and politics 162, 164–166, 170, 173–174, 177; and segregation 198–200, 210; and society 225, 228–229, 233–234, 236–237; and surplus-*jouissance* 248–252, 254; translation of 282; and uneasiness/discontent/unhappiness 261, 264; and value 268–269, 272
Lacan, J.: Aggressiveness in Psychoanalysis (*AP*) 9–10, 137–138, 166, 259–260; Allocution sur les psychoses de l'enfant (*APE*) 107, 206; An issue of Ones (*AIO*) 100–101; Beyond the Reality Principle (*BRP*) 143, 227, 243; Clôture des Journées de l'École freudienne de Paris (*CDJ*) 286; Les complexes familiaux dans la formation de l'individu (*CF*) 9, 228–229, 241, 243; Conférence à Genève sur le symptôme (*CG*) 148; Conférences et entretiens dans des universités nord-américaines (*CNA*) 56, 288; Conférence sur la psychanalyse et la formation du psychiatre (*CPP*) 107; *De la psychose paranoïaque dans ses rapports avec la personnalité* (*DPP*) 7, 26, 226–227; The Direction of the Treatment and the Principles of Its Power (*DTP*) 78, 202; Discourse to Catholics (*DTC*) 87; Du discours psychanalytique (*DDP*) 20, 28, *38*, 40, *40*, 70, 160, 204, *251*, *287*, 288, *289*; D'une réforme dans son trou (*RDT*) 207; *Écrits* (*EC*) 64; L'etourdit (*LE*) xxxiv, 142, 181, 211, 287; Foundation Act (*FA*) 209, 257–258; Freud Forever: An Interview with Panorama (*FFI*) 17, 20; The Freudian Thing or the Meaning of the Return to Freud in Psychoanalysis (*FT*) 9, 85, 94, 145, 147, 232; The Function and Field of Speech and Language in Psychoanalysis (*FFS*) 10, 33, 76–77, 85, 88, 90–91, 93, 144, 177, 179, 181, 193, 205, 231, 285; *Impromptu n°2* (*IM2*) 39; The Instance of the Letter in the Unconscious or Reason Since Freud (*IL*) 90, 92, 100, 232, 242, 244; Intervention au 1re Congrès mondial de psychiatrie (*ICM*) 242–243; Interventions sur l'exposé de P. Mathis: "Remarques sur la fonction de l'argent dans la technique analytique" (*IEM*) 57; Kant with Sade (*KS*) 32, 42, 78, 195; Knowledge, ignorance, truth and enjoyment (*KIT*) 189; Letter of Dissolution (*LD*) 56, 171, 257; Lituraterre (*LTE*) 244; Logical Time and the Assertion of Anticipated Certainty (*LT*) 166–168; La méprise du sujet supposé savoir (*MSS*) 128; The Mirror Stage as Formative of the I Function as Revealed in Psychoanalytic Experience (*MS*) 8, 166, 230; Monsieur A (*MA*) 55; Motifs du crime paranoïaque (*MDP*) 241; *Le mythe individuel du névrosé, ou poésie et vérité dans la névrose* (*MIN*) 165, 231; Le nombre treize et la forme logique de la suspicion (*N13*) 209; The Place, Origin and End of My Teaching (*POE*) 243; Le plaisir et la règle fondamentale (*PRF*) 180; Position of the Unconscious (*PU*) 12, 78, 235; Préface à l'édition anglaise du Séminaire XI (*PEA*) 93; Preface of one Thesis (*PTH*) 207–208; Presentation on Psychical Causality (*PPC*) 74–76, 231; Presentation on Transference (*PT*) 59; Proposition du 9 octobre 1967 sur le psychanalyste de l'École (*P9O*) 26, 128, 169, 204, 206, 208, 211; La psychiatrie anglaise et la guerre (*PAG*) 168, 206, 209; Psychanalyse et médecine (*PEM*) 254; Psychoanalysis and Its Teaching (*PIT*) 88, 92; On a Question Prior to Any Possible Treatment of Psychosis (*QTP*) 77; Radiophonie (*RA*) 13, 52, 99, 133, 149, 151, 160, 204, 243, 264; Remarks on Daniel Lagache's Presentation (*RDL*) 148; Responses to Students of Philosophy Concerning the Object of

298  Index

Psychoanalysis (*RSF*) 50, 147–148, 159, 203, 243; Science and Truth (*ST*) 58, 92–93, 147, 170, 178, 201, 205; *The Seminar of Jacques Lacan. Book I* (*SI*) 85–91, 102, 202, 219, 285; *The Seminar of Jacques Lacan. Book II* (*SII*) xxvi–xxvii, 28, 50, 65, 85–86, 88, 90, 233, 250; *The Seminar of Jacques Lacan. Book III* (*SIII*) 17, 87, 90–91, 145, 232, 241; *The Seminar of Jacques Lacan. Book IV* (*SIV*) 55–56, 58–59, 94, 172, 220, 242; *The Seminar of Jacques Lacan. Book IX* (*SIX*) 10, 51, 87, 90, 94; *The Seminar of Jacques Lacan. Book V* (*SV*) xxxiii, 8, 55, 85–86, 90, 102, 148, 233, 253; *The Seminar of Jacques Lacan. Book VI* (*SVI*) xxviii, 56–57, 66, 94, 233–234, 242; *The Seminar of Jacques Lacan. Book VII* (*SVII*) 50–51, 58–59, 66–67, 91, 94, 104, 142, 170–171, 209–210, 228, 235; *The Seminar of Jacques Lacan. Book VIII* (*SVIII*) 50, 52, 87, 91, 93, 214, 219–220; *The Seminar of Jacques Lacan. Book X* (*SX*) 12, 51–52, 90, 171–172, 286; *The Seminar of Jacques Lacan. Book XI* (*SXI*) 11, 51, 67–68, 204–205, 209, 235, 253, 288; *The Seminar of Jacques Lacan. Book XIX* (*SXIX*) 58, 80–81, 88, 111, 205, 257; *The Seminar of Jacques Lacan. Book XVII* (*SXVII*) xxix, 18, 28, 33, 37–39, 42, 69–70, 91, 104–106, 119, 121, 130, 137–138, 143, 159, 171, 179, 188, 191, 194, 200, 204–205, 234–236, 249–254, 261–265, 269, 272, 286–288; *The Seminar of Jacques Lacan. Book XX* (*SXX*) 57, 70–71, 93, 130, 143, 147, 149, 151, 202, 204–205, 230, 272; *The Seminar of Jacques Lacan. Book XXIII* (*SXXIII*) 71, 211; Seminar on "The Purloined Letter" (*PL*) 126, 149, 169, 173; *Le Séminaire* (*S0*) 231; *Le Séminaire. Livre IX* (*SIX*) 10, 51, 87, 90, 94; *Le Séminaire. Livre XII* (*SXII*) 92, 145, 235; *Le Séminaire. Livre XIII* (*SXIII*) 25–29, 34, 87, 93, 149, 205, 234, 236; *Le Séminaire. Livre XIV* (*SXIV*) 13, 17, 34, 56, 61, 96, 100, 127, 144, 146, 151, 181, 204; *Le Séminaire. Livre XV* (*SXV*) 13, 19, 89, 93, 100, 179, 180; *Le Séminaire. Livre XVI* (*SXVI*) 13, 16, 19, 27, 32–33, 35, 37, 50–51, 55, 61, 68, 80, 91–92, 99–100, 102–103, 115–116, 120, 122, 128–132, 136–137, 143–144, 146, 149, 173, 178, 182, 191–192, 194, 202, 210, 236, 240, 260–261, 268, 273; *Le Séminaire. Livre XVIII* (*SXVIII*) 56, 92, 108, 147–148, 193, 201, 211, 273; *Le Séminaire. Livre XXI* (*SXXI*) 142–144, 149–151, 258–259; *Le Séminaire. Livre XXII* (*SXXII*) 56, 149; *Le Séminaire. Livre XXIV* (*SXXIV*) 25, 93, 144, 149, 150–151; *Le Séminaire. Livre XXV* (*SXXV*) 55, 92–93, 145, 272; *Le Séminaire. Livre XXVII* (*SXXVII*) 177–178, 184; The Situation of Psychoanalysis and the Training of Psychoanalysts in 1956 (*SPT*) 87, 91, 169, 208; Of Structure as the Of Structure as the Inmixing of an Otherness Prerequisite to Any Subject Whatever (*IMX*) 203; On the Subject Who is Finally in Question (*SQ*) 150, 205; The Subversion of the Subject and the Dialectic of Desire in the Freudian Unconscious (*SSD*) 33, 285, 287; The Symbolic, the Imaginary, and the Real (*SIR*) 87; *Talking to Brick Walls* (*PAM*) 35–37, 92, 206–207, 256, 285–286, 288; Television (*TV*) 31, 36, 111, 117, 150, 170; A Theoretical Introduction to the Functions of Psychoanalysis in Criminology (*FPC*) 96, 99–100, 230–231, 260; The Third (*TT*) 211; Variations on the Standard Treatment (*VST*) 85; The Youth of Gide, or the Letter and Desire (*YG*) 85–86

Laclau, E. xxxvii
*lalangue* 70, 211, 258–259
Langer, F. 63
language: and alienation 2–3, 10; and automatism 16–18; and capitalism 31, 33, 36–38; and economy/*oikonomia* 64–65, 67, 70; and history 86–88; and ideology 96, 100; and labour/work 117; and market 130; and materialism 144–149; and money 160; and politics 163, 165–166, 168, 170–171, 174; and segregation 197, 201, 203, 211; and slavery 214; and society 227, 230, 231; and superstructure 242–244; and surplus-*jouissance* 247, 253; and uneasiness/discontent/unhappiness 257; *see also* linguistic/s

Laplanche, J. xxxii
Larriera, S. xxviii, 20
Lauretis, T. 139
law 25, 60, 77, 94, 126, 158, 159, 161, 162, 202, 203, 251, 259, 260, 267, 269, 274n3, 278
Le Bon, G. 200, 247
leftism/the left 49, 100, 190
Lenin, V. 7, 106, 150, 178, 188–189, 191, 195, 206, 240
Leninism 150
Lévi-Strauss, C. 52, 55–57, 59, 65, 100, 127, 165, 230, 231, 285
liberty *see* freedom/liberty
libidinal: and capitalism 31–33, 41; and economy/*oikonomia* 63, 65; and labour/work 116, 119, 122; and politics 170–173; and segregation 200, 203, 205; and society 234; and surplus-*jouissance* 247, 248
libido 2, 65, 118, 123n10, 170, 173, 200, 243, 247, 254
linguistics: and alienation 10; and capitalism 31, 35–36; and economy/*oikonomia* 65, 67; and freedom/liberty 76–77; and history 86–87, 90–91; and ideology 96, 100; and labour/work 112; and materialism 149; and politics 170, 174; and superstructure 242–243; and surplus-*jouissance* 253; translation of 277–278; *see also* language
Lorde, A. 139
love: and alienation 1, 9; and consumption 59–60; and materialism 147; and money 154, 160; and politics 171; and segregation 200, 202; and slavery 214–224; and surplus-*jouissance* 247–248
Lukács, G. 7

machine: and automatism 17–19, 21; and labour/work 112, 121; and politics 166; and proletarian/labourer/worker 179, 184; and society 232–234, 236; and surplus-*jouissance* 250, 252
manufacture 17, 165, 264, 268
market 126–133; and alienation 3; and automatism 16; and bourgeoisie 25, 31; and capitalism 32, 35, 37, 39, 42; and labour/work 115, 118–121; and money 157; and politics 162, 171; and revolution 194–195; and segregation 198–199, 204; and society 229

marriage 51, 158, 229
Marx, K., (and Friedrich Engels): *Capital. A Critique of Political Economy*, Vol. I (*CAI*) 4, 8, 17, 19, 32, 50, 66, 68, 115, 137–138, 146–147, 154–156, 165–166, 170, 173, 177, 198–199, 230, 234, 248, 261, 264; *Capital. A Critique of Political Economy*, Vol. II (*CAII*) 234; *Capital. A Critique of Political Economy*, Vol. III (*CAIII*) 199; Carta de Marx a Freud (*CAF*) 228; *A Contribution to the Critique of Political Economy* (*CPE*) 56–57, 165, 239, 240; *Critique of Hegel's Philosophy of Right* (*CHP*) 50, 164; Critique of the Gotha Programme (*CGP*) 47, 71; Difference Between the Democritean and Epicurean Philosophy of Nature (*DDE*) 180, 228; *Early Writings* (*EW*) 3–5; *Economic and Philosophic Manuscripts of 1844* (*EPM*) 56, 164, 179, 226, 234, 236–237; *The Eighteenth Brumaire of Louis Bonaparte* (*BLB*) 190; The Election Results in the United States (*TER*) 198; The German Ideology (*GI*) 24, 66, 97–98, 137, 145–147, 226, 233, 235; *Grundrisse. Foundations of the Critique of Political Economy* (*GR*) 4, 25, 147, 164, 227, 232; On the Jewish Question (*OJQ*) 56, 163, 208, 235; Manifesto of the Communist Party (*MCP*) 24, 29, 47, 136–137, 174, 177, 179, 229; *Marx on suicide* (*MOS*) 60–61; *The Poverty of Philosophy* (*PP*) 56, 234; The Programme of the Parti Ouvrier (*PPO*) 198; A Provisional Rules of the Working Men's International Association (*PRW*) 198; Theses on Feuerbach (*TOF*) 46, 91, 236; *Value, Price, and Profit* (*VPP*) 156
Marxian xxviii, 2, 65, 67, 103–105, 119, 123n8, 124n16, 225, 236, 290n1, 290n2
Marxism xxvii, xxix, xxxi–xxxv, xxxvii, xxxviii, xl, xli, 29, 31, 34–37, 46, 55, 86, 91–94, 99, 101, 105, 143, 147, 151, 178, 179, 181, 197, 203, 240, 241, 243, 262, 278
masochism 32, 42–43, 171, 269
mass 200; *Massenpsychologie* 168, 200, 208; masses 107, 164, 168, 200, 201, 208
Master discourse *see* discourse of the Master

master/tyrant 134–139; and politics 166, 170; and proletarian/labourer/worker 188; and revolution 189, 194–195; and segregation 201, 205, 207, 209–210, 214; and slavery 215–223; and society 237; and surplus-*jouissance* 248, 250–252; translation of 281; and uneasiness/discontent/unhappiness 259–265; and value 273
materialism 142–151; and bourgeoisie 25; and history 86, 91–93; and ideology 96; and politics 163–164; and segregation 203; and society 227; and superstructure 241
mathematics and *mathemes* 285–289, *287, 289*
Maupertuis, P. L. M. de 267, 270
Mauss, M. 57–58, 161, 230, 231
mental: mental disorder 21; mental health 169, 199; mental illness 206, 207
metalanguage xl, xli
metapsychology 94, 114, 228
method 3, 146, 147, 189
methodology xxiv
militance 34, 35, 48
Miller, J.-A. xxix, 48, 63–64, 66, 68, 86, 173, 218, 284, 287
Miller, M. 49
Milner, J.-C. 113, 205, 285
mode of production 24, 32, 41, 42, 57, 58, 60, 103, 116, 117, 156, 157, 159, 160, 239, 260, 261, 288
modern 25, 28, 33, 34, 58, 60, 64, 70, 75, 76, 82, 103, 115–121, 137, 140n3, 155, 177, 195, 202, 203, 205–207, 227–229, 232–235, 247, 259, 260, 276, 278
modernity xxv, 2, 116, 118, 205, 246, 247, 276, 277
money 153–161; and alienation 11; and capitalism 40; and consumption 55, 57–58; and freedom/liberty 78; and market 132; and materialism 146; and politics 169; and segregation 198; and society 229, 233, 235; uneasiness/discontent/unhappiness 261, 264; and value 267, 270
Morin, F. 157
mourning 110
myth: and economy/*oikonomia* 70; and history 87, 94; and market 127; and master/tyrant 138; and segregation 202; and slavery 216; and society 225, 228, 231, 237; and uneasiness/discontent/unhappiness 262

narcissism 200, 201
nation 36, 104–106
nature xxix, xxxi, xli, 2, 3, 10, 17, 45, 46, 49, 51, 52, 66, 69, 98, 119, 120, 128, 136, 154, 158, 195, 203, 209, 217, 223, 227, 228, 231–233, 242, 249, 259–261, 269, 274n5
needs 2–4, 6, 17, 35, 37, 46, 69, 71, 89, 110, 146, 158, 164, 232, 246, 261, 264, 280
negativity 6, 33, 36, 37, 40, 42, 163, 164, 183, 247, 248, 252, 253
Negri, A. 211
neurosis 90, 169, 229, 231, 247, 259
neurotic 90, 123n7, 169
Nobus, D. 12
normative 59–60, 112, 260
no sexual relationship 236, 237, 257, 263

Oedipus 26, 56, 59–60, 106, 127, 169, 231
*oikonomia see* economy/*oikonomia*
overdetermination 77, 241
ownership 2, 7, 32, 132; *see also* private property

paranoid 9, 166, 241, 243
Parker, I. 203
party 47, 48, 51, 52, 151, 166, 169, 181–184
patriarchy 58, 60, 139
Pavón-Cuéllar, D. 203, 211
perversion 42, 229, 232–234
phallus 60, 156, 259, 263
phenomena/phenomenology: and alienation 5; and communism 46, 49–50, 52; and history 85, 90; and ideology 98; and labour/work 112; and master/tyrant 135; and materialism 147; and politics 165; and society 230; and superstructure 243; and value 266, 272
philosophy 3, 6–8, 138, 142–144, 151, 163, 185n5, 189, 205, 230, 242, 252, 276–278, xxxiv, xxxv, xxxviii
*plaisir* 114, 278
Plato 78–79, 135, 201–202, 214–216, 218, 220–223
pleasure 27, 28, 42, 61, 65, 66, 110–114, 123n3, 123n7, 159, 185n2, 222, 246, 247, 254, 257, 268–271, 274n5, 274n7, 278, 279, 284

pleasure principle 27, 28, 159, 247, 249, 257, 274n5
policy/ies 61, 128, 225
politics 162–174; and automatism 17; and capitalism 35, 37, 44; and communism 45; and economy/*oikonomia* 69; and imperialism 105; and labour/work 117, 122, 126; and segregation 203, 207, 209–210; and surplus-*jouissance* 246
Pontalis, J. B. xxxii
population 199, 232
post-colonialism 102
postmodern 35
poverty 6, 199, 218
power: and alienation 3; and automatism 17, 19; and bourgeoisie 24; and capitalism 33, 35, 37, 40, 42; and communism 51; and consumption 58–60; and freedom/liberty 82; and history 92; and ideology 97, 99, 101–104; and imperialism 108; and labour/work 115–116, 120–121; and market 129; and master/tyrant 134–135; and money 156; and politics 162, 164, 171–172, 174; and proletarian/labourer/worker 177; and revolution 188, 190–194; and segregation 199; and society 228; and surplus-*jouissance* 248–249; and uneasiness/discontent/unhappiness 258, 260–261, 264; and value 266, 268–269
praxis 6, 99, 143, 162, 164, 193, 257
price 32, 64, 71n1, 120, 127, 131, 151, 157, 158, 162, 210, 268
primitive 2, 46, 58, 98, 227, 248
private property: and alienation 3, 5; and capitalism 32, 34; and communism 45; and consumption 57, 60–61; and market 132; and politics 163–164; and society 226–227, 234
production 3, 4, 13, 16–18, 20, 21, 24–27, 31–37, 39–42, 46, 56–61, 69–71, 97–99, 104, 105, 111–113, 116–122, 123n6–123n8, 126–130, 137, 138, 143, 146, 147, 156, 159, 160, 162, 165, 166, 170, 177, 198, 222, 227, 232, 233, 235–237, 239, 240, 257, 261, 264, 268–270, 280, 281, 288
profit 3, 57, 114, 157, 199, 200, 210, 226, 234, 274n7, 279
progress: and alienation 3; and bourgeoisie 26; and communism 46; and freedom/liberty 74; and labour/work 122; and market 128; and politics 165; and segregation 198, 206; and society 229–230, 235; and uneasiness/discontent/unhappiness 257
proletarian/labourer/worker 177–185; and alienation 4, 5, 11, 13; and automatism 17–21; and capitalism 31–32, 37–39, 42–43; and consumption 58, 60; and economy/*oikonomia* 68, 70; and labour/work 111, 117–121; and market 131–132; and money 156; and politics 164, 166, 174; and revolution 188, 192; and segregation 199; and society 229; and superstructure 242; and surplus-*jouissance* 251, 254; and uneasiness/discontent/unhappiness 261, 262, 264; and value 268
Proudhon 5
psychoanalysis xxvi, xxvii, xxviii, xxx–xxxviii, xl, xli, 1, 16, 31, 32, 34–36, 41, 44, 48, 49, 55, 56, 58, 64, 65, 81, 83n4, 85, 86, 89, 90, 110, 113–115, 118, 122, 126, 127, 150, 151, 157, 162, 168, 170–172, 174, 177, 181, 183, 184, 185n1, 190, 193, 198, 201, 205, 208, 209, 211, 247, 250, 252, 256–260, 262, 263, 265, 266, 277, 278, 282
psychology 25, 26, 28, 49, 51, 64, 67, 90, 168, 200, 201, 208, 225, 227, 228, 242
psychosis 71, 77, 78

racism 107, 128, 197–198, 202–204, 273
Real xl, 18, 67, 71, 86, 91, 250, 252, 258
reality xxvii, xli, 23, 24, 26, 33, 34, 36, 41, 44, 83n1, 99, 105, 136, 143, 144, 146, 150, 181, 190, 191, 223, 227, 229, 231, 232, 236, 240, 241, 247, 281, 286
Recalcati, M. 22
reification 7, 46, 47, 99, 100, 252
religion: and alienation 4; and bourgeoisie 25; and capitalism 31, 35; and communism 50; and labour/work 113; and money 160; and politics 163; and segregation 205; and society 235
repetition 18, 22n3, 41, 91, 113, 120, 121, 189, 190, 196n2, 232, 246, 248, 249, 254, 269, 274n6
repression: and capitalism 32, 36; and economy/*oikonomia* 69; and history 90–91; and labour/work 110–111; and money 161; and politics 169; and revolution 192; and segregation 199;

and society 230, 235; and surplus-*jouissance* 247; and uneasiness/discontent/unhappiness 257
revolution xxvii, 188–195; and automatism 19; and bourgeoisie 25, 29; and capitalism 33–35, 39; and communism 51; and economy/*oikonomia* 68; and freedom/liberty 78; and imperialism 108; and proletarian/labourer/worker 177–178, 180, 184; and superstructure 243; and uneasiness/discontent/unhappiness 256
Ricardo 165, 173, 198, 199
Rickman, J. 168, 209
rights: and bourgeoisie 25, 28; and consumption 57, 60; and economy/*oikonomia* 71; and politics 163–164, 169; and segregation 207, 211; and society 230, 235
Roudinesco, É. Xxxiii
Rousseau (ian) 2, 83n1, 162, 269
ruling class 6, 29

Sartre, J.-P. 91, 93, 208
satisfaction: and economy/*oikonomia* 66–67, 70; and labour/work 110–111, 112–113, 116; and market 127; and money 159–160; and proletarian/labourer/worker 183, 185; and surplus-*jouissance* 246–247, 254
savoir 69, 248, 250, 251, 254
science xxv, 20, 25–28, 33–36, 46, 49, 50, 58, 107, 119, 138, 143, 163, 165, 167, 203–208, 264, 283
segregation xxxvii, 107, 127–128, 197–211, 236
*Selbstentfremdung* 3
self: and alienation 3, 8–11; and automatism 16, 22; and capitalism 43; and communism 45, 47, 51; and economy/*oikonomia* 65; and imperialism 106–107; and labour/work 114, 117, 119, 121; and master/tyrant 135–136; and materialism 144; and politics 166, 169, 170; and revolution 195; and segregation 201, 208, 210; and slavery 216, 223; and society 226–227; and superstructure 242; and surplus-*jouissance* 247; translation of 277–278; and uneasiness/discontent/unhappiness 258, 260
self-esteem 210

semblant 70, 130–131, 174, 263
servitude 83n2, 135, 164, 221, 222, 230
sexuation 64, 70, 174
signifier xxvi, xxix, xxxiii, xxxvi; and alienation 10–13; and automatism 17–18, 20; and bourgeoisie 26; and capitalism 33, 38–39; and communism 52; and economy/*oikonomia* 64–68, 70; and freedom/liberty 74, 76, 78; and history 86–92; and labour/work 118–119; and market 130–131; and master/tyrant 138; and materialism 142, 144–151; and money 160; and politics 163, 169–170, 173–174; and revolution 191; and segregation 201, 209; and society 225, 230–237; and superstructure 244; and surplus-*jouissance* 248, 250–251, 253–254; translation of 277, 283; and uneasiness/discontent/unhappiness 258, 262–264
Sismondi 5
slave xxxvii, 214–224; and bourgeoisie 27; and capitalism 34, 38; and imperialism 103; and master/tyrant 134–138; and politics 164, 166; and revolution 192; and segregation 201, 210; and society 228, 230; and surplus-*jouissance* 250; translation of 282; and uneasiness/discontent/unhappiness 259–262
slavery 214–224
Smith, A. 165, 199, 226, 267
socialism 48, 69, 71, 105, 161
social movement(s) 57, 193
society xli, 225–237; and alienation 3, 5–6; and automatism 21; and bourgeoisie 24–29; and capitalism 32, 39; and communism 45–52; and consumption 57, 59; and economy/*oikonomia* 66–67, 70; and ideology 99; and materialism 145–146; and politics 163, 165; and proletarian/labourer/worker 183–184; and segregation 198, 202–203; and superstructure 239; and surplus-*jouissance* 247–249, 254; and uneasiness/discontent/unhappiness 256–257, 259–262, 264–265
Socrates 34, 167, 201, 215–219, 222–224, 236, 257
Soler, C. 181–182, 287
sovereignty: and bourgeoisie 25; and economy/*oikonomia* 64, 66, 68, 70; and master/tyrant 135; and politics 174; and

revolution 194; and segregation 209, 211
Soviet Union/Soviet 48, 49, 51, 147, 150, 208, 242, 280
species 8, 133, 138
speculative 47, 150, 286
speech: and alienation 10; and economy/*oikonomia* 65; and history 90; and labour/work 117, 121; and market 128; and materialism 144; and politics 170–171, 174; and proletarian/labourer/worker 181; and revolution 191; and segregation 209; and society 233; and surplus-*jouissance* 246, 247, 250–251, 253; and uneasiness/discontent/unhappiness 258
Spinoza (ian) 51, 55, 83n1
Stalin, J. 48–49, 93, 100, 107, 147, 242–243
State 83n1, 105, 163, 169, 171, 189, 195, 202, 235, 239
Stavrakakis, Y. xxxvii
strike 19, 71, 76, 117, 122, 178, 179, 182, 184, 262
structural 17, 24, 26, 29, 31–33, 35, 36, 42, 45, 65, 77, 104, 117, 118, 130, 139, 158, 165, 167, 184, 191, 192, 194, 198, 199, 201, 203, 208, 226, 227, 230, 231, 237, 243, 280
structuralism 35, 37, 43, 52, 64, 70, 230, 235
structuralist 35, 55, 65, 68, 86, 87, 89, 91, 99, 100, 124n17, 228, 236
subject: and alienation 10–13; and automatism 16–21; barred subject 69; and bourgeoisie 24–25, 27–29; and capitalism 31–33, 35–44; and consumption 56–59, 61; divided subject 18, 20, 179, 205, 263, 264; and economy/*oikonomia* 63–71; and freedom/liberty 74, 76, 78, 82; and history 85, 87, 89, 90, 93; and imperialism 106; and labour/work 111, 115, 118–122; and market 126, 128–129, 131–132; and master/tyrant 134, 136–139; and materialism 144–146, 150–151; and money 160; and politics 167–171, 173; and proletarian/labourer/worker 177–183, 185; and revolution 192–193; and segregation 201–209; and slavery 220, 221; and society 226–227, 230–233, 235–236; subjectivity xl, xli, 4, 11, 28, 41, 43, 85, 89, 118, 124n13, 124n16, 168, 201, 205, 233, 247, 253, 259, 276–278; and superstructure 241; and surplus-*jouissance* 246–247, 249–254; translation of 276–278; and uneasiness/discontent/unhappiness 258–265; and value 269
subjectivity: and alienation 4, 10–11; and automatism 20; and bourgeoisie 28; and capitalism 36, 41, 43–44; and freedom/liberty 77; and history 85, 89; and labour/work 118; and politics 167, 168; and segregation 201, 205; and society 233; and surplus-*jouissance* 247, 253; and uneasiness/discontent/unhappiness 259
sublimation 70, 231, 234–235, 247
subordination 20, 48–49, 67, 97, 118, 136, 146
subversion: and capitalism 35, 39; and economy/*oikonomia* 69–70; and market 129; and proletarian/labourer/worker 181; and segregation 211; and society 227; and uneasiness/discontent/unhappiness 256
superstructure 239–244; and consumption 60–61; and ideology 100; and materialism 145, 147; and politics 165; and segregation 197; translation of 279
surplus-*jouissance* xxx, 246–255, *251*; and automatism 16–18, 21; and bourgeoisie 23; and capitalism 37, 41; and consumption 56; and economy/*oikonomia* 64, 68–70; and ideology 100; and politics 173
surplus-value: and automatism 16, 19, 21; and bourgeoisie 28; and capitalism 32, 34, 37, 39, 41; and economy/*oikonomia* 64, 68–69, 71; and imperialism 103–105; and labour/work 115–118, 120–122; and market 128–130; and master/tyrant 137–138; and materialism 146; and money 153–154, 156, 159–160; and politics 166, 170; and segregation 200–201; and society 225, 236; and surplus-*jouissance* 248–249, 254; translation of 279, 284; and uneasiness/discontent/unhappiness 264; and value 266, 268–273
symbolic xl, xli, 10, 12, 18, 21, 25, 29, 56, 65, 67, 69, 71, 76–78, 86–89, 91, 92, 102, 103, 113, 117, 119, 120, 142, 144,

145, 147–151, 159, 161, 170, 201–203, 207, 211, 228, 231, 235, 236, 250, 252, 253, 259, 261
symptom: and bourgeoisie 25; and capitalism 41–42, 44; and communism 47; and consumption 56; and economy/*oikonomia* 71; and freedom/liberty 82; and history 92; and ideology 100; and imperialism 104; and labour/work 117, 119; and market 128, 132; and master/tyrant 138; and materialism 145, 149–150; and proletarian/labourer/worker 177–185; and segregation 211; and surplus-*jouissance* 247–248, 251; and uneasiness/discontent/unhappiness 259
system xxxiv, 3, 16–18, 20–23, 31, 33, 34, 42, 49, 60, 65, 121, 126, 131, 164, 169, 171, 184, 193, 197, 200, 210, 250, 269, 270

theory xxvi, xxxiv, 1, 3, 6, 17, 29, 31, 36, 37, 67, 85, 86, 97–100, 103, 105, 110, 113, 114, 118, 126, 129, 132, 145, 147, 162, 164, 170, 171, 178, 181, 182, 193, 250, 267, 286
Tomšič, S. 40–44, 205, 211
topology: Cross Cap 132; and economy/*oikonomia* 70; graph 247, 286; and ideology 100; Klein Bottle 132; Klein Group 286; and market 132; projective plane 132; and superstructure 244; torsion 28, 204; translation of 279, 282–283; and value 267
totality 6, 67, 118, 241
transference: and politics 171; and slavery 220, 221; and uneasiness/discontent/unhappiness 258
truth: and capitalism 38, 42; and economy/*oikonomia* 69, 70; and freedom/liberty 76, 78; and history 92; and ideology 100; and imperialism 104; and labour/work 122; and market 126, 131–133; and master/tyrant 138; and materialism 147, 149–151; and politics 168; and proletarian/labourer/worker 177–179, 181–185; and revolution 190, 194–195; and segregation 198, 204, 211; and slavery 217, 221–222; and society 231; and surplus-*jouissance* 248, 251–252; and uneasiness/discontent/unhappiness 261–265

Tse-Tung, M. 205
tyrant *see* master/tyrant

*Überbau* 239, 244n1
*Unbewusst* 113, 123n11
unconscious xxvii; and alienation 10, 13; and automatism 16–21; and capitalism 31–32, 36; and economy/*oikonomia* 63–64, 70; and freedom/liberty 81–82; and history 85, 88; and imperialism 106; and labour/work 110–117, 119–120, 122; and market 126–128; and materialism 148–150; and money 158; and politics 162, 164–165, 170–173; and proletarian/labourer/worker 177–179, 181–183, 185; and revolution 189, 193; and segregation 201–202; and society 228, 231, 233; and superstructure 244; and surplus-*jouissance* 246–251; translation of 277, 283; and uneasiness/discontent/unhappiness 257–258, 262, 264; and value 272
uneasiness/discontent/unhappiness 256–265; and politics 164–166, 169; and proletarian/labourer/worker 183; and society 226, 231; translation of 281
unhappiness *see* uneasiness/discontent/unhappiness
*Unheimlich* 123n11, 128
Union 19, 48, 49, 51, 108, 128, 208, 280
University's discourse *see* discourse of the University
utilitarianism: and communism 50; and economy/*oikonomia* 64, 66, 67; and politics 171; and society 228–230, 236; and uneasiness/discontent/unhappiness 260; and value 266, 274

valorisation 115, 119, 210, 234, 248; and capitalism 41; and labour/work 115–117, 119; and materialism 146; and segregation 210; and surplus-*jouissance* 248
value xxviii, xxxvii, 266–274; and alienation 3, 13; and automatism 19; and capitalism 32, 34, 37, 39; and consumption 55–56, 59–61; and economy/*oikonomia* 64, 68–71; and ideology 98–100; and imperialism 103–105; and labour/work 111, 115–121; and market 126–132; and master/tyrant 138; and materialism 146–147, 153; and

money 154–161; and politics 164–166, 173; and proletarian/labourer/worker 182; and revolution 195; and society 231; and surplus-*jouissance* 248–249, 254–255; translation of 279, 280; and uneasiness/discontent/unhappiness 259, 261, 264; *see also* surplus-value
*Verdrängung* 69
*Verwirklichung* 68
vocabulary xxvi–xxxviii, 4
Voloshinov, V. N. 242
*Vorstellung* 89;
*Vorstellungsrepräsentanz* 113
*Vorstellungsrepräsentanz* 113

wage 4, 20, 179
wage labour 4, 5, 264
War 49, 51, 194, 206

wealth 6, 42, 46, 58, 59, 154, 157, 166, 222, 226, 234, 261, 269, 280
Williams, R. xxxii, xxxvi, 241
women: and consumption 56–61; and economy/*oikonomia* 65; and market 127; and master/tyrant 138–139; and money 158; and segregation 198; and society 229, 237; and uneasiness/discontent/unhappiness 263
work *see* labour/work
worker *see* proletarian/labourer/worker
working class 29, 45, 137, 185n4, 198, 199, 229
*Wunsch* 112

*Zapatismo* xxii
Žižek, S. xxxvii, 18, 43–44, 188–190, 252
Zupančič, A. 41–42, 44, 205, 249, 252

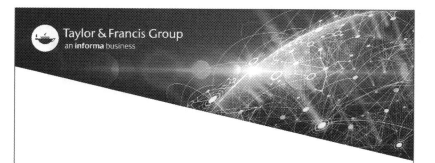

Printed in the United States
by Baker & Taylor Publisher Services